AMERICAN COMMODITY FLOW

A Geographical Interpretation of Rail and Water Traffic
Based on Principles of Spatial Interchange

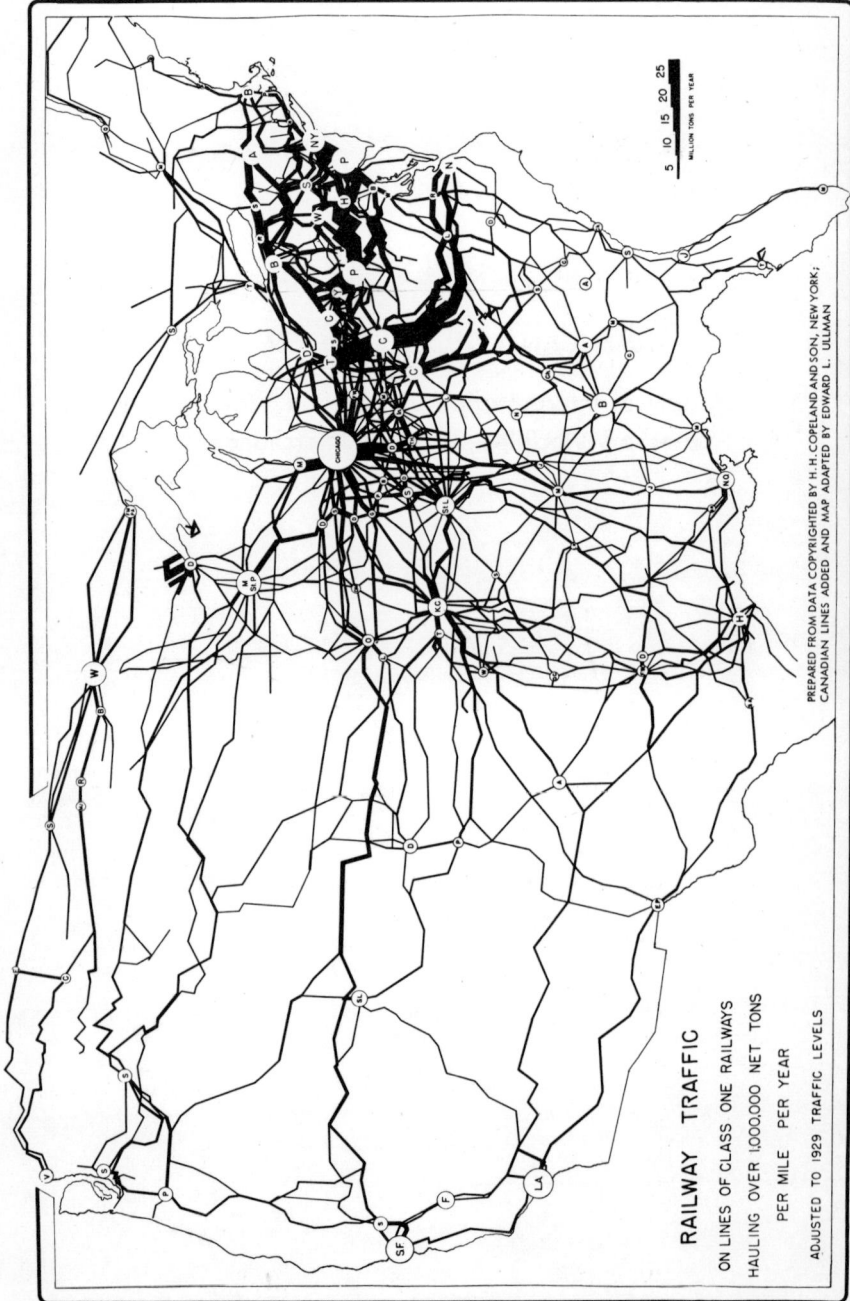

RAILWAY TRAFFIC

ON LINES OF CLASS ONE RAILWAYS

HAULING OVER 1,000,000 NET TONS

PER MILE PER YEAR

ADJUSTED TO 1929 TRAFFIC LEVELS

PREPARED FROM DATA COPYRIGHTED BY H. H. COPELAND AND SON, NEW YORK;
CANADIAN LINES ADDED AND MAP ADAPTED BY EDWARD L. ULLMAN

5 10 15 20 25

MILLION TONS PER YEAR

AMERICAN COMMODITY FLOW

A Geographical Interpretation

of Rail and Water Traffic

Based on Principles of Spatial Interchange

By
Edward L. Ullman

1957
UNIVERSITY OF WASHINGTON PRESS
Seattle

Lithographed in the United States of America

Foreword

THIS VOLUME contains a description and an interpretation, through text and maps, of rail and water traffic flows in American domestic and foreign trade.

The discussion in the first four chapters is illustrated with maps of state-to-state rail traffic for twenty representative states, based on the Interstate Commerce Commission 1 per cent sample Carload Waybill Statistics, and with new maps of rail and other traffic. In Chapters I and II are a summary description and interpretation of the American flow pattern. Chapter III and the first part of Chapter IV set forth the general analysis and theory indicated by the new maps and data. Flow maps of American domestic and foreign ocean trade, and origin and destination maps for United States coastal traffic, are presented and discussed in Chapter V.

For discussion of the reliability, character, and use of the data in the ICC 1 per cent sample on which the state-to-state rail traffic maps are based, the reader is referred to the Interstate Commerce Commission's publication, Waybill Statistics, Their History and Uses. [1] Briefly, the sample data

---

1. Interstate Commerce Commission, Bureau of Transport Economics and Statistics, Waybill Statistics, Their History and Uses (Washington, D. C., 1954). This report also lists several other general reports and special uses made of waybill and traffic data. See also Edward L. Ullman, "Maps of State-to-State Rail Freight Movement for 13 States of the United States in 1948," Report No. 3, ONR Contract N5 ORI-07633 (1951; privately distributed). This report has maps for ten states not included in the present volume.

For some other reports illustrating the use of traffic flow

are more reliable for large flows than for small flows; they provide an excellent indication of major connections, the main subject of this report. For many of the individual states the sample flows have been compared with actual annual tonnage, and in most cases little serious discrepancy has been found. In addition, maps have been prepared for several states for two or more succeeding years; virtually no change in general patterns developed. One of the states, Washington for 1949,

---

data, see: Edward L. Ullman, "American Commodity Flow: The Cases of Connecticut, Iowa and Washington," Report No. 12, ONR Transportation Geography Project (1955); privately distributed), also published in German in Die Erde, No. 2, 1955, pp. 129-64; Leo W. Sweeney, "The Iowa Economy as Portrayed by Rail Freight Traffic Movement," Iowa Business Digest, XXII, No. 12 (December, 1951), 1-8; Edwin H. Lewis, Minnesota's Interstate Trade (Minneapolis: University of Minnesota Press, 1953); Ray S. Kelley, Jr., Origins and Destinations of New England's Rail Traffic, National Planning Association, Committee of New England (Boston, March, 1952); National Planning Association, Committee of New England, The Economic State of New England, Arthur Bright and George Ellis, eds. (New Haven: Yale University Press, 1954); U.S. Federal Reserve Bank of San Francisco, "Twelfth District Interregional Trade, 1950," Monthly Review, September, 1952, pp. 79-81, and later studies from the same source which translate tonnages into values (see also Social Science Research Council, Interregional Linkages: Proceedings of the Western Committee on Regional Economic Analysis [Berkeley, Calif., 1954]). Another study using flow data in part to calculate a region's balance of payments is Paul B. Simpson, Regional Aspects of Business Cycles and Special Studies of the Pacific Northwest (University of Oregon, 1953), especially sections in chapter vi and in Appendix C.

Two foreign country rail studies of freight traffic are Erwin Scheu, Deutschlands wirtschaftsgeographische Harmonie (Breslau: F. Hirt, 1924), and Aage Aagesen, Geografiske Studier over Jernbanere i Danmark (Copenhagen: H. Hagerups Boghandel, 1949). Another study, confined to passenger rail traffic, is Bruno Castiglioni, La Rete ferroviaria italiana e il movimento dei viaggiatori (Padua: R. Zannoni, Editore, 1936).

may be compared with a 1948 map published in <u>Die Erde</u>.[2]
Comparison of the 1948 and 1949 maps reveals almost identical patterns and indicates the consistency of the sample as
well as the validity of establishing a bench mark based on one
year.

Some flows have not been reported because their indication
would violate the so-called "disclosure rule," which federal
agencies are becoming more and more efficient in enforcing,
to the detriment of scholarship. In most cases the loss is not
significant, because only the smaller flows, those which are
apt to have fewer than three shippers, are likely to be suppressed. Sometimes, however, the omissions are serious.
For example, the important movements of alumina from Alabama and Louisiana to Washington (shown in the Washington figures for 1948 and 1949) are reported as only 40, 300 tons from
Alabama and 0 from Louisiana in 1950, when normally several
hundred thousand tons annually are received from each of the
states every year. Presumably the reason for the suppression
in 1950 was that a small number of giant companies originated
and/or terminated the movements. Thus it was impossible to
portray a fundamental aspect of the American economy, as
well as one of the longest heavy-volume land hauls in the world.
How many other important connections of this kind have been
suppressed is not known, although the number involved in a
five- or six-fold commodity breakdown, as used in this report,
cannot be too great.

---

2. "American Commodity Flow: The Cases of Connecticut,
Iowa and Washington."

Acknowledgments

FOR PERMISSION to reproduce the traffic flow map based on their copyrighted data I am grateful to H. H. Copeland and Son. I also wish to thank the Interstate Commerce Commission and the other agencies which cooperated in providing data. I am particularly indebted to Mr. John W. Barriger, President of the Pittsburgh and Lake Erie Railroad Company, for his aid and encouragement.

Much of the research for this study was undertaken as part of a contract awarded by the Office of Naval Research, whose support is gratefully acknowledged. The results, in the form of a mimeographed report, were privately distributed among a small number of interested persons.

Professor Donald Patton, of the University of Maryland, prepared the inland waterways map and data on some state-to-state pipeline and water traffic. Warmest thanks are due to him and also to the following associates and graduate students in the Department of Geography of the University of Washington. Francis Anderson, a research assistant on the project, carefully and patiently compiled most of the state-to-state maps. The Ohio and Pennsylvania maps were prepared by Clyde Browning and James Brooks, respectively. Burton F. Kelso, Howard D. Vogel, and Robert P. Hinkle drafted the ocean flow maps for Chapter V and aided in other ways. Douglas Carter, Waldo Tobler, Willis Heath, Professor John Sherman, and others also contributed invaluable cartographic assistance. William Siddall prepared the bibliography and index. Professor Donald Hudson and other colleagues also aided unselfishly in countless ways.

Edward L. Ullman

Rome, 1957

Contents

Maps

xvi

Tables

Notes on Reading the Maps

Movements on the state-to-state rail traffic maps in Chapter IV are shown by dots. The number of dots on the origin maps in each of the states thus is proportionate to the tonnage moving from the individual states to the state indicated in the title; on the destination maps the number is proportionate to the volume received from the title state. Dots within the title state represent intrastate origins and destinations (identical for both origin and destination). Origin and destination maps are provided for total movements and are also broken down into major commodity groupings according to the ICC standard five-fold classification of major commodities, with six states having an additional commodity classification for petroleum products (combined from products of mines--crude petroleum; and manufacturing and miscellaneous--refined products). Two states (Pennsylvania and Ohio) have still other breakdowns. The specific commodity subdivision for each state is indicated in the list of maps and on the maps themselves. For the specific commodity movements, each dot generally represents 10,000 tons (1 per cent sample multiplied by 100); each block of 10 dots represents 100,000 tons, as the legend on each plate indicates. For a few heavy commodity movements for Ohio and Pennsylvania the values are 50,000 and 500,000 tons, respectively, as indicated on the legends. (Dots on the Ohio maps are also smaller, and the scale of the Pennsylvania maps is larger, than for the other states.) For total movements in all states each dot equals 50,000 tons and each block of 10 dots 500,000 tons, as indicated on the respective legends.

For the origin and destination maps of Water-Borne Commerce between U.S. Coastal Regions in Chapter V, three types of dots are used on each map, as indicated on the leg-

ends, to indicate: (1) shipments from the title region (destinations); (2) shipments into the title region (origins); and (3)
shipments within the title regions (intraregional movements).
Each dot has a value of 50,000 tons, and each block of 10 dots
500,000 tons (as on the total maps for rail state-to-state
movements).

The tonnage scale on the various flow maps (rail, water,
etc.) varies from map to map, as each legend indicates, in
accordance with the graphic requirements of the data. Some
approximate comparisons are as follows. The Railway Traffic
flow map (frontispiece) has about two and two-thirds times
as much tonnage per width of line as the inland waterway map
(Barge and Raft Traffic); about three times that of the three
U.S. Domestic Trade ocean flow maps (each of which is on
the same scale); about one and two-thirds times that for the
U.S. Foreign Trade dry cargo map; and about three and one-
half times that for the U.S. Foreign Trade tanker traffic map.
The last two maps are reported in cargo tons of 2,240 lbs.;
all others in short tons of 2,000 lbs. By way of comparison
a metric ton is 2,204 lbs. All data refer to net weight tons
of freight, not gross, which includes tare, and not measure-
ment or cubic tons.

AMERICAN COMMODITY FLOW

A Geographical Interpretation of Rail and Water Traffic
Based on Principles of Spatial Interchange

I

American Internal Commodity Flow:

Rail and Water Traffic

WHAT IS the pattern of spatial connections in the American economy? Where, for example, do the Northwest and the South sell their lumber? What is the reach of the growing California market? Where do the New England states obtain their food? What precisely are the major connections--routes of transport--in the country? These and a host of other questions have never been satisfactorily and precisely answered. The answer is best given by map representation, the main feature of this report. The results are a surprisingly logical response to American geography and to the effects of distance, with little cross hauling on a large scale, and yet with some distinctive spatial patterns not envisaged by a priori assumptions. The result also is a new representation of the geography of linkages and connections to be set alongside the well-known static geography of distinctive production and consumption regions and climatic and terrain patterns. For the first time, therefore, data are becoming available for completing the fundamental depiction of American economic geography and for the formulation of some new principles of spatial interaction.

The pattern of American transport routes and freight traffic flows is shown by the frontispiece map of railway traffic. [1] Although the map is based on prewar data, on the scale used

---

1. The map is based on original data collected in the field by H. H. Copeland and Son; it appears in Edward L. Ullman, "The Role of Transportation and the Bases for Interaction," in Man's Role in Changing the Face of the Earth, William L. Thomas, Jr., ed. (Chicago: University of Chicago Press, 1956), p. 874.

it is essentially current today.[4] Only lines carrying more than 1,000,000 net tons of freight per year are shown; these lines probably represent about 90 per cent of American rail traffic measured in ton miles. Highways are not shown, but their inclusion would hardly change the pattern since highways even in 1954 carried only about 15 per cent of the ton miles compared to the railroads' approximate 50 per cent, and the highways generally parallel the railways. The actual estimated percentages for the various forms of transportation in 1948 are shown in Table 1.

TABLE 1
PERCENTAGE OF TOTAL TON MILES BY TYPES
OF TRANSPORT, UNITED STATES, 1948*

(Excluding Coastal Shipping)		(Including Coastal Shipping)	
Railway	64. 4	Railway	54. 6
Highway	8. 7	Highway	7. 0
Inland waterways and		Inland waterways, Great	
Great Lakes	15. 0	Lakes, coastal and	
		intercoastal shipping	28. 9
Pipelines (petroleum)	11. 9	Pipelines (petroleum)	9. 5
Airways	....	Airways	....
Total	100. 0	Total	100. 0

*U. S. Interstate Commerce Commission, Volume of Inter-city Freight Traffic, Public and Private, by Kinds of Transportation, 1939-49, ICC Statement No. 5046, File No. 10-D-7 (Washington, D. C., Sept., 1950), Tables 1 and 2.

The map of United States railroads (p. 3) showing trackage, or physical capacity, correlates quite well with the traffic flow map (frontispiece). Lines are classified into six categories from approximately greatest capacity to least as follows: (1) four-track lines (principally the Pennsylvania and New York Central railroads funneling traffic over or through the Appalachian Mountains); (2) three-track; (3) two-track; (4) centralized traffic control single-track; (5) automatic block single-track; (6) all other single-track. Centralized traffic control (CTC) is a recently developed form of remote signaling and switch control which increases capacity to the equivalent of perhaps one and one-half tracks on the average; automatic block signals (shown on the maps only on lines where

2. Perhaps the major change would be a slight thickening of the transcontinentals, particularly to the southwest, and of traffic along the Pacific Coast.

2

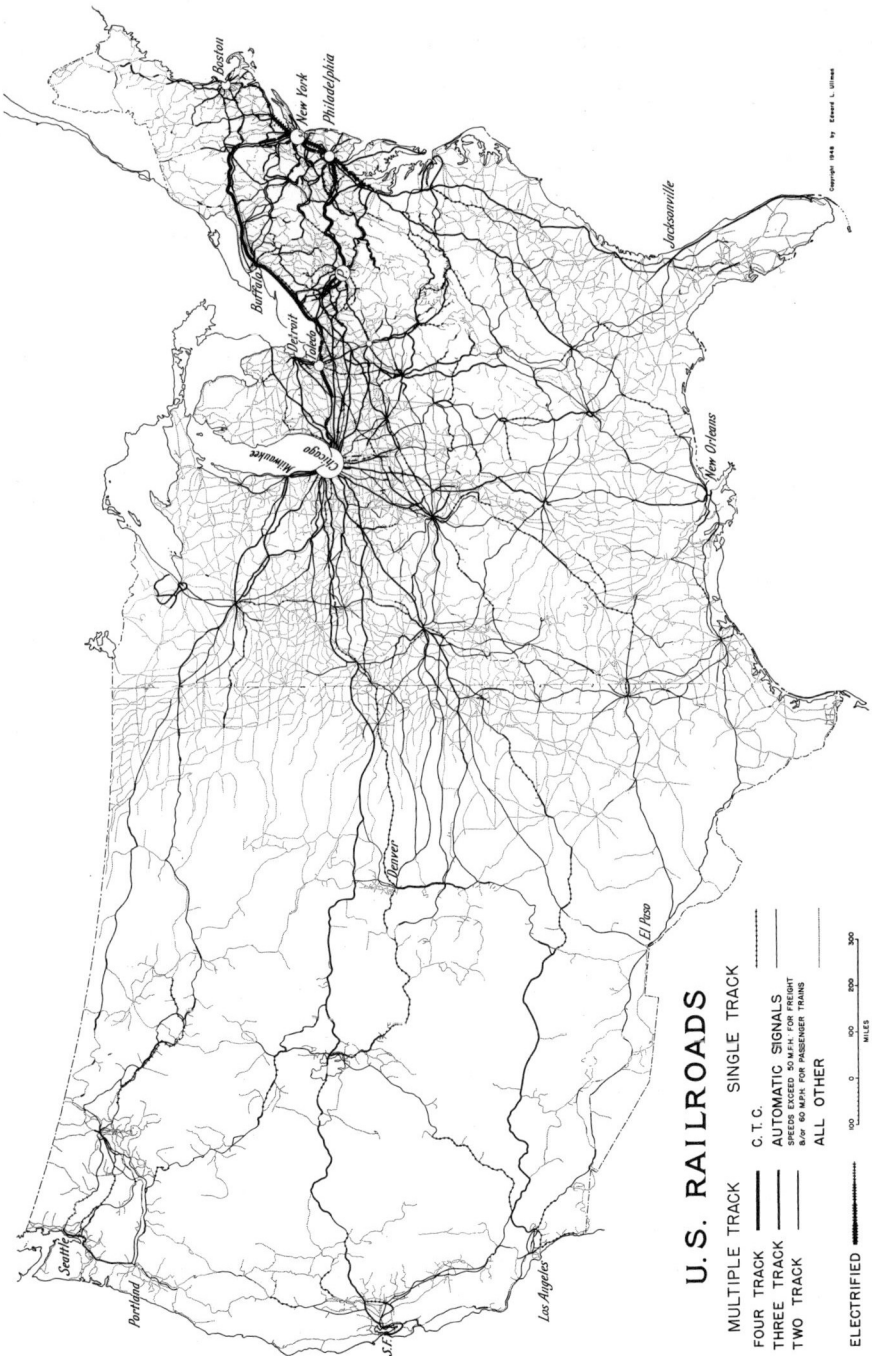

U.S. RAILROADS

MULTIPLE TRACK   SINGLE TRACK

FOUR TRACK
THREE TRACK
TWO TRACK

C.T.C.
AUTOMATIC SIGNALS
SPEEDS EXCEED 50 M.P.H. FOR FREIGHT
&/or 60 M.P.H. FOR PASSENGER TRAINS
ALL OTHER

ELECTRIFIED

MILES
100   0   100   200   300

Copyright 1946 by Edward L. Ullman

3

speed limits also exceed fifty miles per hour for freight or sixty miles per hour for passenger trains) also increase the capacity of single-track lines, but not as much as CTC.

Space precludes detailed analysis of all that the maps show. [3] The two most important general features are the predominantly east-west, cross-grain pattern of rail flows, and the marked dominance of the industrial belt and adjacent coal-producing and rich farming areas which feed fuel and food to the belt.

The cross-grain pattern of American transportation

Relief in the United States generally runs north-south, but traffic more generally east-west. This occurs in spite of the remarkable sensitivity of railroads to heavy gradients. Where possible the railroads use dioric streams or gaps crossing some of the grain of the country, such as the Columbia, in the West, or in the East the New, Kanawha, Potomac, Susquehanna, Juniata, and especially Mohawk rivers. [4] Only the last cuts entirely across the Appalachians; yet traffic through its gap via the New York Central, while heavy, is less than on the Pennsylvania or some other lines which climb over the mountains.

The western transcontinentals exhibit an even more marked cross-grain alignment. This is further reflected in the origin and destination maps for states like Arizona and Montana (at

_____

3. For further details and analysis see the author's "The Railroad Pattern of the United States," Geographical Review, XXXIX (1949), 242-56, from which the trackage map in this report is reproduced. Additions to CTC and automatic block have occurred since 1948, the date of this map, as well as some decrease in multiple track; the present map, however, serves its intended purpose of indicating the relative importance of the routes as well as, or better than, a more recent one. For a larger scale map in color (with some correction of details), see the author's U. S. Railroads Classified according to Capacity and Relative Importance (New York: Simmons-Boardman Publishing Corp. , 1951).

4. The word dioric was constructed from the Greek dia oros, "through mountains." For its first use, see Edward L. Ullman, "Rivers as Regional Bonds: The Columbia-Snake Example," Geographical Review, XLI (1951), 212.

4

end of Chapter IV), which show marked east-west connections but almost no north-south ties. (The Grand Canyon, of course, effectively limits direct northern connections for most of Arizona.)

Only in the following corridors does a north-south alignment, parallel to the grain of the country, predominate over long distances: (1) along the southeastern Piedmont and Coastal Plain; (2) down the Mississippi Valley and contiguous lowland with lines to the Gulf and to Texas; and (3) the mid-continent lines in the corridor west of the Ozarks and east of the arid Great Plains. All three of these corridors focus on the industrial belt, as does the rest of the rail pattern.

The inland waterways flow map shows less than 5 per cent of the United States flow pattern, but also one naturally more geared to the grain of the country as well as focusing on the industrial belt.[5] Prior to the opening of the Erie Canal in 1825 and of the railroads thereafter, the American Middle West shipped goods south via the Mississippi, thence via coastal ships around to New York and other eastern seaboard ports.[6] The existence of this traffic spurred construction of the trans-Appalachian canals and railroad lines and joined together the two core areas of America.

Traffic flows and the American industrial belt

The other major feature which emerges from the rail flow pattern is the focusing of the transport net on the industrial belt. The industrial belt, because of its marked dominance in America, naturally has the greatest volume of transportation; it also aligns the routes of the rest of the country since it is the great market. Raw materials are shipped to it, finished products shipped out; as a result, traffic going into the belt is two or three times heavier than the return flows of lighter weight, higher value, finished products. (This phenomenon can readily be seen on the origin and destina-

---

5. See Donald J. Patton, "The Traffic Pattern on American Inland Waterways," Economic Geography, XXXII (1956), 29-37.

6. See George R. Taylor, The Transportation Revolution, 1815-1860, Vol. IV of The Economic History of the U.S. (New York: Rinehart & Co., 1951).

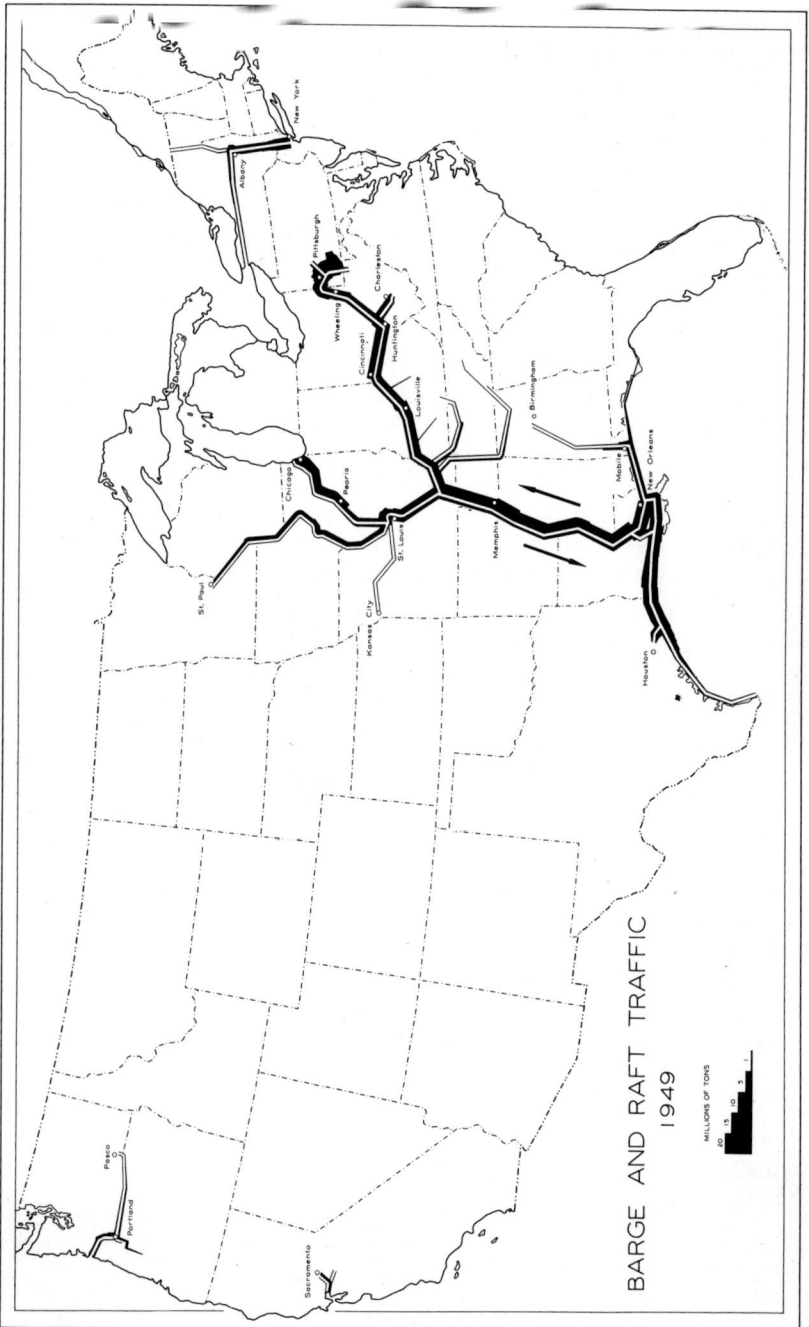

BARGE AND RAFT TRAFFIC
1949

MILLIONS OF TONS

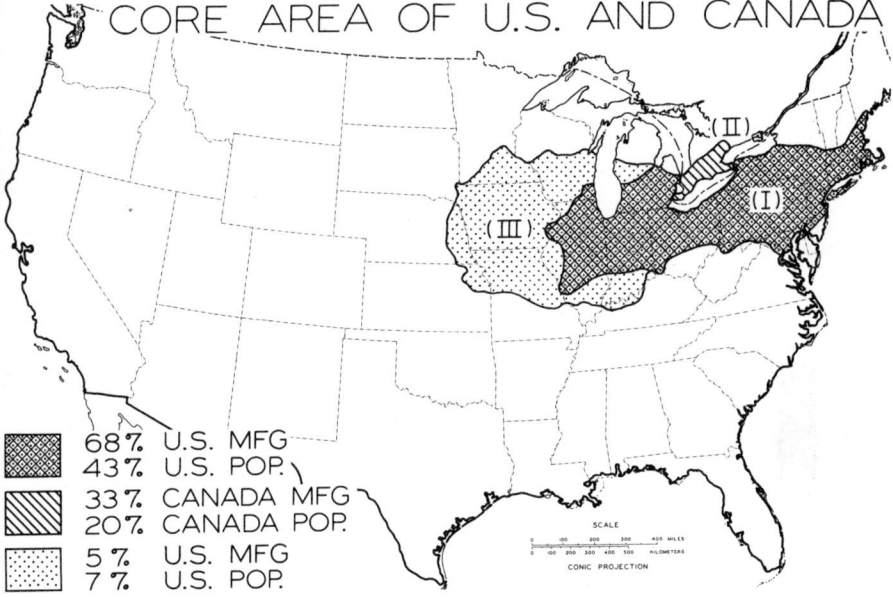

CORE AREA OF U.S. AND CANADA

68% U.S. MFG
43% U.S. POP.
33% CANADA MFG
20% CANADA POP.
5% U.S. MFG
7% U.S. POP.

CORE AREAS OF THE UNITED STATES AND CANADA

Additional data for these regions: Area I: 7. 7 per cent U. S. area; 52 per cent U. S. income; 70 per cent of persons listed in Who's Who. Area III: 6. 9 per cent U. S. area; 7. 3 per cent U. S. income. Areas I and III combined: 14. 6 per cent U. S. area; 50. 3 per cent U. S. population; 59. 3 per cent U. S. income; 73. 3 per cent U. S. industrial employment. Area II: . 4 per cent Canada area; 19. 8 per cent Canada population; 33 per cent Canada industrial employment. Areas I and II combined: 3. 7 per cent U. S. and Canada area; 41. 2 per cent U. S. and Canada population; 65. 9 per cent U. S. and Canada industrial employment. Areas I, II, and III combined: 6. 9 per cent U. S. and Canada area; 47. 7 per cent U. S. and Canada population; 70. 8 per cent U. S. and Canada industrial employment.

7

tion maps for New England and other areas in Chapter IV.)

Other Major Features of the American Flow Pattern

Coal has traditionally accounted for almost one-third of the American rail tonnage up until World War II, and even today is about one-quarter. This enormous flow can be seen in the central Appalachians of Pennsylvania, West Virginia, and Kentucky, and in the interior fields of southern Illinois, in all of which the heavy originating lines can be picked out on the flow map. On the origin and destination maps for the Far West the importance of Utah and Wyoming coal can be readily observed.

Especially prominent is the heavy flow in the East from the Pocahontas Area via the Norfolk and Western, Chesapeake and Ohio, and Virginian railways, with about two-thirds of the coal moving north and west to the interior and one-third east to Hampton Roads for water shipment, particularly up the coast to New England. (See maps of West Virginia rail coal shipments, Great Lakes, and eastern seaboard coal trade, on the following page.)[7] Appalachian coal is all-important to the American economy; it is in or near the center of the industrial belt and in addition moves great distances for such an apparently low value resource, reaching areas as remote as Maine, Ontario, North Dakota, and Georgia. This surprisingly long reach reflects: (1) route economies based on volume movement and mechanical loading, and the utilizing, for part of the haul, of cheap water transport on the Atlantic seaboard and on the Great Lakes, to the heads of Lakes Superior, Michigan, and Ontario (made even cheaper by "ballast" rates

---

7. Map A, Great Lakes Coal Traffic, is reproduced from a Corps of Engineers map in U. S. Department of the Army, Corps of Engineers, Transportation on the Great Lakes (Washington, D. C., 1932; revised 1937), p. 322; B, West Virginia Coal Shipments, was compiled from the ICC Carload Waybill Statistics, One Per Cent Sample of Terminations (Washington, D. C.); C, Coal Shipments along the Eastern Seaboard, was reproduced from U. S. Board of Investigation and Research, The Economics of Coal Traffic Flow, 79th Cong., 1st sess., Senate Doc. 82 (Washington, D. C., 1945).

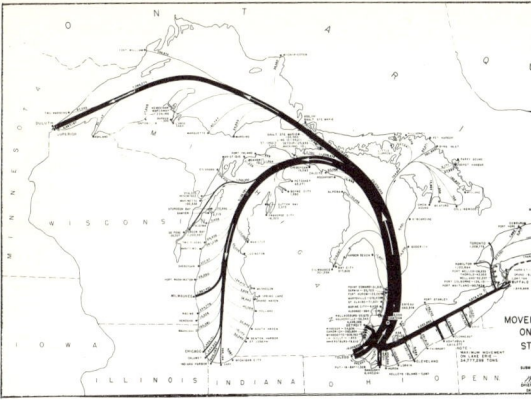

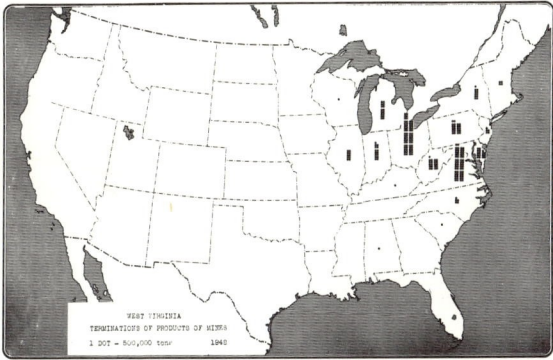

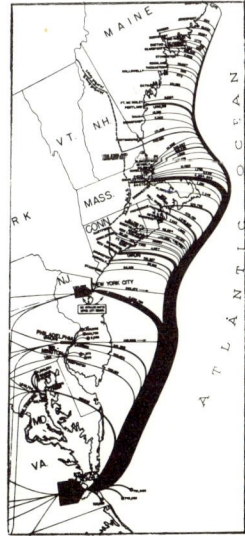

Movement of coal:
A, on Great Lakes;
B, from West Vir-
ginia; C, along east-
ern seaboard

for return hauls against the heavy movement of iron ore down part of the lakes); (2) the high quality and coking characteristics of Pocahontas and Pennsylvania coal, not possessed to the same degree by other fields and thus placing this coal partially in the category of a localized resource in general demand.

Iron ore also is near the industrial belt in transportation cost terms, since cheap Great Lakes water transport can be used to bring it to the belt. The heavy density of short lines on the rail flow map at the northwestern end of Lake Superior shows the rail haul of this ore from the Mesabi Range down to Lake Superior for transshipment. [8]

A new and vital resource which the industrial belt has in only negligible quantities is petroleum and natural gas, already the major source of energy in the United States. Fortunately for the industrial belt, oil is cheaply transported by pipeline or tanker, and gas by pipe; as a result the 1,000-1,500-mile distance from the southwestern fields is no major handicap. This movement by pipeline and tanker (see domestic tanker traffic maps in Chapter V) has become an important feature of the American traffic pattern. Already natural gas lines span the continent and cover more route miles than railroads, a direct function, in part, of the production of natural gas several times farther away from the industrial belt than

---

8. For flow maps of Great Lakes traffic in iron ore, coal, and wheat, and movements of iron ore to and from lake ports, see U.S. Department of the Army, Corps of Engineers, Transportation on the Great Lakes. These maps are also reproduced in Stuart Daggett, Principles of Inland Transportation (4th ed.; New York: Harper & Bros., 1955), where they can be readily consulted. Part III, pp. 127-226, of this work treats transportation geography in the United States and provides a most useful supplement to the present report.

Lake traffic is almost entirely bulk cargo, principally iron ore, followed by coal and limestone, with considerable wheat, especially on the Canadian side. The total traffic is large, representing the largest single flow in America. The Soo Canal traffic is about the same as Suez and for years was greater, before Middle East oil increased in flow. See Albert G. Ballert, "The Soo and the Suez," Science, CXXII (Oct. 28, 1955), 822-23.

coal. Cheapness of modern, large diameter pipelines and the efficiency and cheapness of production of natural gas enable it to compete, even though it is more remote. The construction of these pipelines represents the major change in the American transport pattern in the last two or three decades.

Tanker transport in volume is utilized for carrying petroleum from the Gulf to the eastern seaboard and from California to the Pacific Northwest, although Alberta oil is beginning to be pumped down to Washington via a new pipeline. (For maps of petroleum movements and of total traffic see Chapter V.)

Three other persistent, major generators of the American flow pattern, which can be observed on the origin and destination maps, should also be noted:

1. The location of the principal agricultural regions of the United States, namely, the fertile corn belt adjacent to or in the western part of the industrial belt, and the contiguous spring and winter wheat belts farther west, the most important agricultural and animal products shipping areas of the country.

2. The location of the principal forest areas of the United States, the Pacific Northwest, and the South, and to a much smaller extent the forest remnants of northern New England and northern Michigan, Wisconsin, and Minnesota.

3. The location of the relatively small, off-season citrus and other fruit and early vegetable producing areas in the United States subtropics, particularly Florida and California. These climatically localized specialty areas persistently show up in the state origin and destination maps, although the tonnage produced is not as great as in the other areas enumerated above. California reaches clear across the country, but Florida is restricted largely to the area from Illinois east for large shipments. [9] The contribution of these areas is a reflection of the commercialized, year-round diet of the Amer-

---

9. This "reach" is interrelated with the blanketing of large parts of the East in freight rates from California. See Stuart Daggett and John P. Carter, The Structure of Transcontinental Railroad Rates (Berkeley, Calif.: University of California Press, 1947). To a degree the same holds true for Florida, but because of shorter distances the effect is not as great.

icon public and gives rise to some of the longest land hauls in the United States and indeed in the whole world.

In addition, inspection of the state-to-state origin and destination maps reveals in every case heavy traffic within each state and between adjacent states. This indicates the very real effects of friction of distance or transport costs on the movement of many products such as ubiquitous, low-value bulk items like common sand, gravel, bricks, or other primary "weight-losing" raw materials like ores or logs. There is also much interchange of higher value products used in complex manufacturing and assembly operations.

II

The Location of Railroad Offices and Yards

THE LOCATION of railroad offices and yards reveals unsus-
pected interrelations between commodity flow and American
geography. The explanation of this distribution illustrates
some of the consequences of an interaction approach to area
analysis.

On the home office maps note the striking concentration of
headquarters in gateway cities around the edges of the industrial belt. [1] This is a logical arrangement and an integral
feature of the American spatial economy. Home offices for
most of the lines running from the eastern seaboard to the
interior are in the coastal gateways: New York for the New
York Central and others, Philadelphia for the Pennsylvania,
Baltimore for the Baltimore and Ohio, and so forth. On the
southern and western margins of the industrial belt are Washington for the Southern Railway, Louisville for the Louisville
and Nashville, St. Louis for the southwestern roads, and
Chicago, Omaha, and the Twin Cities for the western transcontinentals. (The concentration of offices in Cleveland is

---

1. Home office locations were obtained from the Official
Guide of the Railways and Steam Navigation Lines of the United States (New York: National Railway Publishing Co., 1950);
net revenue for each railway company is from the ICC Sixty-
third Annual Report of the Statistics of Railways in the United
States . . . (Washington, D.C., 1951). The concentration of
offices in Cleveland is a result of the unusual control of several lines obtained by the Van Sweringens initially in the
1920's, when they moved the offices to their huge new office
building in the new Terminal Station. Some of these lines do
not even touch Cleveland.

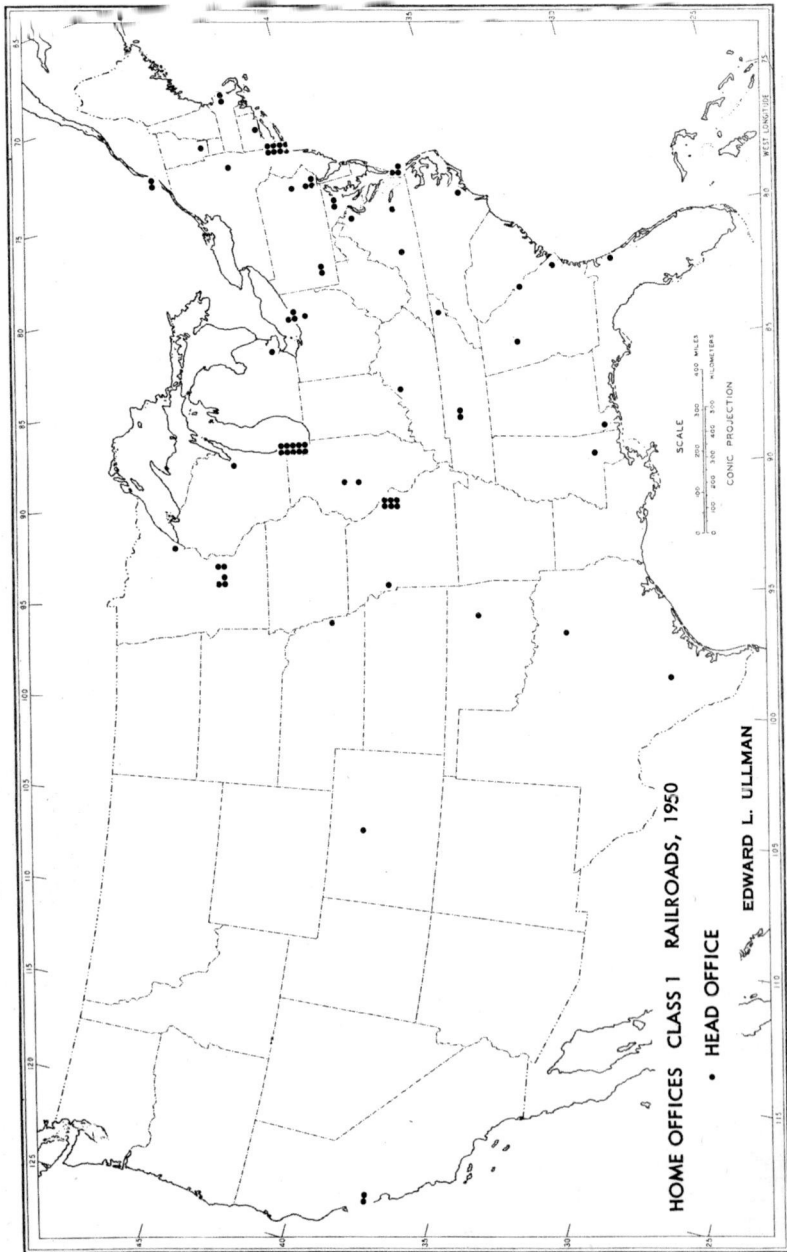

HOME OFFICES CLASS 1 RAILROADS, 1950

• HEAD OFFICE

EDWARD L. ULLMAN

14

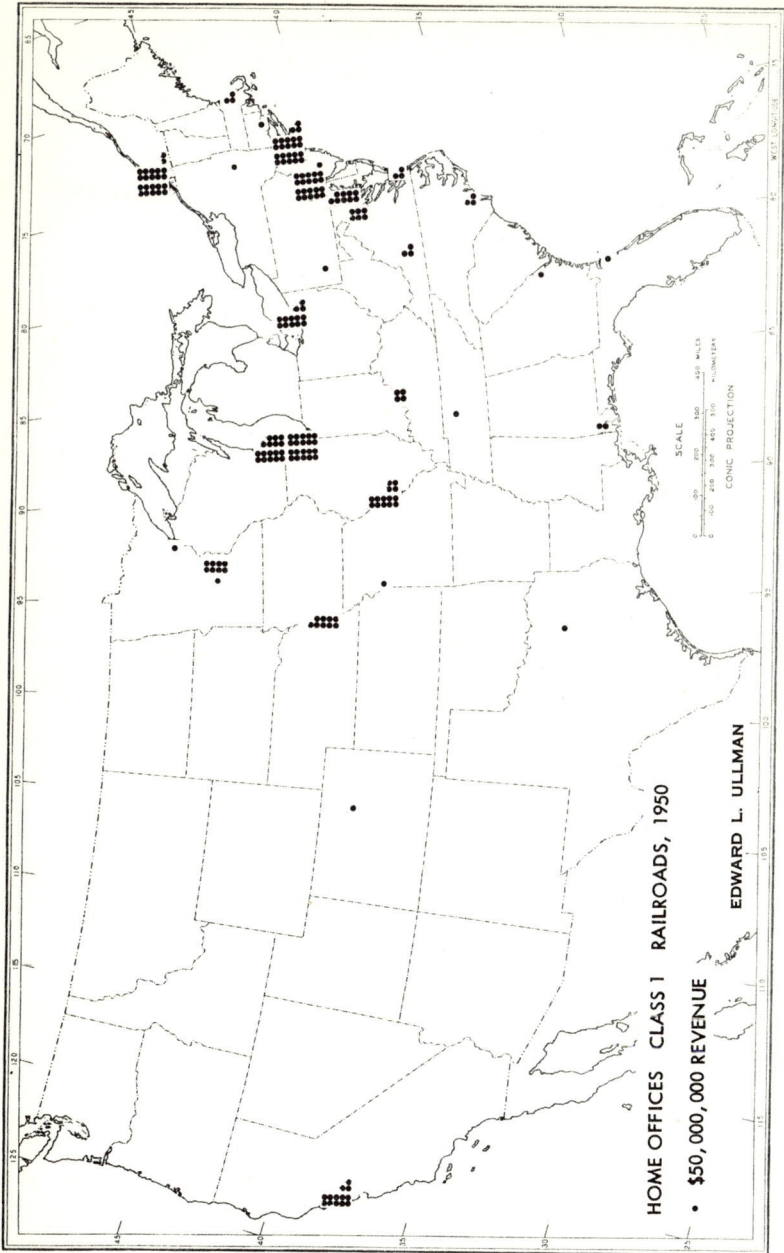

HOME OFFICES   CLASS 1   RAILROADS, 1950

• $50,000,000 REVENUE

EDWARD L. ULLMAN

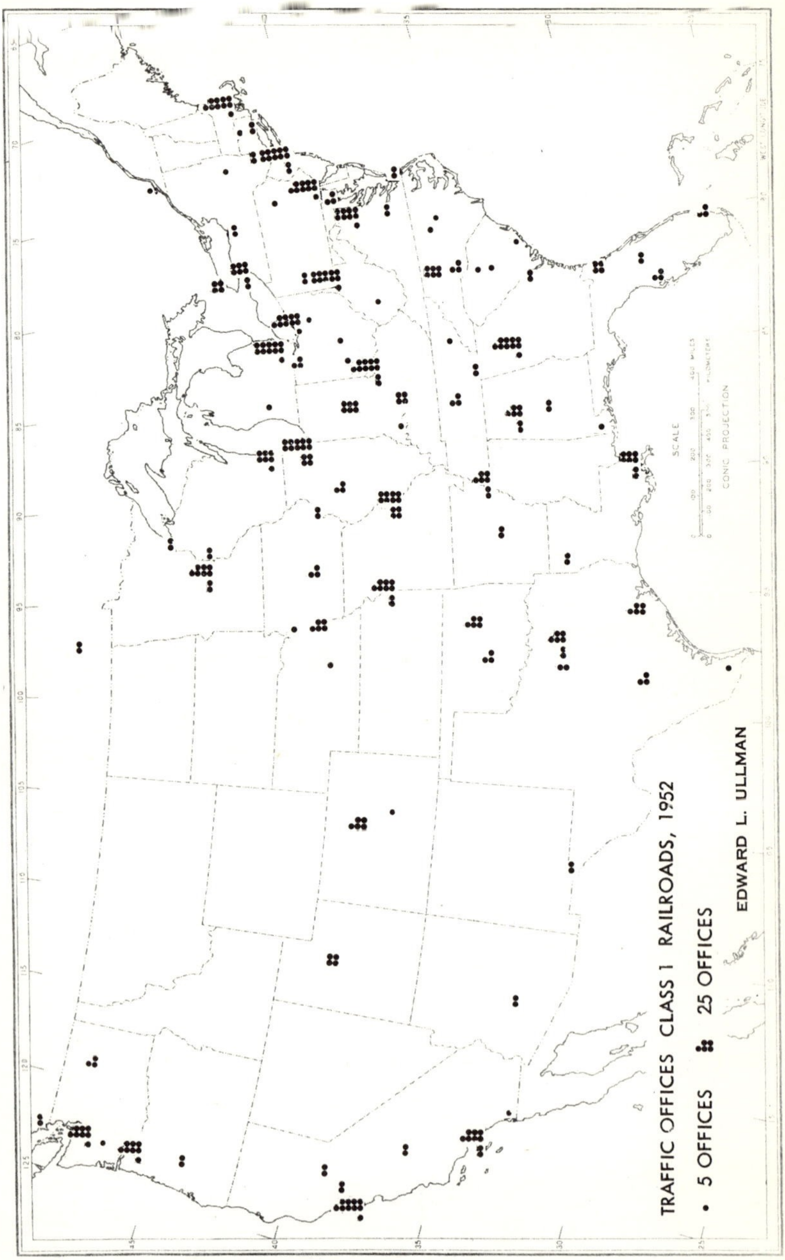

TRAFFIC OFFICES CLASS 1 RAILROADS, 1952
• 5 OFFICES
25 OFFICES
EDWARD L. ULLMAN
SCALE
CONIC PROJECTION

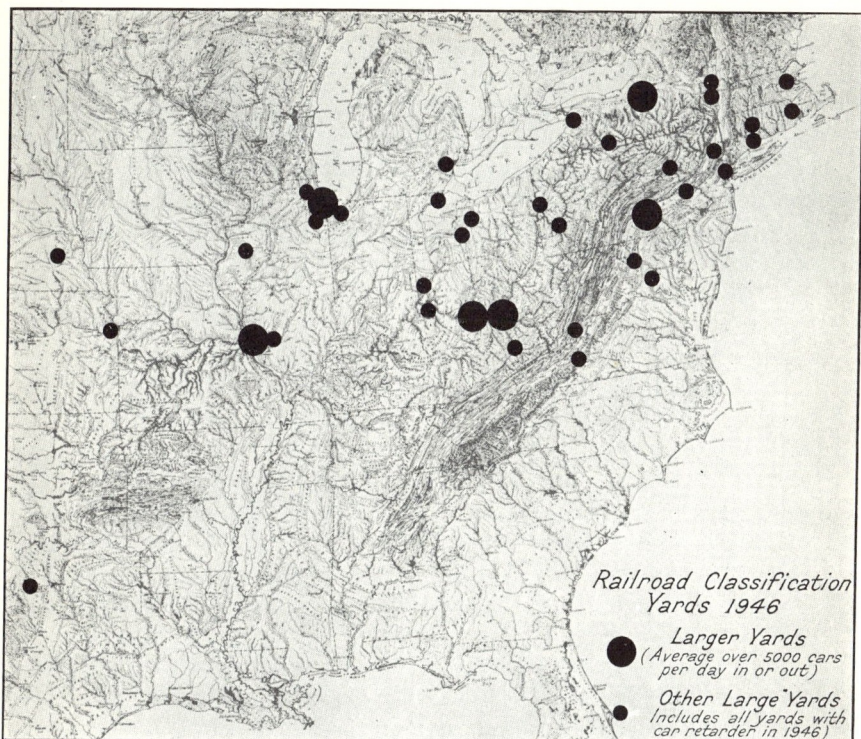

Railroad Classification
Yards 1946

Larger Yards
(Average over 5000 cars
per day in or out)

Other Large Yards
Includes all yards with
car retarder in 1946)

Location of principal freight classification yards in the United States, 1946. Location of larger yards based on Freight Terminal Survey of Association of American Railroads, 1946; other large yards from same source plus all yards with car retarders (indicative of the larger and busier yards), as reported by Union Switch and Signal Company and General Railway Signal Company. (Base reproduced from Erwin Raisz: Map of Landforms of the United States, 1939.)

a special page not altering the conclusions; see explanation at end of note 1.) Major centers outside the belt include port gateways, the original starting points for construction of some systems inland, for example: Wilmington, North Carolina, for the Atlantic Coast Line; Mobile for the Gulf Mobile and Ohio; and San Francisco for the Southern Pacific (originally Central Pacific).

The map of traffic solicitation offices shows a quite different pattern. [2] As would be expected, the great concentration of offices is in the industrial belt. Number of offices correlates fairly well with size of cities, with some notable exceptions. Thus, Chicago and New York are at the top. Philadelphia, presumably because it is so close to New York, is smaller than either Detroit or Pittsburgh. These latter two cities, although not having many lines, are the capitals respectively of the huge automobile and steel industries, which ship in volume all over the country. Pittsburgh is also the home office for some large industries. According to traffic men, Pittsburgh, because of its home office character, specifies the routing of much freight which does not originate or terminate in that city.

Baltimore is an example of a large city (about one million population) with very few traffic offices, mainly because so much of the business is handled out of nearby Washington, D. C. Eugene, Oregon, has the same number of offices (thirteen) as Baltimore, although it is only about one-tenth the size. This is a postwar phenomenon reflecting Eugene's rise to become the leading lumber center of the nation. This lumber, as the state-to-state maps show, is shipped in quantity over all of the United States except to the competing Southeast. Railroads naturally seek to service this volume, long-haul business, the mainstay of the Pacific Northwest traffic.

Other traffic solicitation offices reflect still other traffic characteristics, as the maps show, but space precludes detailed treatment. A somewhat more sharply differentiated pattern, with the larger places showing up as even larger, would undoubtedly emerge if some measure of the relative importance of each of the offices such as volume of business

2. Data for this map were obtained by listing the number of traffic offices by cities as reported by the Official Guide of the Railways for 1952.

or number of employees were available. Unfortunately such data are not readily obtainable from the numerous railroad companies.

A still different pattern is the distribution of the largest classification yards of United States railroads in 1946. As will be noted from the map, the largest yards are not concentrated primarily either in the largest cities or in gateways. The principal yards are athwart the main flows as shown on the frontispiece map, and most of them are naturally in the industrial belt where traffic is heavy. Specifically, they are especially located at the entrances or exits to the Appalachians where rail routes are constricted or fan out in entering or leaving the barrier zone. They are thus, logically, at the funnel points for traffic.

The largest yard is Enola, at Harrisburg on the Pennsylvania, where its tracks fan out on leaving the Appalachians, followed by DeWitt at Syracuse on the New York Central; two large yards on the west side of the Appalachians serving the enormous coal flows, respectively, of the Chesapeake and Ohio and the Norfolk and Western railroads; and, of equal or greater importance, the two large yards at the two major rail centers of the United States, Chicago and St. Louis.

Since 1946 additional car retarder yards, the indicator used to indicate most active use, have been constructed. Some of them are at the entrances or exits of the Cascade-Sierra range, just as has been noted for the Appalachians. They include Pasco, on the Northern Pacific, and Oroville and Roseville in the Central Valley of California on the Western Pacific and Southern Pacific, respectively. Still others are elsewhere, in large centers or at strategic points fairly long distances outside such centers.

19

III

The Bases for Transportation and Interaction

A STUDY of the state-to-state traffic flow maps in Chapter IV brings to light specialized production and consumption areas and the effect of distance. As a basis for explanation of these patterns and physical interaction in general, the following system is proposed:[1]

1. Complementarity[2]

It has been asserted that circulation or interaction is a result of areal differentiation. To a degree this is true, but mere differentiation does not produce interchange. Many areas in the world differ from one another but have no interconnections.

In order to have interaction between two areas there must be a demand in one and a supply in the other. Thus a steel industry in one area would use the iron ore produced in another but not the copper produced in still another. Specific complementarity is required before interchange takes place.

---

1. The section that follows is taken, with some abbreviations and modifications, from the author's paper on "The Role of Transportation and the Bases for Interaction," published, as part of the Wenner-Gren Foundation International Symposium held in 1955 at Princeton, in Man's Role in Changing the Face of the Earth, William L. Thomas, Jr., ed. (Chicago: University of Chicago Press, 1956), pp. 862-80. The system is also included in the author's paper on "Geography as Spatial Interaction," Annals of the Association of American Geographers, XLIV (1954), 283-84.

2. The term "complementary" is commonly used in economics and international trade. I am indebted to Mathilda Holzman for suggesting its use in the present context.

So important is complementarity that relatively low-value bulk products move all over the world, utilizing, it is true, relatively cheap water transport for most of the haul. Some cheap products in the distant interior of continents, however, also move long distances. Thus, when the steel mills were built in Chicago, they required coking coal and reached out as far as West Virginia to get suitable supplies, in spite of the fact that the distance was more than five hundred miles by land transport and the coal was relatively low value.

Complementarity is a function both of natural and cultural areal differentiation and of areal differentiation based simply on the operation of economies of scale.[3] One larger plant may be so much more economical than several smaller ones that it can afford to import raw materials and ship finished products great distances; thus, interaction may take place between two apparently similar regions, such as shipment of some specialized logging equipment from the Pacific Northwest to forest areas of the South. In this case the similarity in other respects of the two regions provides the market and encourages the interaction. This, however, is insufficient to affect significantly many total interactions because specialized products based on distinctive natural or other local advantages dominate the total trade of many regions. Thus, total shipments from Washington or Oregon to southern states are low because of the dominance of forest products in each. As another example, the United States, with its high labor costs, presumably ships few labor-intensive products to cheap-labor countries like Japan, although the exact nature of this classic characterization of United States foreign trade, based on "factors of production" as set forth by Ohlin and others, is now a matter of dispute among economists.[4]

---

3. Bertil Ohlin, Interregional and International Trade (Cambridge, Mass.: Harvard University Press, 1933). It should be noted that national competition among companies may also result in greater geographical concentration and longer hauls. Many companies seek a national market because they are unable to obtain all the business in one region, which might be sufficient to support a regional monopoly but not several regional producers.

4. See Wassily W. Leontieff, "Domestic Production and Foreign Trade," Proceedings of the American Philosophical

7. Intervening opportunity

Complementarity, however, generates interchange between two areas only if no intervening complementary source of supply is available. Thus, few forest products moved from the Pacific Northwest to the markets of the interior Northeast sixty years ago, primarily because the Great Lakes area provided an intervening source. Florida attracts more amenity migrants from the Northeast than does more distant California (see map). Probably many fewer people go from New Haven to Philadelphia than would be the case if there were no New York City in between as an intervening opportunity. This, presumably, is a manifestation of Stouffer's law of intervening opportunity, [5] a fundamental determinant of spatial interaction, and the second factor proposed for a system of explanation.

Under certain circumstances, intervening opportunity might ultimately help to create interaction between distant complementary areas by providing a nearby complementary source which would make construction of transport routes profitable and thus pay for part of the cost of constructing a route to the more distant source. On a small scale this process is followed in building logging railroads; the line is extended bit by bit as supplies of timber near the mill are exhausted, and ultimately trains are run long distances between mill and supply. If the line had had to be constructed the long distance initially, it might never have been built. On a larger and more complex scale this is what happens in transcontinental railroads--every effort is made to develop way business, and, as

Society, XCVII (1953), 332-49, reprinted in Economia Internazionale, VII (February, 1954); P. T. Ellsworth, "The Structure of American Trade: A New View Re-examined," Review of Economics and Statistics, XXXVI (August, 1954), 279-85; Boris C. Swerling, "Capital Shortage and Labor Surplus in the United States," Review of Economics and Statistics, XXXVI (August, 1954), 286-89. Note Swerling's conclusion that the major feature of United States imports is that they consist largely of raw materials and other items as determined by natural conditions of climate, mineral resources, and so forth.

5. Samuel Stouffer, "Intervening Opportunities: A Theory Relating Mobility to Distances," American Sociological Review, V (1940), 845-67.

this business develops, it contributes to some of the fixed costs for long-distance interchange.

3. Transferability

A final factor required in an interaction system is transferability or distance, measured in real terms of transfer and time costs. If the distance between market and supply were too great and too costly to overcome, interaction would not take place in spite of perfect complementarity and lack of intervening opportunity. Alternate goods would be substituted where possible; bricks would be used instead of wood, and so forth.

Thus, we might consider that the factor of intervening opportunity results in a substitution of areas, and the factor of transferability or distance results in a substitution of products.

It is a mistake, therefore, to assume that all places, even giant commercial centers, are linked equally with other producing areas and centers of the world. Distance and intervening opportunity drastically trim down the relative quantity of these dramatic, long-distance relationships which international trade enthusiasts like to emphasize. Great Britain and the United States provide two contrasting examples. To reach enough complementary sources, Britain must trade with the world. The United States, on the other hand, can reach sufficiently complementary areas merely by trading within its own borders to account for the overwhelming bulk of its trade, with almost half of the value of the remainder coming from Canada and the nearby Caribbean, although some of course comes from the farthest reaches of the world and more will probably follow as the United States exhausts its own raw materials. [6]

---

6. On a weight basis the percentage would be even higher. Specific value percentages of total United States foreign trade are as follows: 1950: 21 per cent U.S. exports to Canada, 21 per cent to Caribbean (including Mexico, Central America, West Indies, north coast South America) or 42 per cent of total U.S. exports; 22 per cent of U.S. imports from Canada, 22 per cent from Caribbean, total 44 per cent of U.S. imports; 1938: 15 per cent U.S. exports to Canada, 12 per cent to Caribbean, total 27 per cent; 14 per cent imports from Canada, 15 per cent from Caribbean, total 29 per cent. These

To sum up--a system explaining material interaction can be based on three factors: (1) complementarity, a function of areal differentiation promoting spatial interaction; (2) intervening complementarity (or "opportunities") between two regions or places; (3) transferability (distance) measured in real terms including cost and time of transport and effect of improvement in facilities.

The system proposed applies primarily to interaction based on physical movement, principally of goods, but also to a large extent for people. It does not apply to spread of ideas or most other types of communication, except as they accompany the flow of goods or people, which admittedly is often the case. Intervening opportunity, for example, would seem to facilitate rather than check the spread of ideas. Similarity of two regions also would probably facilitate the spread of ideas more than difference or complementarity, although the latter would be important for some cases.

An empirical formula often employed to describe many types of interaction is a gravity model which states that interaction between two places is directly proportionate to the product of the populations or some other measures of volume of two places and inversely proportionate to the distance (or distance modified by some exponent) between the two areas. This measure is often written $\dfrac{P_1 P_2}{d^n}$ (population of place 1 times population of place 2 divided by d, the distance between the two places, with d modified by some exponent, n). This model, however, is useless in describing many interactions because it assumes perfect or near perfect complementarity, a condition which seldom obtains for physical flows. Some form of the model apparently does come close to describing many interchanges, even for goods in a few cases, but apparently primarily for many more or less universal, undifferentiated types of flow such as migration of some people, or telephone calls between

---

percentages were calculated from figures in U. S. Maritime Administration, Review of Essential United States Foreign Trade Routes (Washington, D. C. , May, 1953). See also Tables 4 and 5 in Chapter VI, which, however, do not include Great Lakes and land trade with Canada.

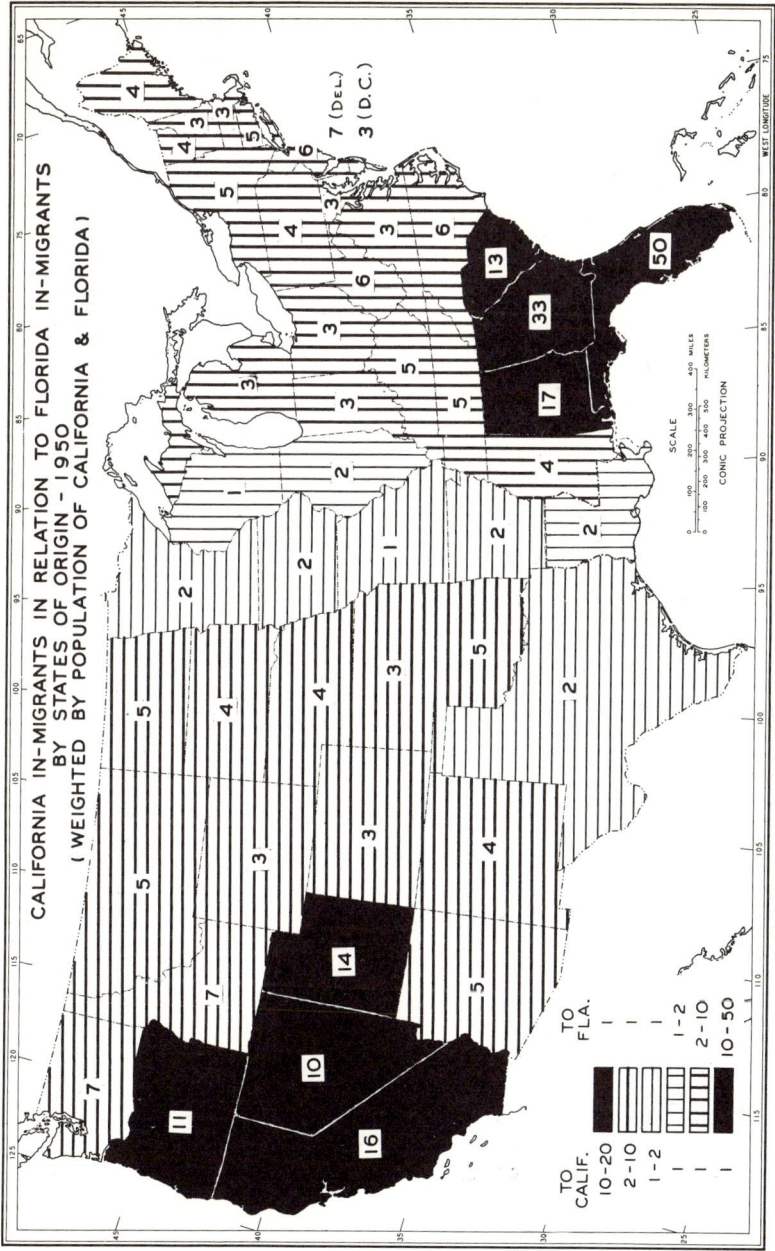

CALIFORNIA IN-MIGRANTS IN RELATION TO FLORIDA IN-MIGRANTS
BY STATES OF ORIGIN – 1950
(WEIGHTED BY POPULATION OF CALIFORNIA & FLORIDA)

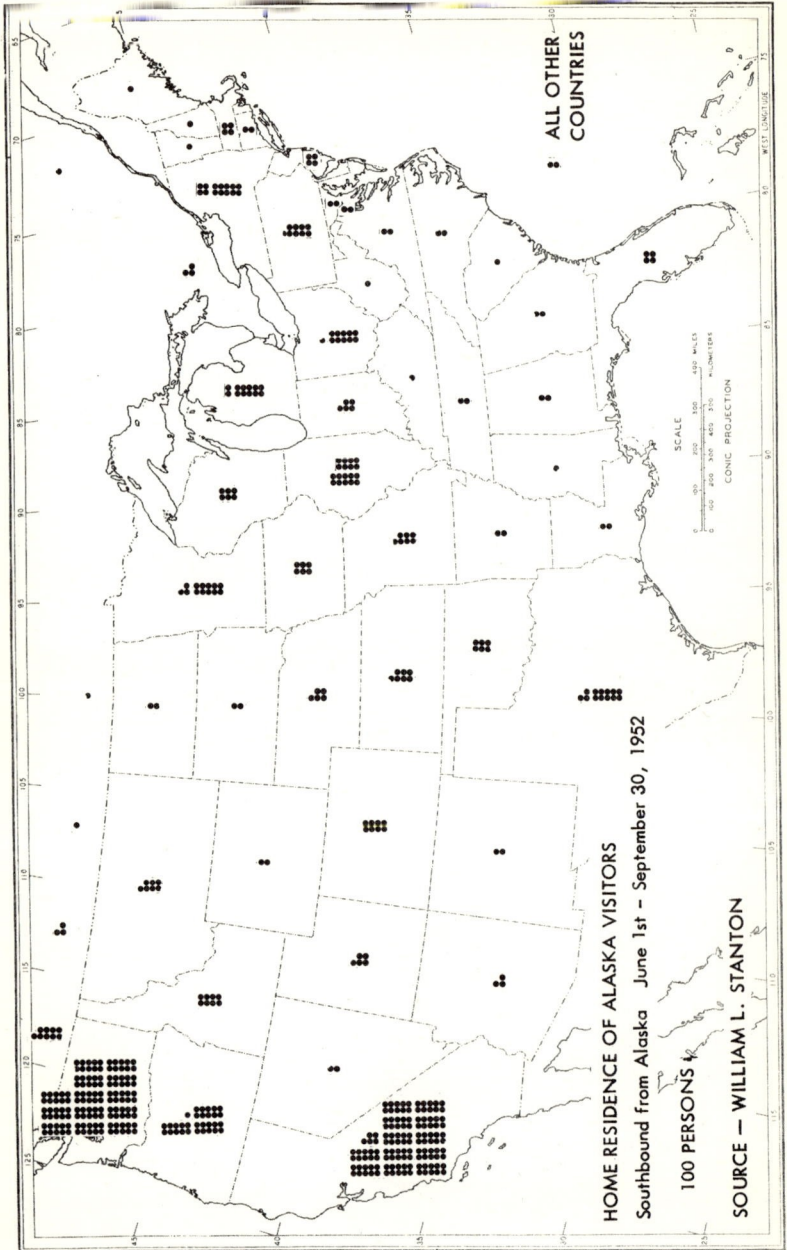

HOME RESIDENCE OF ALASKA VISITORS

Southbound from Alaska   June 1st – September 30, 1952

100 PERSONS

SOURCE – WILLIAM L. STANTON

ALL OTHER
COUNTRIES

SCALE

CONIC PROJECTION

cities. It has been developed by Zipf, Stewart, Dodd, and others. [7]

The map showing origin of visitors to Alaska exhibits a somewhat regular distribution, outside of Pacific Coast states, which correlates fairly well with a p/d (population/distance) relationship. William Stanton demonstrates this when the state data are grouped by geographic census regions. [8] Washington and California, however, show far greater numbers of visitors than the normal p/d relationship. This is not surprising. Seattle is the capital of Alaska for many activities; its ties are therefore close. (Perhaps even this relationship could be equated with a p/d measure if it were recognized that d from Seattle is almost 0.) California is a more puzzling case. It may well be that the extensive travel habits of Californians and relatively close business ties with San Francisco, coupled with the fact that Alaska is a relatively nearby region with a different scenic lure, result in the large numbers. In this case, intervening opportunities for northern scenery in the rest of the country would cut down the number of visitors from eastern United States to Alaska.

---

7. George K. Zipf, Human Behavior and the Principle of Least Effort (Cambridge, Mass.: Addison-Wesley Press, 1949); John Q. Stewart, "Empirical Mathematical Rules concerning the Distribution and Equilibrium of Population," Geographical Review, XXXVII (1947), 461-85; Stuart C. Dodd, "The Interactance Hypothesis: A Gravity Model Fitting Physical Masses and Human Groups," American Sociological Review, XV (1950), 245-56; Joseph A. Cavanaugh, "Formulation, Analysis and Testing of the Interactance Hypothesis," American Sociological Review, XV (1950), 763-66.

8. William L. Stanton, "The Purpose and Source of Seasonal Migration to Alaska," Economic Geography, XXXI (1955), 138-48. Data for the map were obtained from William L. Stanton, Associate Professor of Marketing, University of Washington, and were a result of an original research project conducted by Professor Stanton.

IV

State-to-State Rail Freight Movements

THE MOST important feature of the pattern of state-to-state rail flows, shown on the maps for twenty representative states which follow, is the concentration of flows in the region of state of origin and destination. [1] This obtains even if the state is located in a sparsely populated, relatively unproductive region. The localization of flows is a very real reflection of the cost of movement--of the friction of distance--and the importance of transferability in the interaction system proposed in Chapter III. Although this gross characterization applies to the major part of the tonnage flows, it is not characteristic of a significant minority of longer flows, which reflect instead complementarity and intervening opportunity in our system.

The localization is also not as true if the volume of flows is measured by value instead of by weight. Several sample maps upon estimated value have been prepared, but they are not reproduced because too many errors or uncertainties result to make them completely reliable. [2] Nevertheless, it is quite clear that a state such as Washington has many more long-distance connections, primarily to the industrial belt, when flows are measured in value terms. This, of course, could be inferred from the dominance of manufacturing flows

---

1. See Notes on Reading the Maps (pp. xxi-xxii) for explanation of symbols used on state-to-state flow maps.

2. In part because converting weights to values requires data on specific commodity composition, resulting in smaller flows and therefore lesser sample reliability, and in part because more movements are suppressed for specific flows because of possible violation of the vexing disclosure rule.

from the industrial belt, on the one hand, and the heavy, but low-value shipment of forest products (logs) within Washington, on the other hand. In many cases, also, the balance of traffic is evened out or even reversed when measured in value, as would be expected. In general terms, of course, heavy commodities subject to great weight loss in processing tend to be processed close to the source of supply, in line with standard industrial location theory, and lighter weight, higher value end products, able to stand higher transport costs, are shipped greater distances. Nevertheless, even in value terms, local short movements are great. [3]

Many of the short-tonnage flows themselves are also a response to excellent complementarity and lack of intervening opportunity in nearby areas, so that it is difficult if not impossible to isolate out transferability of distance as the independent variable explaining the distribution. This is particularly true in the core area of the country, the Northeast and Middle West, where resources, production, population, and markets are so large that much complementarity can be achieved merely by short movements.

Stated in another way, the average length of freight haul for railroads, which represented more than half the total ton miles of all forms of transport in the United States in 1948, was 405 miles, made up of overlapping long, medium, and short hauls. Truck hauls were much shorter, and water and pipeline movements probably somewhat longer. This average length of haul, as well as the flows on the maps, generally represents only single hauls in one stage of processing, i. e., hog from farm to packer, or pork products from packer to market, but not both, to say nothing of corn from farm to hog, to packer, to consumer, and so forth. Inclusion of movement through all stages, although increasing average length of haul, would also bring in much backtracking, so that the net geographical distance covered from original producer to final consumer would not be increased nearly as much as the total transport haul.

---

3. The same holds true for Europe, where countries generally have greater value of trade with their near neighbors than with more distant ones. See W. Beckerman, "Distance and the Pattern of Intra-European Trade," Review of Economics and Statistics, XXXVIII (February, 1956), 31-40.

What does the foregoing localization of flows mean? I sus-
pect it indicates, among other things, a modification of the
meaning attached by some to the traditional concept of the
United States as the largest national market in the world,
admittedly characterized by a remarkable unity of culture
and hence presumed capable of supporting mass production
in all lines on a scale impossible in the rest of the world. It
is true that the size of the United States market is a great
advantage, but the United States market is also made up of
regional markets, perhaps not unlike some of the separate
countries of Europe if the international boundaries were blurred.
The existence of these markets depends upon the regional
economies of scale possible and the distance from competition
of the main United States producing and consuming areas.
California, and even the whole West Coast, is the outstanding
example; it is separated from the rest of the country by a
wide, relatively unproductive area but is growing rapidly,
creating its own market so that new thresholds for mass production and branch plants presumably are being reached.
However, even within the industrial belt (not to mention the
South and Midwest), regional markets exist; the iron and
steel industry, for example, long centered in the Pittsburgh
area, several decades ago reached out to Chicago essentially
to supply the market and is now expanding vigorously in the
Philadelphia region to supply the populous eastern seaboard.
Increasing economies in the use of fuels and raw materials,
common to many industries, appear to be creating more of
a market orientation of industry than formerly. (In the case
of iron and steel, of course, the opening up of overseas ore
sources to supplement Mesabi on Lake Superior is an additional
pull to the East Coast.)

The best approach to a concept of the American market
may be to think of a series of overlapping regions, "self-
sufficient" in many goods but each affecting its neighbor and thus
creating a sort of wave- or chainlike reaction, modified here
and there by relative traffic deserts and character of transport (such as cheap water routes)--an interconnected, feder-
ated, national economy. It definitely is not one market for
most producers, and yet it provides the opportunity for one
market for a significant, critical number of specialized or
volume producers of finished products or of naturally localized primary products like certain minerals or fruits. Perhaps ideas and culture, as represented by national advertis-

ing, magazines, brand names, and uniform language, move more readily across the United States than do goods, but they in turn set the stage for the flow of goods.

THE CASES OF IOWA, CONNECTICUT, AND WASHINGTON AS SAMPLE ANALYSES

Analysis of the flow patterns, both for rail and for other major forms of transport, of three representative states follows. In the preceding chapters major features of other flows have been touched upon; the reader is also referred to the maps for twenty states which follow for verification of the previous generalizations and for his own analysis. The major features of the analysis are best shown by the maps, in any case, and in far less space than a text would permit. [4]

Three states with approximately the same population and labor force, but with contrasting economies (affecting complementarity) and in contrasting locations (affecting transferability), have been chosen as comparative examples in order to

---

4. Traffic for Iowa and Connecticut is presented for origins and destinations, for total shipments, and also subdivided into six major commodity groups: Products of Agriculture, Animals and Products, Products of Mines (excluding petroleum), Products of Forests, Petroleum and Products, and Manufactures and Miscellaneous (excluding petroleum). Washington follows the standard ICC five-fold classification: Products of Agriculture, Animals, Mines, Forests, and Manufactures and Miscellaneous. In this case crude oil is listed under Mines, and refined products (gasoline, etc.) are under Manufactures. Inclusion of petroleum under Manufactures or Mines tends to obscure significant relationships because petroleum and products are so important and generally do not come from the same geographic areas as other manufactures or mine products. For this reason a separate petroleum category has been made up for many states in this report. For Washington (and Connecticut), lack of a separate petroleum category is not as serious, however, as for many other states. For destination of Connecticut and Iowa Products of Mines, it is of no importance, since no crude oil moves out of either state. (For other comments on how to read the maps, see the note on pp. xxi-xxii.)

31

isolate the effects of these two characteristics (see Table 2). They are:

1. Connecticut, a small, populous, industrial state on the eastern edge of the United States manufacturing belt, characterized particularly by the high-value, refined nature of its manufactured products and the absence of raw materials.

2. Iowa, in the center of the country, just west of the manufacturing belt, generally considered the richest agricultural state, based on fertile prairie soil, producing particularly corn (fed to hogs) and animal and other agricultural products.

3. Washington, in the remote northwest corner of America, characterized by raw material production, principally forest products, in which it is second in importance only to neighboring Oregon.

TABLE 2
SELECTED CHARACTERISTICS OF CONNECTICUT, IOWA, AND WASHINGTON*

	Population 1950 (1,000's)	Agricultural Workers on Farms Jan., 1945 (1,000's)	Manufacturing Employees 1947 (1,000's)	Volume of Saw Timber on Commercial Forest Lands, 1945 (billions of board ft.)
Connecticut	2,007	31	400	1.6
Iowa	2,621	308	140	5.3
Washington	2,379	100	144	249.5

*U.S. Bureau of the Census, Department of Commerce, Statistical Abstract of the U.S., 1951 (Washington, D.C.: Government Printing Office, 1951), pp. 31, 180, 650, 767.

Iowa

Space will allow only a brief treatment of most of the trade of the individual states. In the discussion of traffic-generating areas earlier, some aspects have already been noted. For Iowa, as well as all the other states, note that the greatest concentration of flows is with nearby areas, reflecting the very real friction of distance on movements of all kinds.

Animals and Products, and Products of Agriculture, two categories in which Iowa is prominent, exhibit somewhat similar aspects: the origin of flows in the western agricultural states (for example, wheat and feed grains from nearby states), and the marketing of the products in the eastern industrial states, with hogs and other live animals moving to the nearby

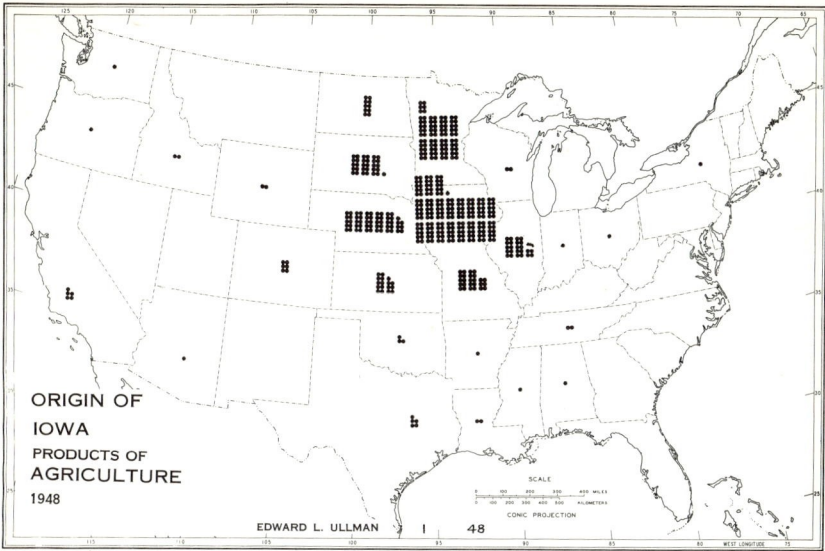

ORIGIN OF
IOWA
PRODUCTS OF
AGRICULTURE
1948

EDWARD L. ULLMAN   I   48

SCALE

CONIC PROJECTION

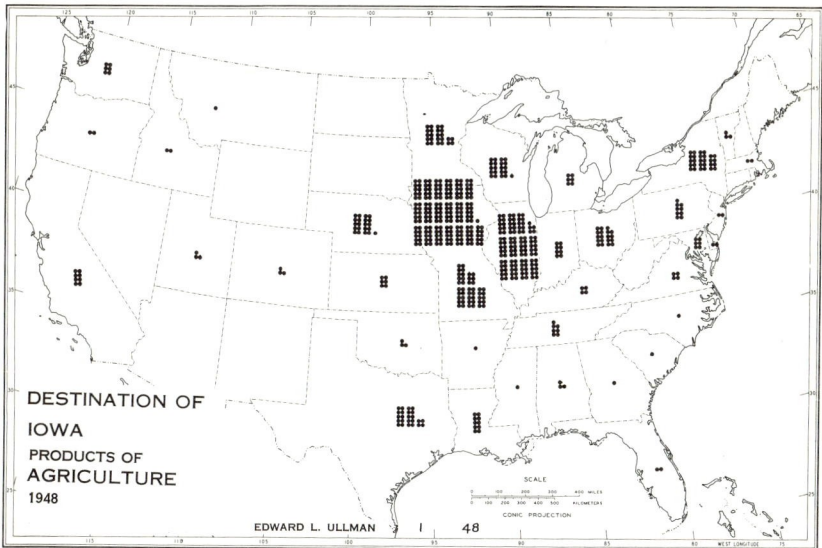

DESTINATION OF
IOWA
PRODUCTS OF
AGRICULTURE
1948

EDWARD L. ULLMAN   I   48

SCALE

CONIC PROJECTION

• 10,000 TONS   100,000 TONS

33

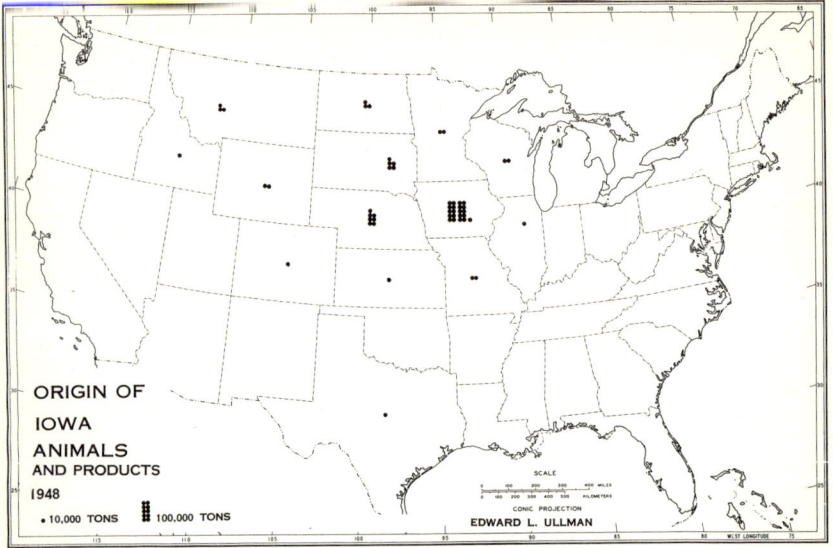

ORIGIN OF
IOWA
ANIMALS
AND PRODUCTS
1948

• 10,000 TONS   ▪ 100,000 TONS

SCALE

CONIC PROJECTION
EDWARD L. ULLMAN

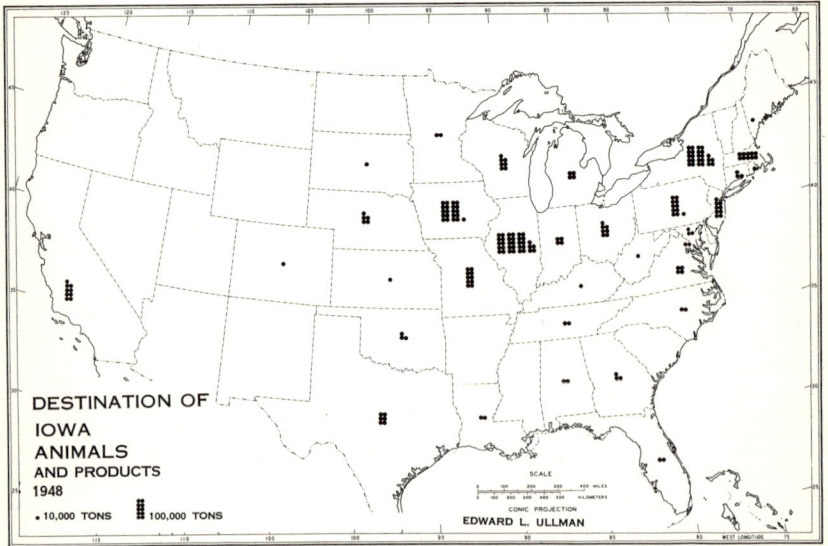

DESTINATION OF
IOWA
ANIMALS
AND PRODUCTS
1948

• 10,000 TONS   ▪ 100,000 TONS

SCALE

CONIC PROJECTION
EDWARD L. ULLMAN

• 10,000 TONS   ▪ 100,000 TONS

34

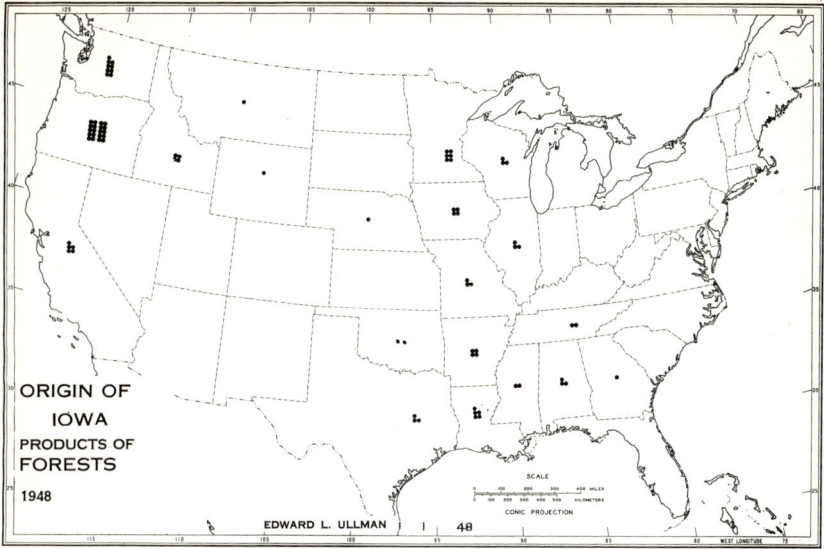

ORIGIN OF
IOWA
PRODUCTS OF
FORESTS
1948

SCALE

EDWARD L. ULLMAN

CONIC PROJECTION

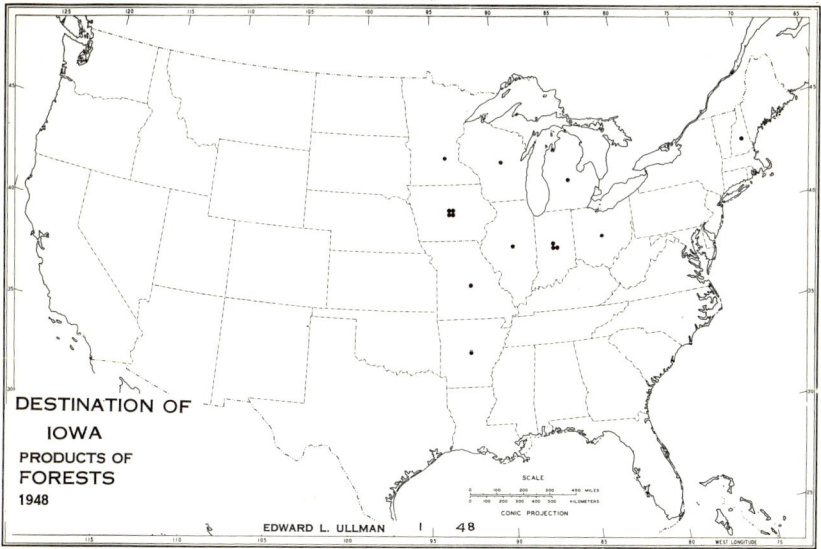

DESTINATION OF
IOWA
PRODUCTS OF
FORESTS
1948

SCALE

EDWARD L. ULLMAN

CONIC PROJECTION

• 10,000 TONS   100,000 TONS

35

ORIGIN OF
IOWA
PETROLEUM PRODUCTS
1948

EDWARD L. ULLMAN

SCALE

CONIC PROJECTION

DESTINATION OF
IOWA
PETROLEUM PRODUCTS
1948

EDWARD L. ULLMAN

SCALE

CONIC PROJECTION

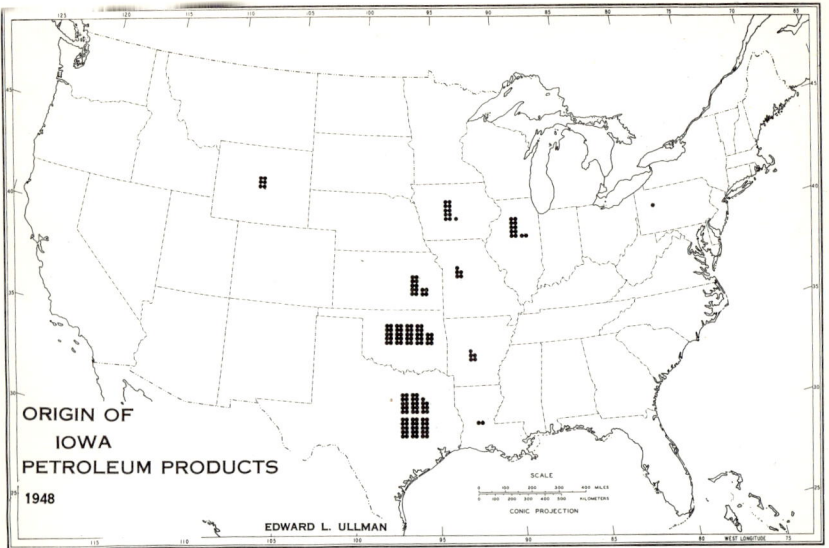

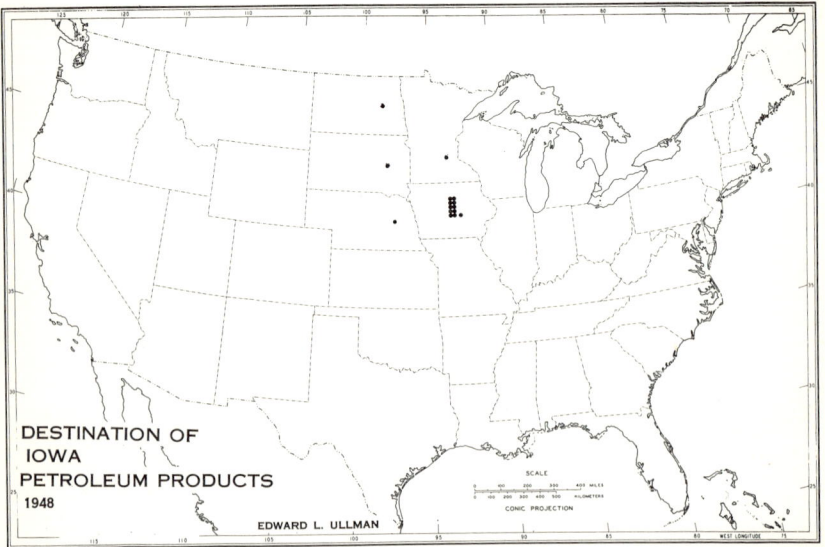

• 10,000 TONS   100,000 TONS

ORIGIN OF
IOWA
PRODUCTS OF MINES
(OTHER THAN PETROLEUM)
1948

EDWARD L. ULLMAN

SCALE

CONIC PROJECTION

DESTINATION OF
IOWA
PRODUCTS OF
MINES
1948

EDWARD L. ULLMAN   48

SCALE

CONIC PROJECTION

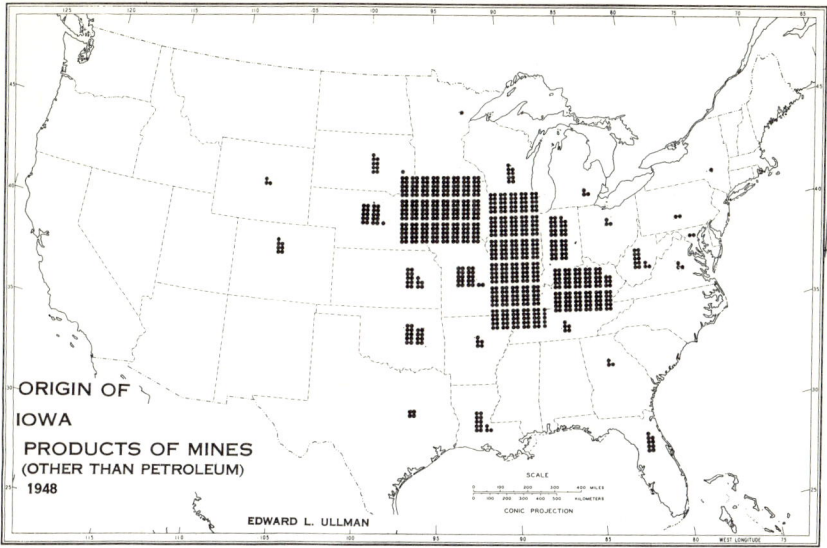

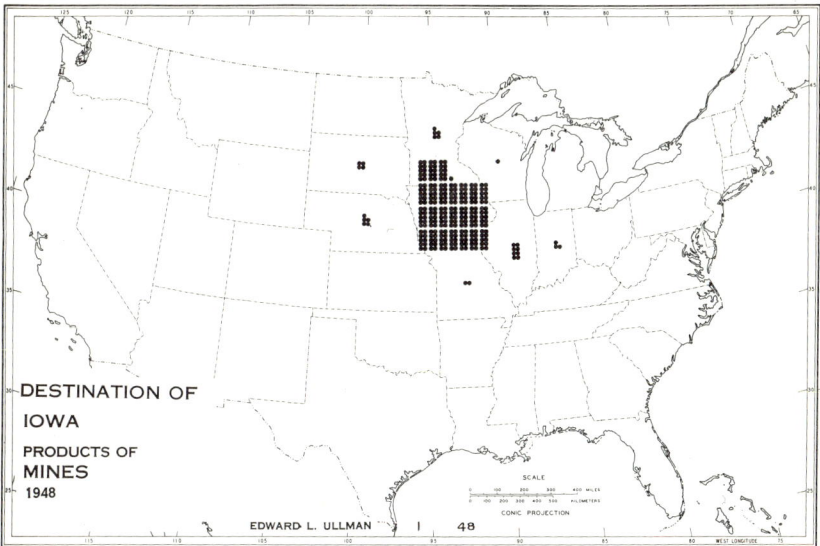

• 10,000 TONS   ▮ 100,000 TONS

37

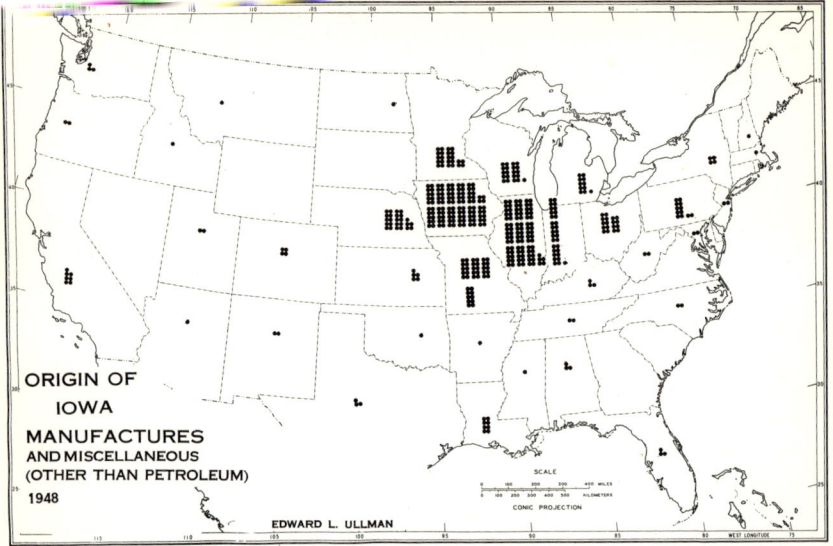

ORIGIN OF
IOWA
MANUFACTURES
AND MISCELLANEOUS
(OTHER THAN PETROLEUM)
1948

SCALE

CONIC PROJECTION

EDWARD L. ULLMAN

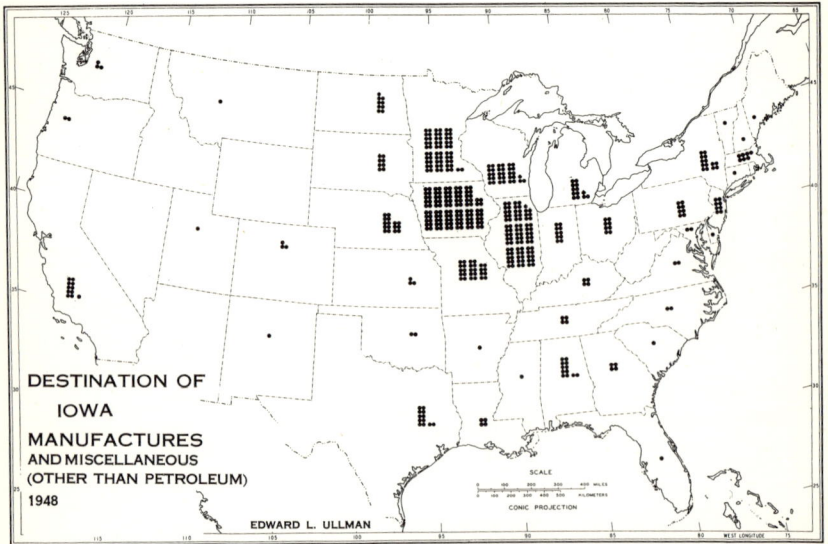

DESTINATION OF
IOWA
MANUFACTURES
AND MISCELLANEOUS
(OTHER THAN PETROLEUM)
1948

SCALE

CONIC PROJECTION

EDWARD L. ULLMAN

• 10,000 TONS   ▮ 100,000 TONS

ORIGIN OF

IOWA

TOTAL
ALL COMMODITIES
1948

EDWARD L. ULLMAN   48   CONIC PROJECTION

DESTINATION OF

IOWA

TOTAL
ALL COMMODITIES
1948

EDWARD L. ULLMAN   48   CONIC PROJECTION

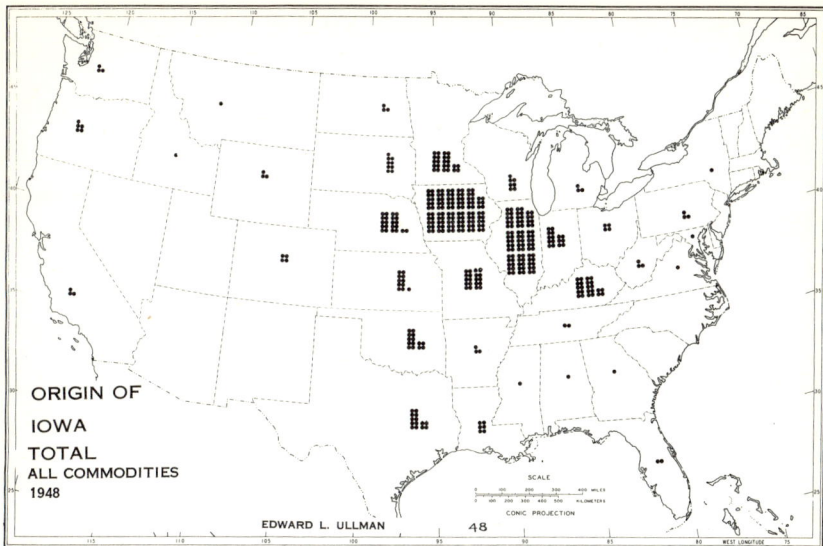

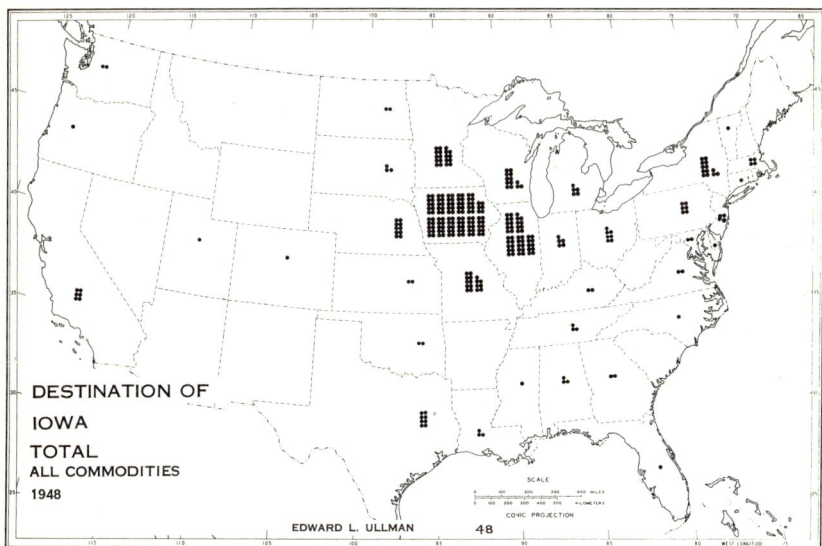

• 50,000 TONS   ▌ 500,000 TONS

39

slates and fresh meats, eggs, and butter to the Atlantic seaboard. [5]

Thus is shown graphically and quantitatively a fundamental feature of United States geography--the flow of heavy raw materials from West to industrial East. (The small reverse movement west to California reflects a flow to the growing California urban market of products such as hogs, not well adapted to the physical conditions in California and thus not produced in sufficient quantity in California or neighboring states to satisfy local needs.)

Products of Mines show particularly origin of coal in the central coal states, Illinois, Indiana, and Kentucky, and even some from Wisconsin, presumably lake-borne Appalachian coal from Milwaukee as well as poorer grade local coal from within Iowa. The principal intrastate mine flows, however, are low-value, ubiquitous sand, gravel, and rock.

Origin of Products of Forests shows particularly reliance on the Pacific Northwest and to some extent on the central South and the nearby lake states of Wisconsin and Minnesota. Shipments of forest products are of course negligible from this prairie state.

Origin of Petroleum and Products indicates the oil states of Texas and Oklahoma as heavy suppliers. More than twice as much petroleum products, however, flows into Iowa by pipeline as by rail. This movement is all refined products and is brought in by a products pipeline. The heavy originating states are Kansas and Oklahoma with some 1, 300, 000 and 2, 400, 000 tons, respectively. [6] These amounts would add 130 and 240 dots to Kansas and Oklahoma, respectively. Mis-

---

5. In addition to rail movements, more than 100, 000 tons of Agricultural Products (mostly wheat and corn) were shipped by barge down the Mississippi to Illinois and Louisiana, respectively (the equivalent of 10 to 13 extra dots for each state). Smaller amounts also went to Arkansas and Texas--approximately equivalent to 7 and 2 dots, respectively (data furnished by Dr. Donald J. Patton, University of Maryland, and calculated from U. S. Corps of Engineers and other data).

6. Figures for pipeline and water movements for 1950 furnished by Dr. Donald J. Patton, who obtained them from company and government officials. Other water traffic (beyond agricultural and petroleum products noted herein) is

souri refineries also contributed approximately 600,000 tons, equivalent to 60 dots.

Manufactures and Miscellaneous show logical concentration in the neighboring parts of the western half of the manufacturing belt. [7] The major flows, however, are bulky items, particularly to and from the neighboring states: cement, other building materials, fertilizers, scrap iron (shipped out to the neighboring steel centers east), etc.

Connecticut

Connecticut, as can be seen from the origin and destination maps, has a much smaller rail trade than Iowa. This reflects primarily a high-value, light industry manufacturing economy, and secondarily tidewater location, which enables much coal and petroleum (the overwhelming bulk of Connecticut's water trade, practically all from the United States), to be brought in by water.

A further characteristic of an industrial New England state (as well as states like Delaware and New Jersey), in contrast to Iowa, is the enormously greater volume of inbound over outbound tonnage shipments. Water receipts accentuate still further this imbalance since Connecticut's water trade is almost all inbound. This weight loss is typical of an industrial area importing raw materials whether it be old England or New England.

Products of Agriculture show an even greater imbalance than total trade. Note the sources in nearby areas (agricultural Vermont as well as New York State, Maine potatoes from Aroostook) and from the Middle West granary. In Animal Products the Middle West shows up even more notably, as would be expected.

Products of Mines are almost all coal and are received principally from the nearby coal fields of the Pennsylvania Appa-

---

negligible except for about 100,000 tons of sand and gravel originated and terminated within Iowa.

7. For a more detailed discussion of other aspects of Iowa rail commodity flow based on the same ICC data as this study, the reader is referred to the thoughtful paper by Leo W. Sweeney, "The Iowa Economy as Portrayed by Rail Freight Traffic Movement," Iowa Business Digest, Vol. XXII, No. 12 (December, 1951).

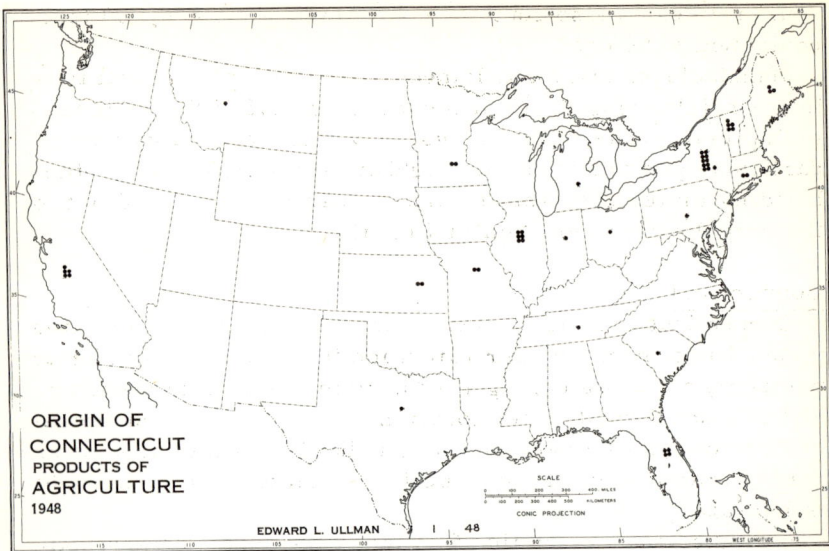

ORIGIN OF
CONNECTICUT
PRODUCTS OF
AGRICULTURE
1948

EDWARD L. ULLMAN   I | 48

SCALE
CONIC PROJECTION

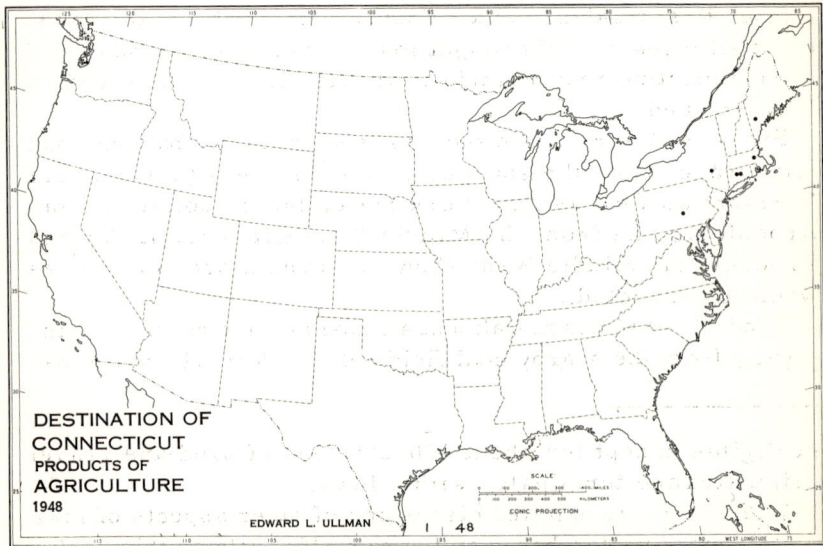

DESTINATION OF
CONNECTICUT
PRODUCTS OF
AGRICULTURE
1948

EDWARD L. ULLMAN   I | 48

SCALE
CONIC PROJECTION

• 10,000 TONS   ▓ 100,000 TONS

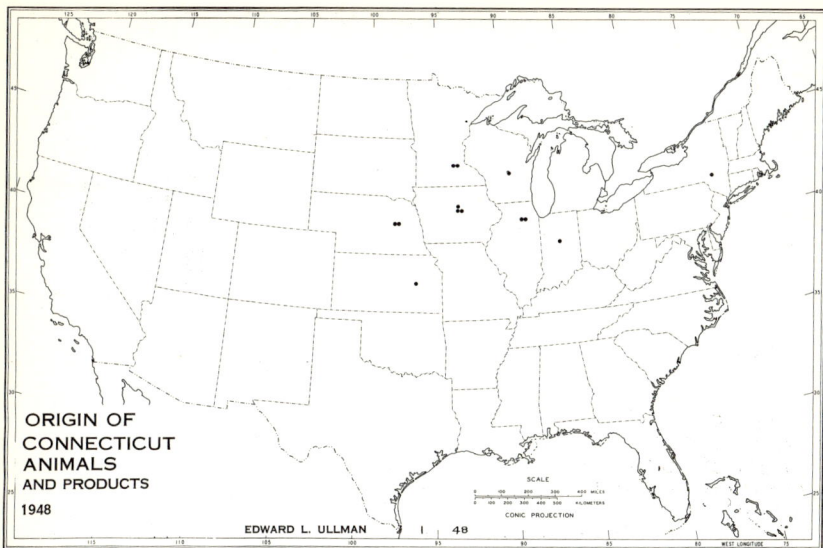

ORIGIN OF
CONNECTICUT
ANIMALS
AND PRODUCTS
1948

EDWARD L. ULLMAN

SCALE

CONIC PROJECTION

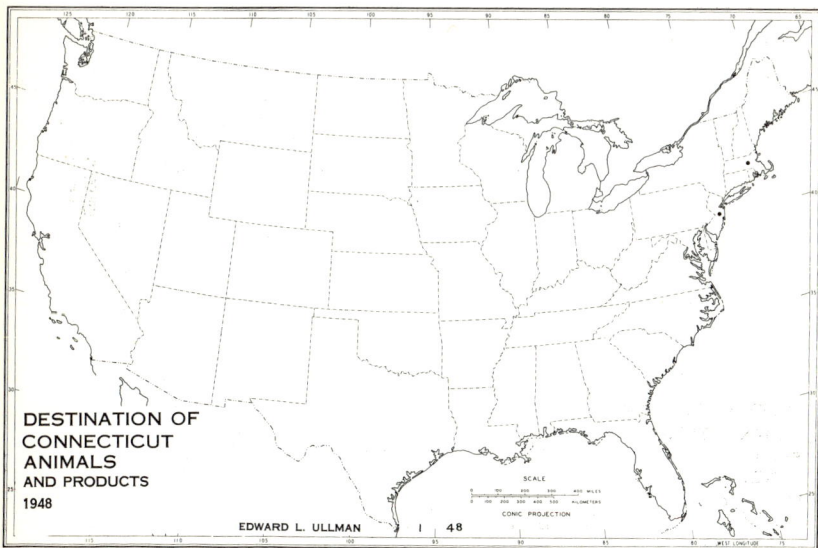

DESTINATION OF
CONNECTICUT
ANIMALS
AND PRODUCTS
1948

EDWARD L. ULLMAN

SCALE

CONIC PROJECTION

• 10,000 TONS   ▊ 100,000 TONS

43

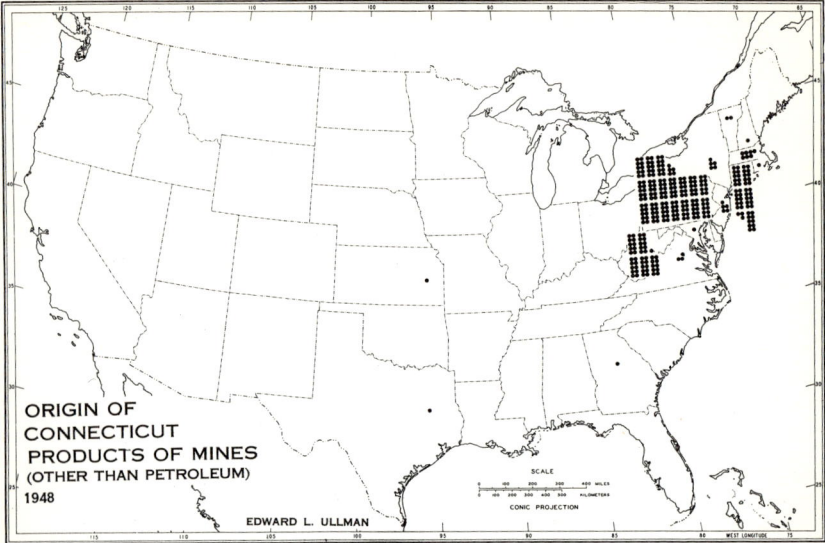

ORIGIN OF
CONNECTICUT
PRODUCTS OF MINES
(OTHER THAN PETROLEUM)
1948

EDWARD L. ULLMAN

SCALE

CONIC PROJECTION

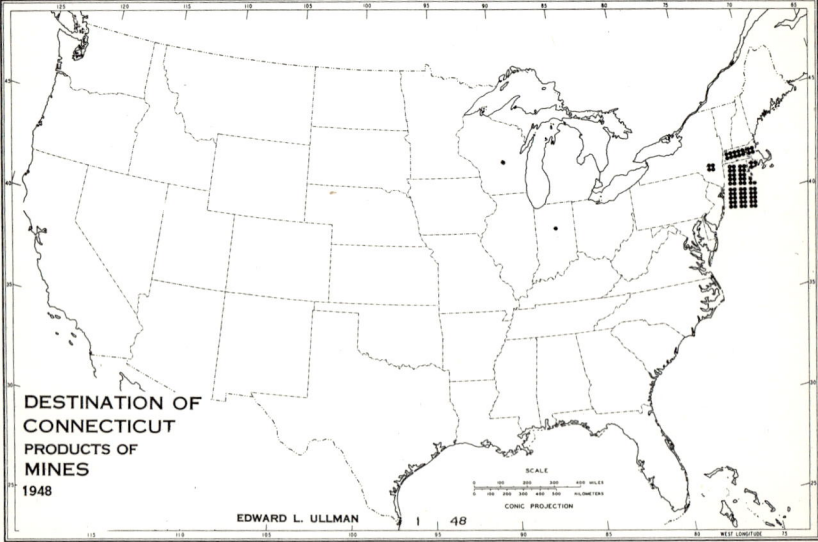

DESTINATION OF
CONNECTICUT
PRODUCTS OF
MINES
1948

EDWARD L. ULLMAN

SCALE

CONIC PROJECTION

• 10,000 TONS   ▮ 100,000 TONS

44

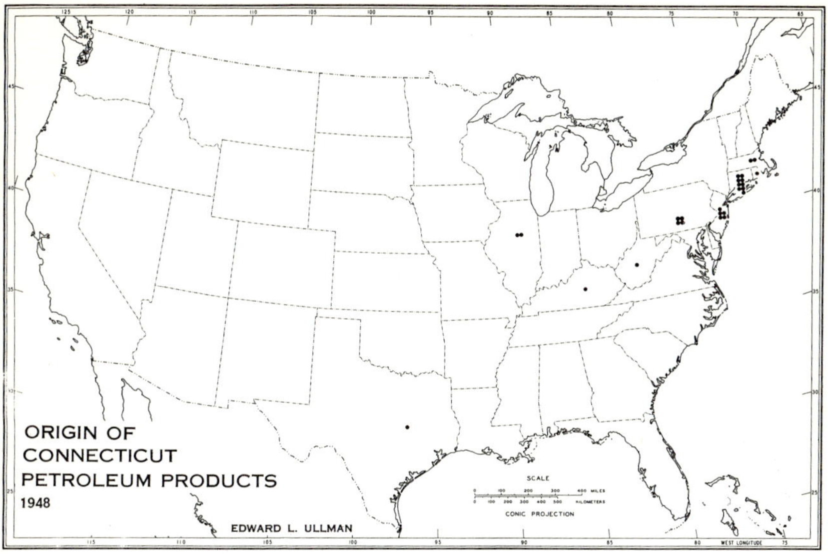
ORIGIN OF
CONNECTICUT
PETROLEUM PRODUCTS
1948
EDWARD L. ULLMAN
SCALE
CONIC PROJECTION
WEST LONGITUDE

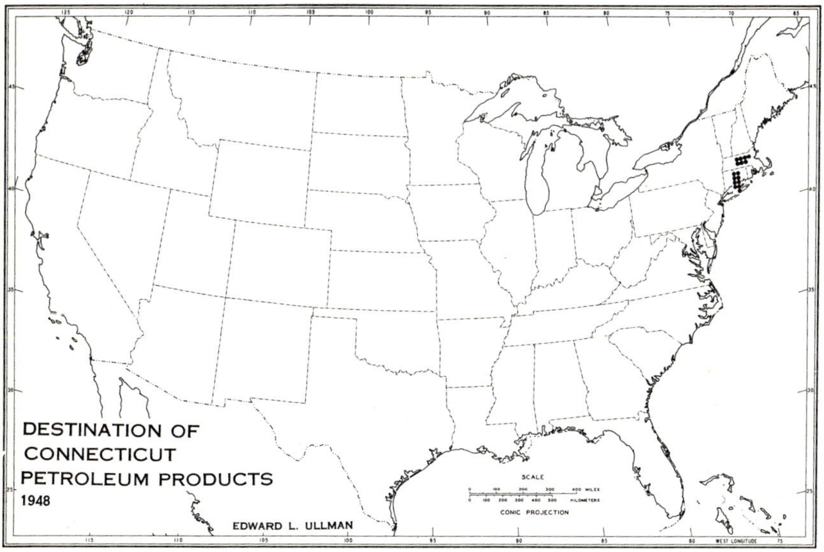
DESTINATION OF
CONNECTICUT
PETROLEUM PRODUCTS
1948
EDWARD L. ULLMAN
SCALE
CONIC PROJECTION
WEST LONGITUDE

• 10,000 TONS 100,000 TONS

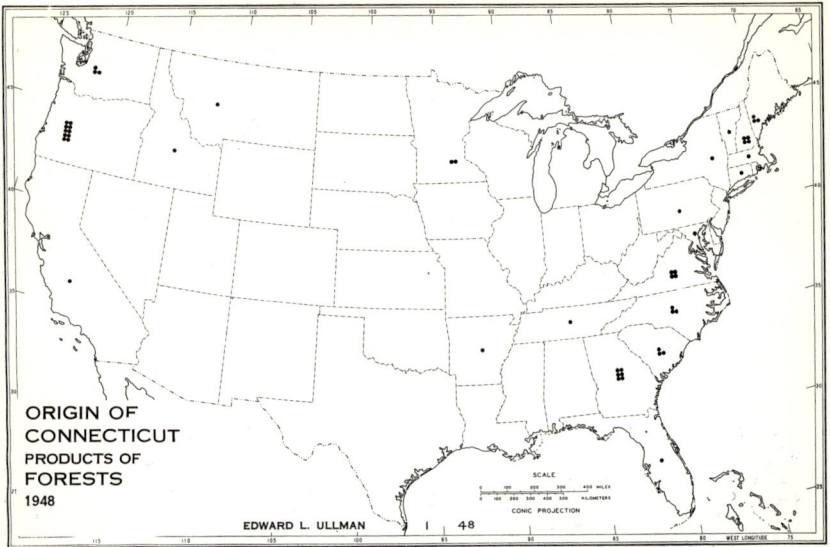

ORIGIN OF
CONNECTICUT
PRODUCTS OF
FORESTS
1948

EDWARD L. ULLMAN   I   48

SCALE

CONIC PROJECTION

WEST LONGITUDE

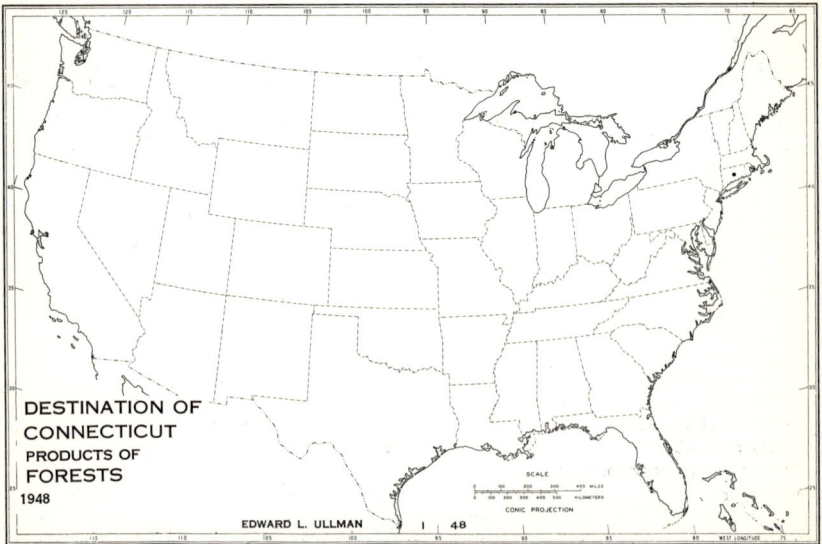

DESTINATION OF
CONNECTICUT
PRODUCTS OF
FORESTS
1948

EDWARD L. ULLMAN   I   48

SCALE

CONIC PROJECTION

WEST LONGITUDE

· 10,000 TONS   ▉ 100,000 TONS

46

ORIGIN OF
CONNECTICUT
MANUFACTURES
AND MISCELLANEOUS
(OTHER THAN PETROLEUM)
1948

SCALE

CONIC PROJECTION

EDWARD L. ULLMAN

DESTINATION OF
CONNECTICUT
MANUFACTURES
AND MISCELLANEOUS
(OTHER THAN PETROLEUM)
1948

SCALE

CONIC PROJECTION

EDWARD L. ULLMAN

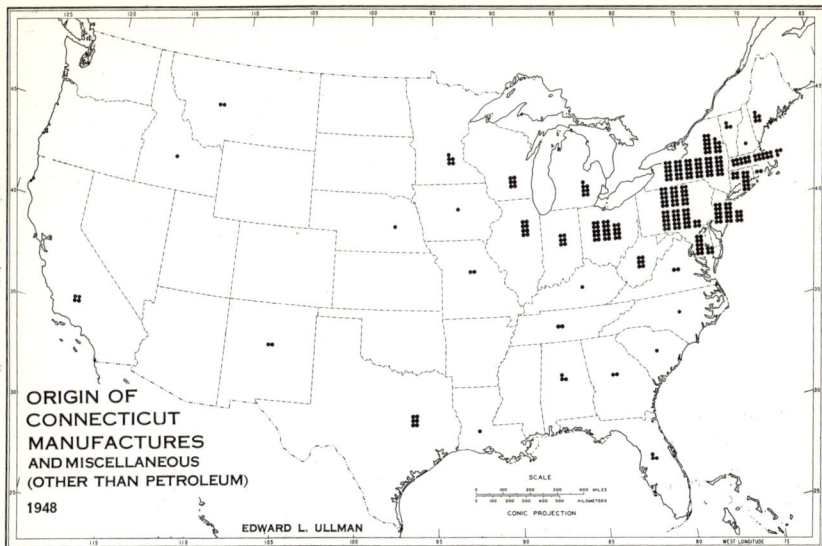

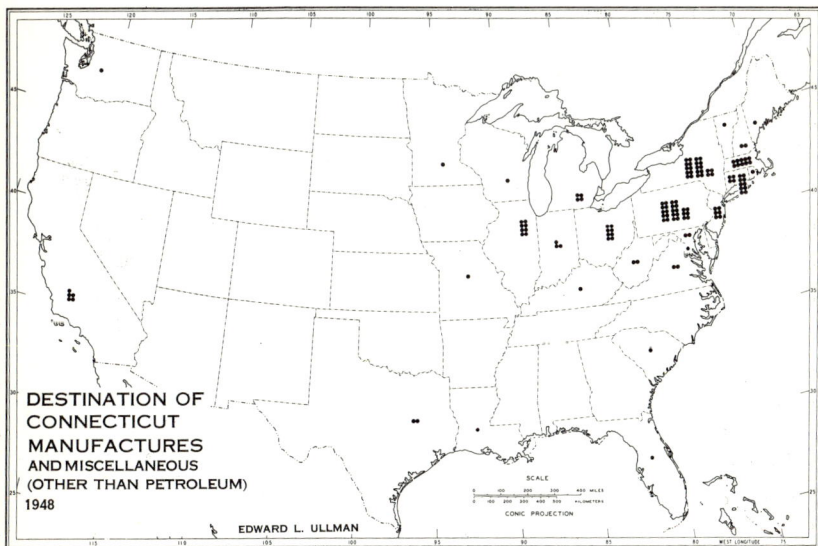

• 10,000 TONS   ▓ 100,000 TONS

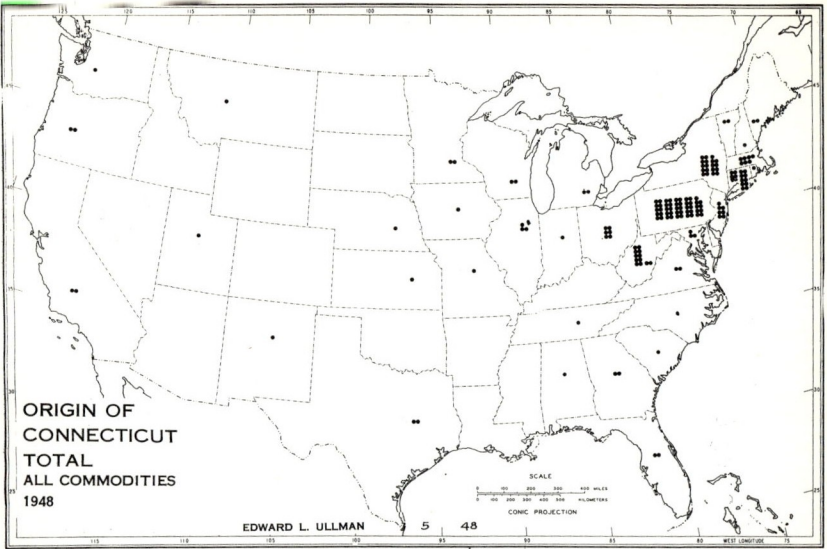

ORIGIN OF
CONNECTICUT
TOTAL
ALL COMMODITIES
1948

EDWARD L. ULLMAN   5   48

SCALE
CONIC PROJECTION

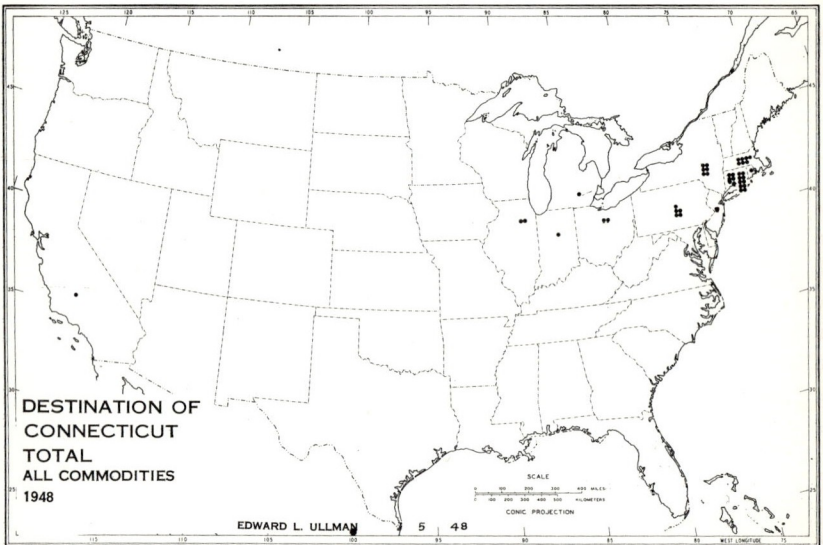

DESTINATION OF
CONNECTICUT
TOTAL
ALL COMMODITIES
1948

EDWARD L. ULLMAN   5   48

SCALE
CONIC PROJECTION

• 50,000 TONS   ▮ 500,000 TONS

48

lachians and from West Virginia. Boat receipts of coal, principally via Norfolk from the middle Appalachians of the Pocahontas region (West Virginia and Virginia), are almost one and one-half times the rail receipts (approximately 3,500,000 tons) and thus would add about 350 dots to West Virginia and Virginia on the Mines map. [8] Part of these shipments into Connecticut ports is shipped out by rail from Connecticut ports inland to Connecticut, and some stone and rock is sent to Massachusetts and New York and shows up on the Destination of Mines map.

The forest areas of nearby New England, the Southeast, and the Pacific Northwest are represented in the movement of Products of Forests to Connecticut. Note that forest products are principally from South Atlantic states rather than from Gulf states, inasmuch as the South Atlantic forest states represent an intervening opportunity.

Origin of Petroleum Products shows how little reaches Connecticut by rail. More than 20 times this amount comes in by tanker, approximately 6,000,000 tons (equivalent to 600 dots on the commodity maps or 120 on the Total map, more than from Pennsylvania). Only 400,000 tons of the petroleum products are of foreign origin; the remainder apparently comes principally from the Gulf, although refineries in the New York area may well contribute large amounts. [9] Destination of rail shipments of Petroleum Products represents shipments inland from Connecticut ports.

Manufactures and Miscellaneous origins and destinations, as would be expected, are heavy for a New England state and are logically concentrated in the eastern half of the industrial belt, just as Iowa's are in the western half. Even in this category Connecticut imports more than it exports, reflecting imports of heavy, semifinished manufactured products like cement from New York and Pennsylvania, and copper, lead, and zinc metal from New York, New Jersey, Pennsylvania, and other states. Exports include lighter weight, more fin-

---

8. Calculations made from U.S. Department of the Army, Corps of Engineers, Commercial Statistics, Water-Borne Commerce of the United States for the Calendar Year 1948, Part II of The Annual Report of the Chief of Engineers, 1949 (Washington, D.C., 1950), pp. 95-115.

9. Ibid.

ished items such as brass and bronze, hardware, jewelry, guns, and high-value machinery for which Connecticut is famous. [10]

Washington

The difference between the Connecticut manufacturing economy and one with a much higher proportion of raw materials and semiprocessed goods is illustrated by total shipments from Washington. Both states have about the same size labor force, but Washington has a much heavier flow of commodities. Note also the much greater distance that many Washington products must move compared with Connecticut commodities, reflecting the effect upon flows of distance from market (principally the manufacturing belt).

Total origin and destination shipments show a superficially even balance for Washington, in sharp contrast to Connecticut. Washington, however, ships far more to the manufacturing belt and Middle West than it receives, as would be expected of a raw material state, in contrast to Connecticut. This surplus of exports is reversed, however, by the imports of coal by rail and petroleum by water from western states, since Washington has no oil and is deficient in easily mined or high-grade coals.

Agricultural Products flow resembles the total pattern. Note, however, that most of the origins from the corn belt are from the nearest part, the northwest quarter--Iowa, Minnesota, Nebraska, and South Dakota--primarily corn and soy-

---

10. For a further analysis of New England rail traffic based on these data, see Ray S. Kelley, Jr., Origins and Destinations of New England's Rail Traffic, National Planning Association, Committee of New England (Boston, March, 1952); and The Economic State of New England, Arthur Bright and George Ellis, eds., National Planning Association, Committee of New England (New Haven: Yale University Press, 1954). The first, and one of the few, studies of this type in the country was R. J. McFall's The External Trade of New England, U.S. Bureau of Foreign and Domestic Commerce (Washington, D.C., 1928). This pioneer study covered all forms of transport and broke the trade down into a variety of commodities, although origins and destinations by areas could not be handled as completely as the present ICC data allow.

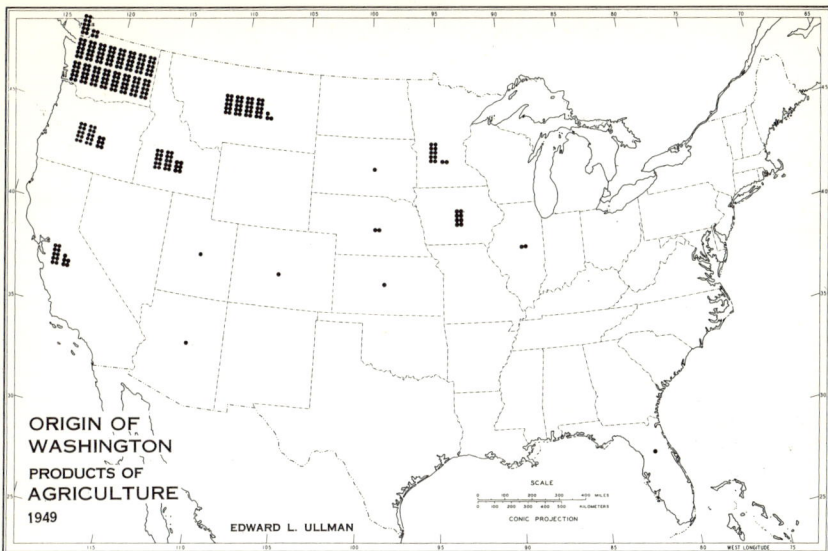

ORIGIN OF
WASHINGTON
PRODUCTS OF
AGRICULTURE
1949

EDWARD L. ULLMAN

SCALE

CONIC PROJECTION

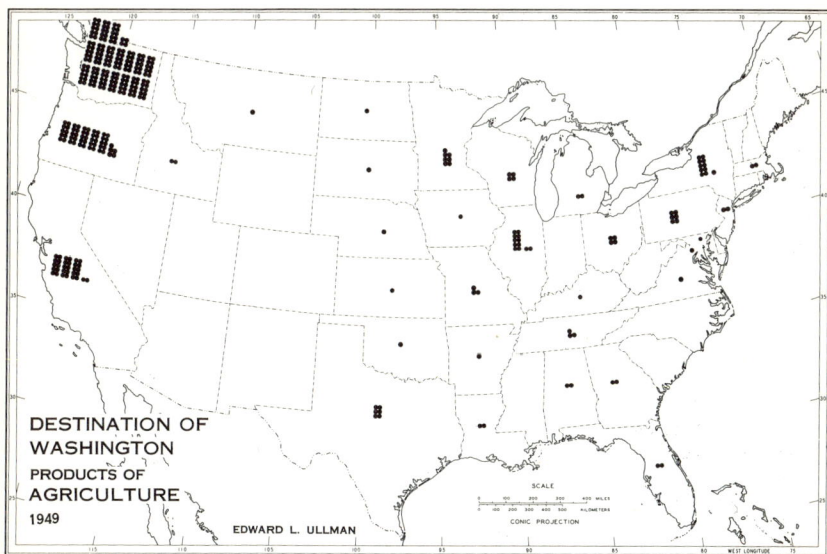

DESTINATION OF
WASHINGTON
PRODUCTS OF
AGRICULTURE
1949

EDWARD L. ULLMAN

SCALE

CONIC PROJECTION

• 10,000 TONS   ▮ 100,000 TONS

51

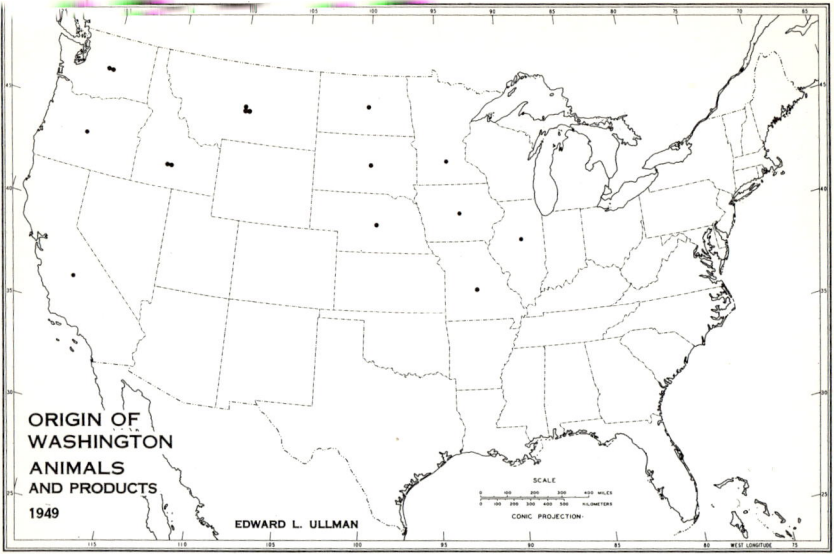

ORIGIN OF
WASHINGTON
ANIMALS
AND PRODUCTS
1949

EDWARD L. ULLMAN

SCALE

CONIC PROJECTION

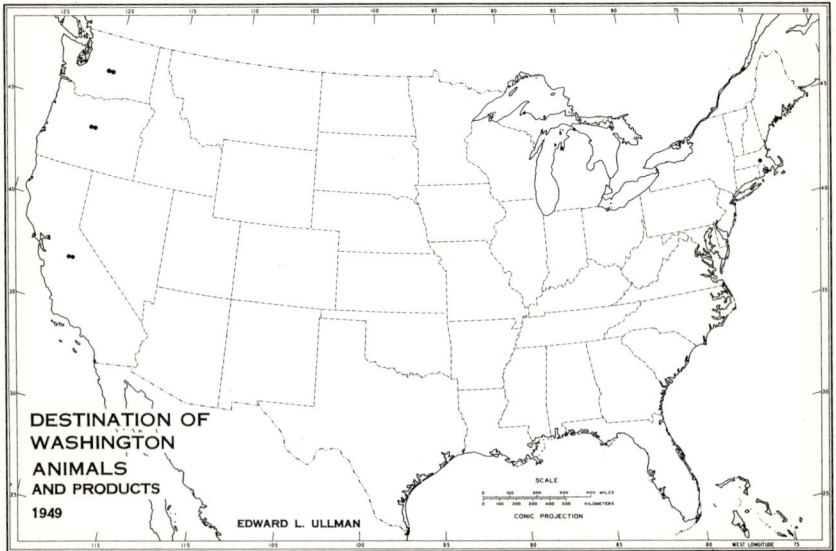

DESTINATION OF
WASHINGTON
ANIMALS
AND PRODUCTS
1949

EDWARD L. ULLMAN

SCALE

CONIC PROJECTION

• 10,000 TONS   ▌ 100,000 TONS

52

ORIGIN OF
WASHINGTON
PRODUCTS OF
MINES
1949

EDWARD L. ULLMAN

SCALE

CONIC PROJECTION

WEST LONGITUDE

DESTINATION OF
WASHINGTON
PRODUCTS OF
MINES
1949

EDWARD L. ULLMAN

SCALE

CONIC PROJECTION

WEST LONGITUDE

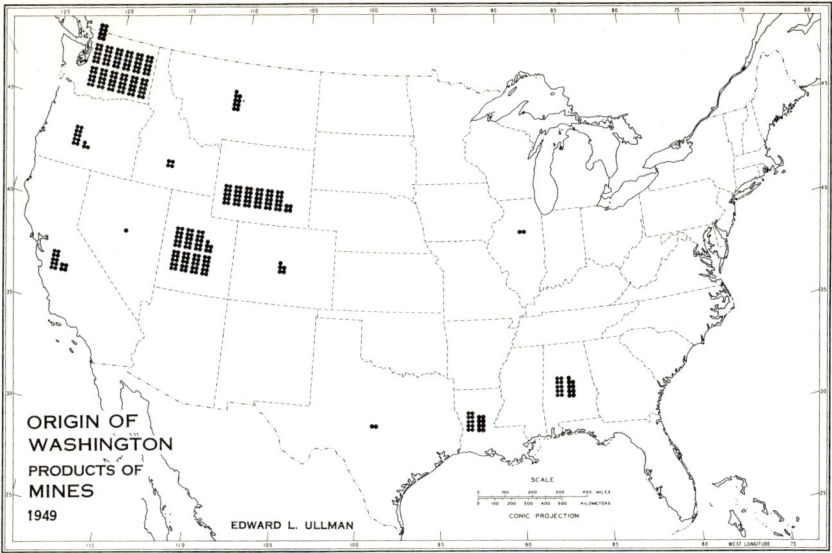

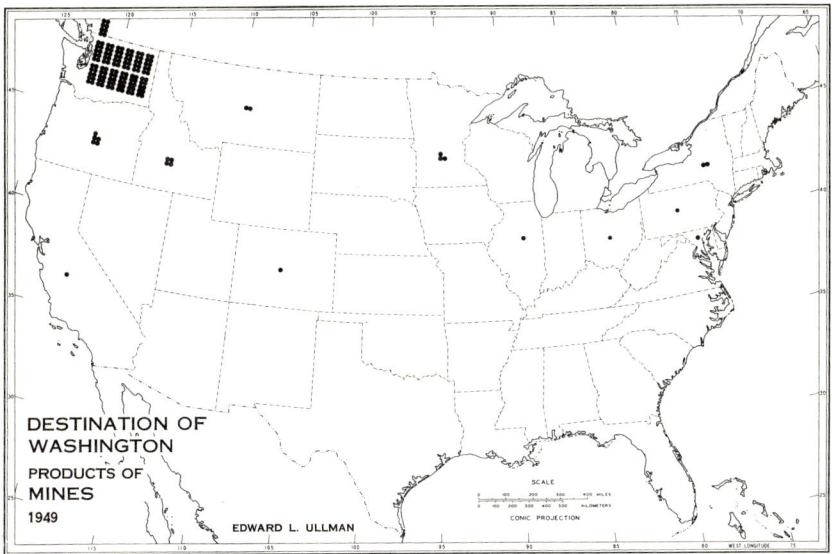

• 10,000 TONS   █ 100,000 TONS

53

ORIGIN OF
WASHINGTON
PRODUCTS OF
FORESTS
1949

EDWARD L. ULLMAN

SCALE

CONIC PROJECTION

WEST LONGITUDE

DESTINATION OF
WASHINGTON
PRODUCTS OF
FORESTS
1949

EDWARD L. ULLMAN

SCALE

CONIC PROJECTION

WEST LONGITUDE

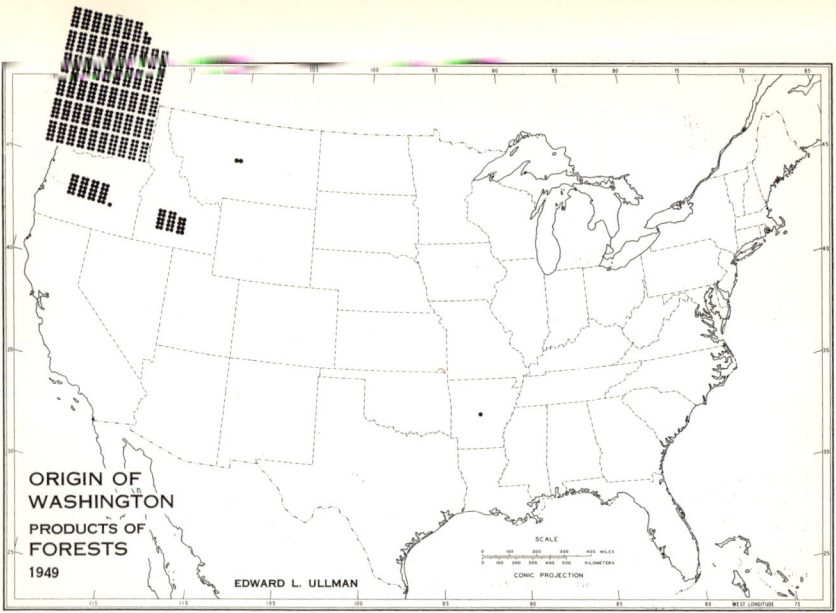

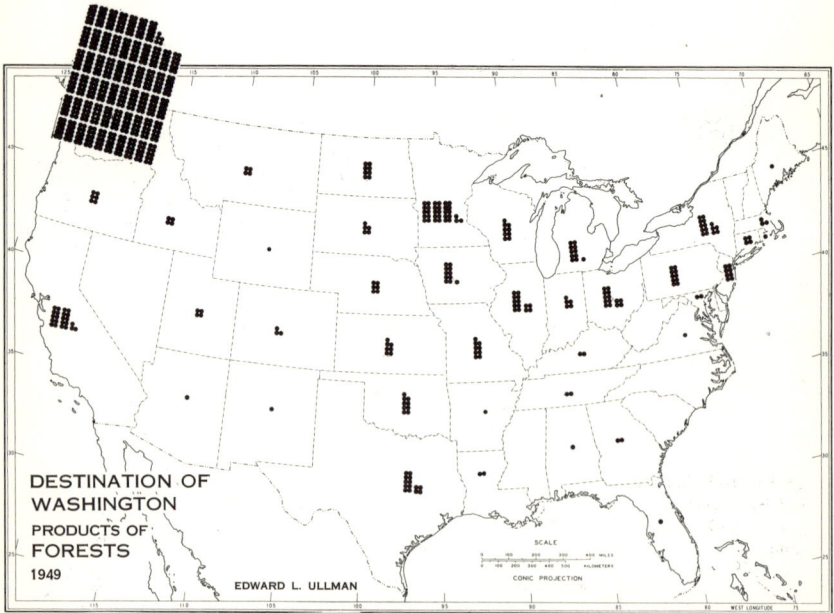

· 10,000 TONS   ▮ 100,000 TONS

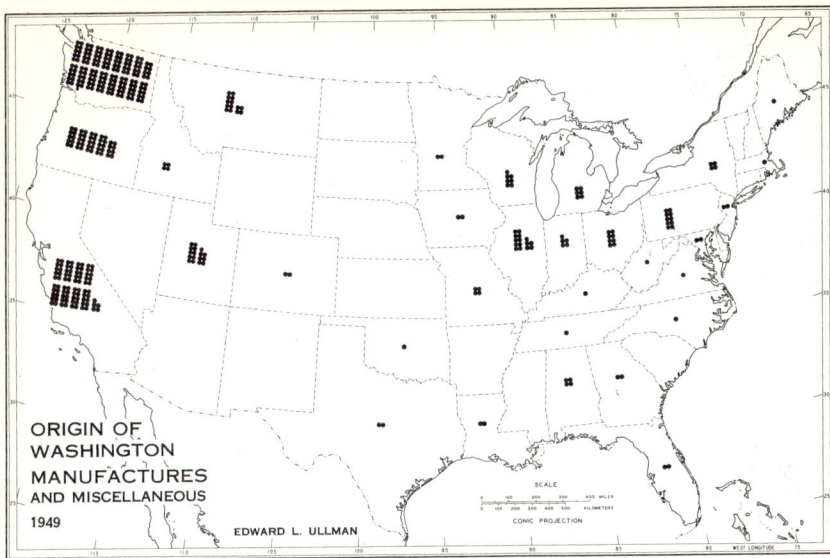

ORIGIN OF
WASHINGTON
MANUFACTURES
AND MISCELLANEOUS
1949

EDWARD L. ULLMAN

SCALE

CONIC PROJECTION

WEST LONGITUDE

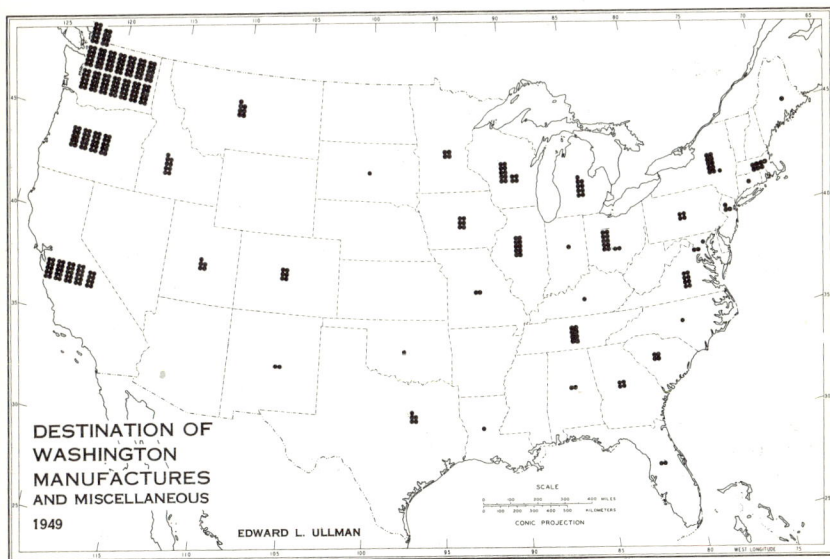

DESTINATION OF
WASHINGTON
MANUFACTURES
AND MISCELLANEOUS
1949

EDWARD L. ULLMAN

SCALE

CONIC PROJECTION

WEST LONGITUDE

• 10,000 TONS   ▌100,000 TONS

55

ORIGIN OF
WASHINGTON
TOTAL
ALL COMMODITIES
1949

EDWARD L. ULLMAN

SCALE

CONIC PROJECTION

DESTINATION OF
WASHINGTON
TOTAL
ALL COMMODITIES
1949

EDWARD L. ULLMAN

SCALE

CONIC PROJECTION

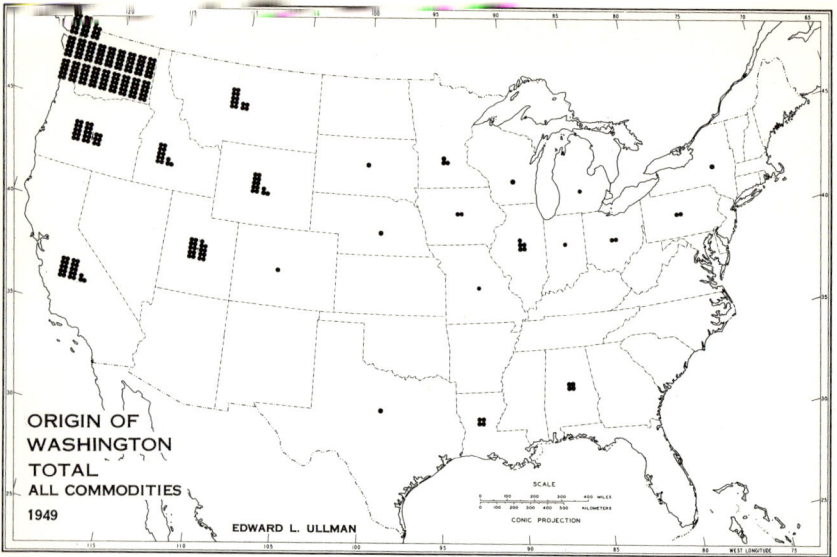

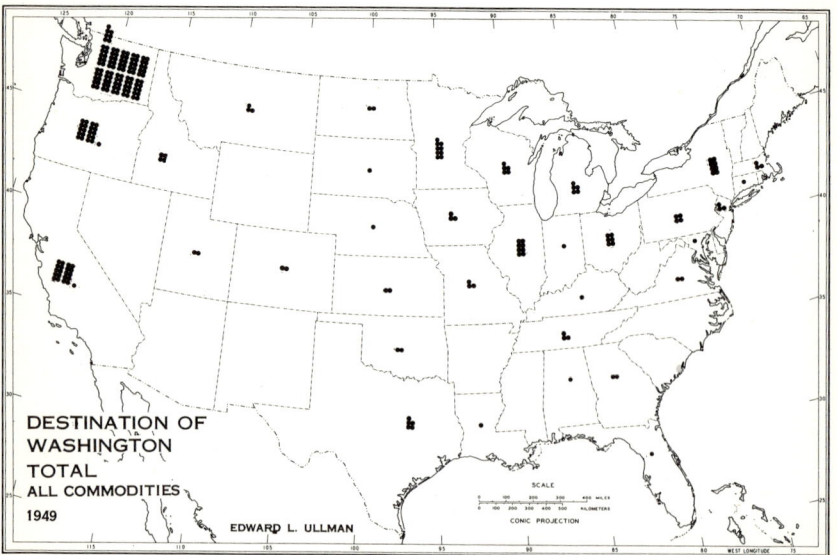

• 50,000 TONS   ▌ 500,000 TONS

bean derivatives. The fact that the same was true in 1948 gives more credence to the small sample. The biggest flows, however, are the intrastate and neighboring state movements of wheat and flour, much of it destined for export from the ports. The most important commodity in the distant exports is apples--logically, since Washington is the leading producer.

Products of Forests, however, show the receipts to be purely local (logs to mills, etc.), but shipments out to the deficit lumber markets of California and the northeastern quarter of the country are heavy. Note, for example, the heavy shipments to relatively nearby Minnesota, the nearest populous state to the East; these shipments are heavier than to Illinois, an even more populous state, because Illinois gets much of its lumber from the central South. [11]

In a splendid recent analysis, Roy Sampson shows how Washington and Douglas fir region lumber is able to compete with southern pine in spite of being almost three times as far from market. [12] Production costs of Douglas fir lumber averaged 15 to 20 per cent below southern pine from 1939 to 1952, with the absolute cost spread between the two regions widening after the war. (This presumably reflects, among other factors, the larger size of Northwest trees and mills, compared to the diminishing supply of larger stands in the cutover South.) In addition, rates per ton mile are less for the long haul, as is normally the case; but, even more significant, southern pine weighs up to 15 per cent more per board foot than Douglas fir, and transport rates are quoted on a weight basis, whereas lumber is sold on a board-foot basis. (For most purposes, the quality of Douglas fir seems to be certainly as high as, if not higher than, most southern pine.) The results of these differences are seen in the map of estimated delivered costs (see following page), which shows the Pacific Northwest competing on equal or superior terms in the industrial belt, the great market of the country.

Water movements of products of forests in Washington are

_____

11. In addition, as will be noted, wood pulp is the most important export listed under manufacturing and is obviously a forest product as well.

12. Roy J. Sampson, "Expanding Domestic Markets for Northwestern Lumber," Pacific Northwest Business, XV (January, 1956), 3-8.

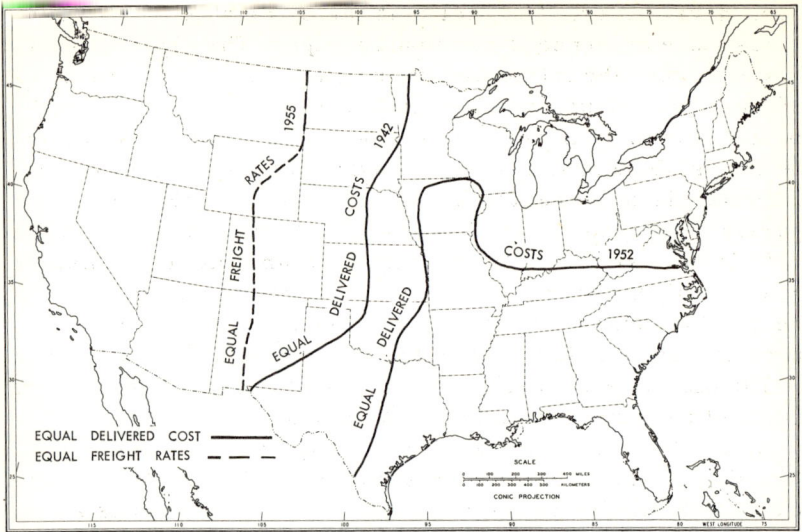

Isolines of equal delivered costs per 1,000 board feet of lumber shipped by rail from Douglas fir region and from Hattiesburg, Mississippi, a center of southern pine production, 1942, 1952, and lines of approximately equal freight rates per unit of weight from the two areas. Note that the industrial belt has equal or lower delivered costs from Douglas fir region. Source: Roy J. Sampson, "Expanding Markets for Northwestern Lumber," Pacific Northwest Business, XV, (January, 1956), 7.

also enormous; logs are rafted throughout Puget Sound and on numerous rivers, as well as being shipped out and along the coast by ship. Rafting of logs is the cheapest way of transporting them and is especially favored by deep, indented, protected Puget Sound and other waterways in humid western Washington. Definite data are difficult to obtain, but "internal" log traffic inbound in Washington is reported at over 8,500,000 tons and outbound 6,300,000. The first figure is greater than the 6,200,000 tons of intrastate Forest Products rail shipments shown in the 1 per cent sample on the maps. [13] Added to this is an indeterminate amount of traffic on the Columbia of perhaps 600,000 tons, as well as about 775,000 tons of domestic shipments, principally to California and the American east coast, as well as some 600,000 tons imported in rafted form from neighboring British Columbia. The net effect would appear to more than double the number of dots within Washington, and perhaps to double the number of dots to California and add about 20 to 30 to the northeastern seaboard states.

For Manufactures and Miscellaneous the principal markets, as well as sources, in addition to neighboring states, are the industrial East and Midwest, and rapidly growing California. The most important commodity is wood pulp, really only a semifinished forest product, with paper products in addition only to California, which is not a paper-producing state. Substantial aluminum bar shipments are also reported to Illinois. The East supplies a variety of manufactured products; so does California, including processed foods, metals and machinery, roofing, glass containers, automobiles and supplies, and petroleum products. Most of the manufactures received from Utah are petroleum products, as are some from Montana.

Petroleum, as has been noted, is not separated from Manufactures or Mines for Washington as for the other two states. Most of the receipts are by water and represent more than half the total domestic and foreign water imports and exports of the state (excluding "internal" traffic). Practically all of

---

13. Internal traffic represents traffic on Puget Sound and on other waterways outside the Columbia River. Calculations for water traffic made from 1948 data in U.S. Department of the Army, Corps of Engineers, Annual Report of the Chief of Engineers, 1949 (Washington, D.C., 1950).

the petroleum comes from California and is the equivalent of an extra 98 dots, of 50,000 tons value each, on the total origins from California, more than five times the number of dots shown originating by rail from California. [14]

Most of the water traffic of Washington, therefore, is petroleum and forest products. Details of the trade are shown in Table 3. A substantial, although unknown, amount of traffic other than petroleum or forest products is transit traffic originating or terminating in another state and shipped through Washington ports. (For the pattern of the total domestic ocean trade of Washington and Oregon ports combined, see the maps in Chapter V. Since Oregon has a similar economy and pattern, the maps showing the two states combined show essentially the same distribution as for Washington alone, except, of course, for greater volume.)

TABLE 3

APPROXIMATE COMPOSITION OF OCEAN TRAFFIC, STATE OF WASHINGTON, 1948[*]
(1,000's of short tons of 2,000 lbs.)

	Foreign		Domestic		Internal	
	Import	Export	Inbound	Outbound	Inbound	Outbound
Total	1,110	1,200	6,120	1,350	12,400	10,300
Forest Products	600[†]	200	180	780	8,700	6,300
Petroleum Products			4,700[‡]			
Petroleum						

*Excludes local (intraharbor) and Columbia River traffic, noted earlier. Source: Annual Report of the Chief of Engineers, U.S. Army, 1949.
†Primarily from Canada.
‡Primarily from California.

_____

14. Since 1954 crude petroleum has been increasing in flow through the recently built Trans-Mountain Pipeline from Alberta, Canada, to new refineries on North Puget Sound. Eventually it is expected that this will become the major source of Washington petroleum, replacing California tanker shipments as California growth uses up its own petroleum. Pipelines for petroleum products only also run from Utah to Pasco in south central Washington and from Montana to Spokane.

ORIGIN OF
ARIZONA
PRODUCTS OF
AGRICULTURE
1950

EDWARD L. ULLMAN

SCALE
CONIC PROJECTION

DESTINATION OF
ARIZONA
PRODUCTS OF
AGRICULTURE
1950

EDWARD L. ULLMAN

SCALE
CONIC PROJECTION

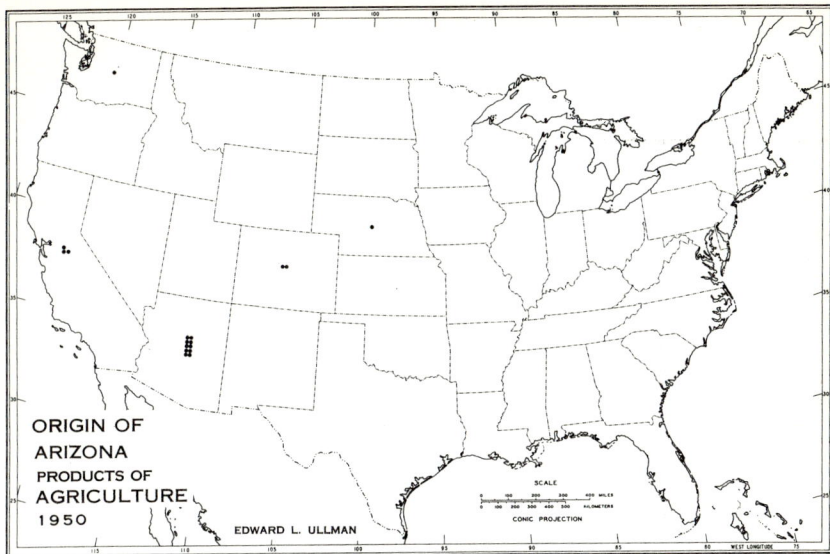

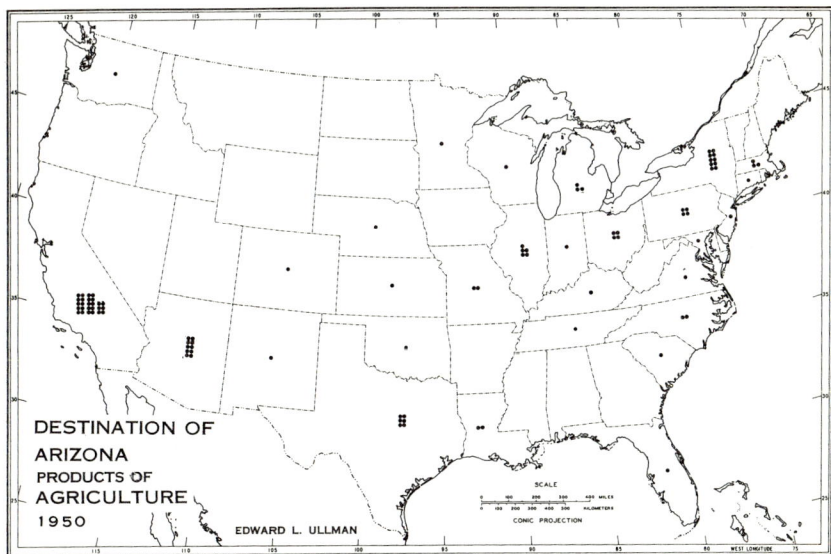

· 10,000 TONS ▓ 100,000 TONS

61

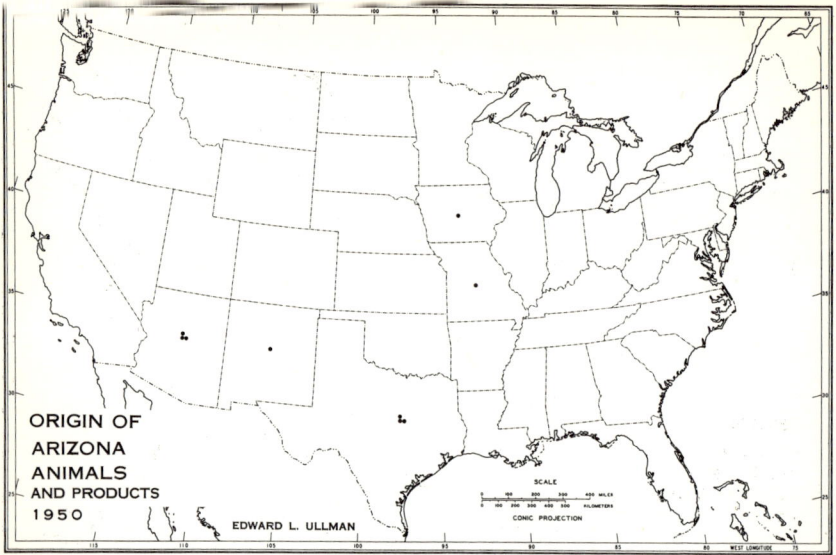

ORIGIN OF
ARIZONA
ANIMALS
AND PRODUCTS
1950

EDWARD L. ULLMAN

SCALE

CONIC PROJECTION

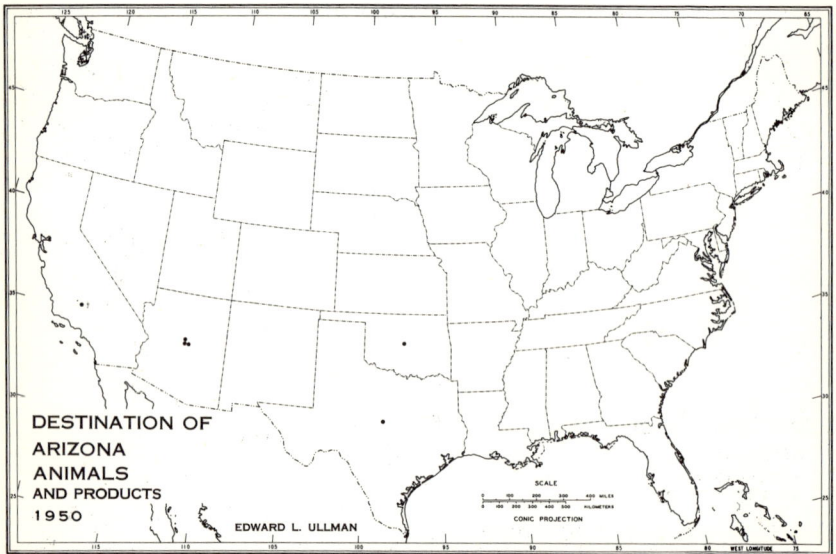

DESTINATION OF
ARIZONA
ANIMALS
AND PRODUCTS
1950

EDWARD L. ULLMAN

SCALE

CONIC PROJECTION

• 10,000 TONS   █ 100,000 TONS

ORIGIN OF
ARIZONA
PRODUCTS OF
MINES
1950

SCALE

CONIC PROJECTION

EDWARD L. ULLMAN

DESTINATION OF
ARIZONA
PRODUCTS OF
MINES
1950

SCALE

CONIC PROJECTION

EDWARD L. ULLMAN

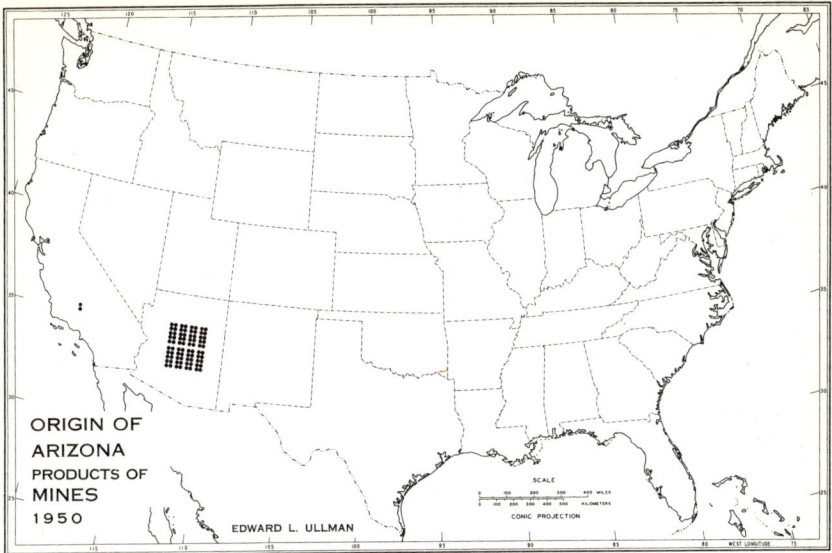

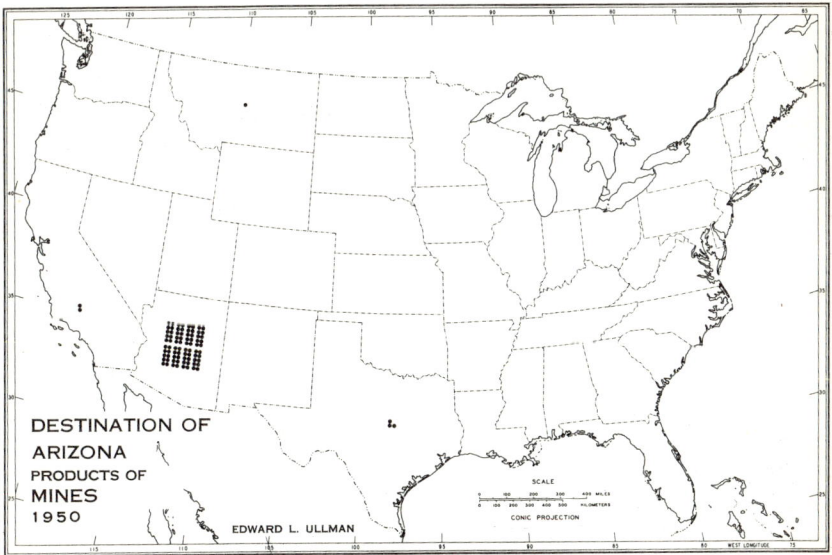

• 50,000 TONS   500,000 TONS

63

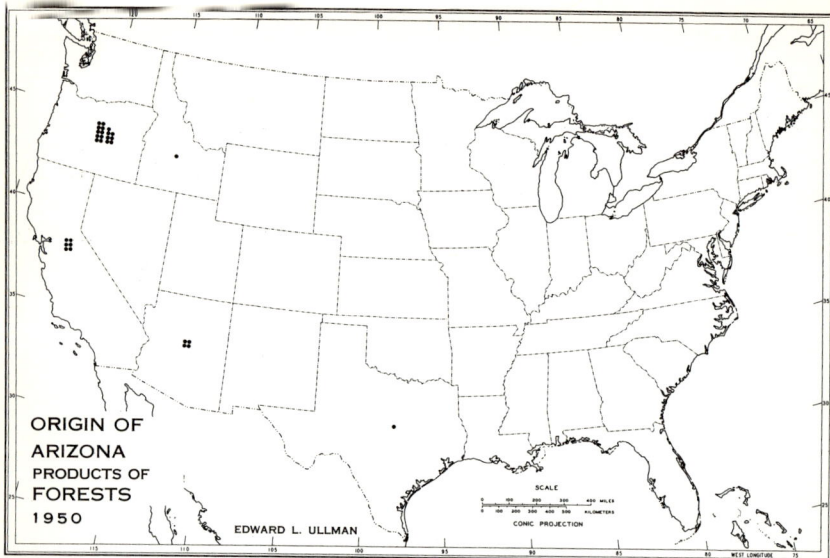

ORIGIN OF
ARIZONA
PRODUCTS OF
FORESTS
1950

EDWARD L. ULLMAN

SCALE

CONIC PROJECTION

WEST LONGITUDE

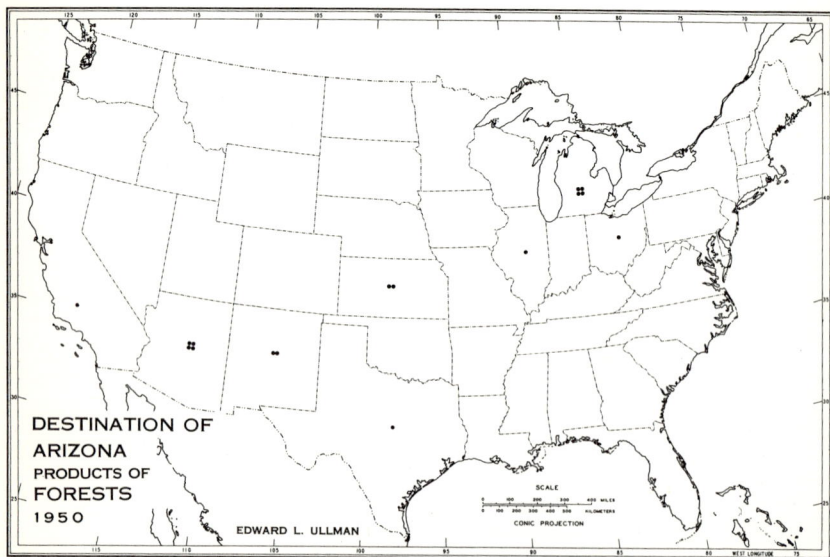

DESTINATION OF
ARIZONA
PRODUCTS OF
FORESTS
1950

EDWARD L. ULLMAN

SCALE

CONIC PROJECTION

WEST LONGITUDE

• 10,000 TONS   ▓ 100,000 TONS

64

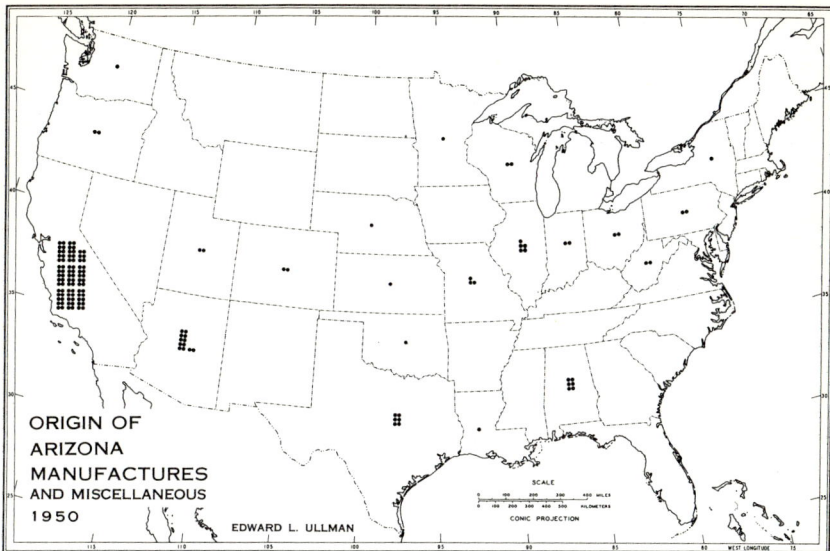

ORIGIN OF
ARIZONA
MANUFACTURES
AND MISCELLANEOUS
1950

EDWARD L. ULLMAN

SCALE

CONIC PROJECTION

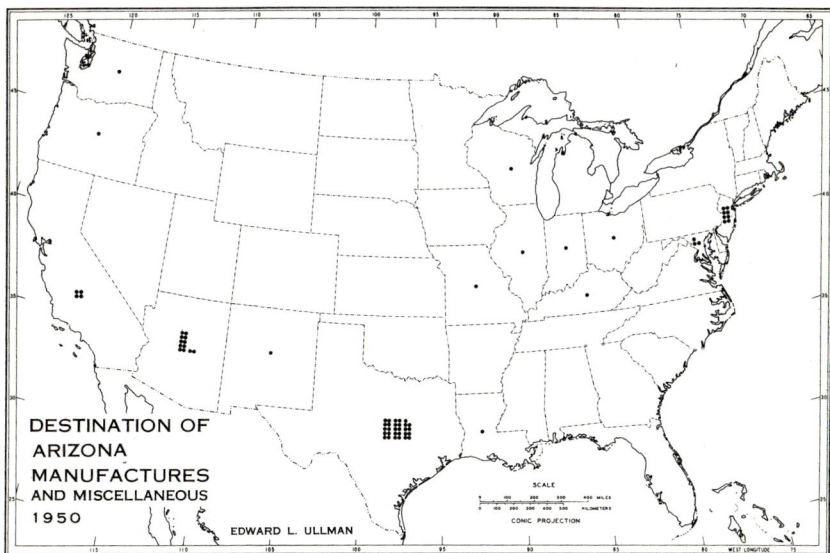

DESTINATION OF
ARIZONA
MANUFACTURES
AND MISCELLANEOUS
1950

EDWARD L. ULLMAN

SCALE

CONIC PROJECTION

• 10,000 TONS   ▉ 100,000 TONS

65

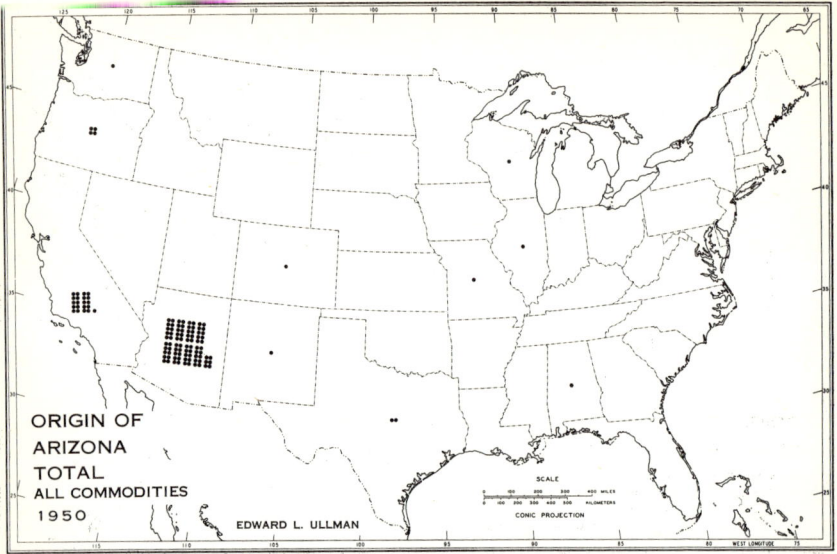

ORIGIN OF
ARIZONA
TOTAL
ALL COMMODITIES
1950

EDWARD L. ULLMAN

SCALE

CONIC PROJECTION

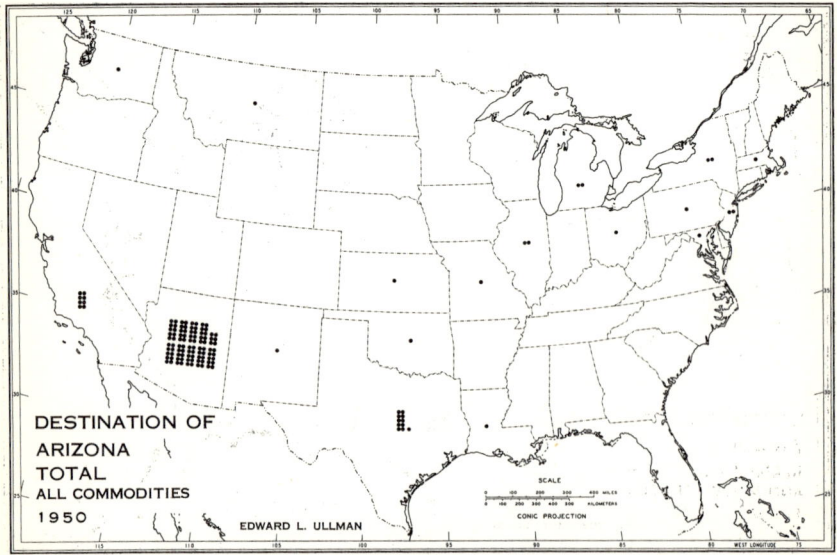

DESTINATION OF
ARIZONA
TOTAL
ALL COMMODITIES
1950

EDWARD L. ULLMAN

SCALE

CONIC PROJECTION

· 50,000 TONS   ▓ 500,000 TONS

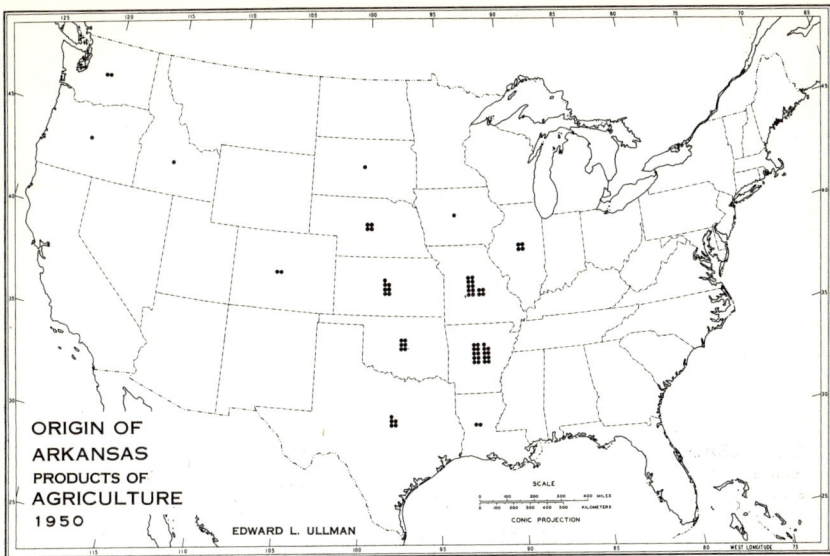

ORIGIN OF
ARKANSAS
PRODUCTS OF
AGRICULTURE
1950

EDWARD L. ULLMAN

SCALE

CONIC PROJECTION

WEST LONGITUDE

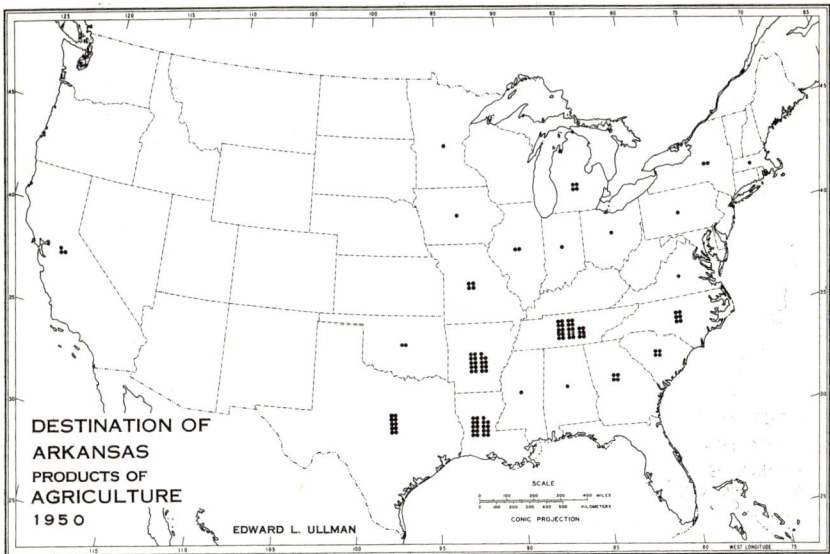

DESTINATION OF
ARKANSAS
PRODUCTS OF
AGRICULTURE
1950

EDWARD L. ULLMAN

SCALE

CONIC PROJECTION

WEST LONGITUDE

• 10,000 TONS ▌ 100,000 TONS

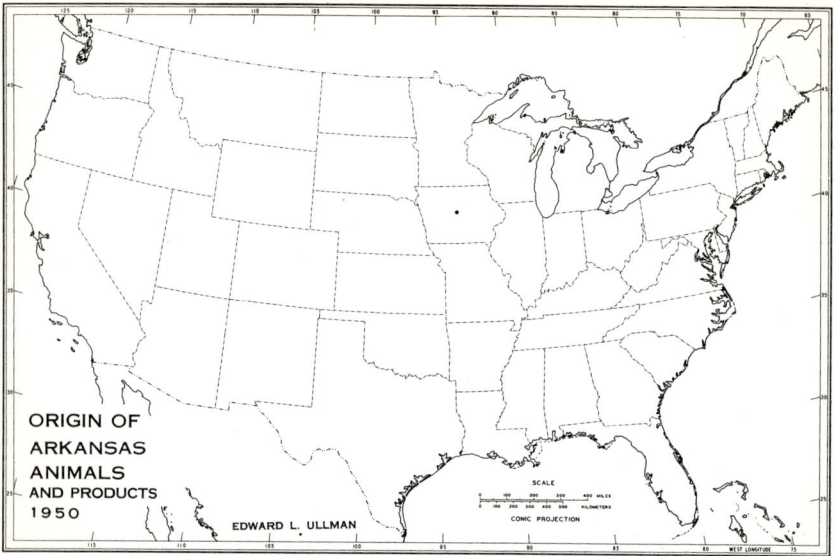

ORIGIN OF
ARKANSAS
ANIMALS
AND PRODUCTS
1950

EDWARD L. ULLMAN

SCALE

CONIC PROJECTION

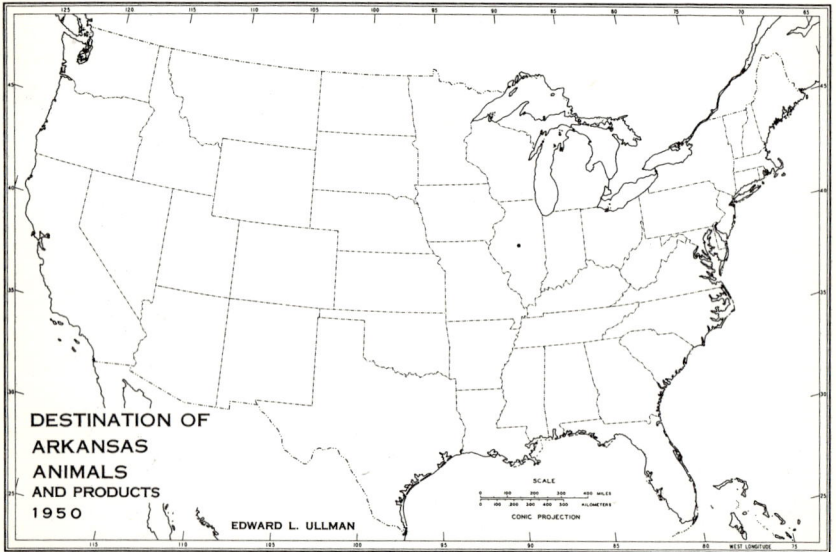

DESTINATION OF
ARKANSAS
ANIMALS
AND PRODUCTS
1950

EDWARD L. ULLMAN

SCALE

CONIC PROJECTION

• 10,000 TONS   ▌100,000 TONS

68

ORIGIN OF
ARKANSAS
PRODUCTS OF MINES
(OTHER THAN PETROLEUM)
1950

EDWARD L. ULLMAN

SCALE

CONIC PROJECTION

DESTINATION OF
ARKANSAS
PRODUCTS OF MINES
(OTHER THAN PETROLEUM)
1950

EDWARD L. ULLMAN

SCALE

CONIC PROJECTION

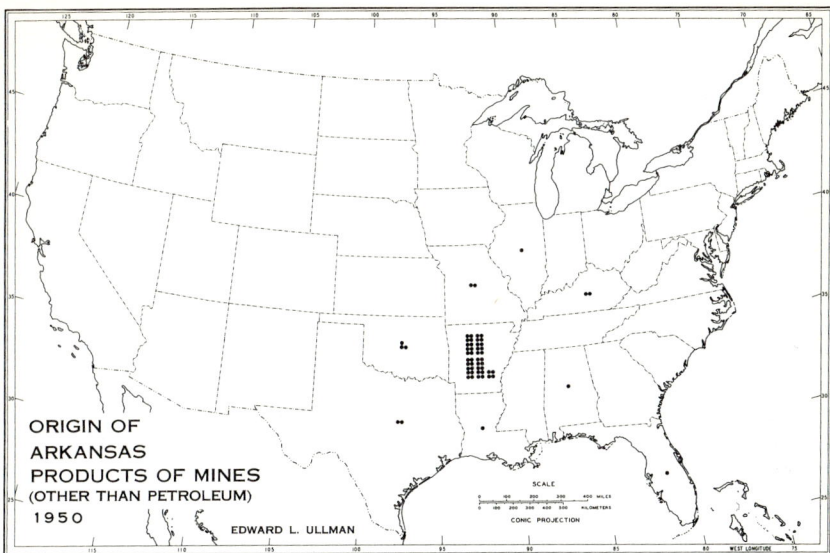

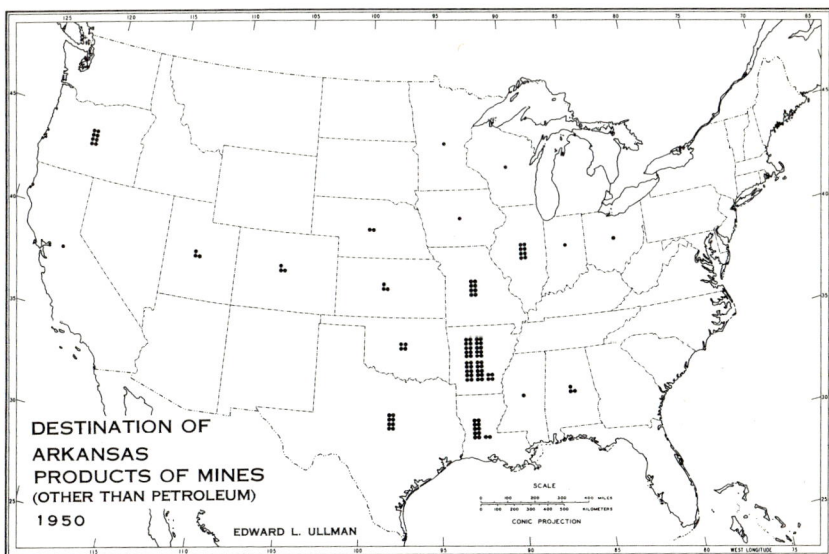

• 50,000 TONS   ▉ 500,000 TONS

69

ORIGIN OF
ARKANSAS
PETROLEUM PRODUCTS
1950

EDWARD L. ULLMAN

SCALE
CONIC PROJECTION

DESTINATION OF
ARKANSAS
PETROLEUM PRODUCTS
1950

EDWARD L. ULLMAN

SCALE
CONIC PROJECTION

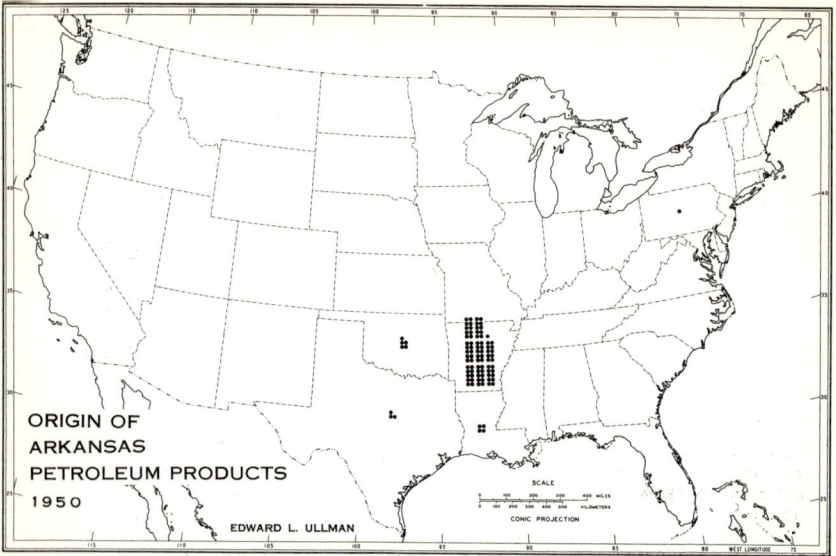

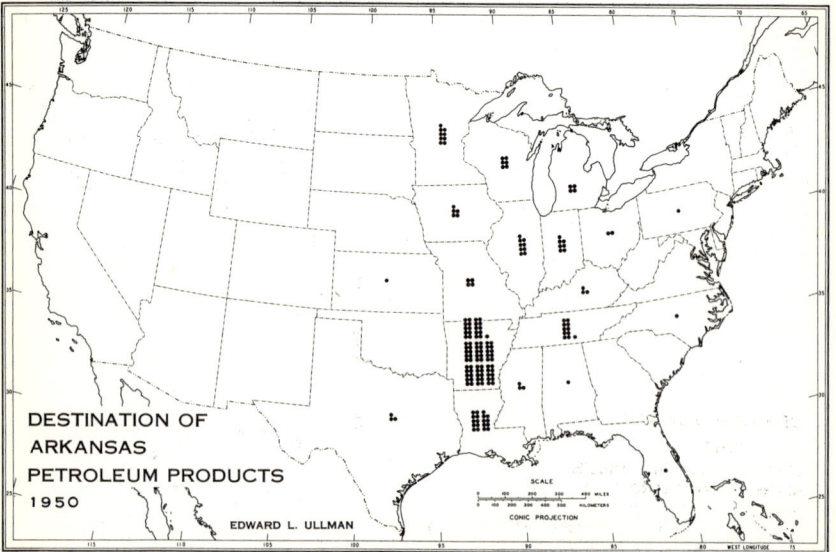

• 10,000 TONS   100,000 TONS

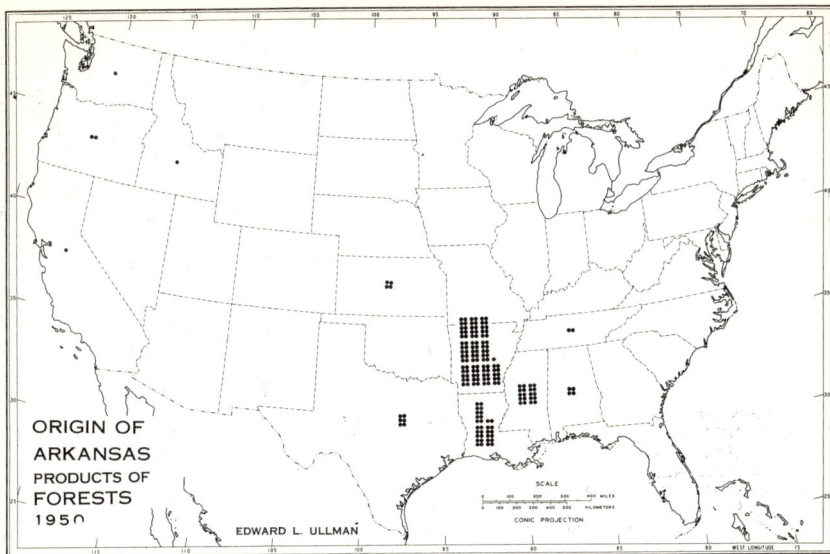

ORIGIN OF
ARKANSAS
PRODUCTS OF
FORESTS
1950

EDWARD L. ULLMAN

SCALE

CONIC PROJECTION

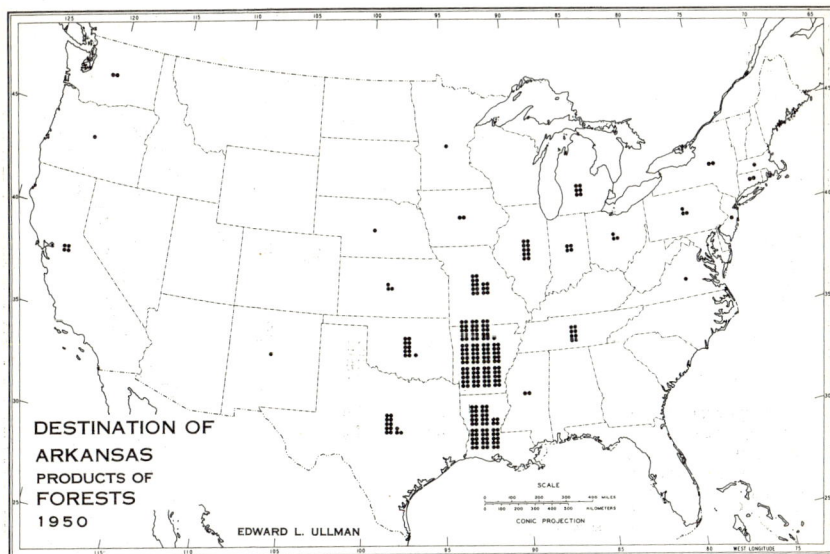

DESTINATION OF
ARKANSAS
PRODUCTS OF
FORESTS
1950

EDWARD L. ULLMAN

SCALE

CONIC PROJECTION

• 10,000 TONS   ▌ 100,000 TONS

71

ORIGIN OF
ARKANSAS
MANUFACTURES
AND MISCELLANEOUS
(OTHER THAN PETROLEUM)
1950

EDWARD L. ULLMAN

SCALE
0   100   200   300   400 MILES
0   100   200   300   400   500 KILOMETERS
CONIC PROJECTION

DESTINATION OF
ARKANSAS
MANUFACTURES
AND MISCELLANEOUS
(OTHER THAN PETROLEUM)
1950

EDWARD L. ULLMAN

SCALE
0   100   200   300   400 MILES
0   100   200   300   400   500 KILOMETERS
CONIC PROJECTION

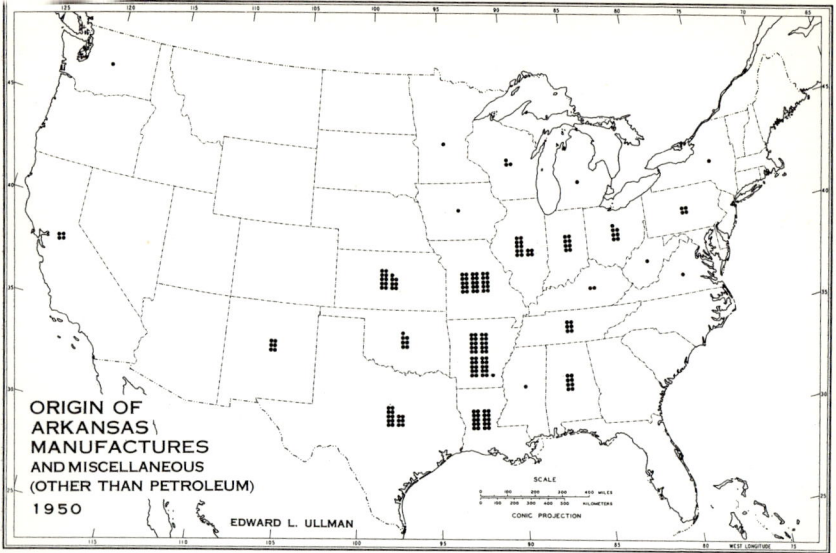

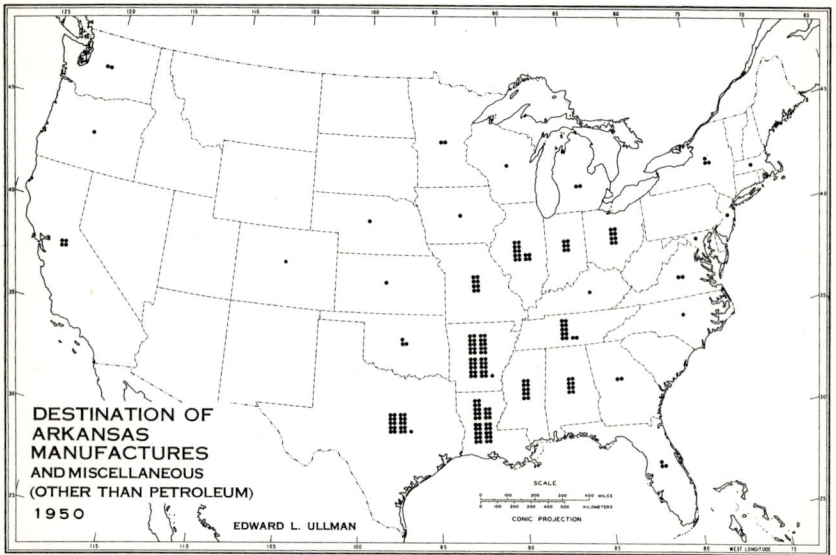

• 10,000 TONS   ▓ 100,000 TONS

72

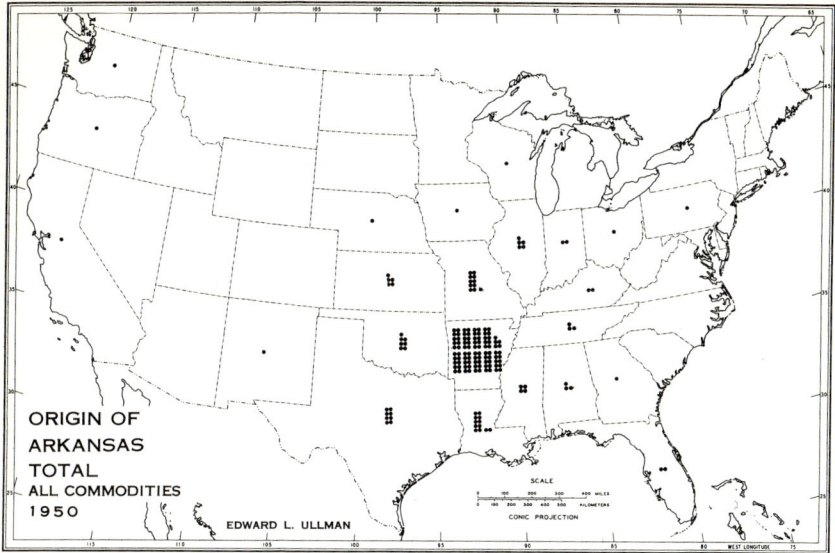

ORIGIN OF
ARKANSAS
TOTAL
ALL COMMODITIES
1950

EDWARD L. ULLMAN

SCALE

CONIC PROJECTION

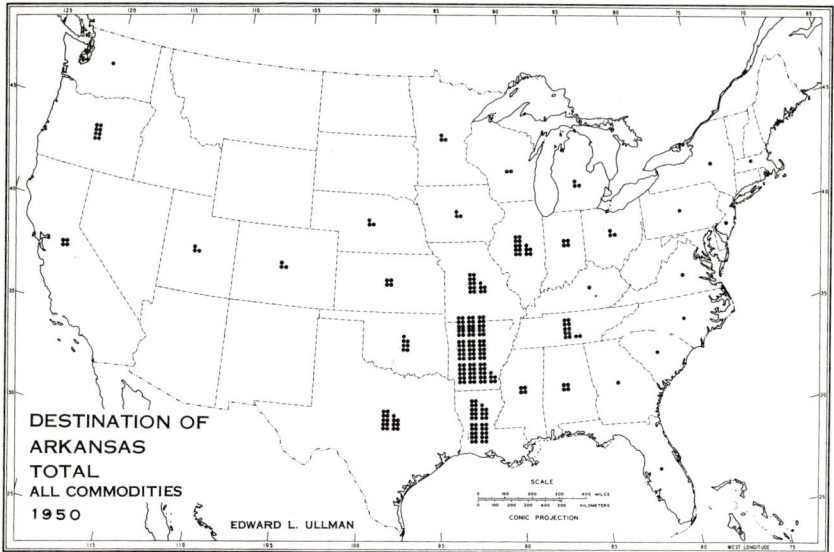

DESTINATION OF
ARKANSAS
TOTAL
ALL COMMODITIES
1950

EDWARD L. ULLMAN

SCALE

CONIC PROJECTION

• 50,000 TONS   █ 500,000 TONS

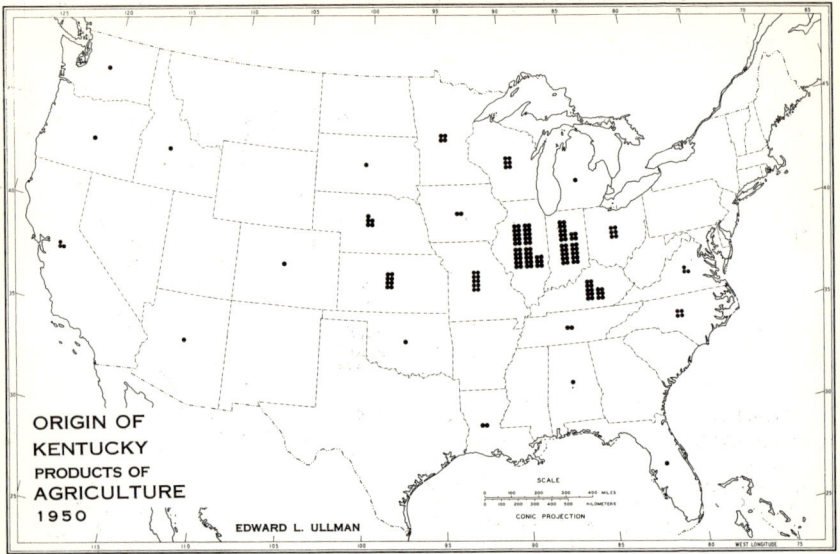

ORIGIN OF
KENTUCKY
PRODUCTS OF
AGRICULTURE
1950

EDWARD L. ULLMAN

SCALE

CONIC PROJECTION

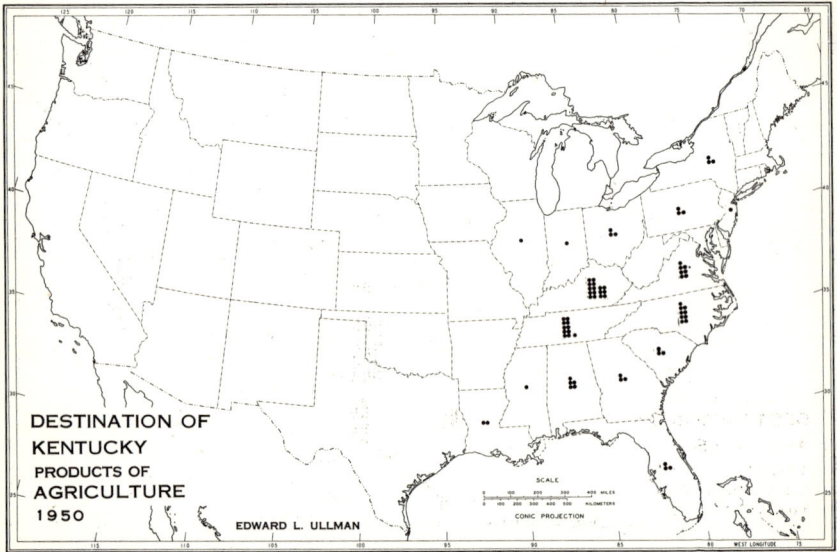

DESTINATION OF
KENTUCKY
PRODUCTS OF
AGRICULTURE
1950

EDWARD L. ULLMAN

SCALE

CONIC PROJECTION

• 10,000 TONS   100,000 TONS

74

ORIGIN OF
KENTUCKY
ANIMALS
AND PRODUCTS
1950

EDWARD L. ULLMAN

SCALE

CONIC PROJECTION

DESTINATION OF
KENTUCKY
ANIMALS
AND PRODUCTS
1950

EDWARD L. ULLMAN

SCALE

CONIC PROJECTION

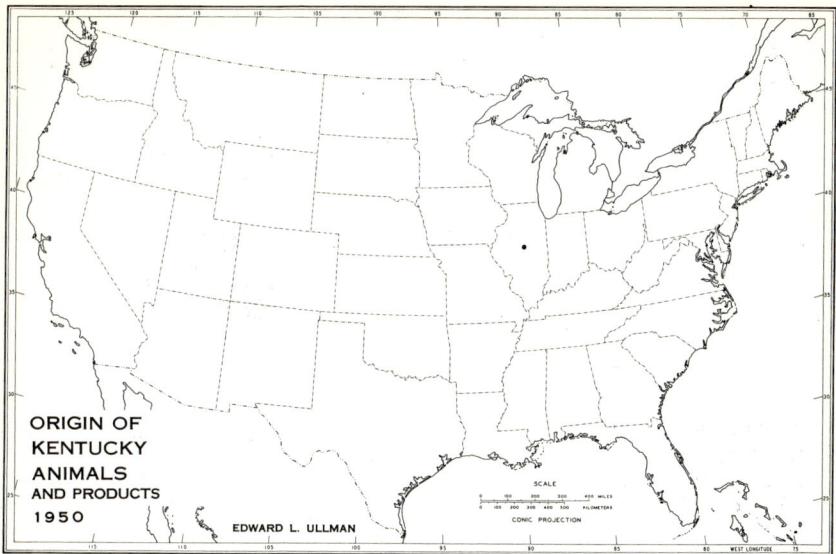

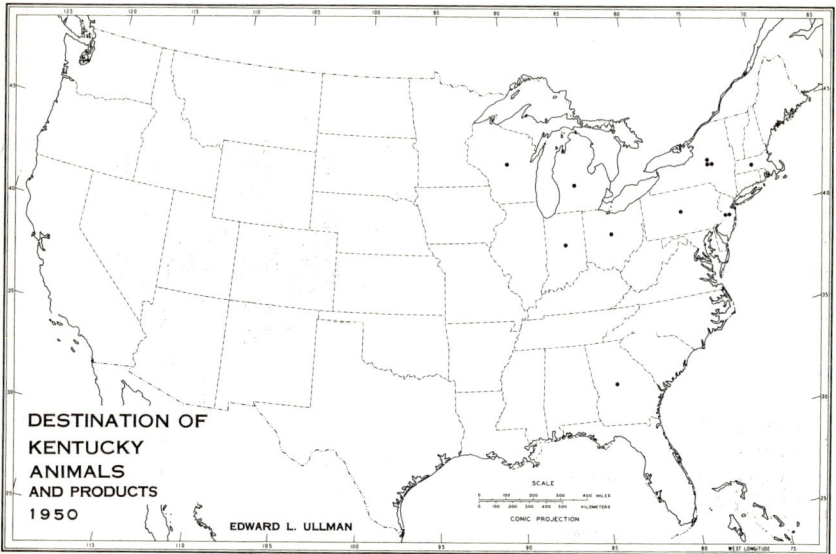

• 10,000 TONS ▊ 100,000 TONS

75

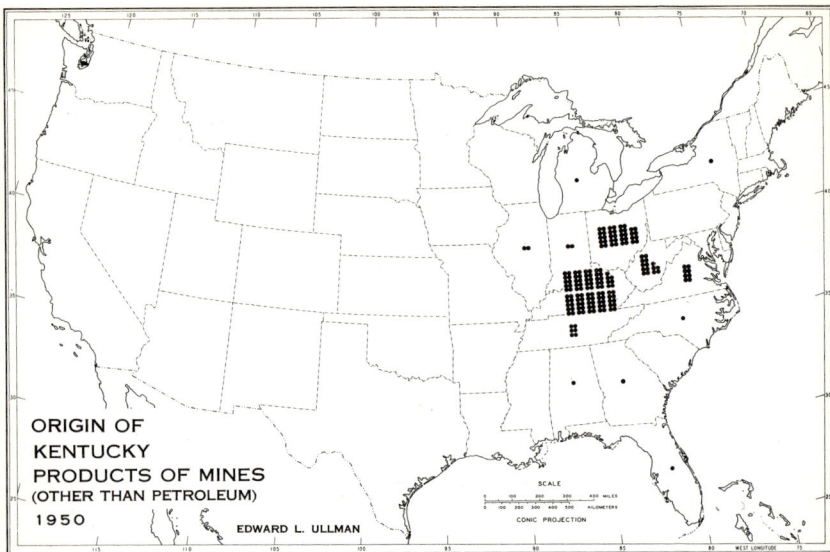

ORIGIN OF
KENTUCKY
PRODUCTS OF MINES
(OTHER THAN PETROLEUM)
1950

EDWARD L. ULLMAN

SCALE

CONIC PROJECTION

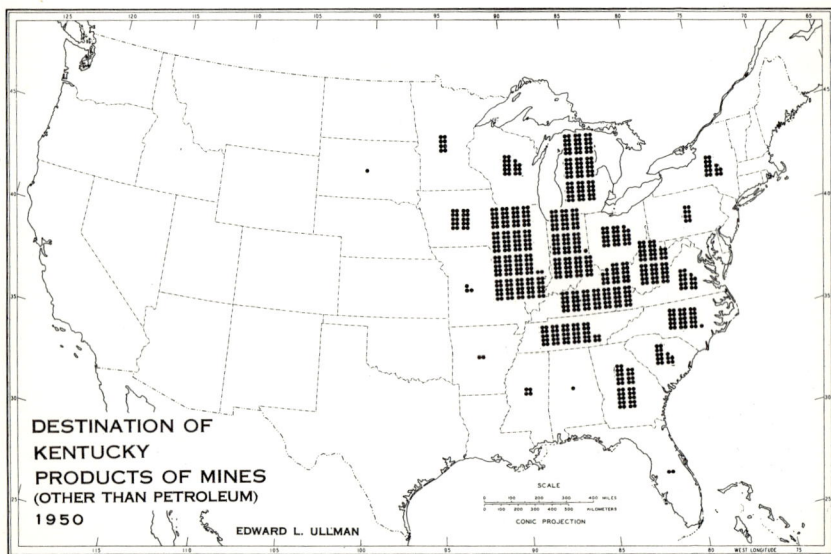

DESTINATION OF
KENTUCKY
PRODUCTS OF MINES
(OTHER THAN PETROLEUM)
1950

EDWARD L. ULLMAN

SCALE

CONIC PROJECTION

· 50,000 TONS ▌ 500,000 TONS

76

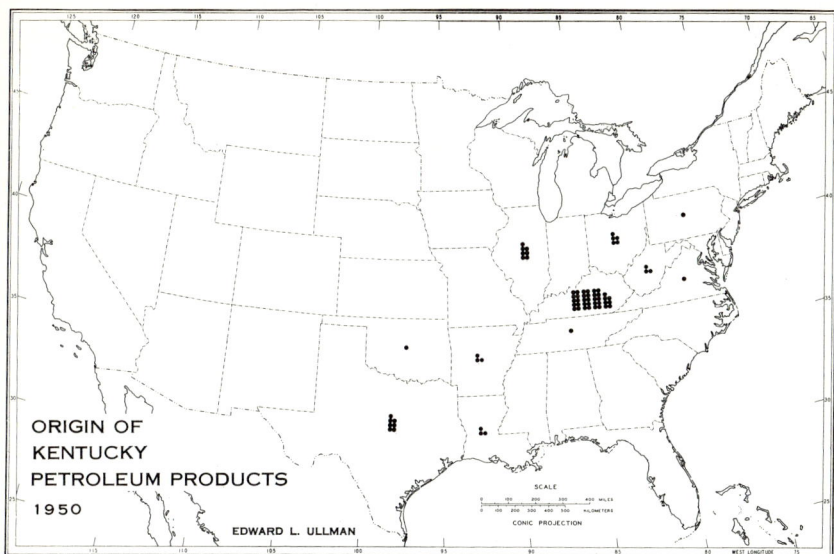

ORIGIN OF
KENTUCKY
PETROLEUM PRODUCTS
1950

EDWARD L. ULLMAN

SCALE

CONIC PROJECTION

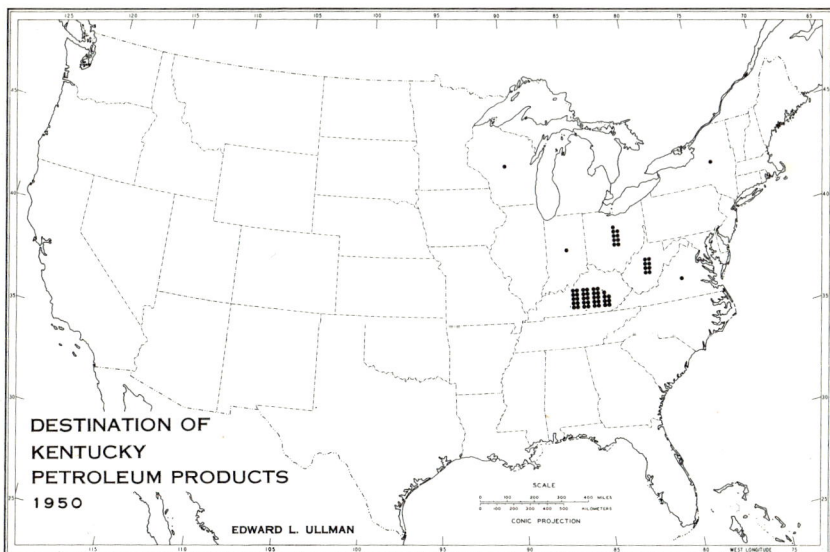

DESTINATION OF
KENTUCKY
PETROLEUM PRODUCTS
1950

EDWARD L. ULLMAN

SCALE

CONIC PROJECTION

• 10,000 TONS   ▮ 100,000 TONS

77

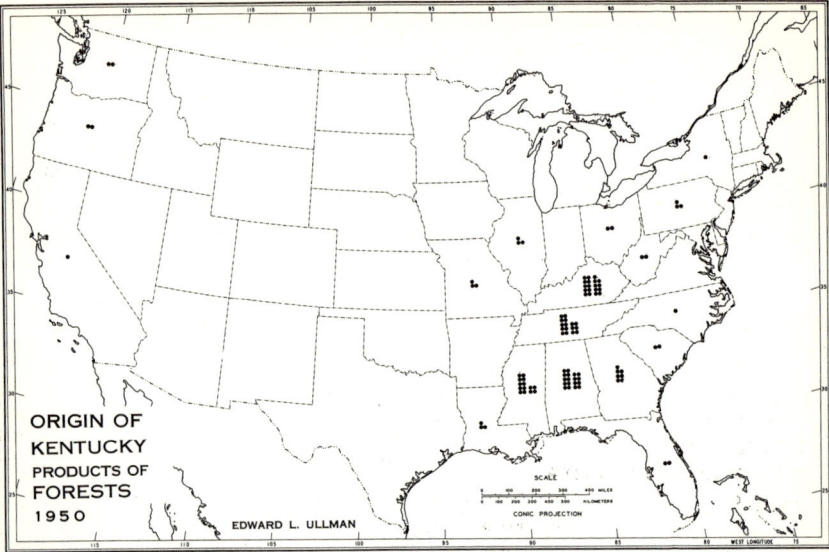

ORIGIN OF
KENTUCKY
PRODUCTS OF
FORESTS
1950

EDWARD L. ULLMAN

SCALE

CONIC PROJECTION

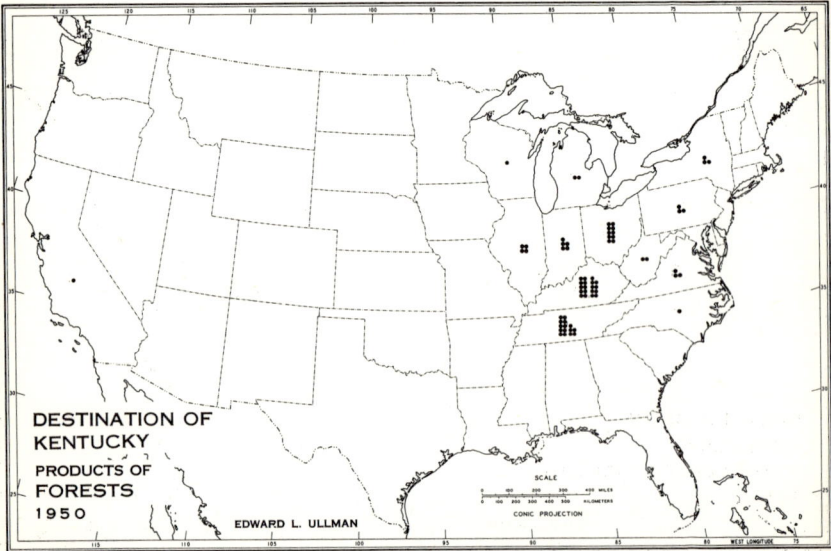

DESTINATION OF
KENTUCKY
PRODUCTS OF
FORESTS
1950

EDWARD L. ULLMAN

SCALE

CONIC PROJECTION

· 10,000 TONS   100,000 TONS

78

ORIGIN OF
KENTUCKY
MANUFACTURES
AND MISCELLANEOUS
(OTHER THAN PETROLEUM)
1950

EDWARD L. ULLMAN

SCALE
CONIC PROJECTION

DESTINATION OF
KENTUCKY
MANUFACTURES
AND MISCELLANEOUS
(OTHER THAN PETROLEUM)
1950

EDWARD L. ULLMAN

SCALE
CONIC PROJECTION

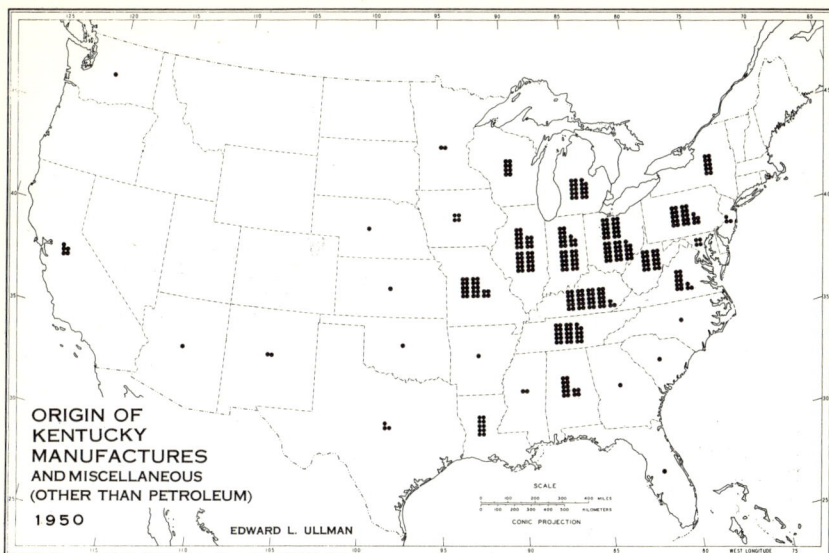

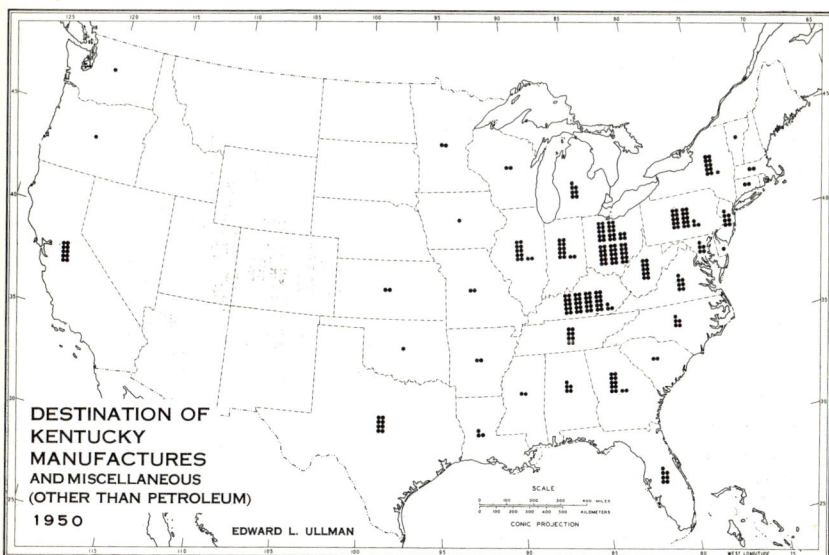

• 10,000 TONS   ▮ 100,000 TONS

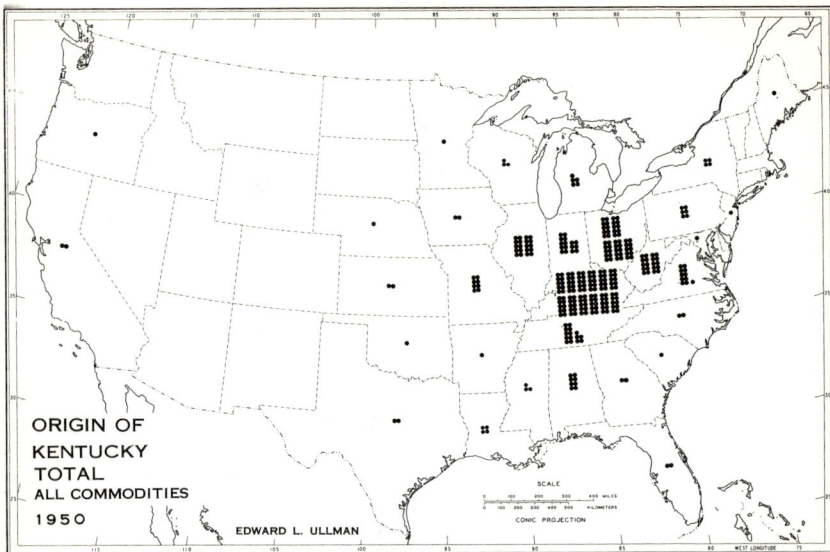

ORIGIN OF
KENTUCKY
TOTAL
ALL COMMODITIES
1950

EDWARD L. ULLMAN

SCALE

CONIC PROJECTION

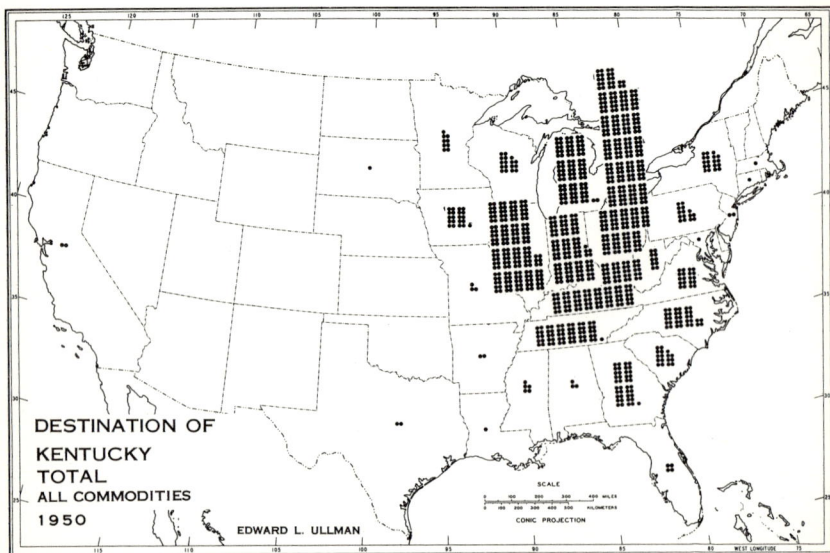

DESTINATION OF
KENTUCKY
TOTAL
ALL COMMODITIES
1950

EDWARD L. ULLMAN

SCALE

CONIC PROJECTION

• 50,000 TONS   500,000 TONS

80

ORIGIN OF
LOUISIANA
PRODUCTS OF
AGRICULTURE
1950

EDWARD L. ULLMAN

SCALE

CONIC PROJECTION

DESTINATION OF
LOUISIANA
PRODUCTS OF
AGRICULTURE
1950

EDWARD L. ULLMAN

SCALE

CONIC PROJECTION

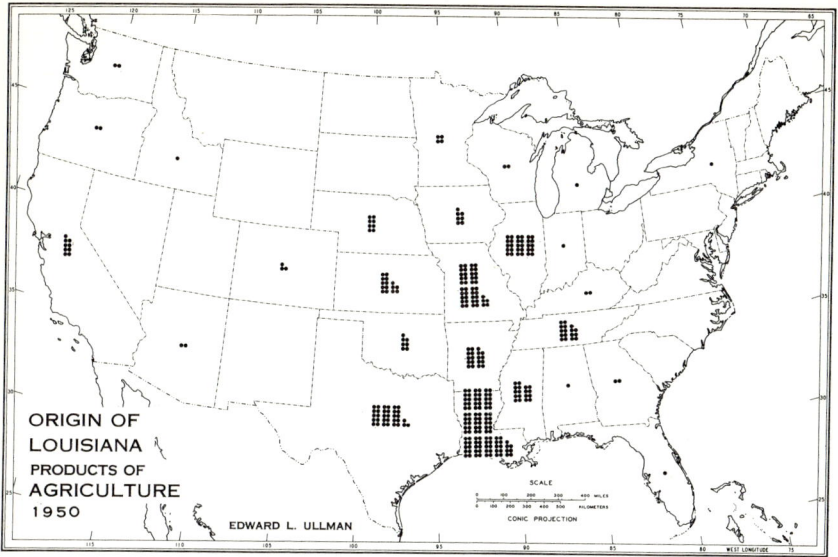

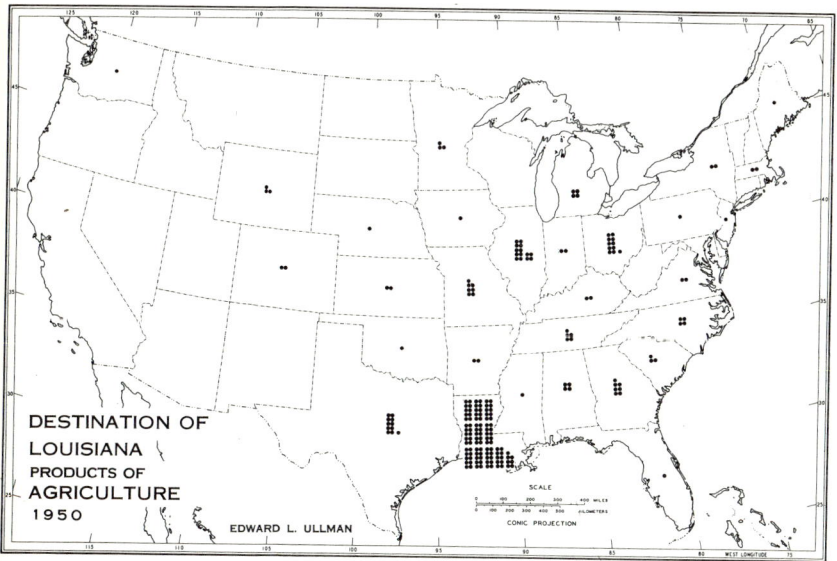

• 10,000 TONS   ▮ 100,000 TONS

81

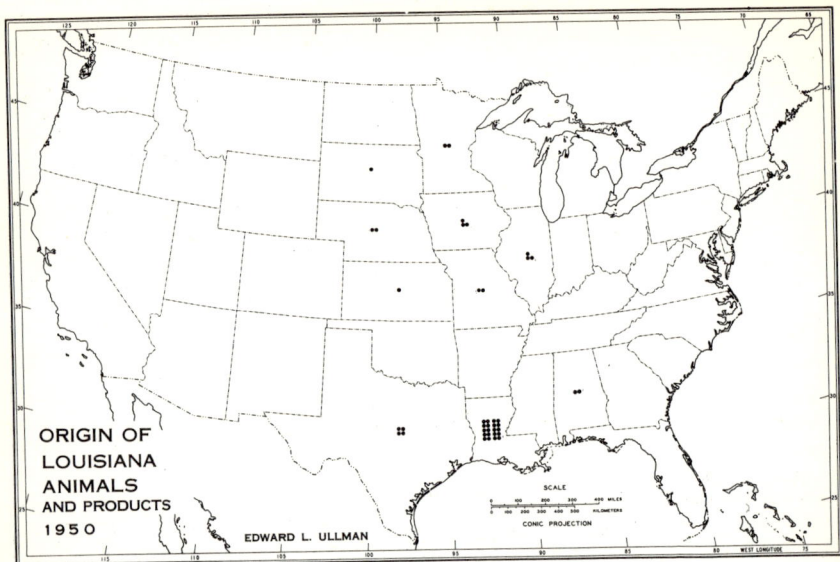

ORIGIN OF
LOUISIANA
ANIMALS
AND PRODUCTS
1950

EDWARD L. ULLMAN

SCALE

CONIC PROJECTION

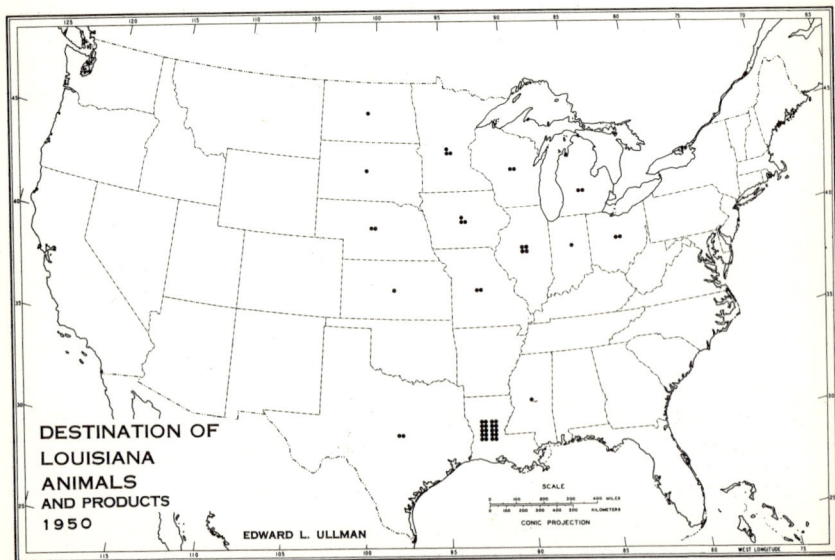

DESTINATION OF
LOUISIANA
ANIMALS
AND PRODUCTS
1950

EDWARD L. ULLMAN

SCALE

CONIC PROJECTION

• 10,000 TONS   ⦚ 100,000 TONS

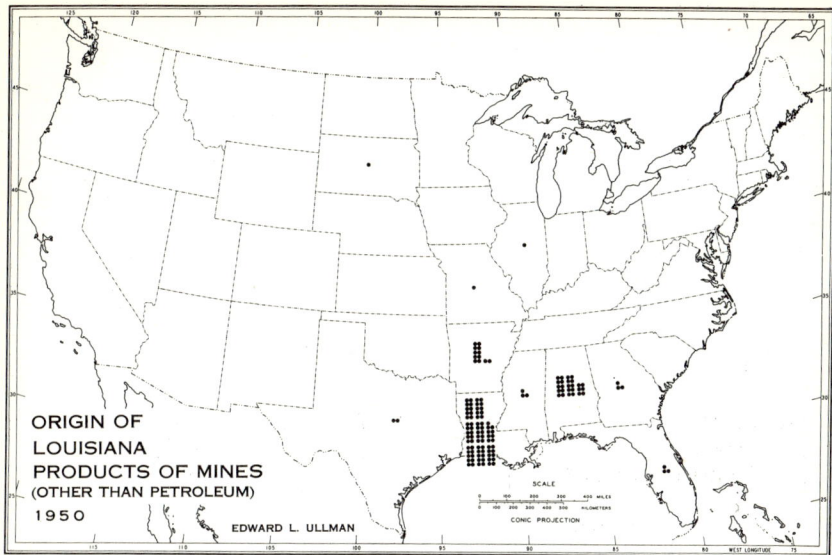

ORIGIN OF
LOUISIANA
PRODUCTS OF MINES
(OTHER THAN PETROLEUM)
1950

EDWARD L. ULLMAN

SCALE

CONIC PROJECTION

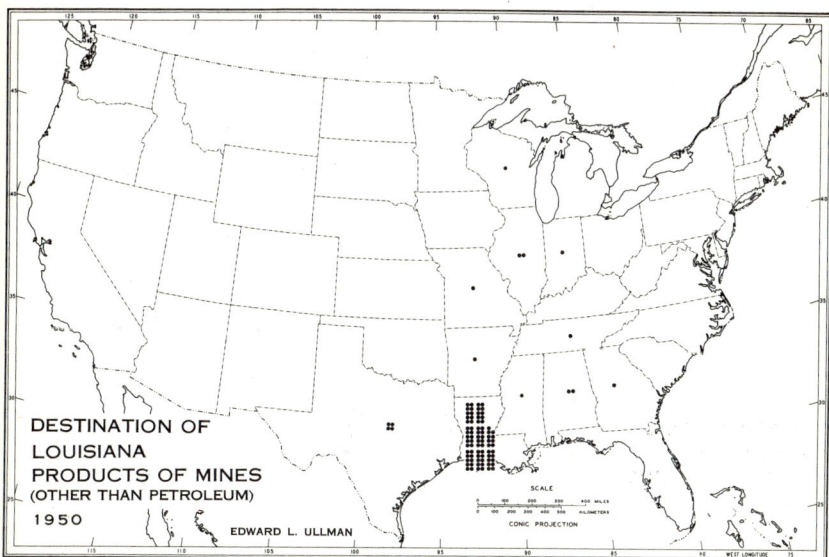

DESTINATION OF
LOUISIANA
PRODUCTS OF MINES
(OTHER THAN PETROLEUM)
1950

EDWARD L. ULLMAN

SCALE

CONIC PROJECTION

• 50,000 TONS ▮▮ 500,000 TONS

ORIGIN OF
LOUISIANA
PETROLEUM PRODUCTS
1950

EDWARD L. ULLMAN

SCALE
CONIC PROJECTION

DESTINATION OF
LOUISIANA
PETROLEUM PRODUCTS
1950

EDWARD L. ULLMAN

SCALE
CONIC PROJECTION

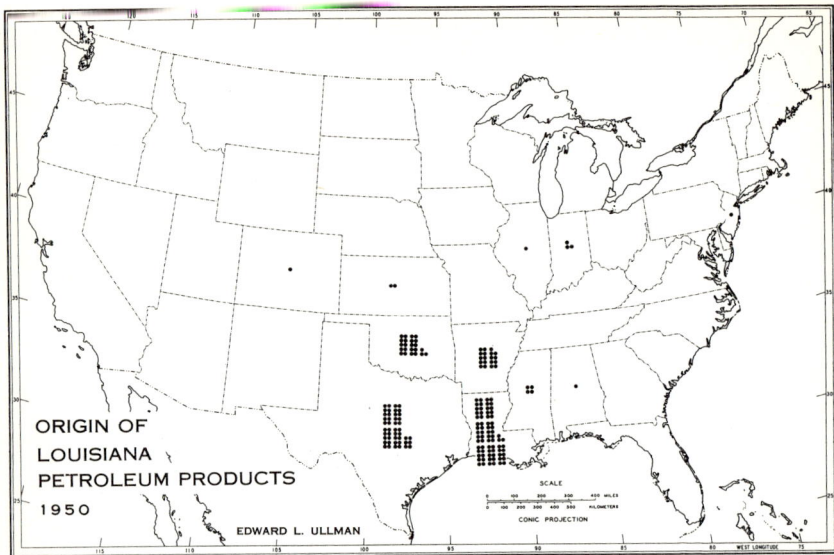

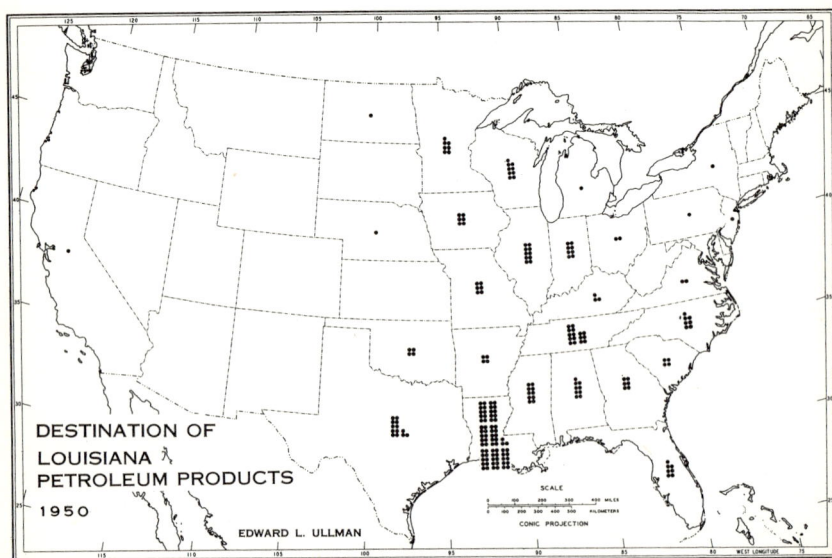

• 10,000 TONS   ▌ 100,000 TONS

84

ORIGIN OF
LOUISIANA
PRODUCTS OF
FORESTS
1950

EDWARD L. ULLMAN

SCALE

CONIC PROJECTION

DESTINATION OF
LOUISIANA
PRODUCTS OF
FORESTS
1950

EDWARD L. ULLMAN

SCALE

CONIC PROJECTION

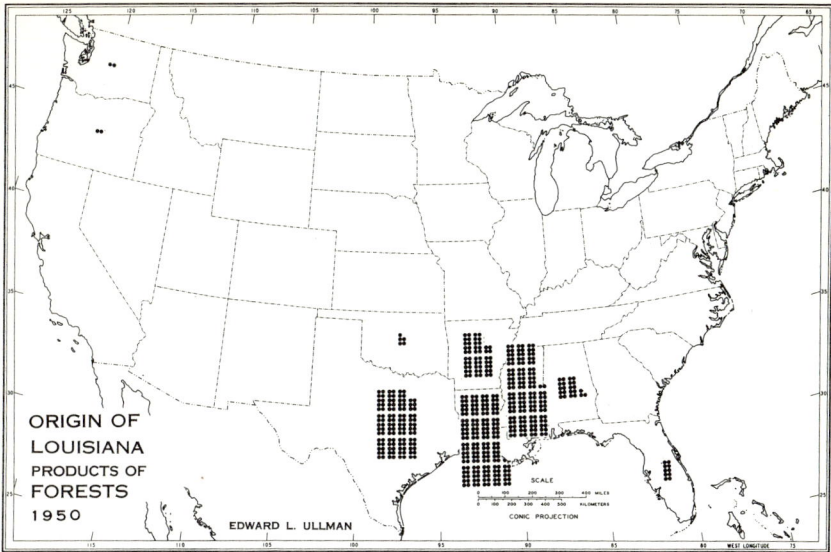

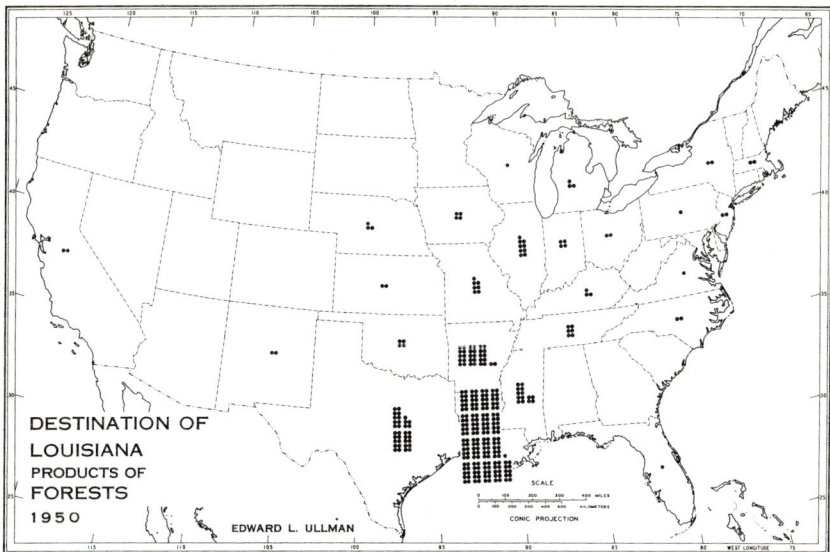

• 10,000 TONS   100,000 TONS

ORIGIN OF
LOUISIANA
MANUFACTURES
AND MISCELLANEOUS
(OTHER THAN PETROLEUM)
1950

EDWARD L. ULLMAN

SCALE
CONIC PROJECTION

DESTINATION OF
LOUISIANA
MANUFACTURES
AND MISCELLANEOUS
(OTHER THAN PETROLEUM)
1950

EDWARD L. ULLMAN

SCALE
CONIC PROJECTION

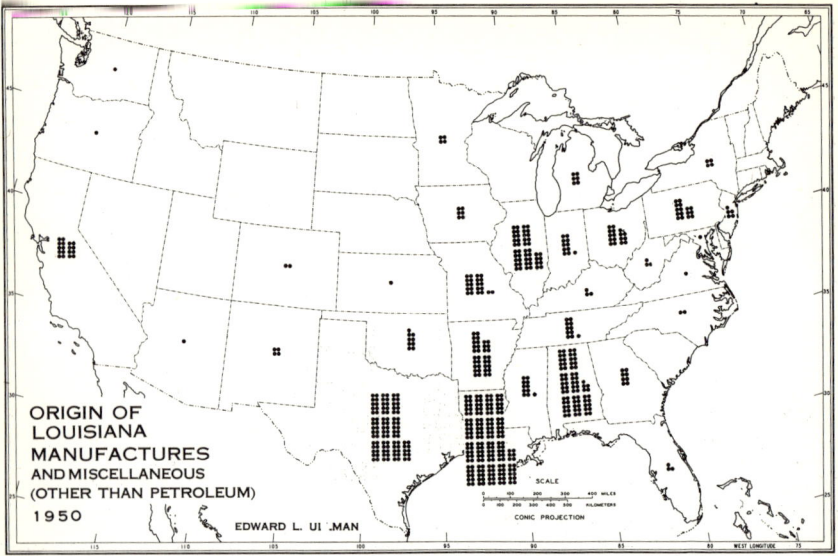

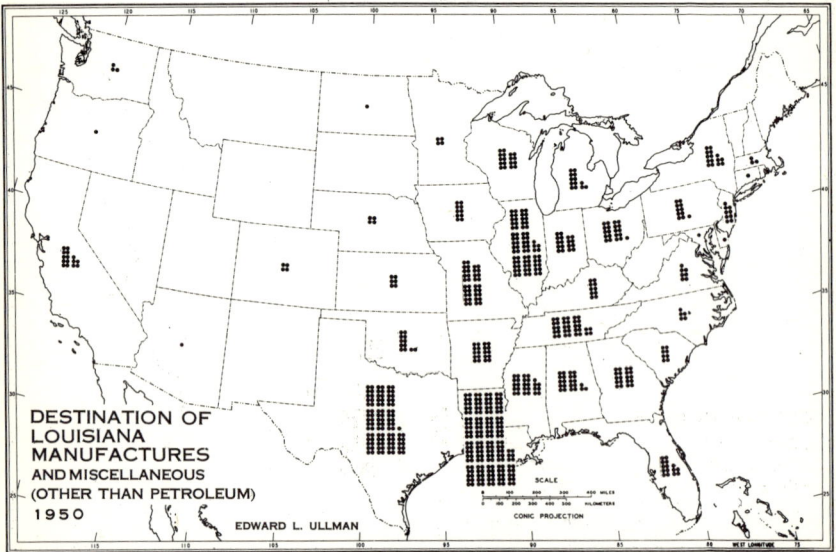

• 10,000 TONS   ▮▮ 100,000 TONS

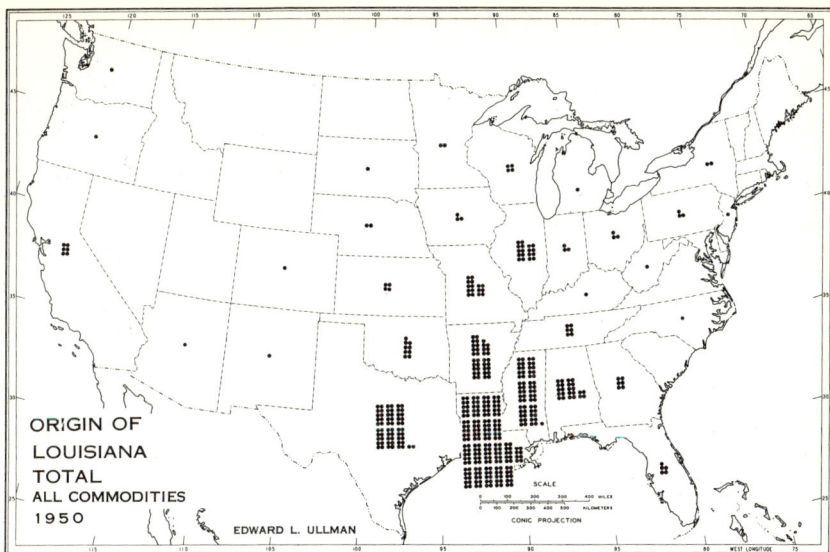

ORIGIN OF
LOUISIANA
TOTAL
ALL COMMODITIES
1950

EDWARD L. ULLMAN

SCALE

CONIC PROJECTION

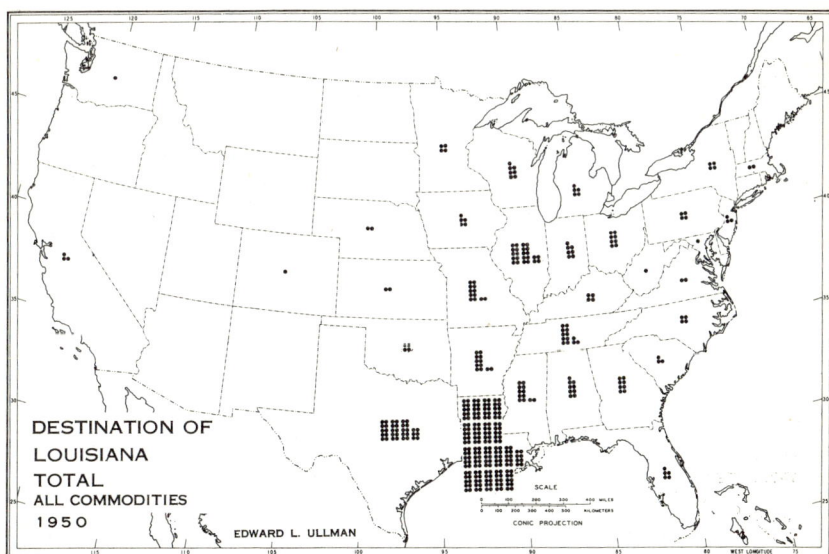

DESTINATION OF
LOUISIANA
TOTAL
ALL COMMODITIES
1950

EDWARD L. ULLMAN

SCALE

CONIC PROJECTION

• 50,000 TONS   ▐▐ 500,000 TONS

87

ORIGIN OF
MAINE
PRODUCTS OF
AGRICULTURE
1950

EDWARD L. ULLMAN

SCALE

CONIC PROJECTION

DESTINATION OF
MAINE
PRODUCTS OF
AGRICULTURE
1950

EDWARD L. ULLMAN

SCALE

CONIC PROJECTION

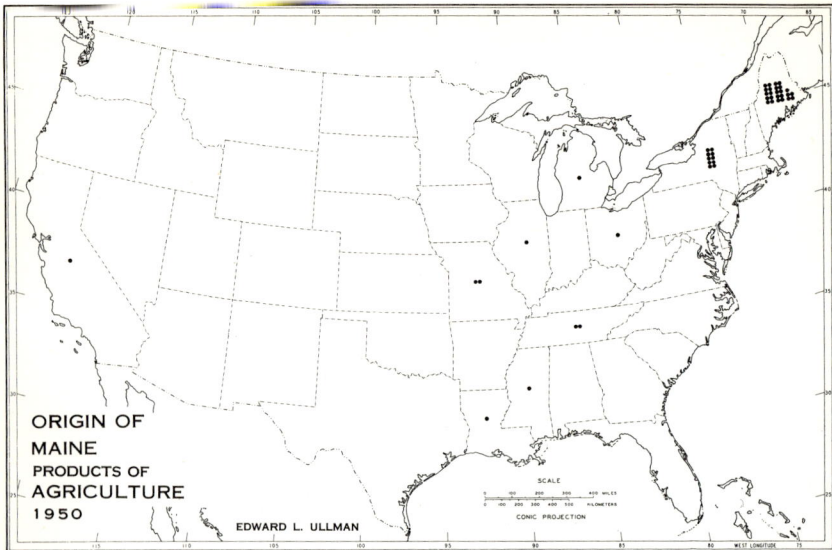

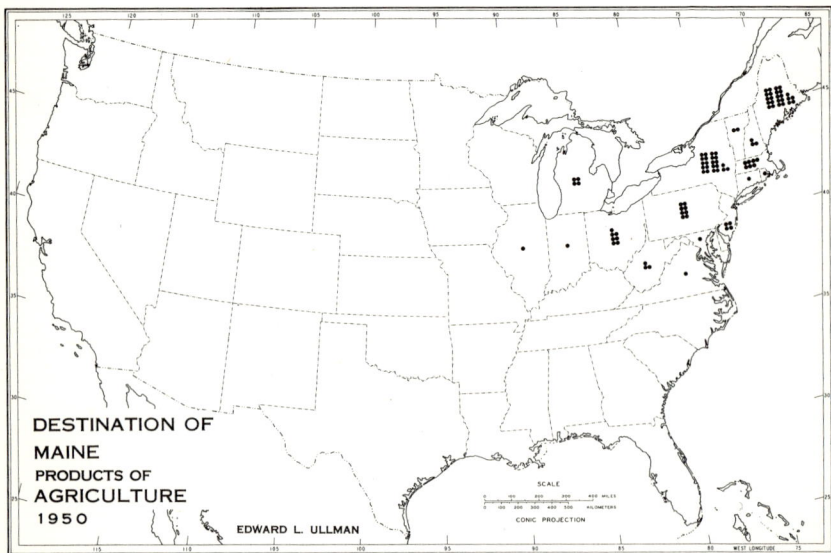

• 10,000 TONS   ▮ 100,000 TONS

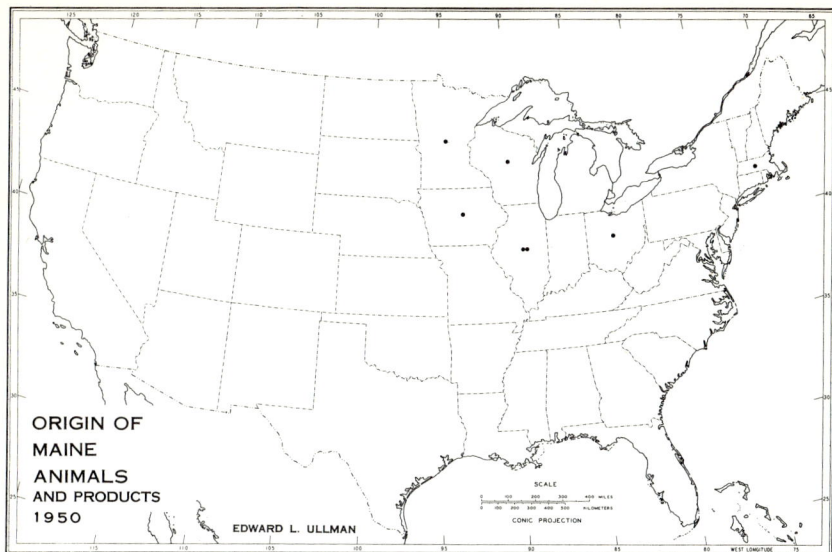

ORIGIN OF
MAINE
ANIMALS
AND PRODUCTS
1950

EDWARD L. ULLMAN

SCALE

CONIC PROJECTION

• 10,000 TONS   ▯ 100,000 TONS

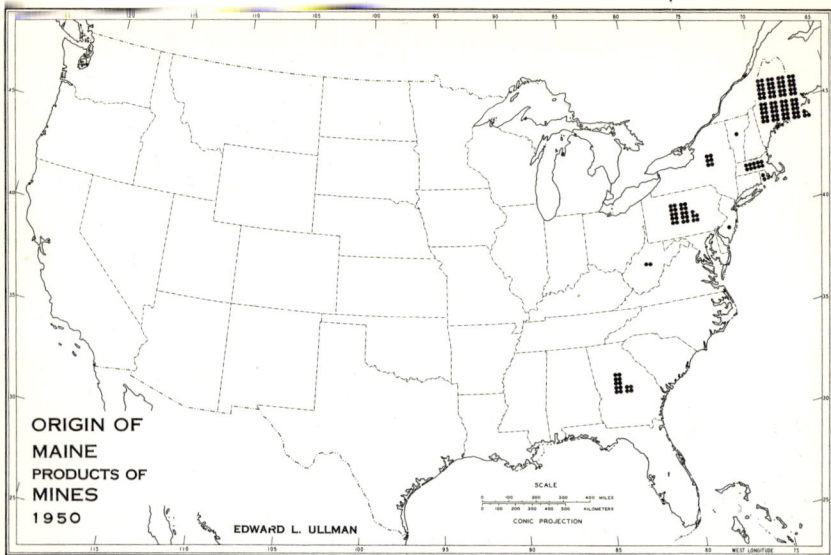

ORIGIN OF
MAINE
PRODUCTS OF
MINES
1950

EDWARD L. ULLMAN

SCALE
CONIC PROJECTION

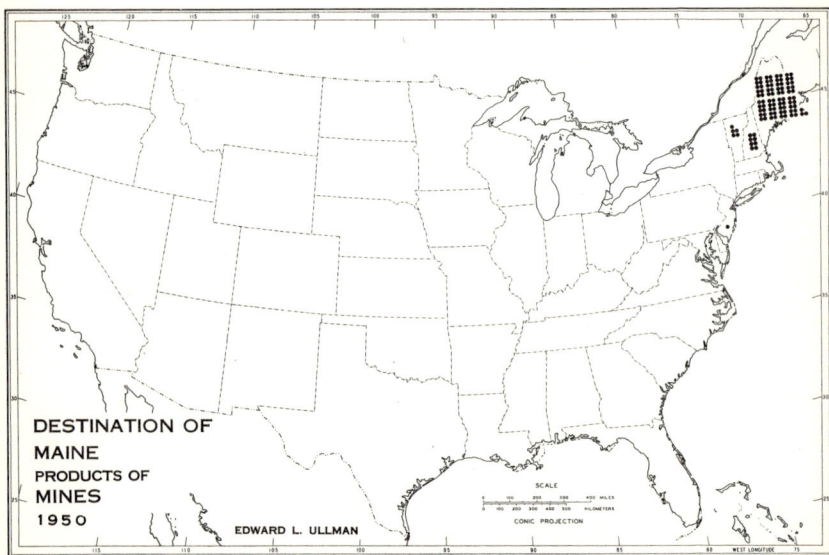

DESTINATION OF
MAINE
PRODUCTS OF
MINES
1950

EDWARD L. ULLMAN

SCALE
CONIC PROJECTION

• 10,000 TONS   ▊ 100,000 TONS

90

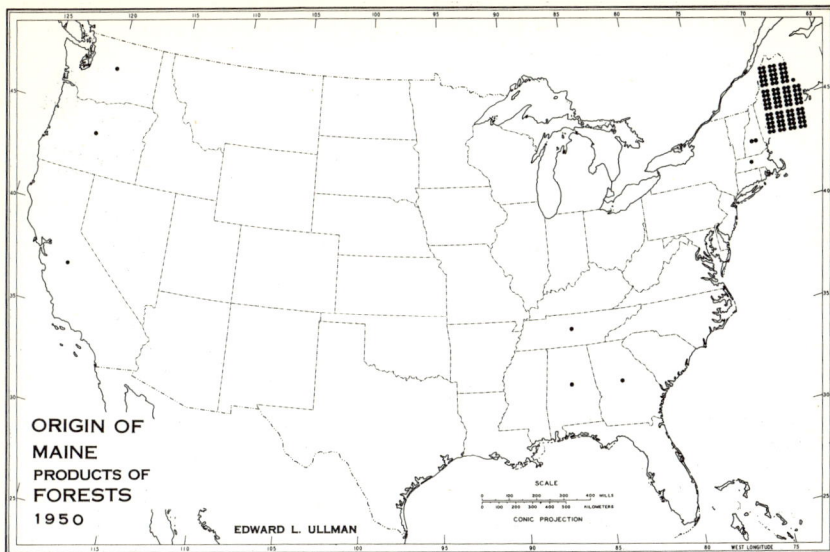

ORIGIN OF
MAINE
PRODUCTS OF
FORESTS
1950

EDWARD L. ULLMAN

SCALE

CONIC PROJECTION

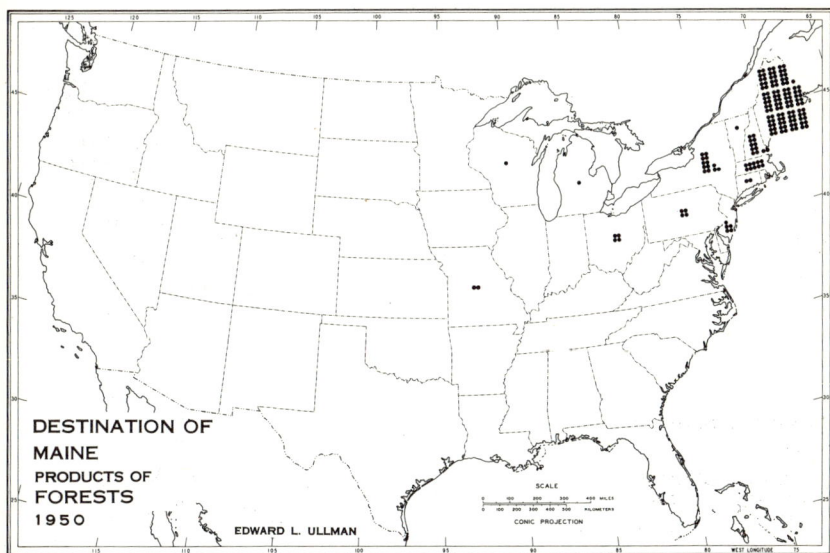

DESTINATION OF
MAINE
PRODUCTS OF
FORESTS
1950

EDWARD L. ULLMAN

SCALE

CONIC PROJECTION

◆10,000 TONS   ▓ 100,000 TONS

91

ORIGIN OF
MAINE
MANUFACTURES
AND MISCELLANEOUS
1950

EDWARD L. ULLMAN

SCALE

CONIC PROJECTION

DESTINATION OF
MAINE
MANUFACTURES
AND MISCELLANEOUS
1950

EDWARD L. ULLMAN

SCALE

CONIC PROJECTION

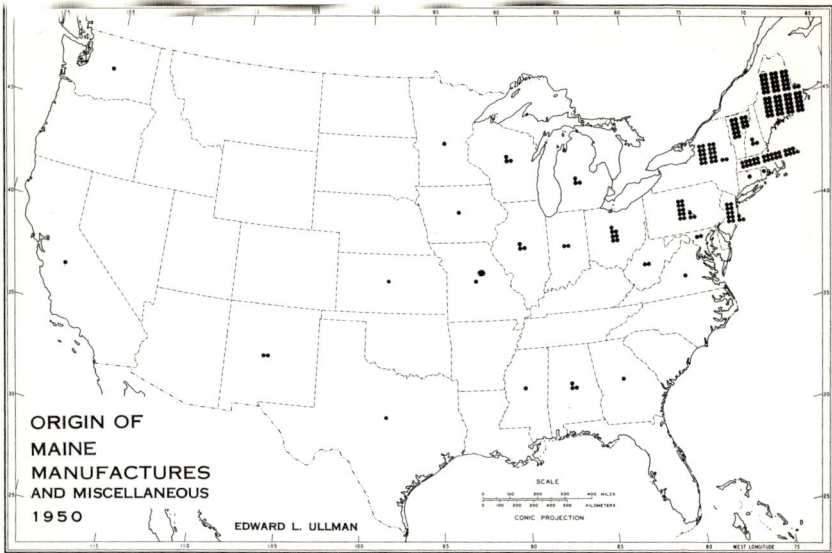

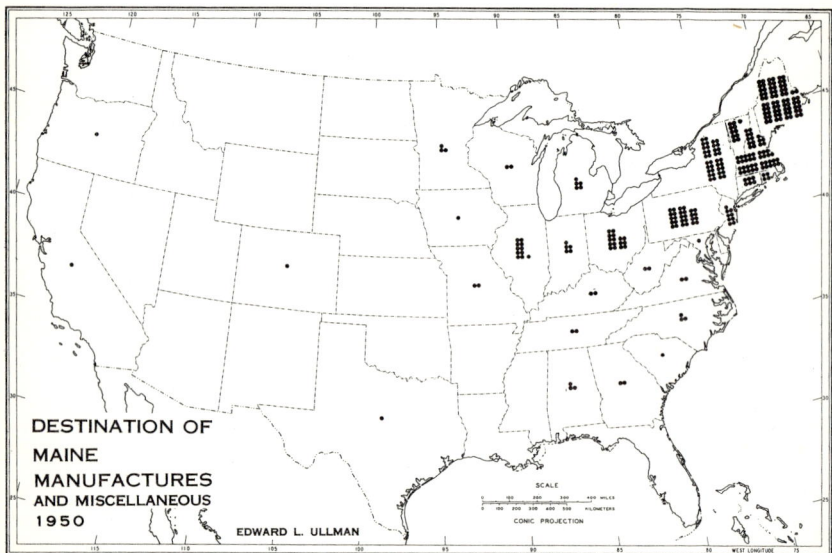

• 10,000 TONS   100,000 TONS

92

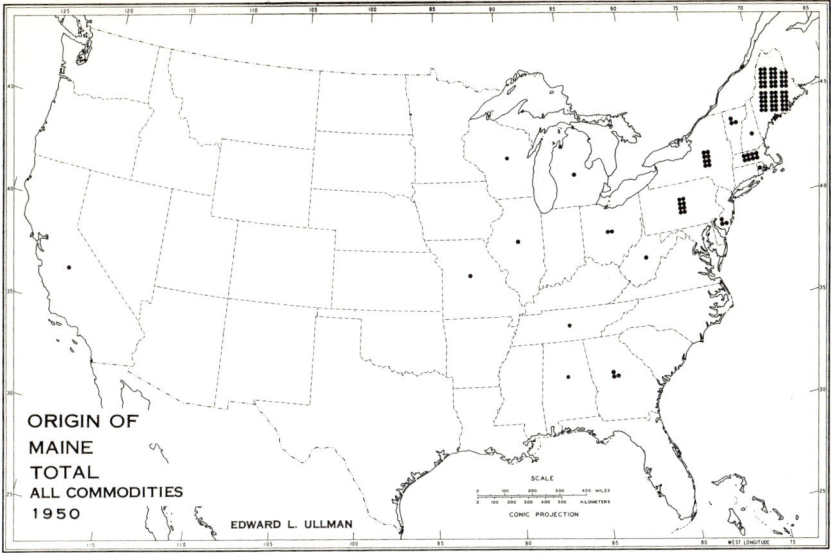

ORIGIN OF
MAINE
TOTAL
ALL COMMODITIES
1950

EDWARD L. ULLMAN

SCALE

CONIC PROJECTION

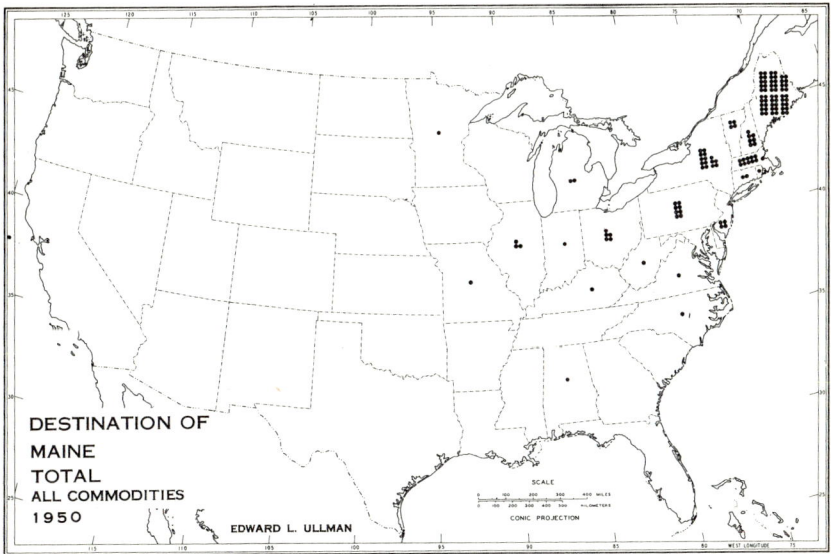

DESTINATION OF
MAINE
TOTAL
ALL COMMODITIES
1950

EDWARD L. ULLMAN

SCALE

CONIC PROJECTION

• 50,000 TONS   ▌ 500,000 TONS

93

ORIGIN OF
MISSISSIPPI
PRODUCTS OF
AGRICULTURE
1950

EDWARD L. ULLMAN

SCALE

CONIC PROJECTION

DESTINATION OF
MISSISSIPPI
PRODUCTS OF
AGRICULTURE
1950

EDWARD L. ULLMAN

SCALE

CONIC PROJECTION

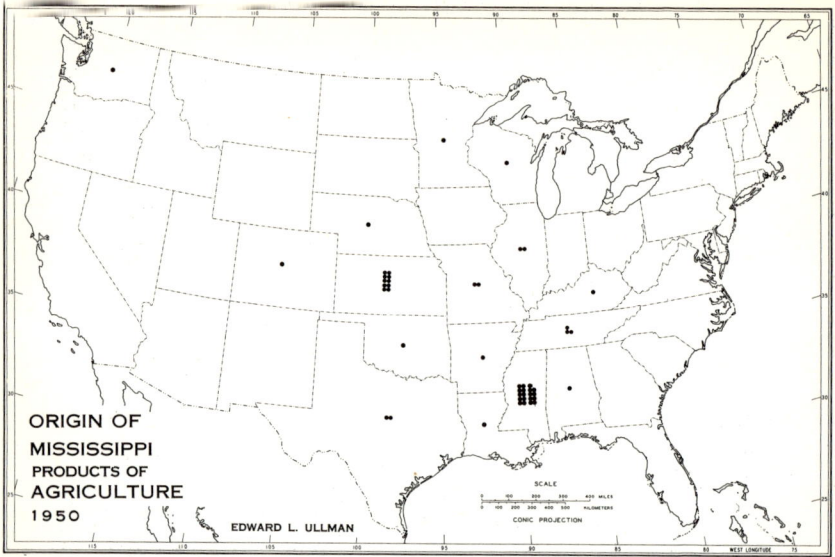

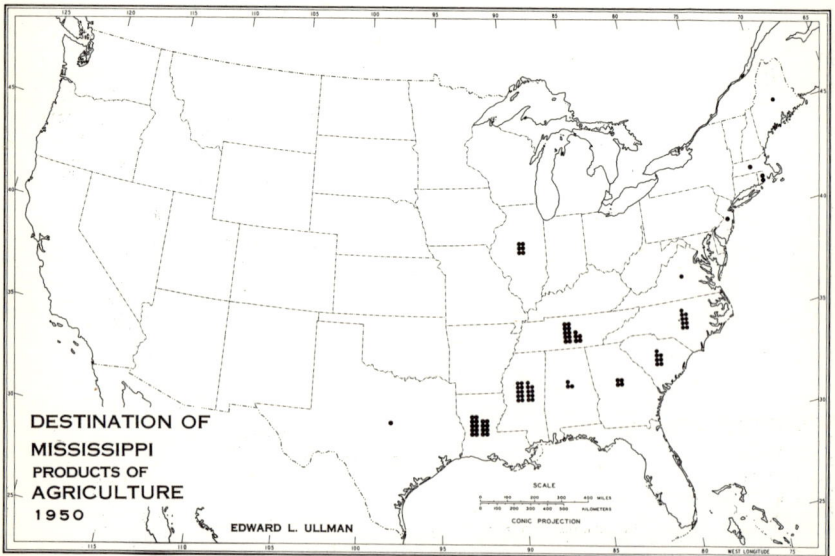

• 10,000 TONS   ▮ 100,000 TONS

ORIGIN OF
MISSISSIPPI
ANIMALS
AND PRODUCTS
1950

EDWARD L. ULLMAN

SCALE
CONIC PROJECTION

DESTINATION OF
MISSISSIPPI
ANIMALS
AND PRODUCTS
1950

EDWARD L. ULLMAN

SCALE
CONIC PROJECTION

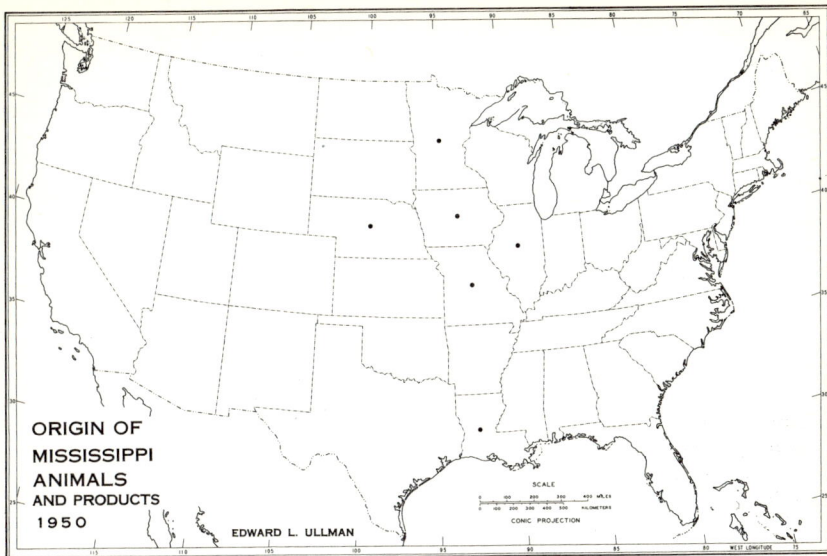

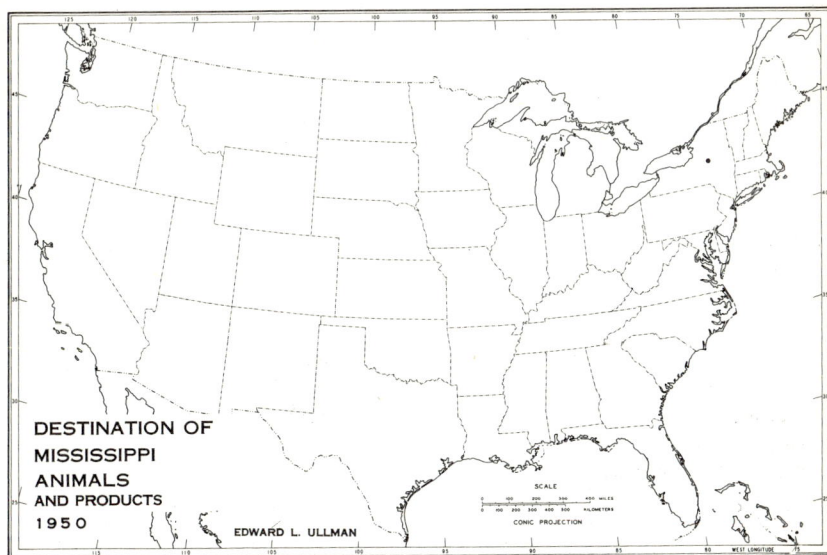

• 10,000 TONS   100,000 TONS

95

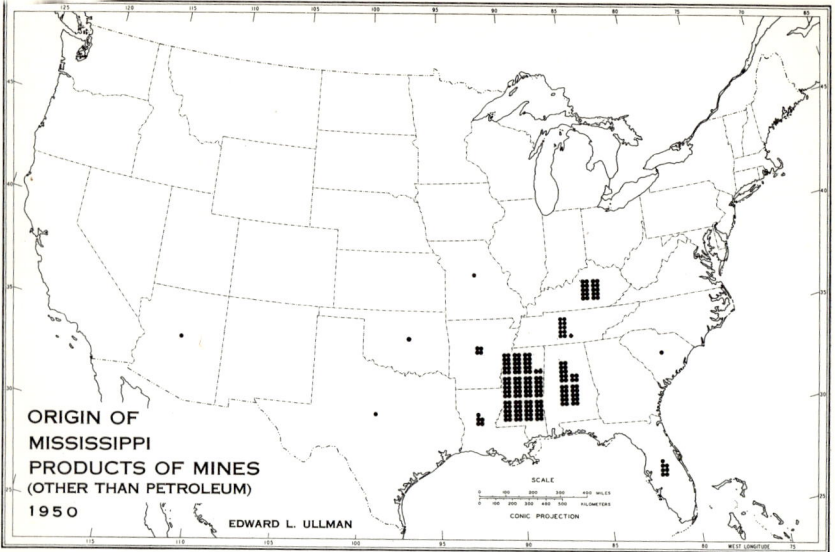

ORIGIN OF
MISSISSIPPI
PRODUCTS OF MINES
(OTHER THAN PETROLEUM)
1950

EDWARD L. ULLMAN

SCALE

CONIC PROJECTION

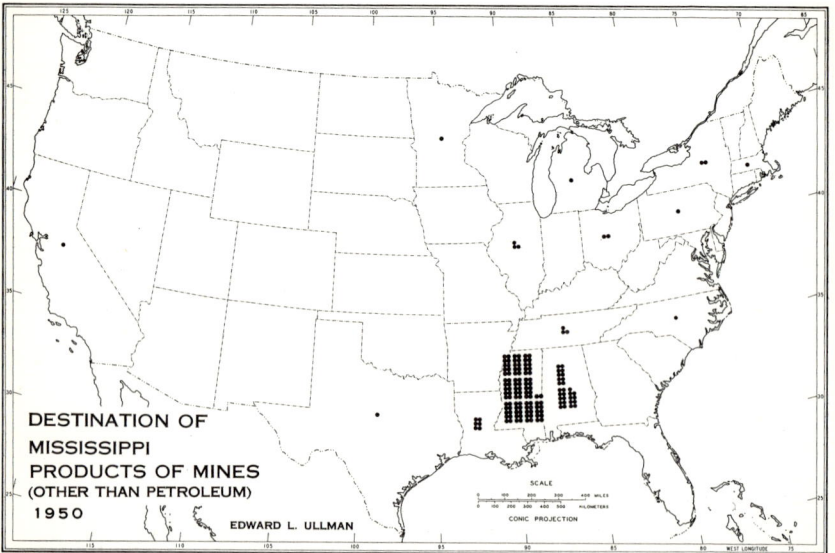

DESTINATION OF
MISSISSIPPI
PRODUCTS OF MINES
(OTHER THAN PETROLEUM)
1950

EDWARD L. ULLMAN

SCALE

CONIC PROJECTION

• 10,000 TONS   ▌100,000 TONS

96

ORIGIN OF
MISSISSIPPI
PETROLEUM PRODUCTS
1950

EDWARD L. ULLMAN

SCALE
CONIC PROJECTION

DESTINATION OF
MISSISSIPPI
PETROLEUM PRODUCTS
1950

EDWARD L. ULLMAN

SCALE
CONIC PROJECTION

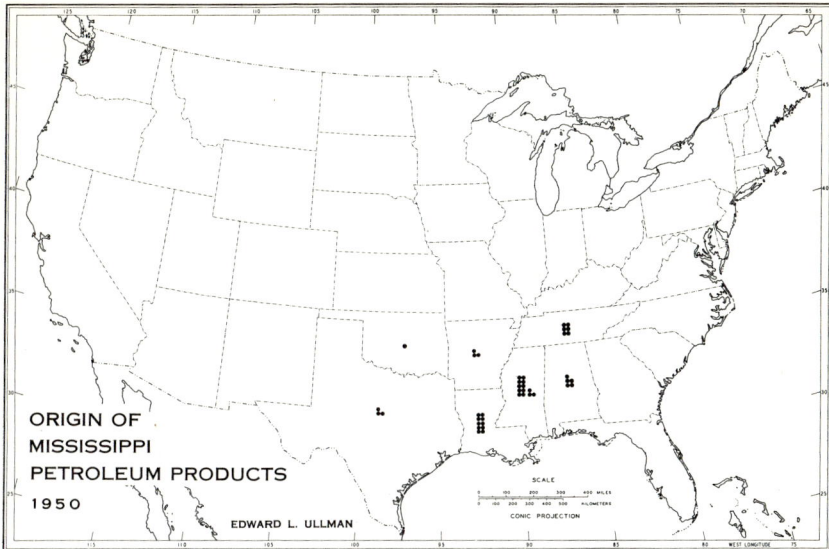

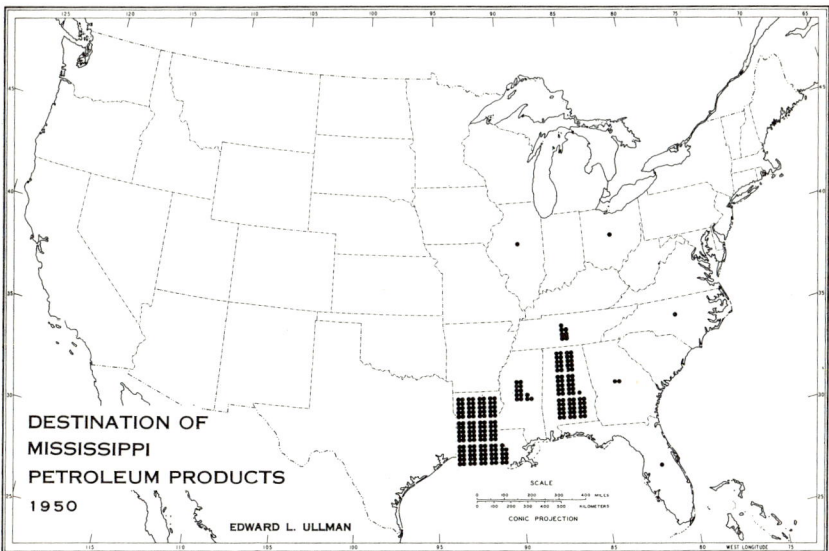

• 10,000 TONS ▤ 100,000 TONS

97

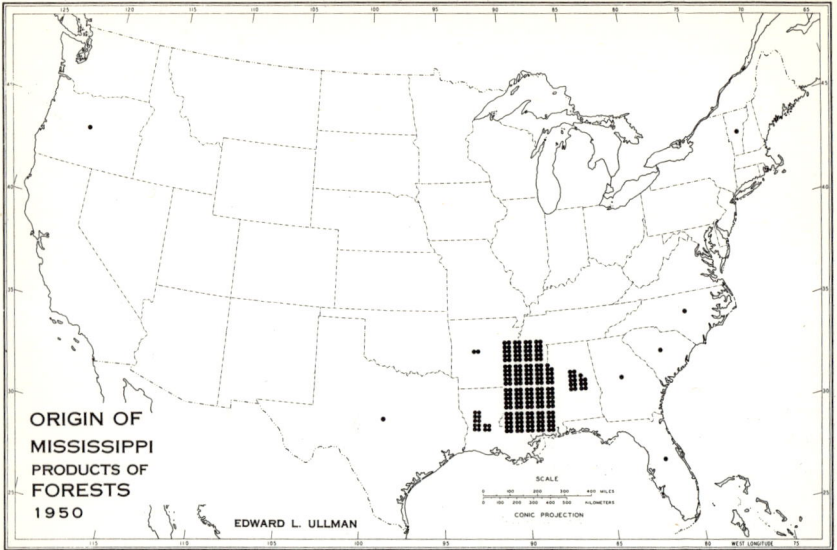

ORIGIN OF
MISSISSIPPI
PRODUCTS OF
FORESTS
1950

EDWARD L. ULLMAN

SCALE

CONIC PROJECTION

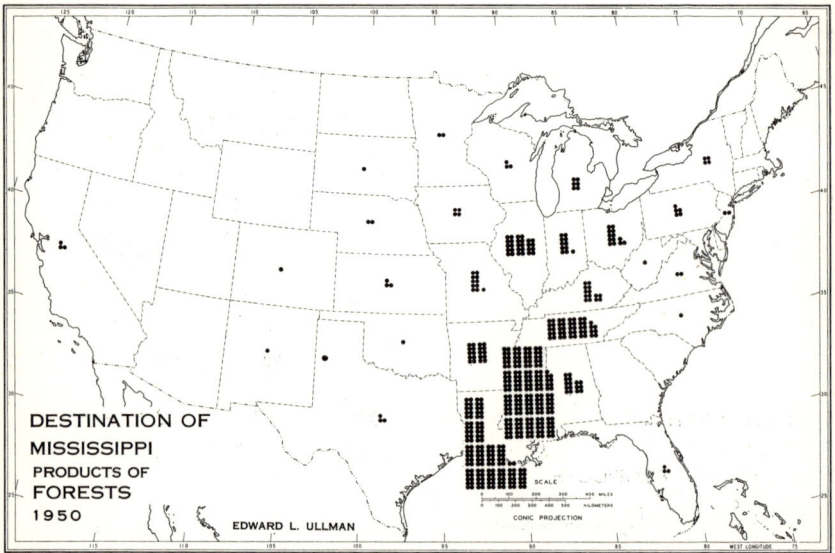

DESTINATION OF
MISSISSIPPI
PRODUCTS OF
FORESTS
1950

EDWARD L. ULLMAN

SCALE

CONIC PROJECTION

• 10,000 TONS   ▌ 100,000 TONS

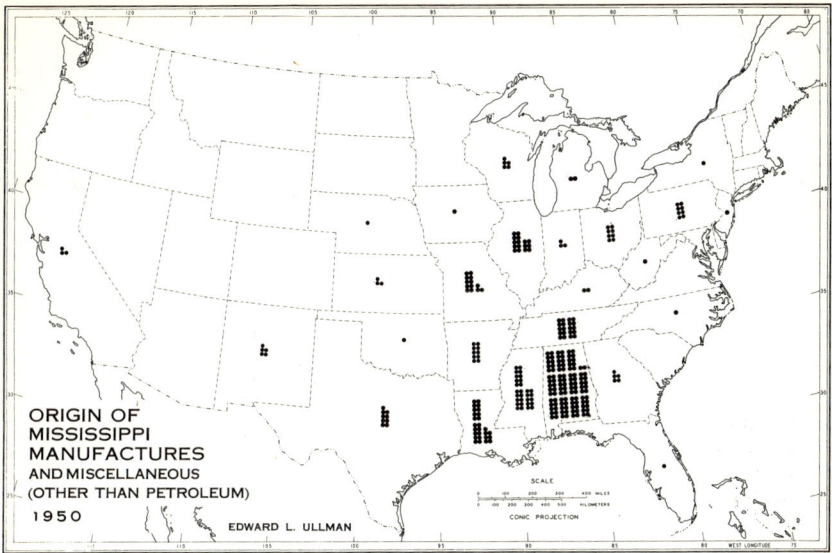

ORIGIN OF
MISSISSIPPI
MANUFACTURES
AND MISCELLANEOUS
(OTHER THAN PETROLEUM)
1950   EDWARD L. ULLMAN

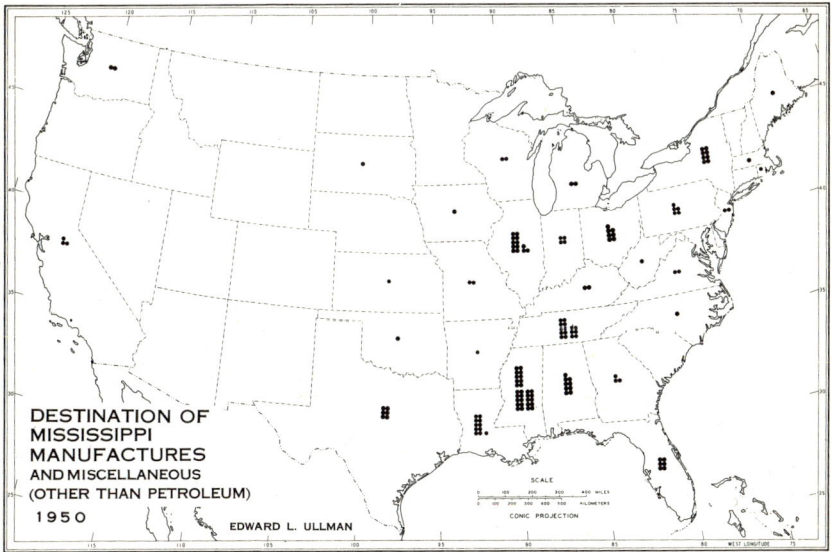

DESTINATION OF
MISSISSIPPI
MANUFACTURES
AND MISCELLANEOUS
(OTHER THAN PETROLEUM)
1950   EDWARD L. ULLMAN

• 10,000 TONS   ⊞ 100,000 TONS

99

ORIGIN OF
MISSISSIPPI
TOTAL
ALL COMMODITIES
1950

EDWARD L. ULLMAN

SCALE

CONIC PROJECTION

DESTINATION OF
MISSISSIPPI
TOTAL
ALL COMMODITIES
1950

EDWARD L. ULLMAN

SCALE

CONIC PROJECTION

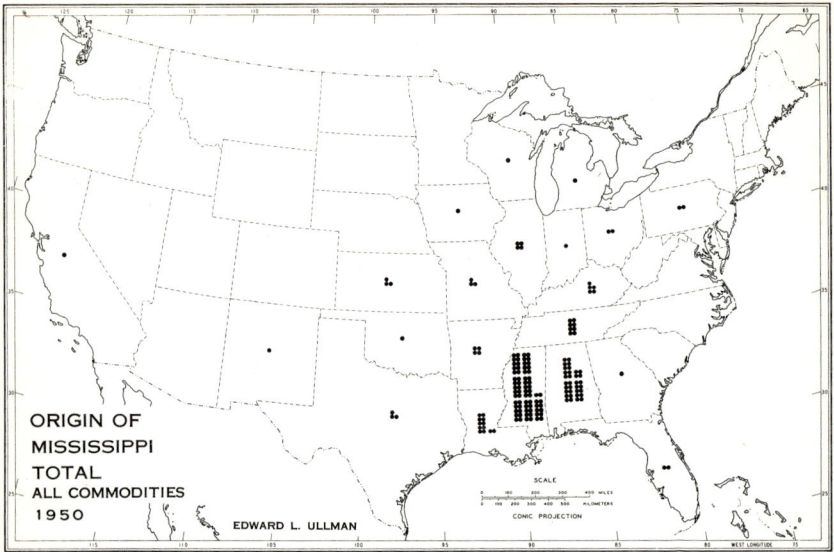

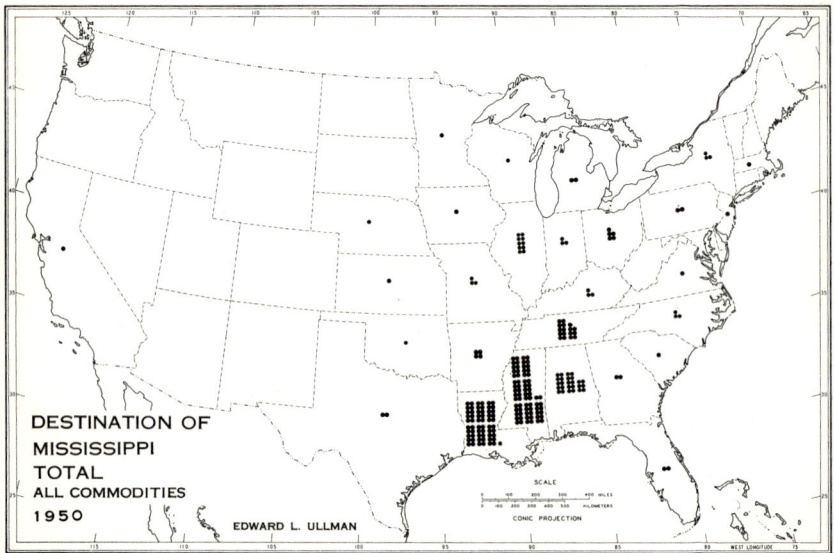

• 50,000 TONS   ▌ 500,000 TONS

100

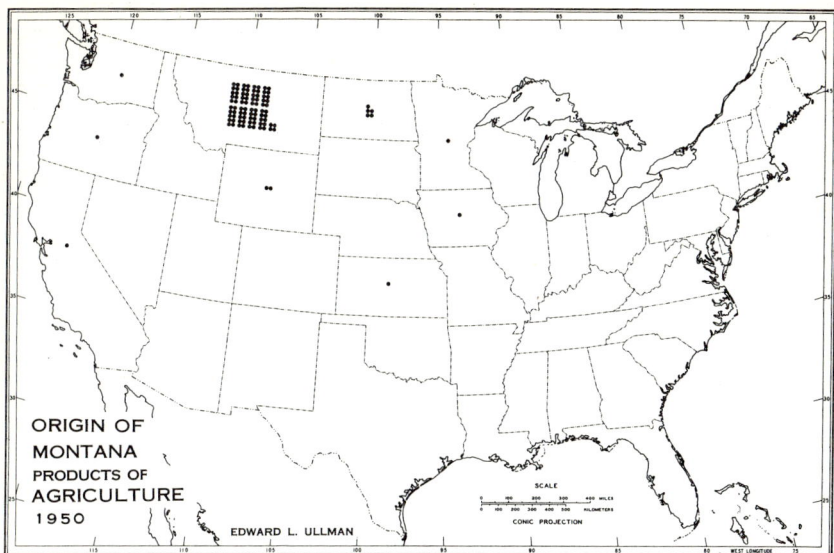

ORIGIN OF
MONTANA
PRODUCTS OF
AGRICULTURE
1950

EDWARD L. ULLMAN

SCALE

CONIC PROJECTION

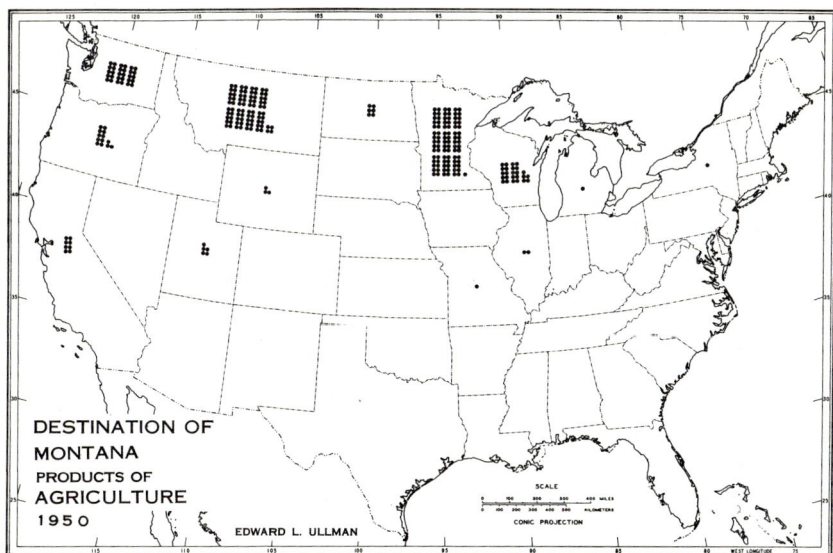

DESTINATION OF
MONTANA
PRODUCTS OF
AGRICULTURE
1950

EDWARD L. ULLMAN

SCALE

CONIC PROJECTION

• 10,000 TONS   ▓ 100,000 TONS

101

ORIGIN OF
MONTANA
ANIMALS
AND PRODUCTS
1950

EDWARD L. ULLMAN

SCALE

CONIC PROJECTION

DESTINATION OF
MONTANA
ANIMALS
AND PRODUCTS
1950

EDWARD L. ULLMAN

SCALE

CONIC PROJECTION

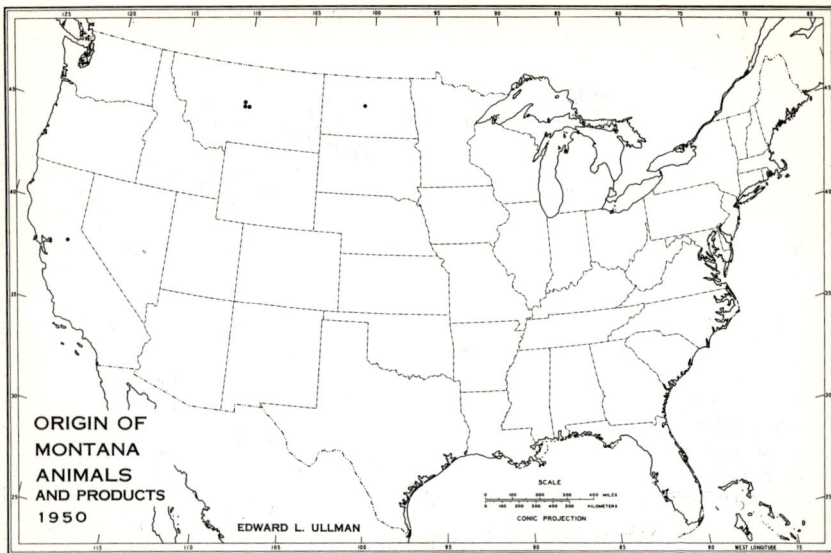

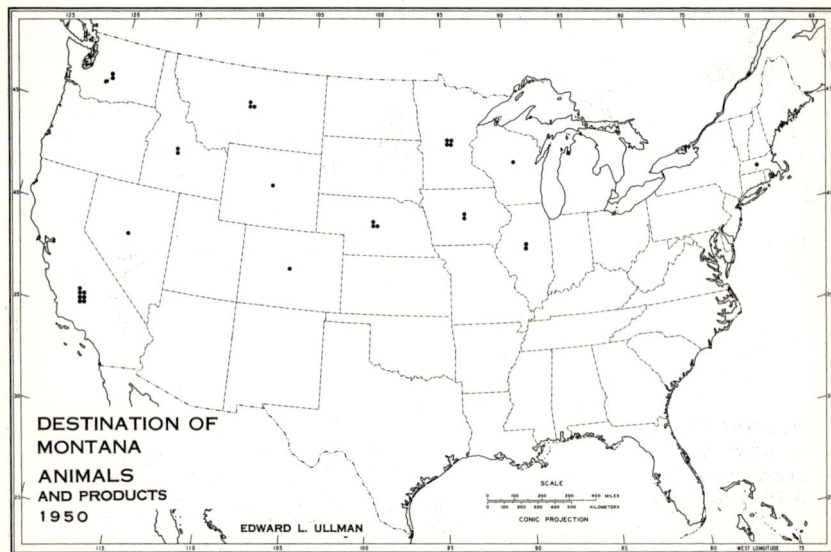

• 10,000 TONS   100,000 TONS

102

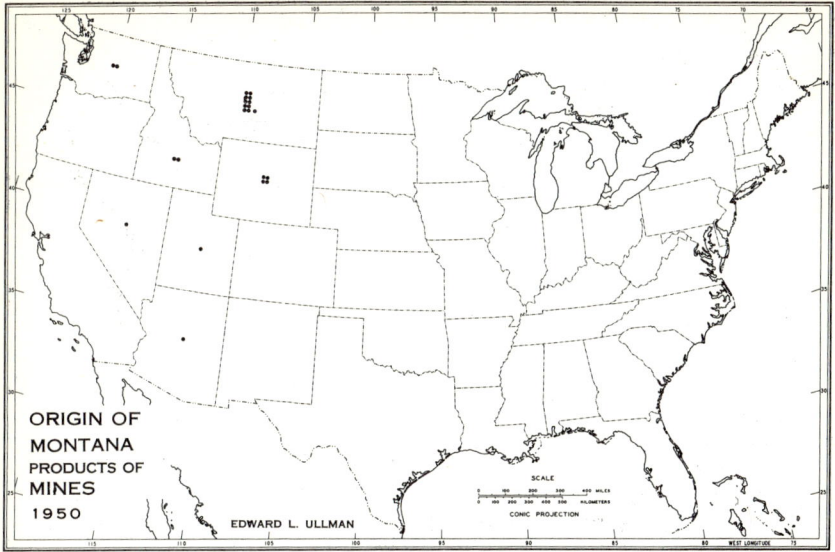

ORIGIN OF
MONTANA
PRODUCTS OF
MINES
1950

EDWARD L. ULLMAN

SCALE

CONIC PROJECTION

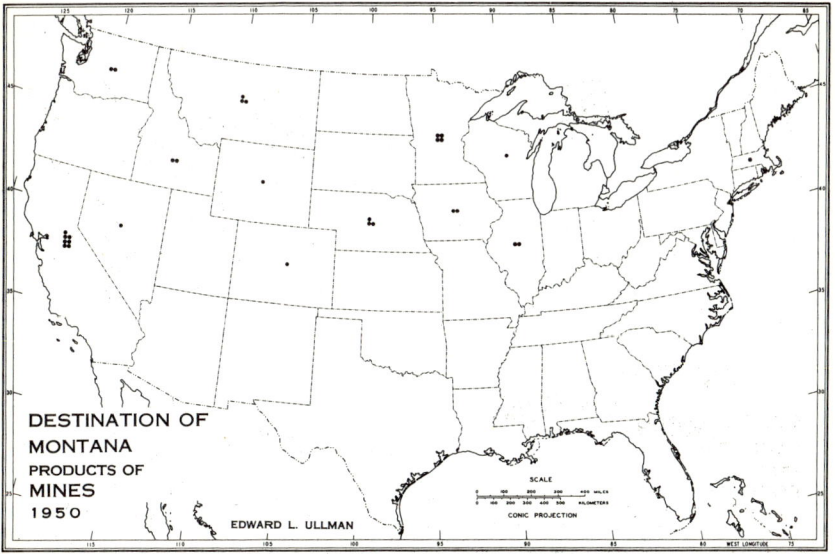

DESTINATION OF
MONTANA
PRODUCTS OF
MINES
1950

EDWARD L. ULLMAN

SCALE

CONIC PROJECTION

• 50,000 TONS   ▊ 500,000 TONS

103

ORIGIN OF
MONTANA
PRODUCTS OF
FORESTS
1950

EDWARD L. ULLMAN

SCALE

CONIC PROJECTION

DESTINATION OF
MONTANA
PRODUCTS OF
FORESTS
1950

EDWARD L. ULLMAN

SCALE

CONIC PROJECTION

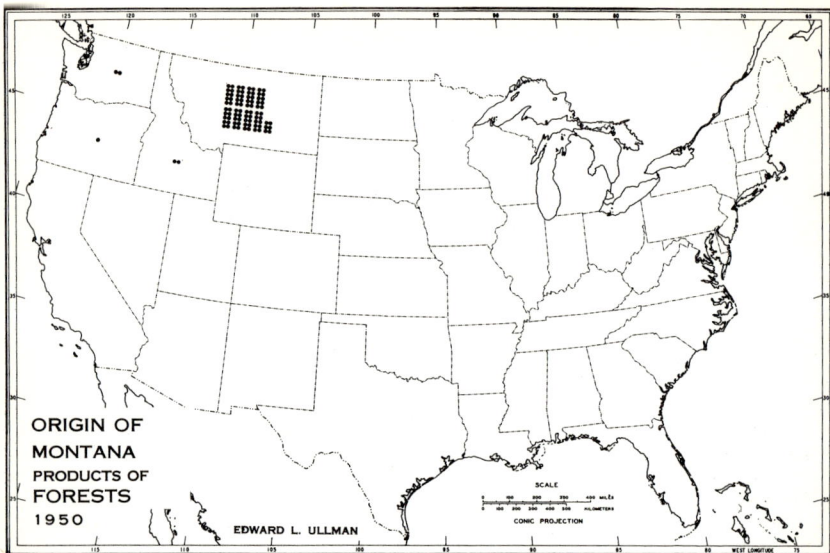

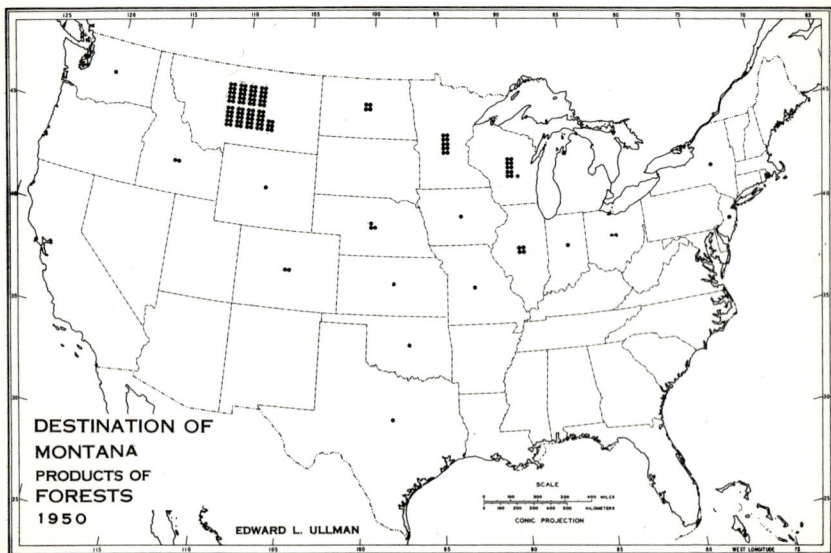

• 10,000 TONS   100,000 TONS

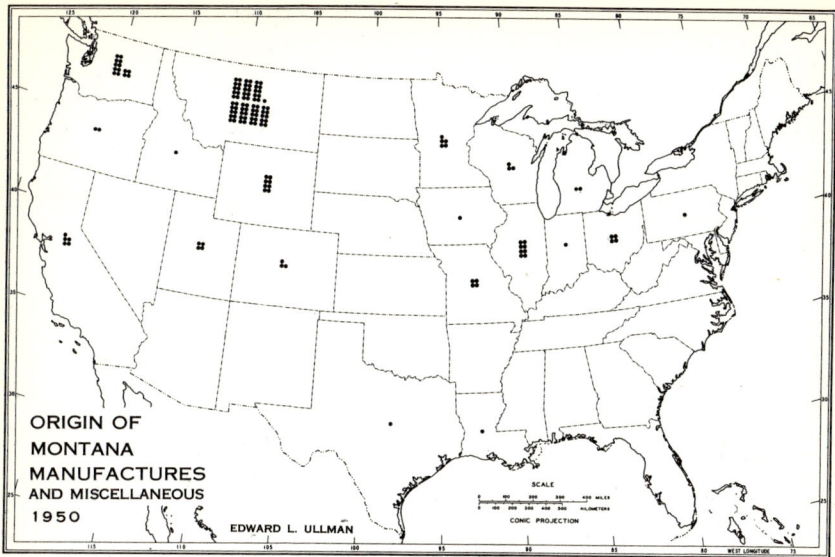

ORIGIN OF
MONTANA
MANUFACTURES
AND MISCELLANEOUS
1950

EDWARD L. ULLMAN

SCALE
CONIC PROJECTION

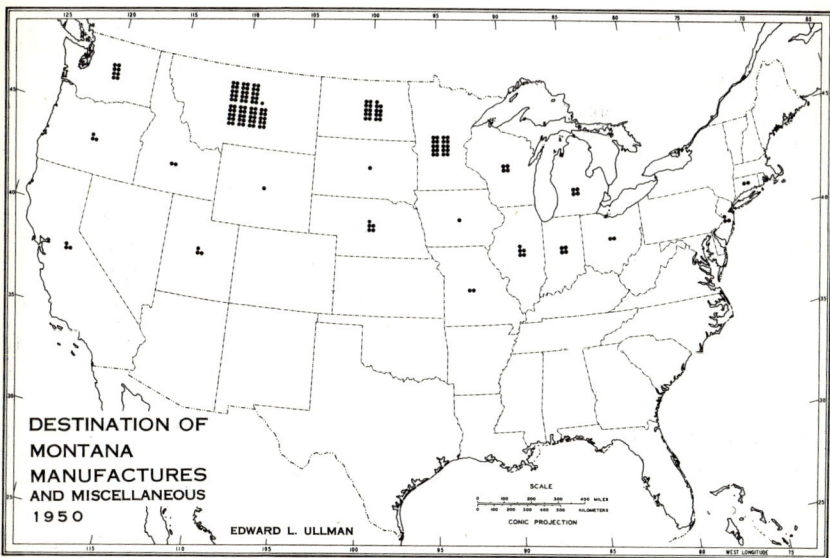

DESTINATION OF
MONTANA
MANUFACTURES
AND MISCELLANEOUS
1950

EDWARD L. ULLMAN

SCALE
CONIC PROJECTION

• 10,000 TONS   ▌ 100,000 TONS

105

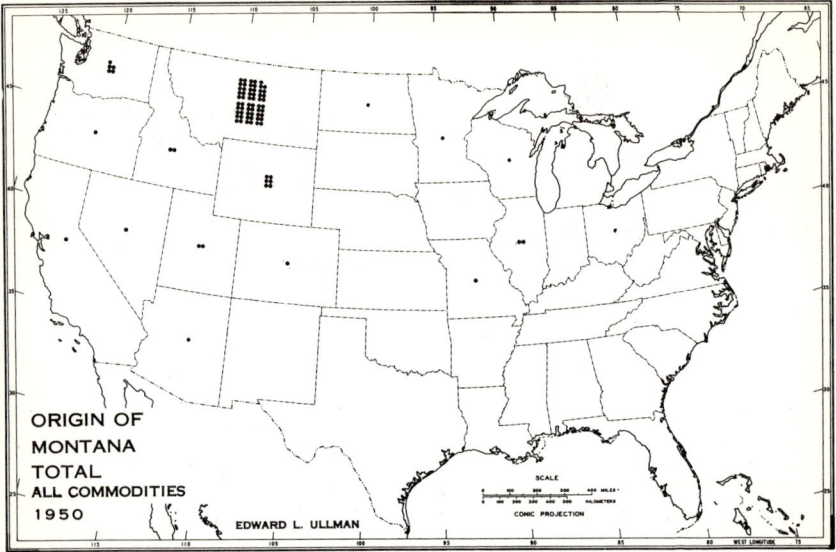

ORIGIN OF
MONTANA
TOTAL
ALL COMMODITIES
1950

EDWARD L. ULLMAN

SCALE

CONIC PROJECTION

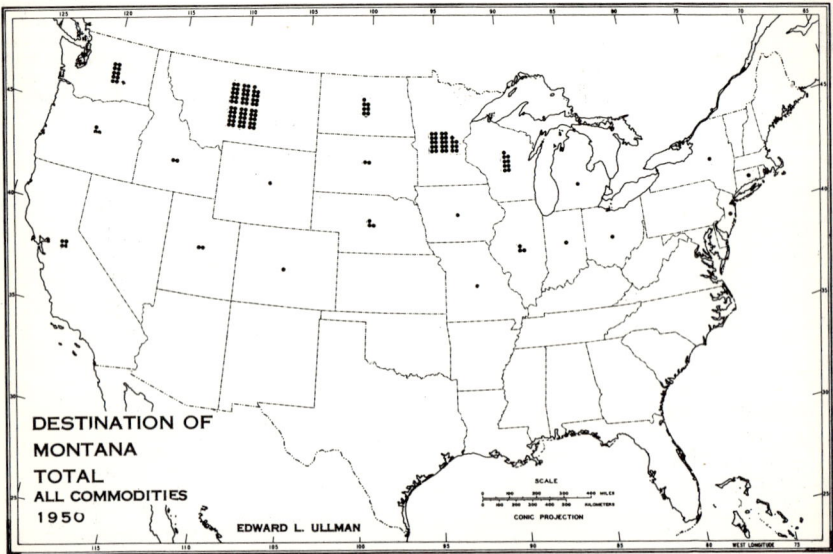

DESTINATION OF
MONTANA
TOTAL
ALL COMMODITIES
1950

EDWARD L. ULLMAN

SCALE

CONIC PROJECTION

• 50,000 TONS   ▌ 500,000 TONS

106

ORIGIN OF
NEW JERSEY
PRODUCTS OF
AGRICULTURE
1950

EDWARD L. ULLMAN

SCALE
CONIC PROJECTION

DESTINATION OF
NEW JERSEY
PRODUCTS OF
AGRICULTURE
1950

EDWARD L. ULLMAN

SCALE
CONIC PROJECTION

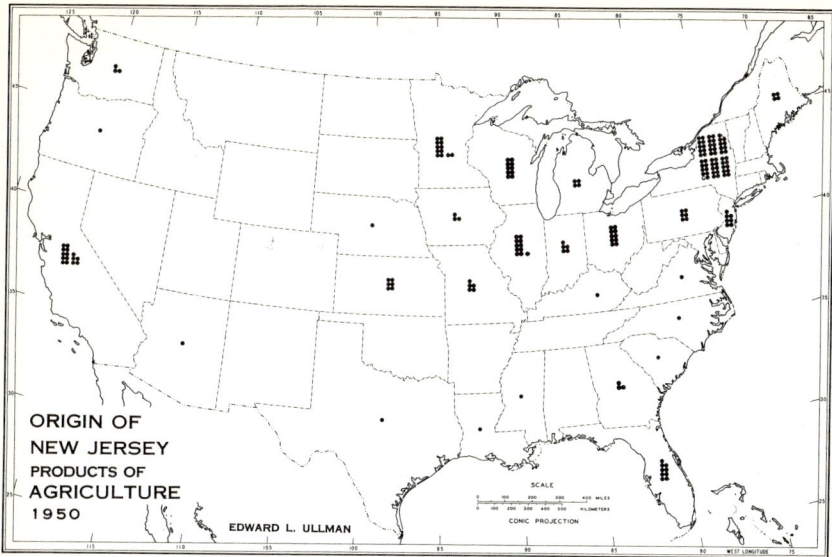

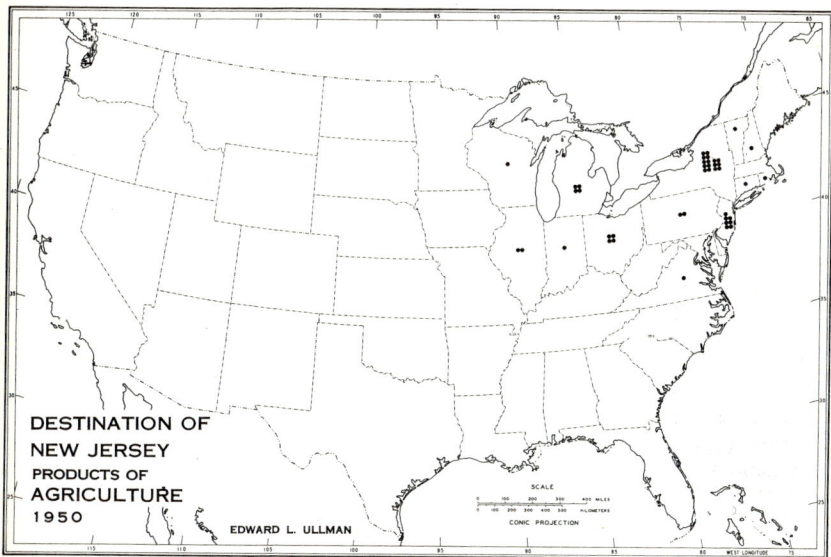

• 10,000 TONS   ▌ 100,000 TONS

ORIGIN OF
NEW JERSEY
ANIMALS
AND PRODUCTS
1950

EDWARD L. ULLMAN

SCALE
CONIC PROJECTION

DESTINATION OF
NEW JERSEY
ANIMALS
AND PRODUCTS
1950

EDWARD L. ULLMAN

SCALE
CONIC PROJECTION

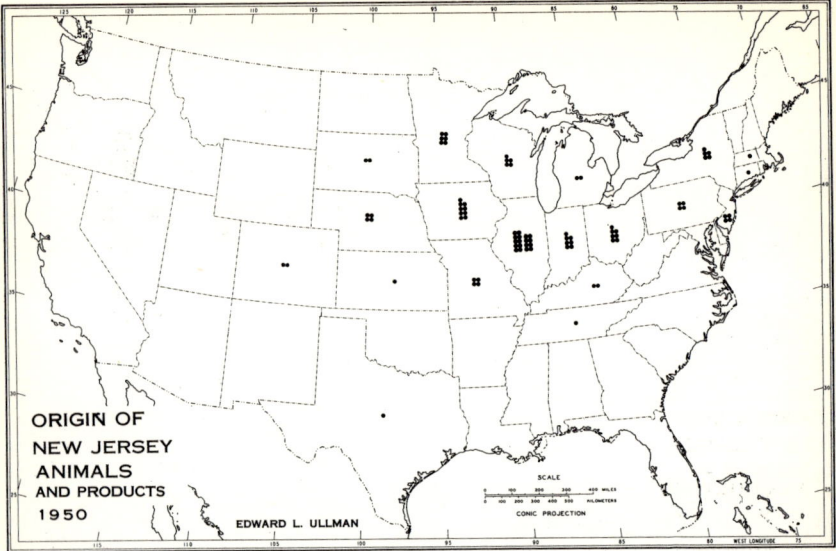

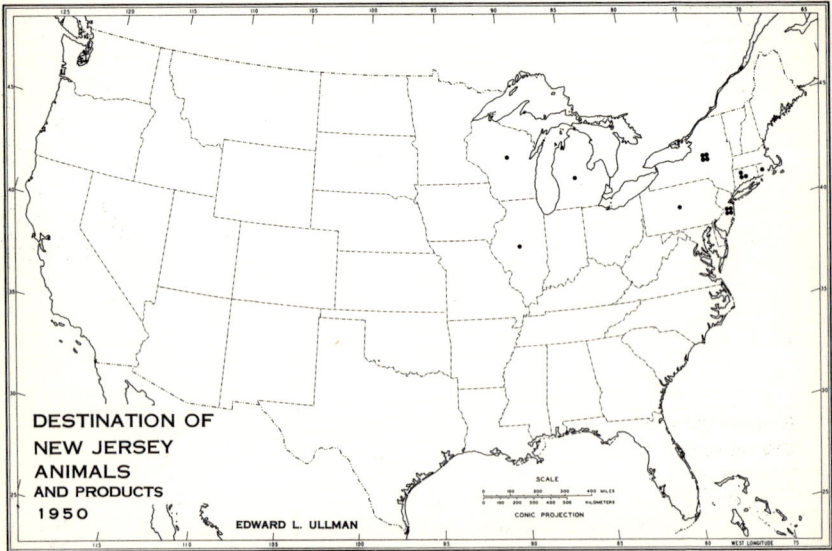

• 10,000 TONS   100,000 TONS

108

ORIGIN OF
NEW JERSEY
PRODUCTS OF
MINES
1950

EDWARD L. ULLMAN

SCALE

CONIC PROJECTION

DESTINATION OF
NEW JERSEY
PRODUCTS OF
MINES
1950

EDWARD L. ULLMAN

SCALE

CONIC PROJECTION

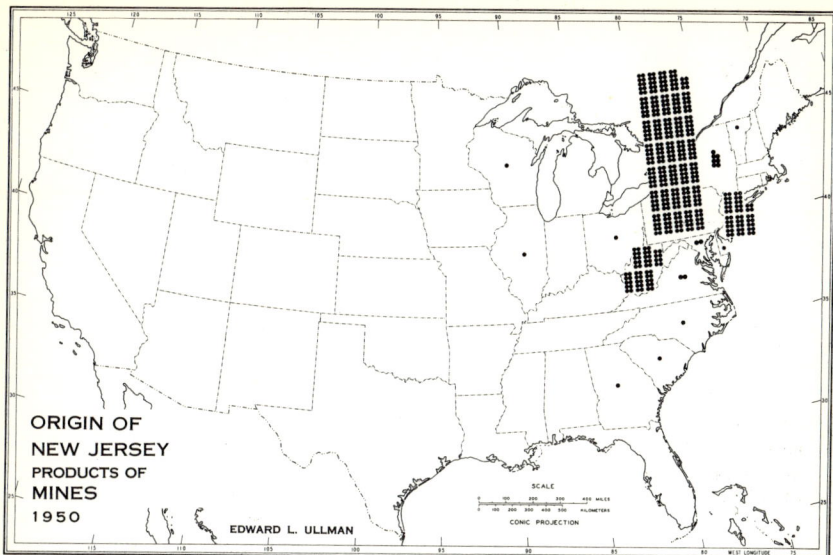

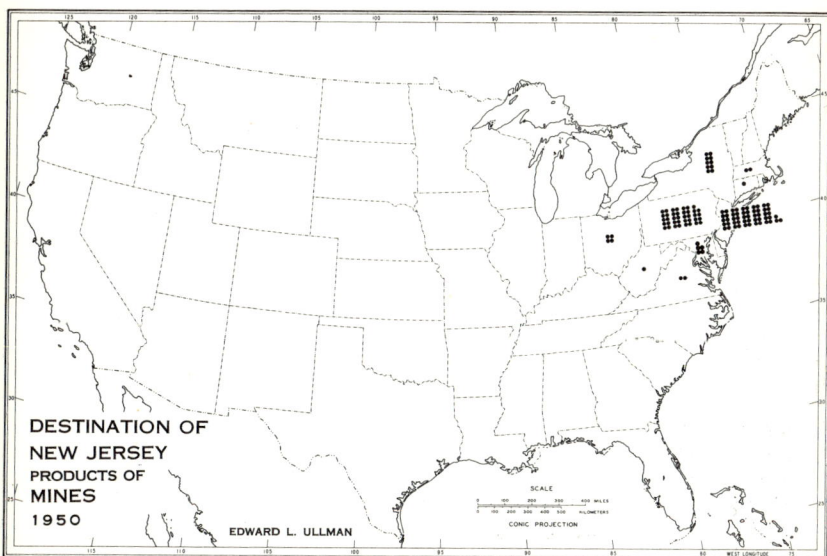

• 50,000 TONS   ▮ 500,000 TONS

109

ORIGIN OF
NEW JERSEY
PRODUCTS OF
FORESTS
1950

EDWARD L. ULLMAN

SCALE

CONIC PROJECTION

DESTINATION OF
NEW JERSEY
PRODUCTS OF
FORESTS
1950

EDWARD L. ULLMAN

SCALE

CONIC PROJECTION

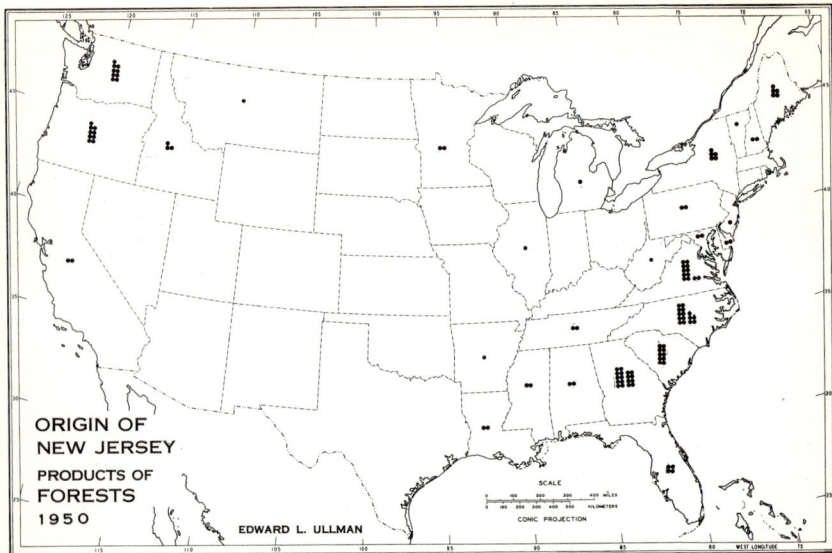

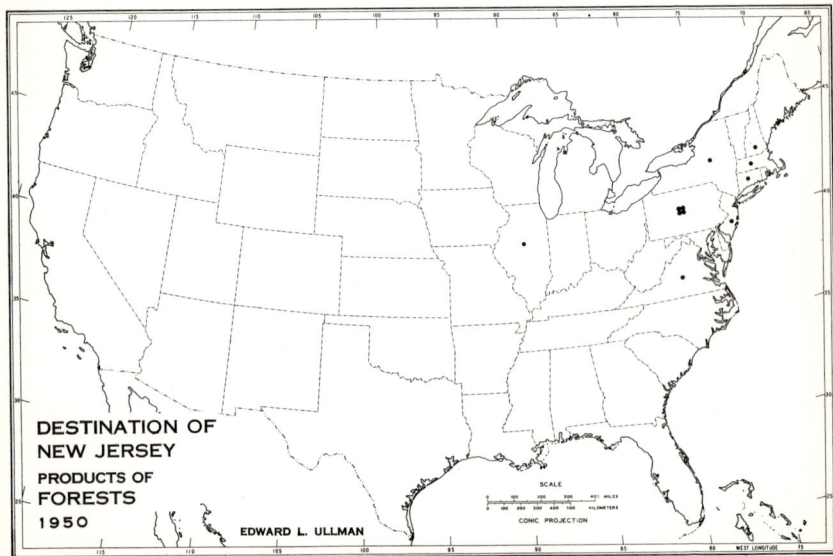

• 10,000 TONS   100,000 TONS

ORIGIN OF
NEW JERSEY
MANUFACTURES
AND MISCELLANEOUS
1950

EDWARD L. ULLMAN

SCALE

CONIC PROJECTION

DESTINATION OF
NEW JERSEY
MANUFACTURES
AND MISCELLANEOUS
1950

EDWARD L. ULLMAN

SCALE

CONIC PROJECTION

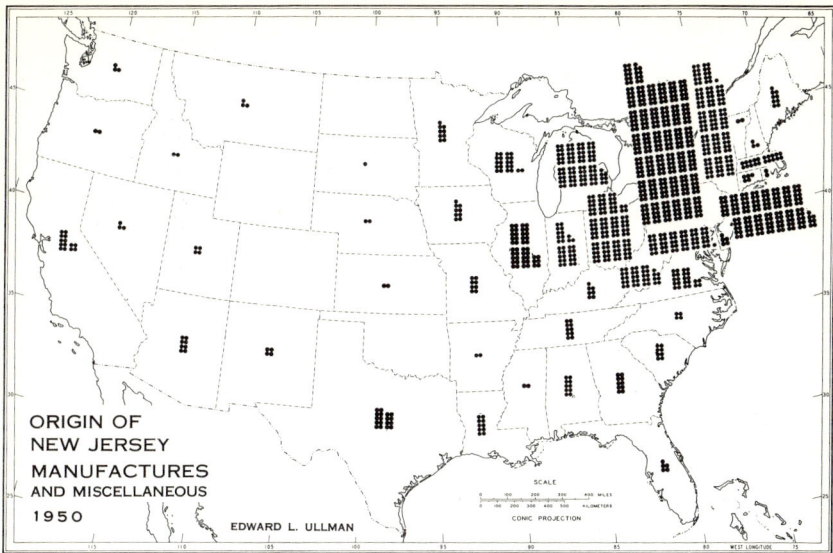

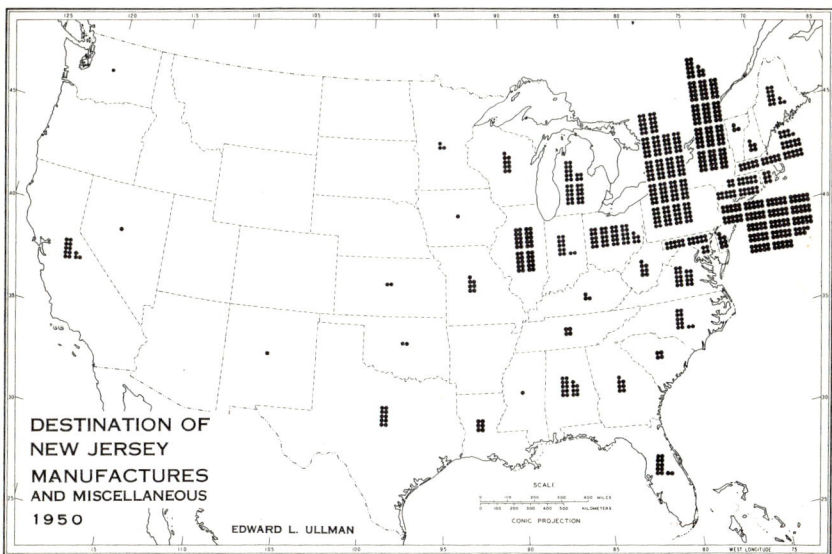

• 10,000 TONS   ▦ 100,000 TONS

111

ORIGIN OF
NEW JERSEY

TOTAL
ALL COMMODITIES
1950

EDWARD L. ULLMAN

SCALE

CONIC PROJECTION

DESTINATION OF
NEW JERSEY

TOTAL
ALL COMMODITIES
1950

EDWARD L. ULLMAN

SCALE

CONIC PROJECTION

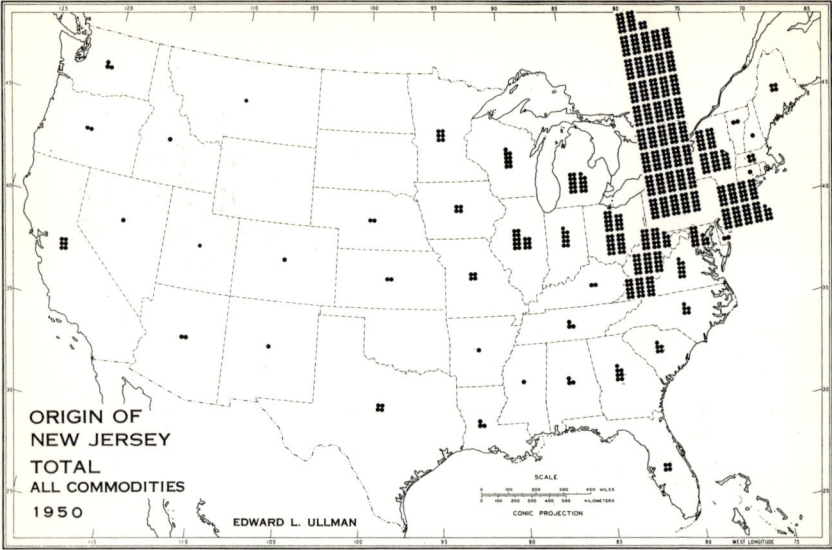

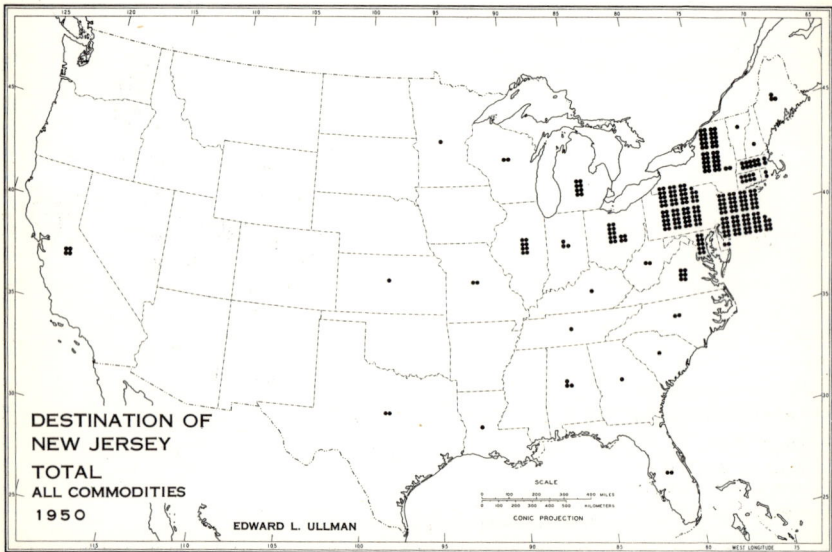

• 50,000 TONS   ▌ 500,000 TONS

112

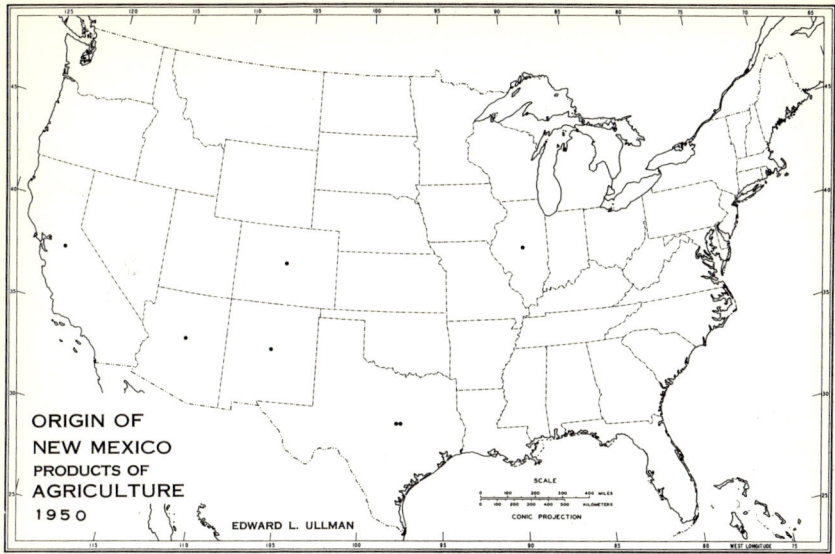

ORIGIN OF
NEW MEXICO
PRODUCTS OF
AGRICULTURE
1950

EDWARD L. ULLMAN

SCALE
CONIC PROJECTION

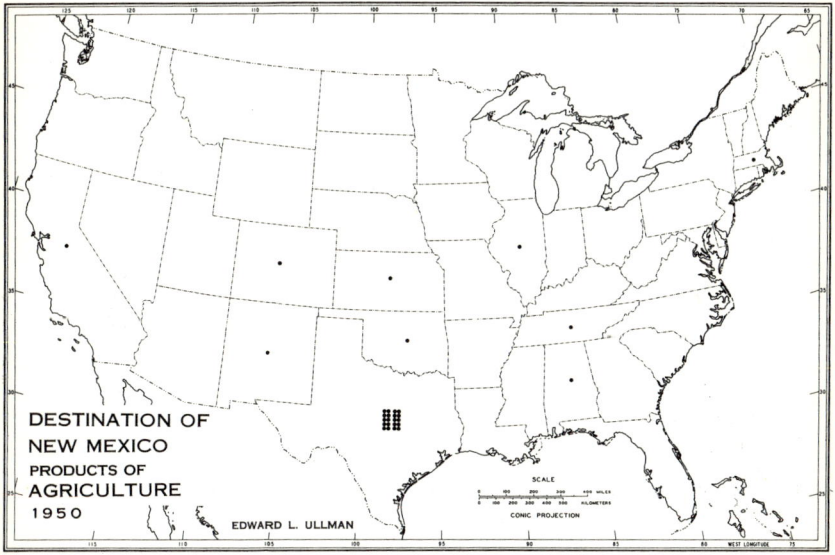

DESTINATION OF
NEW MEXICO
PRODUCTS OF
AGRICULTURE
1950

EDWARD L. ULLMAN

SCALE
CONIC PROJECTION

• 10,000 TONS   ▋100,000 TONS

113

ORIGIN OF
NEW MEXICO
ANIMALS
AND PRODUCTS
1950

EDWARD L. ULLMAN

SCALE

CONIC PROJECTION

WEST LONGITUDE

DESTINATION OF
NEW MEXICO
ANIMALS
AND PRODUCTS
1950

EDWARD L. ULLMAN

SCALE

CONIC PROJECTION

WEST LONGITUDE

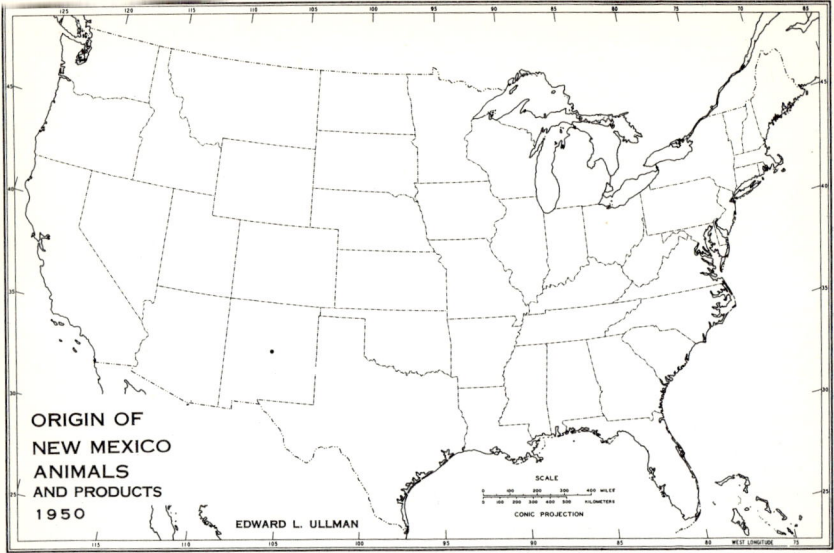

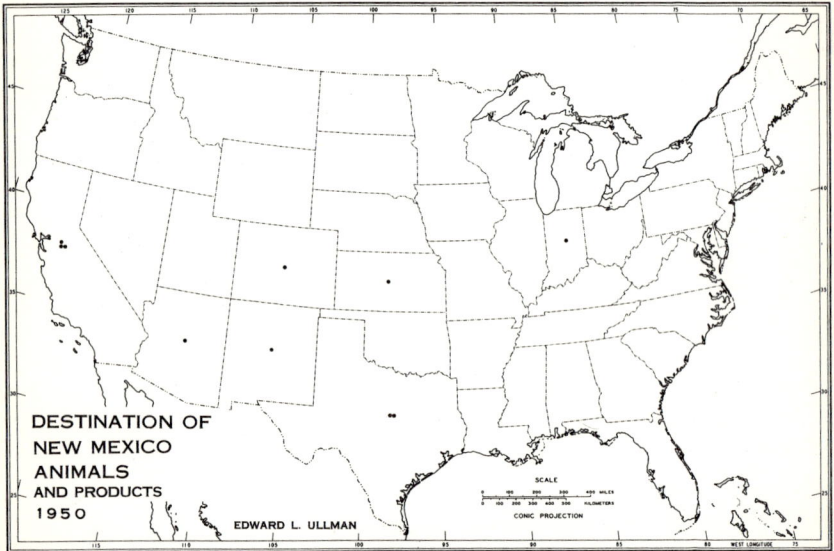

• 10,000 TONS   100,000 TONS

ORIGIN OF
NEW MEXICO
PRODUCTS OF
MINES
1950

EDWARD L. ULLMAN

SCALE
CONIC PROJECTION

DESTINATION OF
NEW MEXICO
PRODUCTS OF
MINES
1950

EDWARD L. ULLMAN

SCALE
CONIC PROJECTION

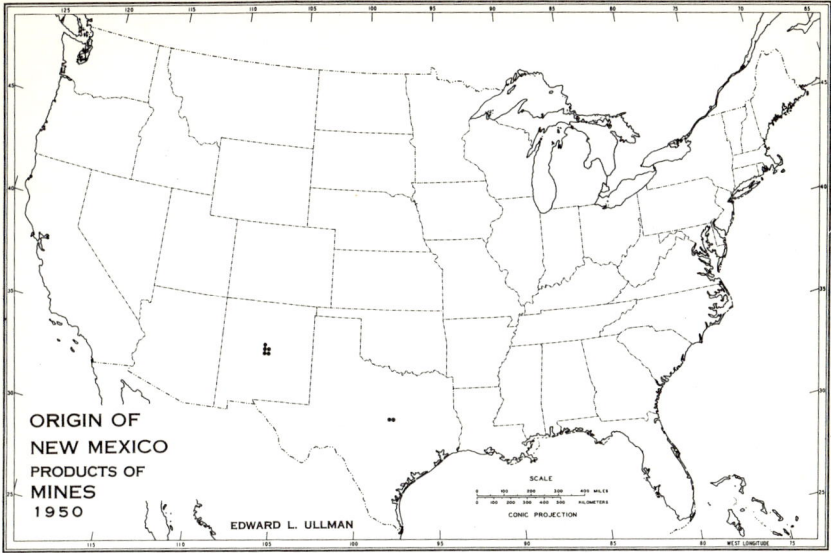

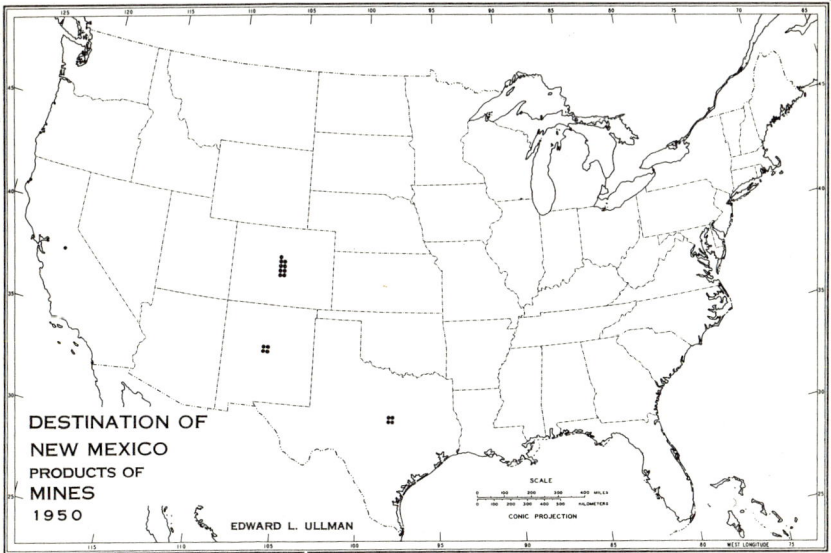

• 50,000 TONS   ▓ 500,000 TONS

115

ORIGIN OF
NEW MEXICO
PRODUCTS OF
FORESTS
1950

EDWARD L. ULLMAN

SCALE

CONIC PROJECTION

DESTINATION OF
NEW MEXICO
PRODUCTS OF
FORESTS
1950

EDWARD L. ULLMAN

SCALE

CONIC PROJECTION

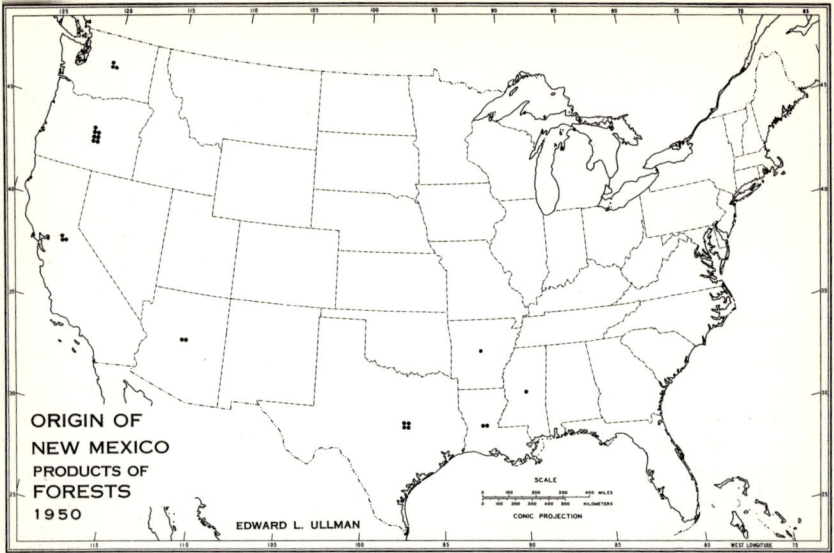

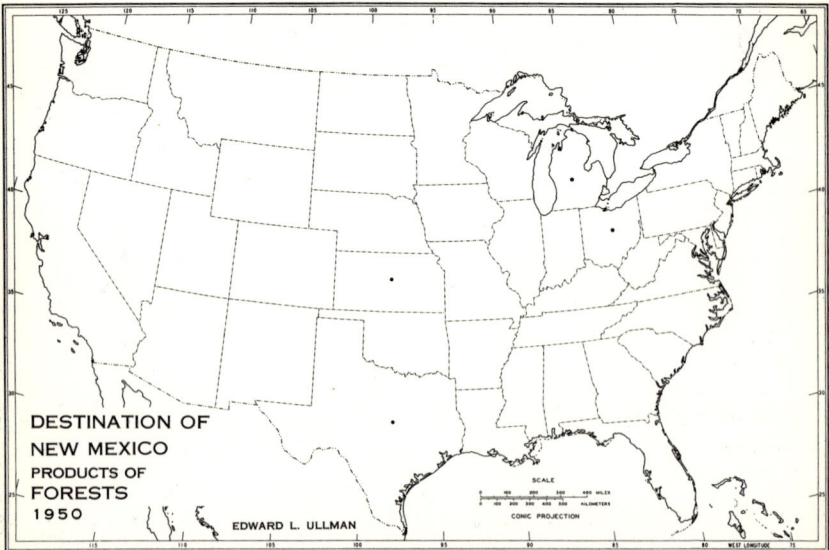

• 10,000 TONS   ▓ 100,000 TONS

116

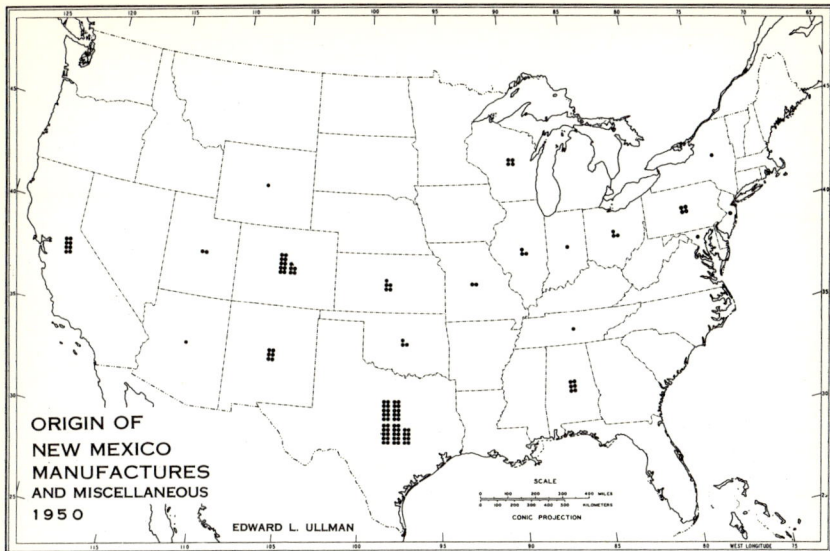

ORIGIN OF
NEW MEXICO
MANUFACTURES
AND MISCELLANEOUS
1950

EDWARD L. ULLMAN

SCALE
CONIC PROJECTION

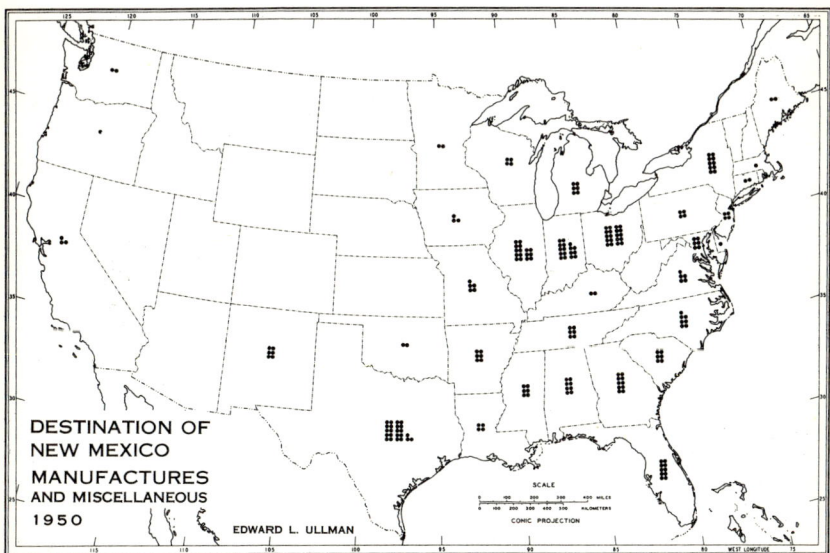

DESTINATION OF
NEW MEXICO
MANUFACTURES
AND MISCELLANEOUS
1950

EDWARD L. ULLMAN

SCALE
CONIC PROJECTION

• 10,000 TONS   ▮ 100,000 TONS

117

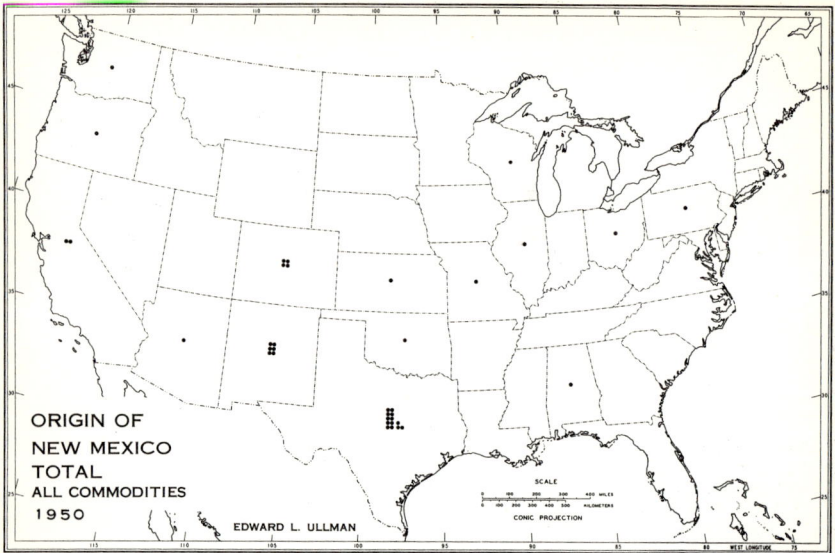

ORIGIN OF
NEW MEXICO
TOTAL
ALL COMMODITIES
1950

EDWARD L. ULLMAN

SCALE

CONIC PROJECTION

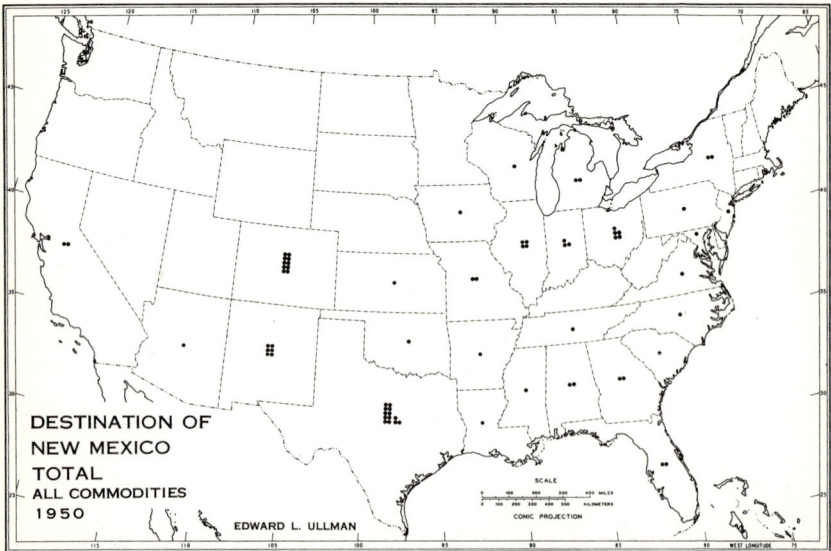

DESTINATION OF
NEW MEXICO
TOTAL
ALL COMMODITIES
1950

EDWARD L. ULLMAN

SCALE

CONIC PROJECTION

• 50,000 TONS   ▓ 500,000 TONS

ORIGIN OF
OHIO
PRODUCTS OF
AGRICULTURE
1950

EDWARD L. ULLMAN

SCALE

CONIC PROJECTION

CLYDE BROWNING

DESTINATION OF
OHIO
PRODUCTS OF
AGRICULTURE
1950

EDWARD L. ULLMAN

SCALE

CONIC PROJECTION

CLYDE BROWNING

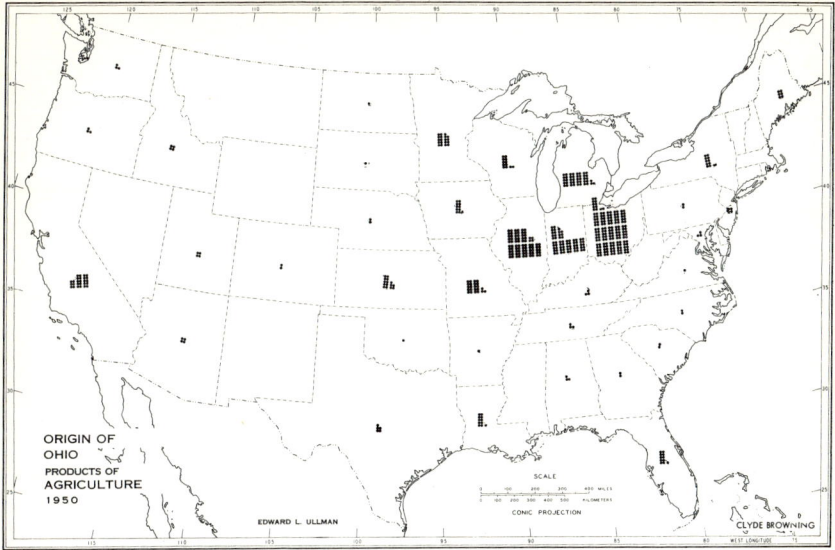

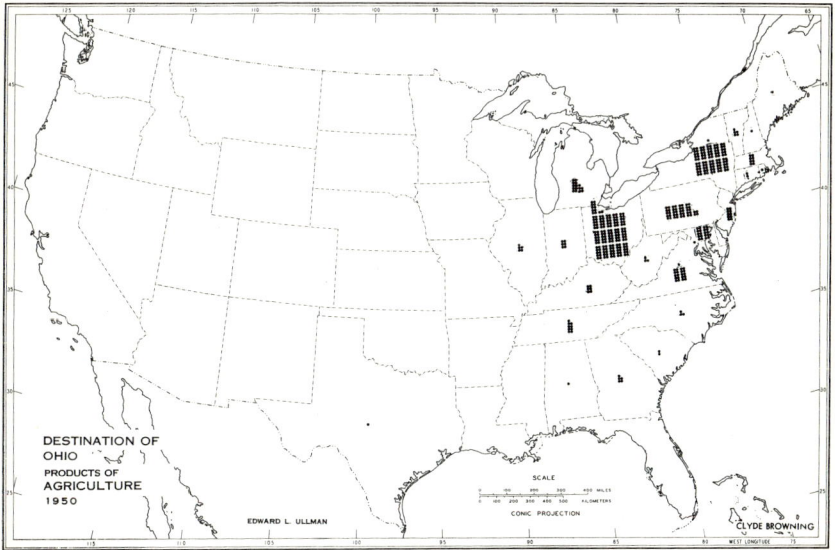

• 10,000 TONS   ▊ 100,000 TONS

ORIGIN OF
OHIO
ANIMALS
AND PRODUCTS
1950

EDWARD L. ULLMAN

SCALE

CONIC PROJECTION

CLYDE BROWNING

DESTINATION OF
OHIO
ANIMALS
AND PRODUCTS
1950

EDWARD L. ULLMAN

SCALE

CONIC PROJECTION

CLYDE BROWNING

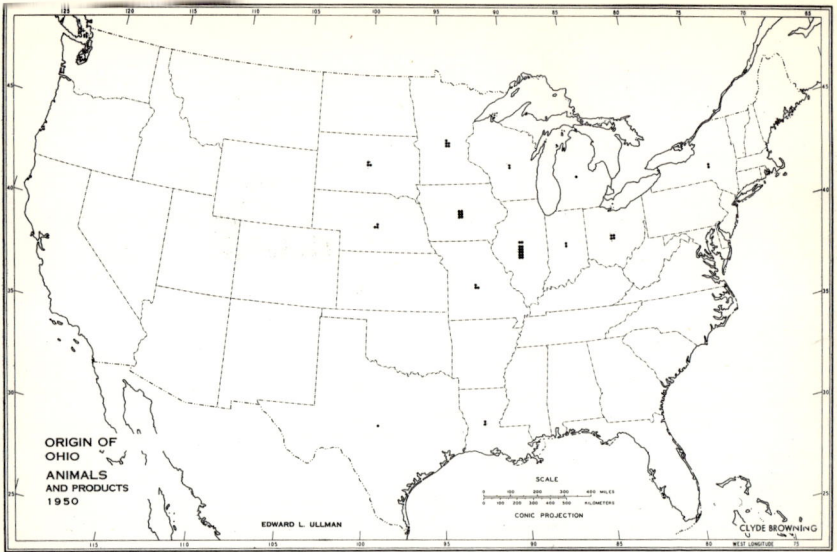

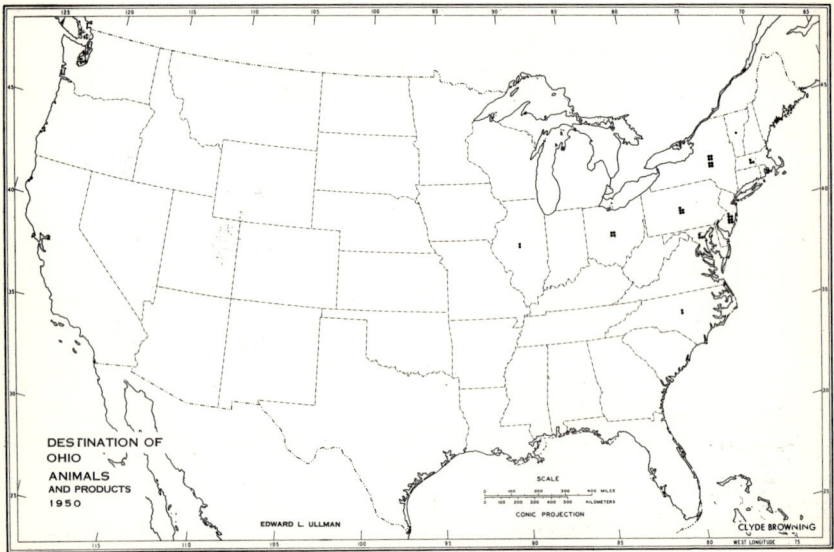

• 10,000 TONS   100,000 TONS

120

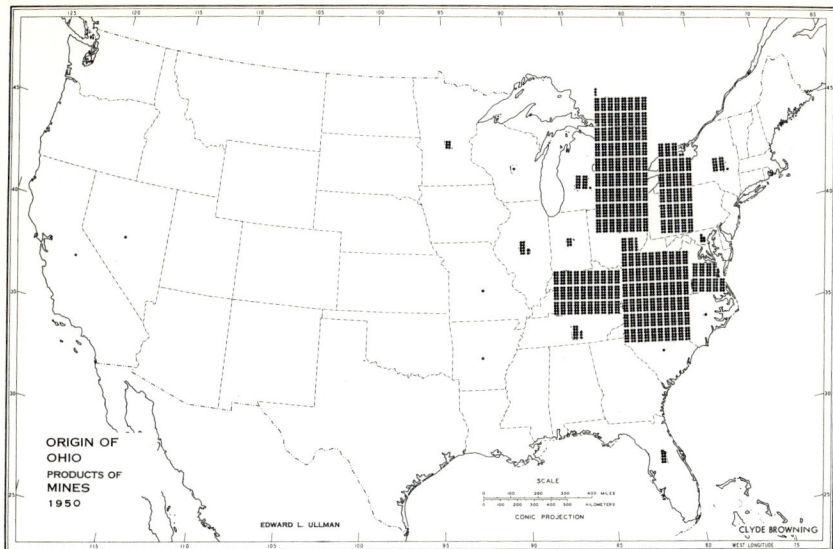

ORIGIN OF
OHIO
PRODUCTS OF
MINES
1950

EDWARD L. ULLMAN

SCALE

CONIC PROJECTION

CLYDE BROWNING

WEST LONGITUDE

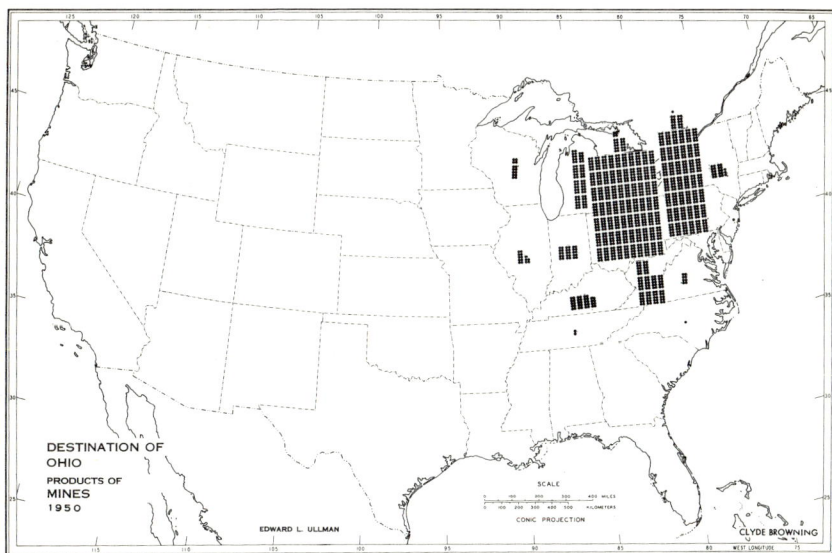

DESTINATION OF
OHIO
PRODUCTS OF
MINES
1950

EDWARD L. ULLMAN

SCALE

CONIC PROJECTION

CLYDE BROWNING

WEST LONGITUDE

• 50,000 TONS   ▮ 500,000 TONS

121

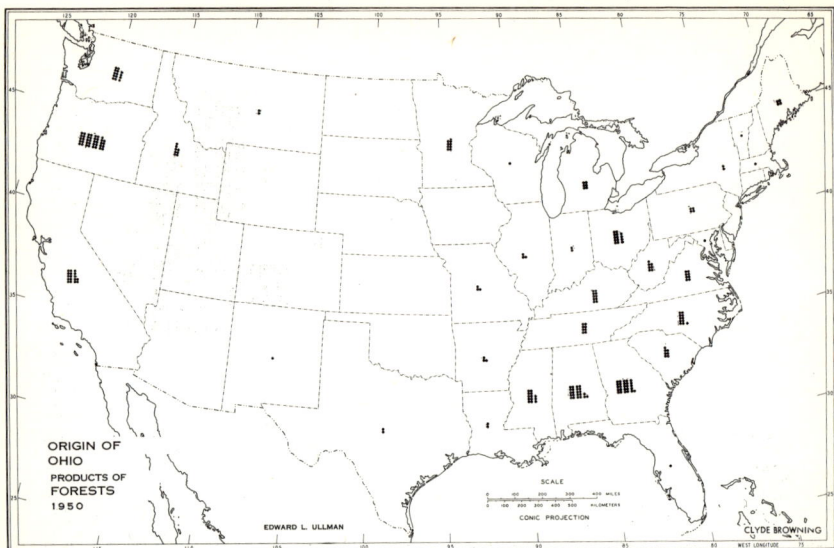

ORIGIN OF
OHIO
PRODUCTS OF
FORESTS
1950

EDWARD L. ULLMAN

SCALE

CONIC PROJECTION

CLYDE BROWNING

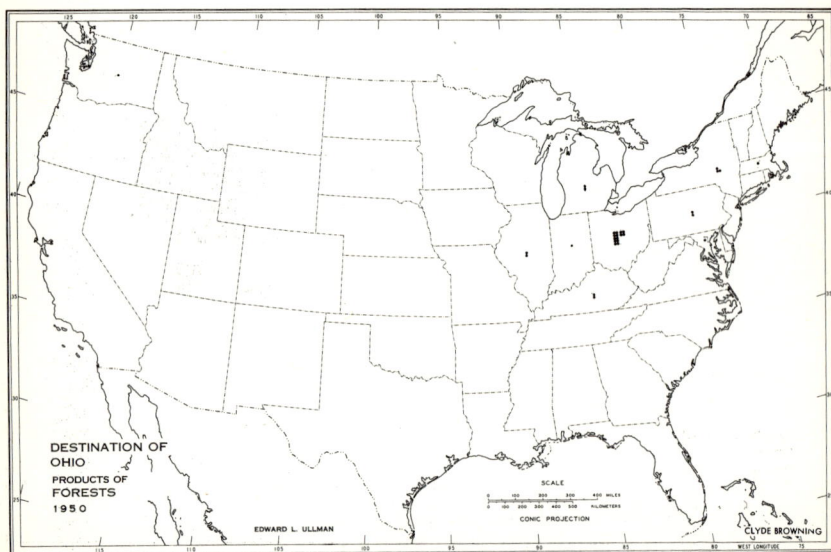

DESTINATION OF
OHIO
PRODUCTS OF
FORESTS
1950

EDWARD L. ULLMAN

SCALE

CONIC PROJECTION

CLYDE BROWNING

• 10,000 TONS   █ 100,000 TONS

122

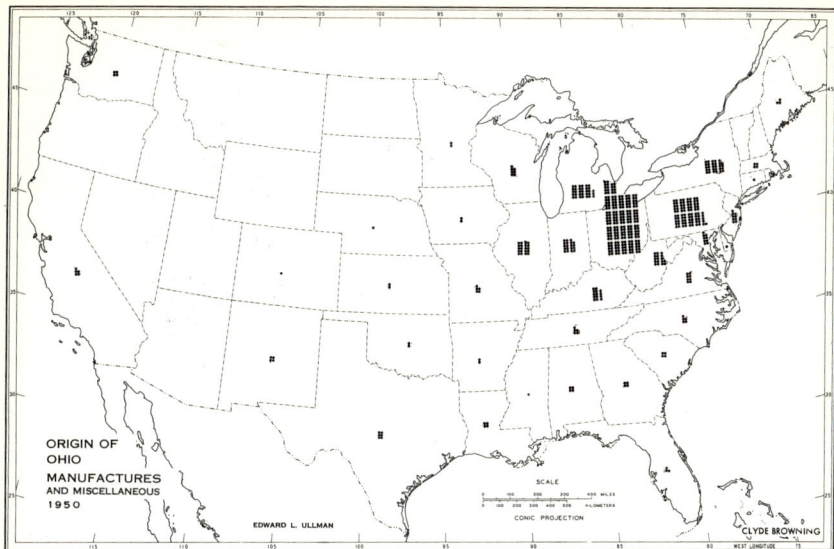

ORIGIN OF
OHIO
MANUFACTURES
AND MISCELLANEOUS
1950

EDWARD L. ULLMAN

SCALE

CONIC PROJECTION

CLYDE BROWNING

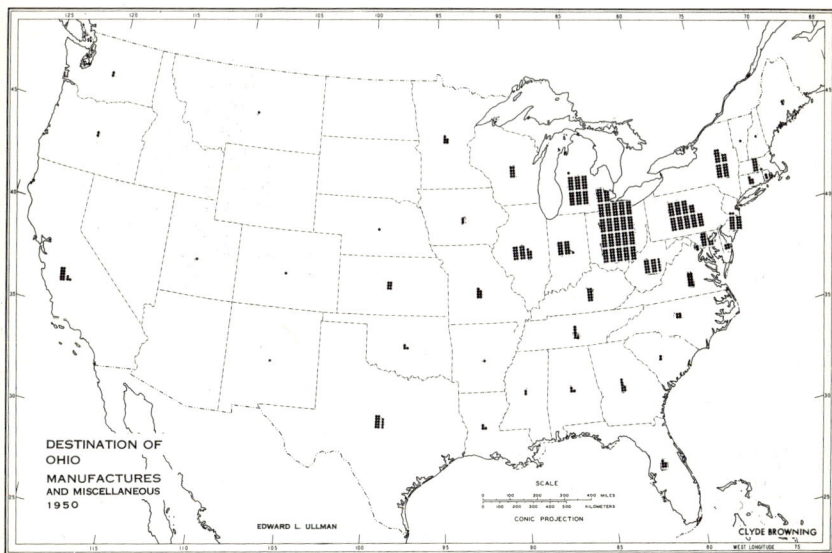

DESTINATION OF
OHIO
MANUFACTURES
AND MISCELLANEOUS
1950

EDWARD L. ULLMAN

SCALE

CONIC PROJECTION

CLYDE BROWNING

• 50,000 TONS   ▓ 500,000 TONS

123

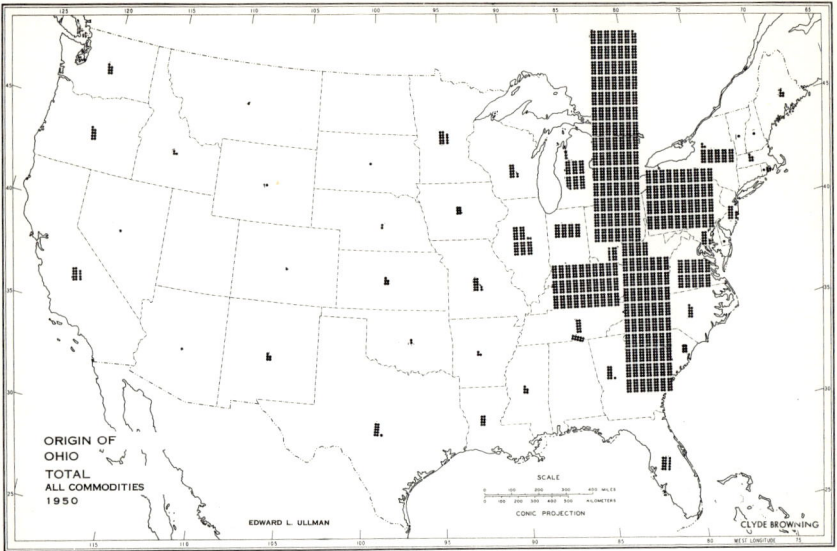

ORIGIN OF
OHIO
TOTAL
ALL COMMODITIES
1950

EDWARD L. ULLMAN

SCALE

CONIC PROJECTION

CLYDE BROWNING

WEST LONGITUDE

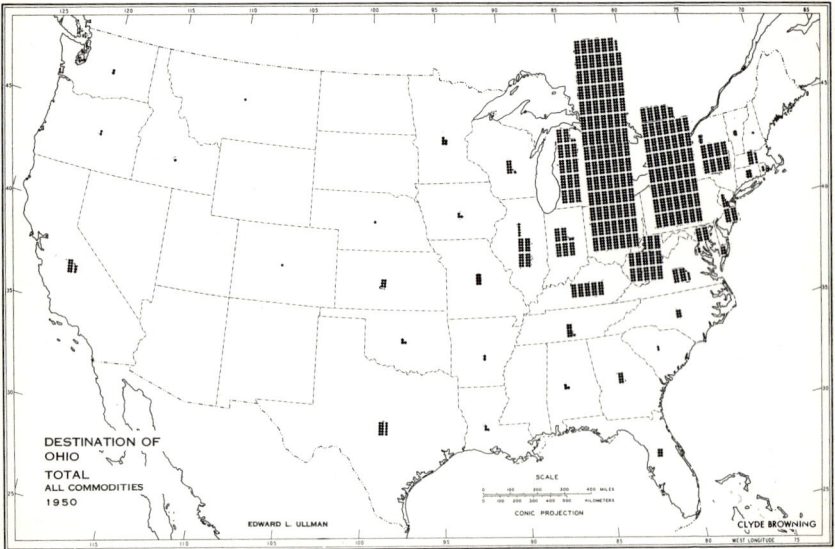

DESTINATION OF
OHIO
TOTAL
ALL COMMODITIES
1950

EDWARD L. ULLMAN

SCALE

CONIC PROJECTION

CLYDE BROWNING

WEST LONGITUDE

• 50,000 TONS   ▓ 500,000 TONS

124

ORIGIN OF
OKLAHOMA
PRODUCTS OF
AGRICULTURE
1950

EDWARD L. ULLMAN

SCALE

CONIC PROJECTION

DESTINATION OF
OKLAHOMA
PRODUCTS OF
AGRICULTURE
1950

EDWARD L. ULLMAN

SCALE

CONIC PROJECTION

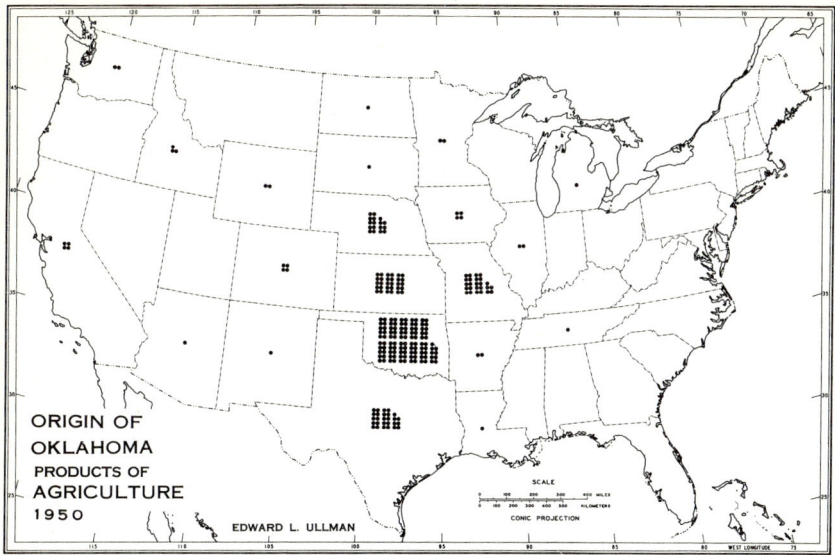

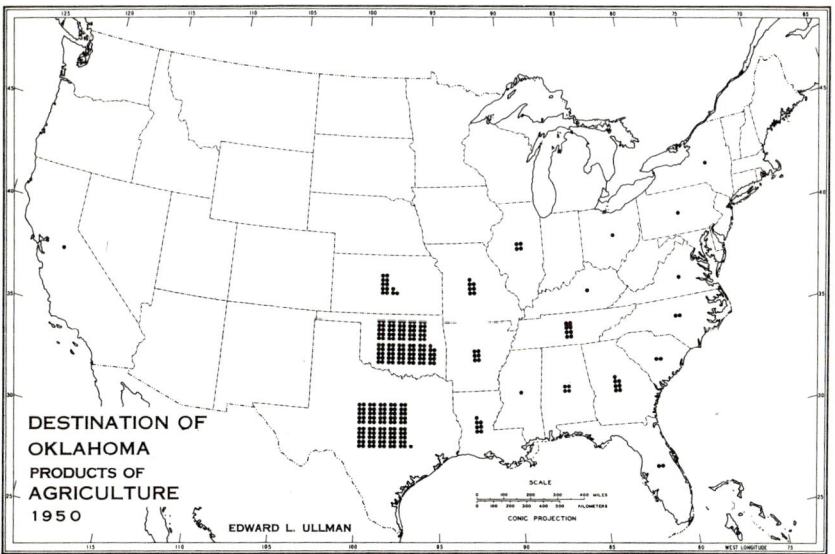

• 10,000 TONS   ▓ 100,000 TONS

125

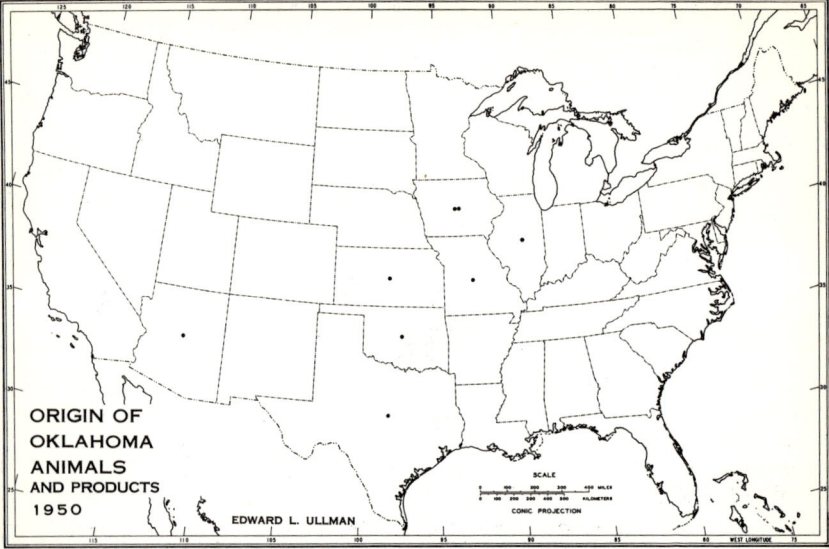

ORIGIN OF
OKLAHOMA
ANIMALS
AND PRODUCTS
1950

EDWARD L. ULLMAN

SCALE

CONIC PROJECTION

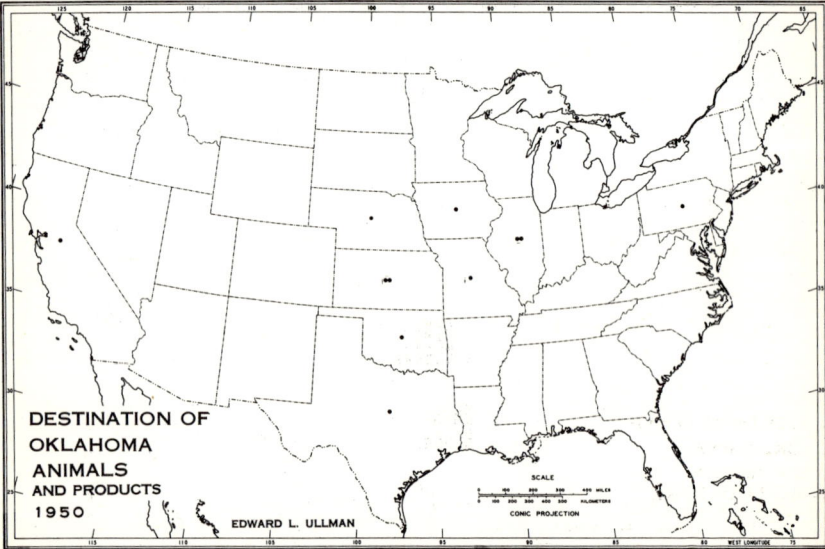

DESTINATION OF
OKLAHOMA
ANIMALS
AND PRODUCTS
1950

EDWARD L. ULLMAN

SCALE

CONIC PROJECTION

• 10,000 TONS   ▮ 100,000 TONS

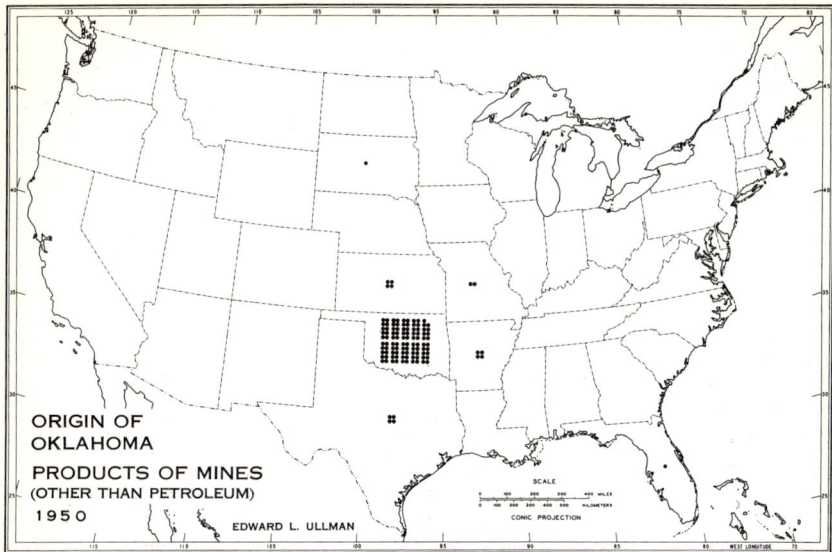

ORIGIN OF
OKLAHOMA
PRODUCTS OF MINES
(OTHER THAN PETROLEUM)
1950

EDWARD L. ULLMAN

SCALE

CONIC PROJECTION

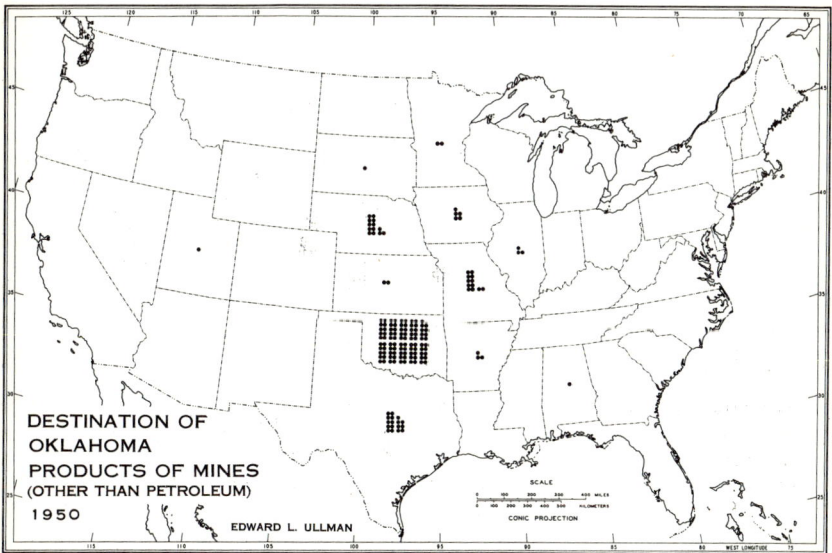

DESTINATION OF
OKLAHOMA
PRODUCTS OF MINES
(OTHER THAN PETROLEUM)
1950

EDWARD L. ULLMAN

SCALE

CONIC PROJECTION

• 50,000 TONS   ▓ 500,000 TONS

127

ORIGIN OF
OKLAHOMA
PETROLEUM PRODUCTS
1950

EDWARD L. ULLMAN

SCALE
CONIC PROJECTION

DESTINATION OF
OKLAHOMA
PETROLEUM PRODUCTS
1950

EDWARD L. ULLMAN

SCALE
CONIC PROJECTION

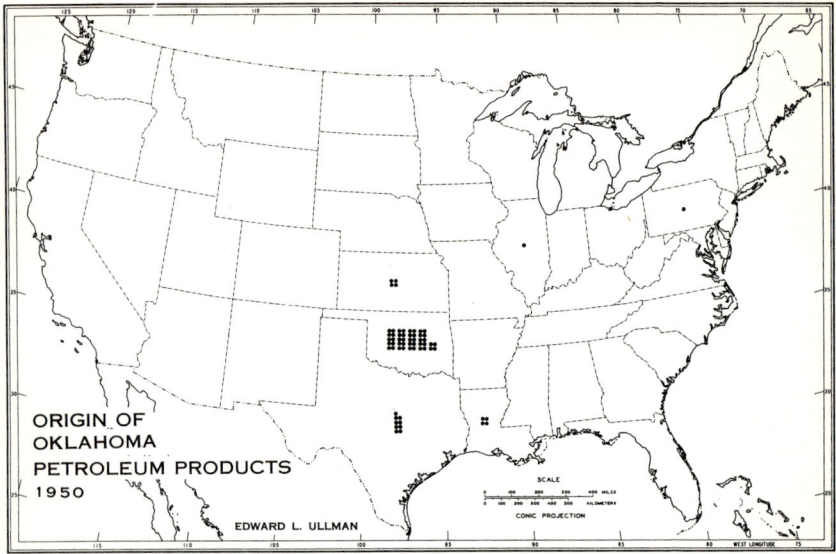

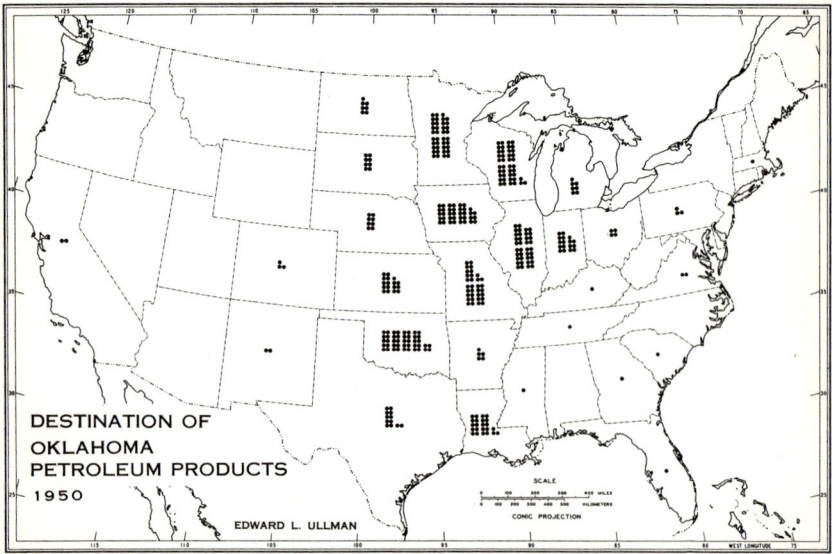

• 10,000 TONS   ▊ 100,000 TONS

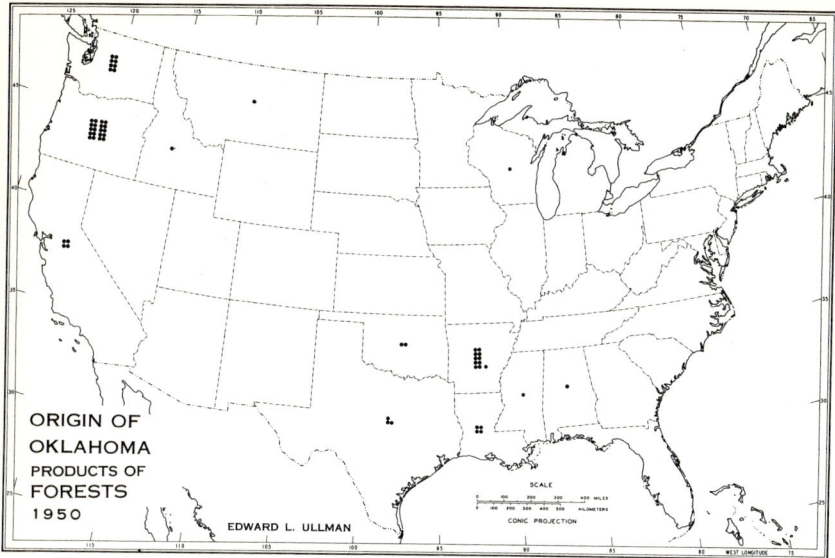

ORIGIN OF
OKLAHOMA
PRODUCTS OF
FORESTS
1950

EDWARD L. ULLMAN

SCALE

CONIC PROJECTION

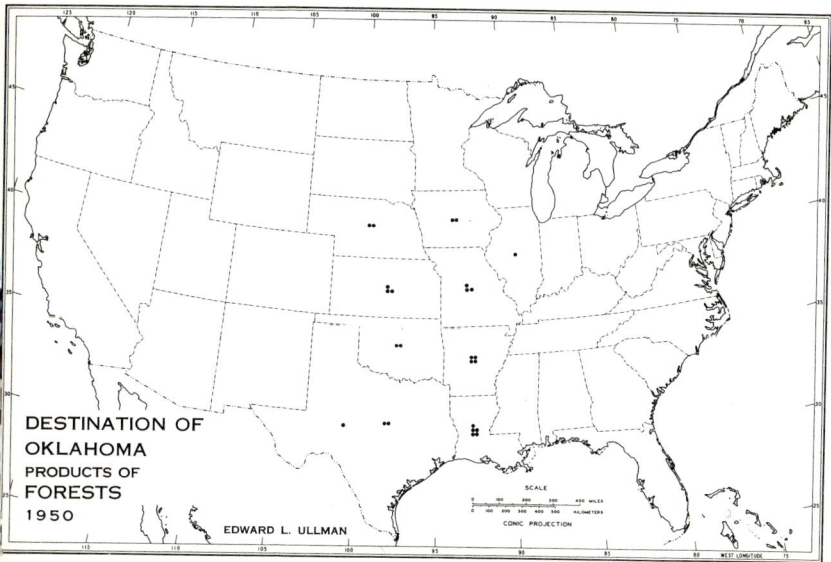

DESTINATION OF
OKLAHOMA
PRODUCTS OF
FORESTS
1950

EDWARD L. ULLMAN

SCALE

CONIC PROJECTION

• 10,000 TONS ▦ 100,000 TONS

129

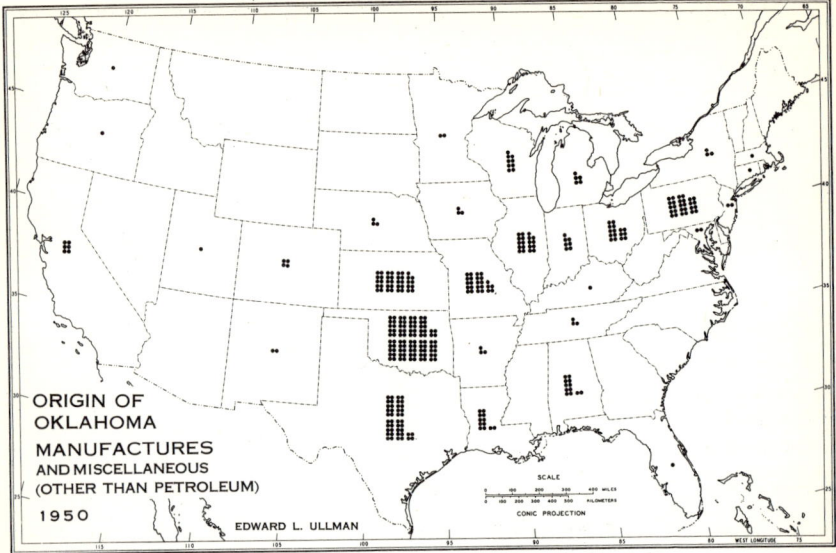

ORIGIN OF
OKLAHOMA
MANUFACTURES
AND MISCELLANEOUS
(OTHER THAN PETROLEUM)
1950

EDWARD L. ULLMAN

SCALE

CONIC PROJECTION

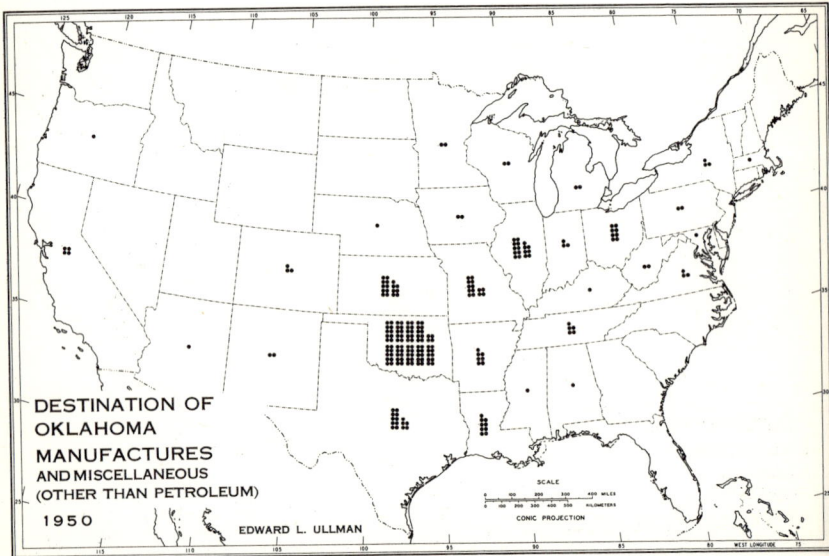

DESTINATION OF
OKLAHOMA
MANUFACTURES
AND MISCELLANEOUS
(OTHER THAN PETROLEUM)
1950

EDWARD L. ULLMAN

SCALE

CONIC PROJECTION

• 10,000 TONS   ▮ 100,000 TONS

130

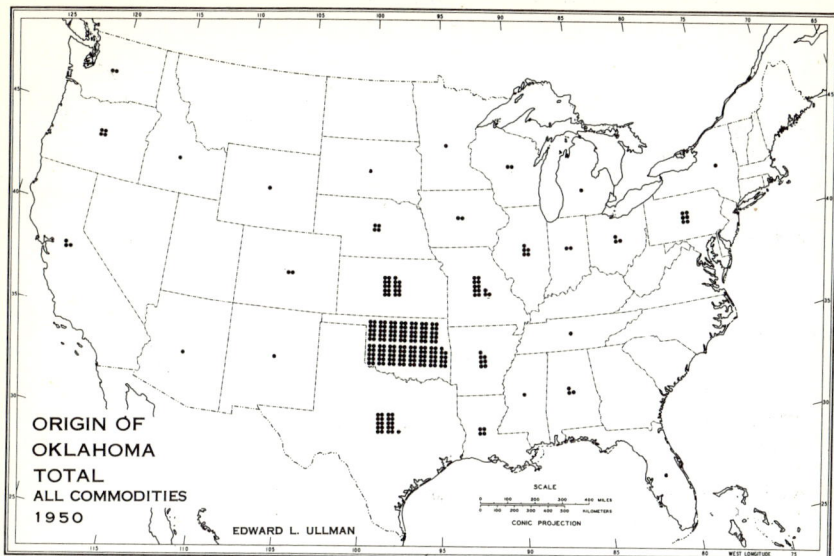

ORIGIN OF
OKLAHOMA
TOTAL
ALL COMMODITIES
1950

EDWARD L. ULLMAN

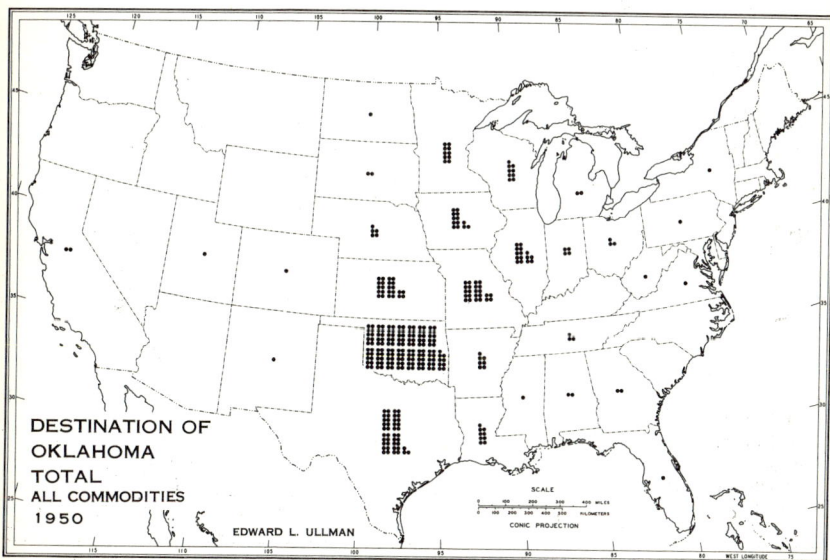

DESTINATION OF
OKLAHOMA
TOTAL
ALL COMMODITIES
1950

EDWARD L. ULLMAN

· 50,000 TONS   500,000 TONS

131

ORIGIN OF OREGON PRODUCTS OF AGRICULTURE 1950

EDWARD L. ULLMAN

SCALE
CONIC PROJECTION

DESTINATION OF OREGON PRODUCTS OF AGRICULTURE 1950

EDWARD L. ULLMAN

SCALE
CONIC PROJECTION

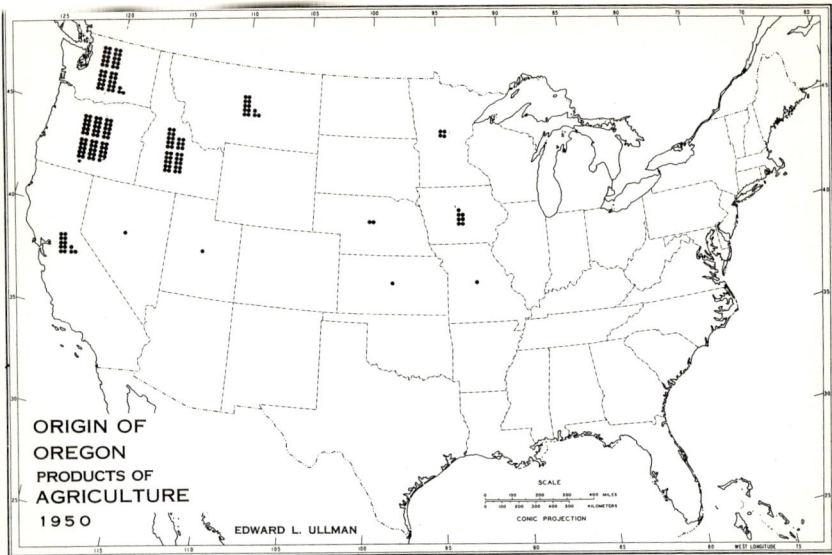

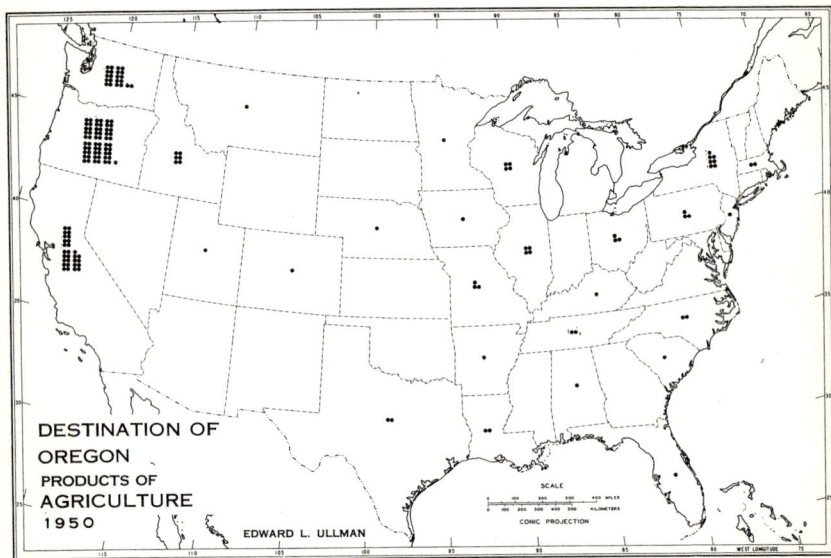

• 10,000 TONS   ▮ 100,000 TONS

132

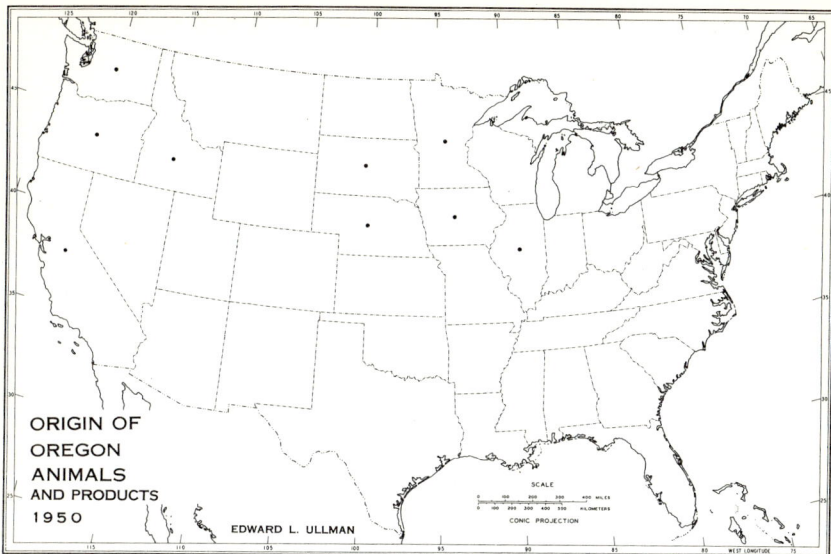

ORIGIN OF
OREGON
ANIMALS
AND PRODUCTS
1950

EDWARD L. ULLMAN

SCALE

CONIC PROJECTION

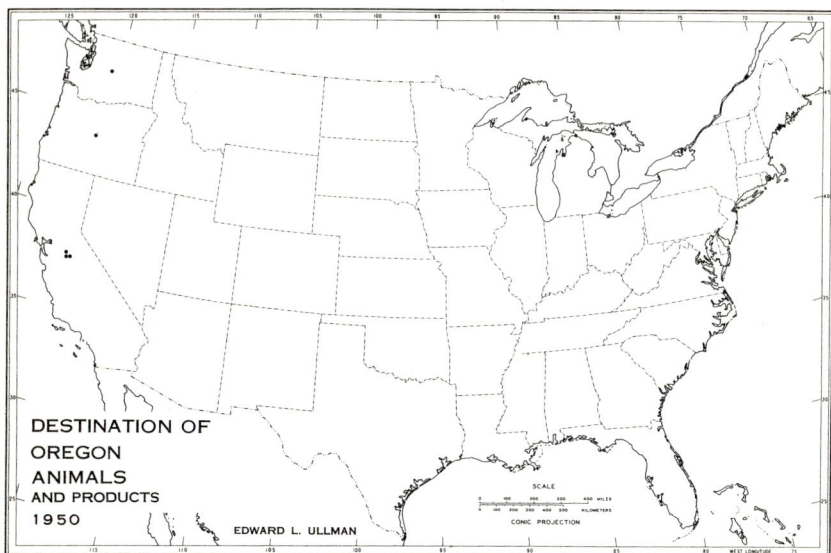

DESTINATION OF
OREGON
ANIMALS
AND PRODUCTS
1950

EDWARD L. ULLMAN

SCALE

CONIC PROJECTION

• 10,000 TONS   100,000 TONS

133

ORIGIN OF
OREGON
PRODUCTS OF MINES
(OTHER THAN PETROLEUM)
1950

EDWARD L. ULLMAN

SCALE
CONIC PROJECTION

DESTINATION OF
OREGON
PRODUCTS OF MINES
(OTHER THAN PETROLEUM)
1950

EDWARD L. ULLMAN

SCALE
CONIC PROJECTION

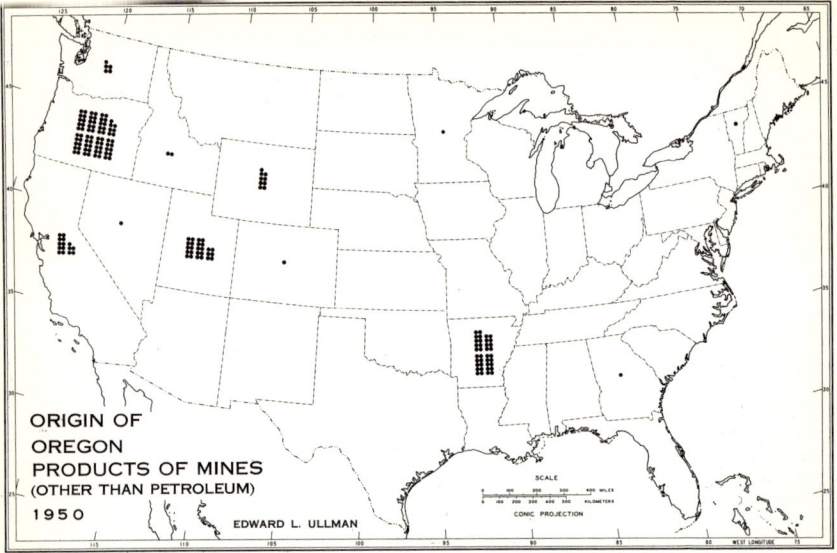

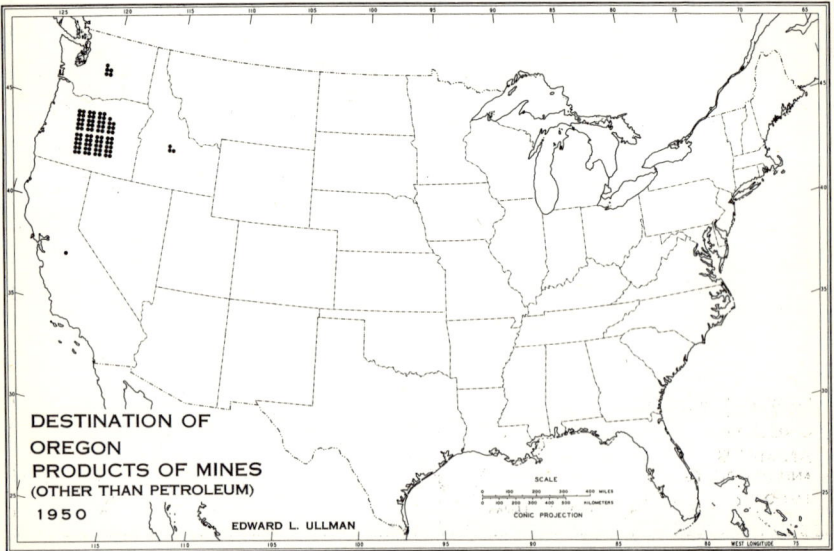

• 10,000 TONS   ▌ 100,000 TONS

134

ORIGIN OF
OREGON
PETROLEUM PRODUCTS
1950

EDWARD L. ULLMAN

SCALE
CONIC PROJECTION

DESTINATION OF
OREGON
PETROLEUM PRODUCTS
1950

EDWARD L. ULLMAN

SCALE
CONIC PROJECTION

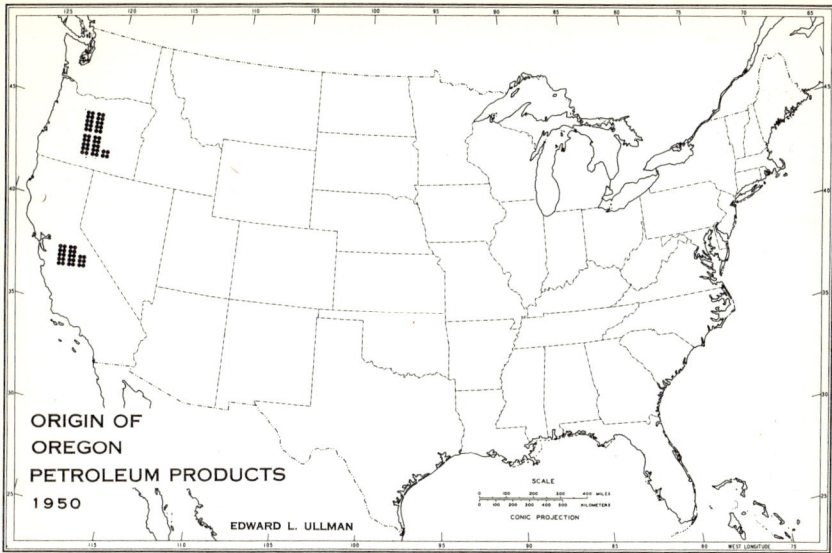

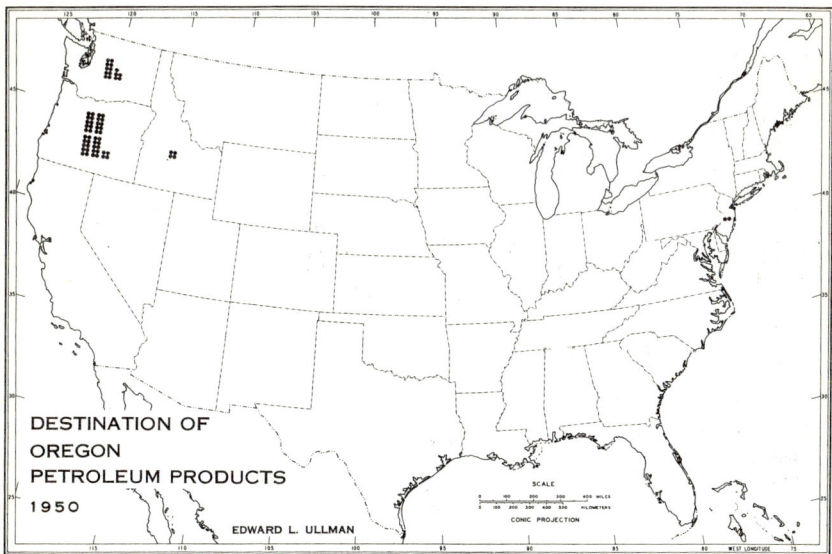

• 10,000 TONS   100,000 TONS

135

ORIGIN OF
OREGON
PRODUCTS OF
FORESTS
1950

EDWARD L. ULLMAN

SCALE

CONIC PROJECTION

DESTINATION OF
OREGON
PRODUCTS OF
FORESTS
1950

EDWARD L. ULLMAN

SCALE

CONIC PROJECTION

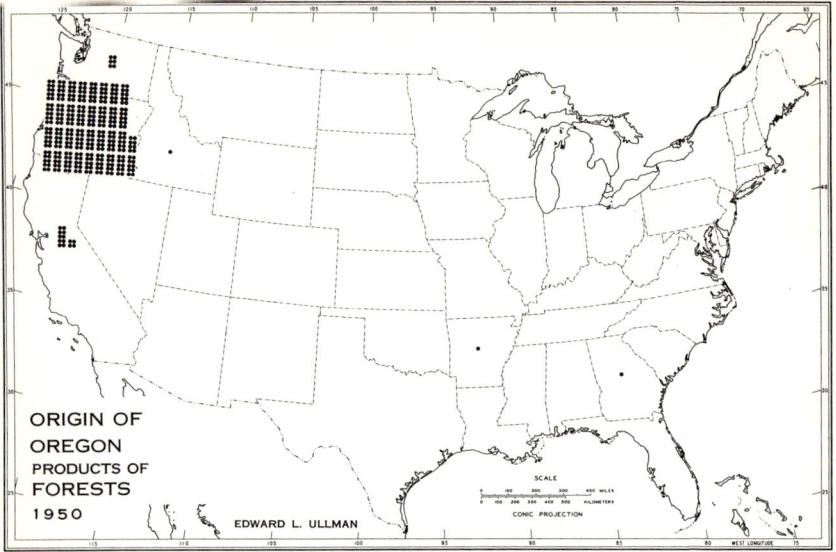

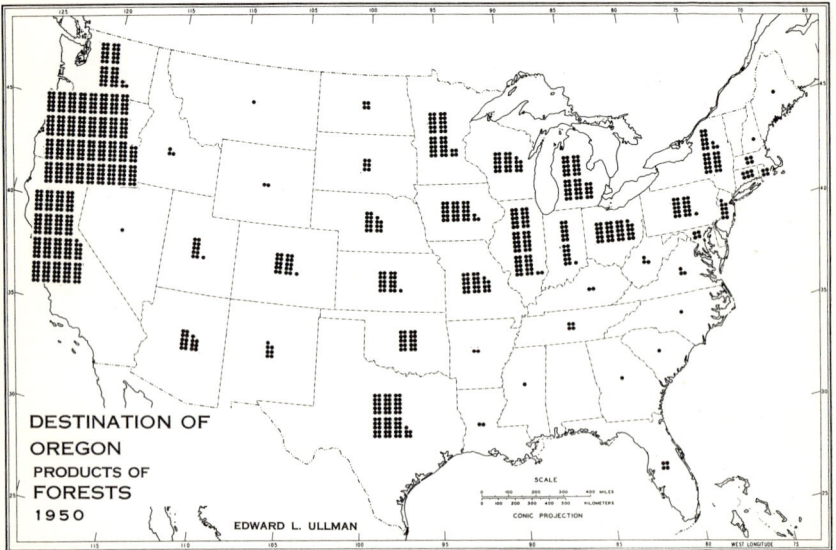

• 10,000 TONS   100,000 TONS

136

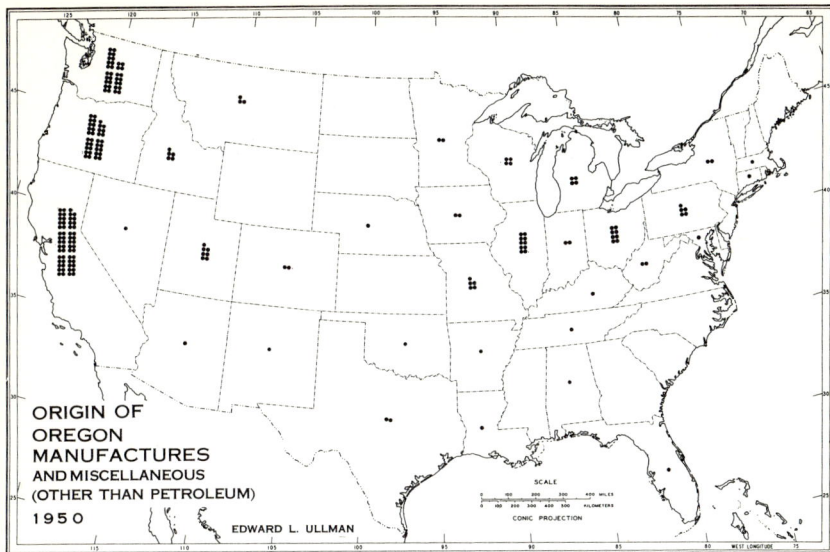

ORIGIN OF
OREGON
MANUFACTURES
AND MISCELLANEOUS
(OTHER THAN PETROLEUM)
1950

EDWARD L. ULLMAN

SCALE
CONIC PROJECTION

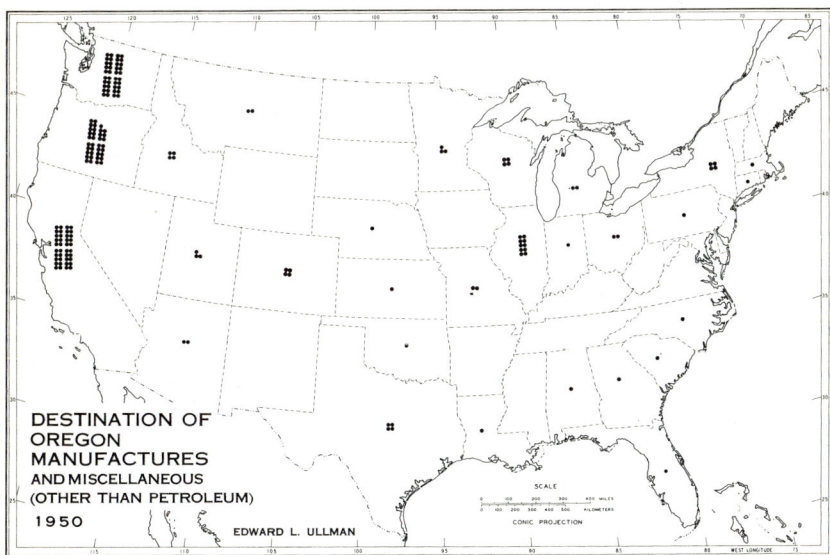

DESTINATION OF
OREGON
MANUFACTURES
AND MISCELLANEOUS
(OTHER THAN PETROLEUM)
1950

EDWARD L. ULLMAN

SCALE
CONIC PROJECTION

• 10,000 TONS   100,000 TONS

137

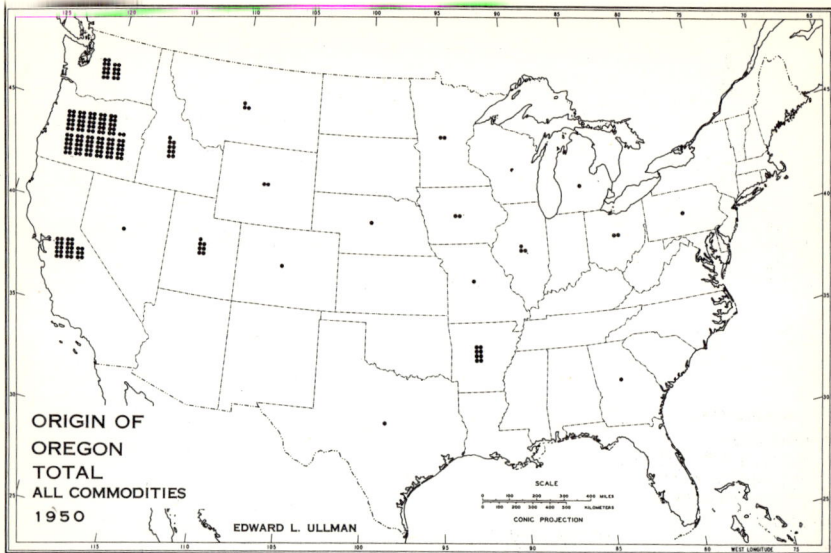

ORIGIN OF
OREGON
TOTAL
ALL COMMODITIES
1950

EDWARD L. ULLMAN

SCALE

CONIC PROJECTION

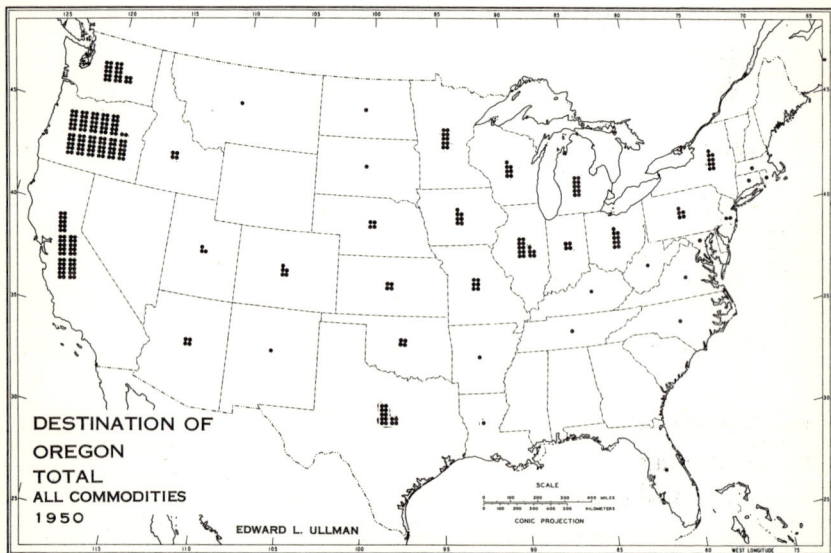

DESTINATION OF
OREGON
TOTAL
ALL COMMODITIES
1950

EDWARD L. ULLMAN

SCALE

CONIC PROJECTION

• 50,000 TONS   500,000 TONS

138

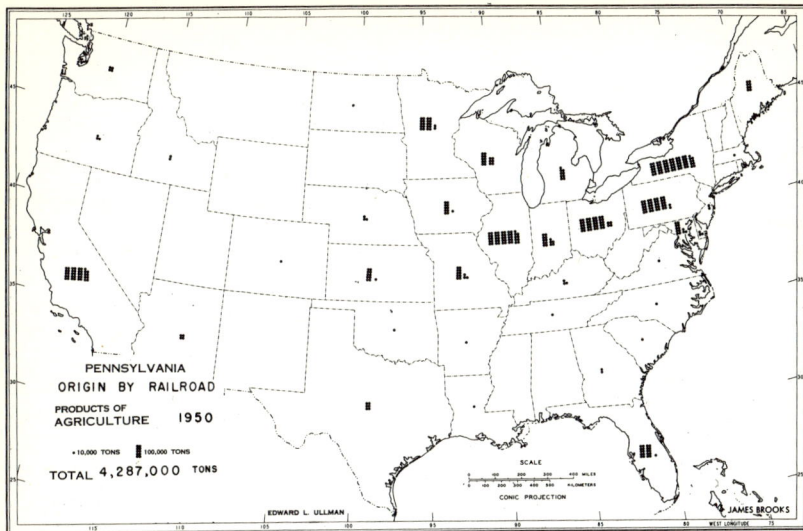

PENNSYLVANIA
ORIGIN BY RAILROAD
PRODUCTS OF
AGRICULTURE   1950

• 10,000 TONS   ▌100,000 TONS
TOTAL 4,287,000 TONS

EDWARD L. ULLMAN

SCALE
CONIC PROJECTION

JAMES BROOKS

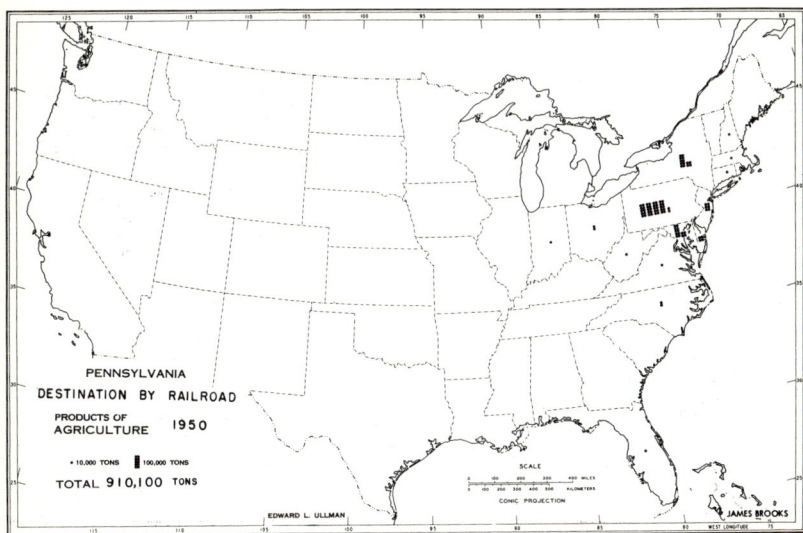

PENNSYLVANIA
DESTINATION BY RAILROAD
PRODUCTS OF
AGRICULTURE   1950

• 10,000 TONS   ▌100,000 TONS
TOTAL 910,100 TONS

EDWARD L. ULLMAN

SCALE
CONIC PROJECTION

JAMES BROOKS

139

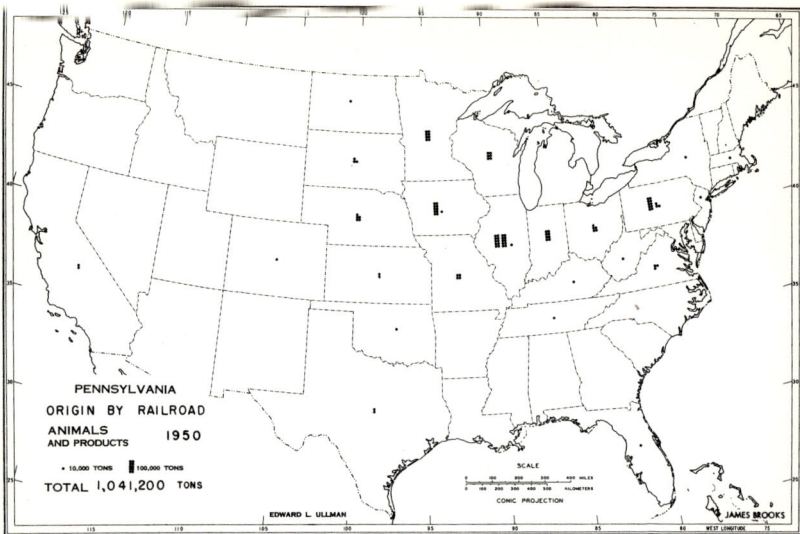

PENNSYLVANIA
ORIGIN BY RAILROAD
ANIMALS
AND PRODUCTS   1950

• 10,000 TONS   ■ 100,000 TONS

TOTAL 1,041,200 TONS

SCALE

EDWARD L. ULLMAN

CONIC PROJECTION

JAMES BROOKS

WEST LONGITUDE

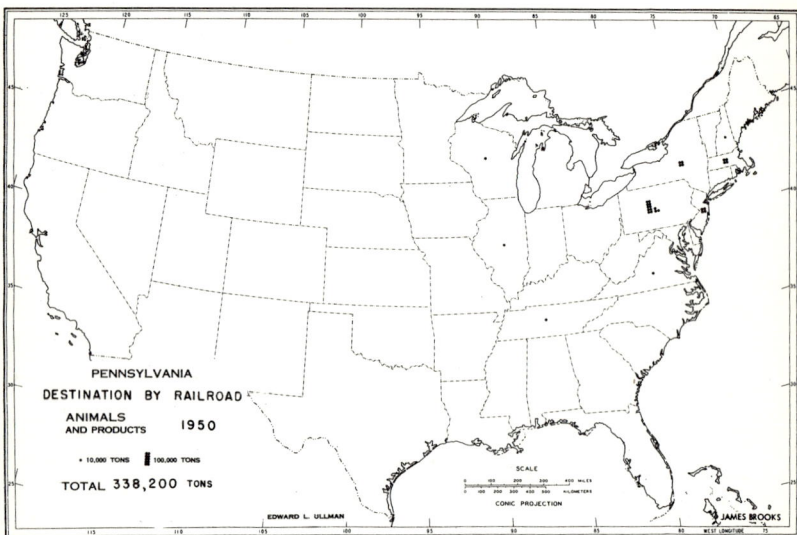

PENNSYLVANIA
DESTINATION BY RAILROAD
ANIMALS
AND PRODUCTS   1950

• 10,000 TONS   ■ 100,000 TONS

TOTAL 338,200 TONS

SCALE

EDWARD L. ULLMAN

CONIC PROJECTION

JAMES BROOKS

WEST LONGITUDE

140

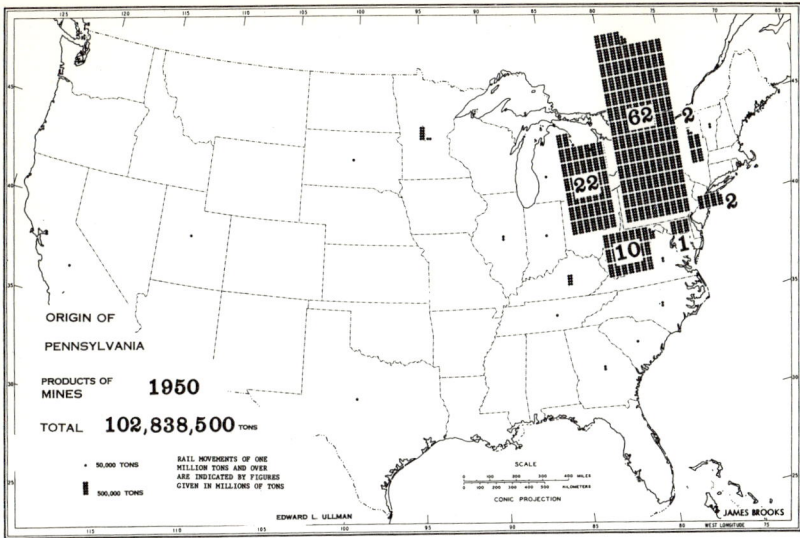

ORIGIN OF
PENNSYLVANIA
PRODUCTS OF
MINES   1950
TOTAL   102,838,500 TONS

• 50,000 TONS
▪ 500,000 TONS

RAIL MOVEMENTS OF ONE
MILLION TONS AND OVER
ARE INDICATED BY FIGURES
GIVEN IN MILLIONS OF TONS

SCALE

CONIC PROJECTION

EDWARD L. ULLMAN

JAMES BROOKS

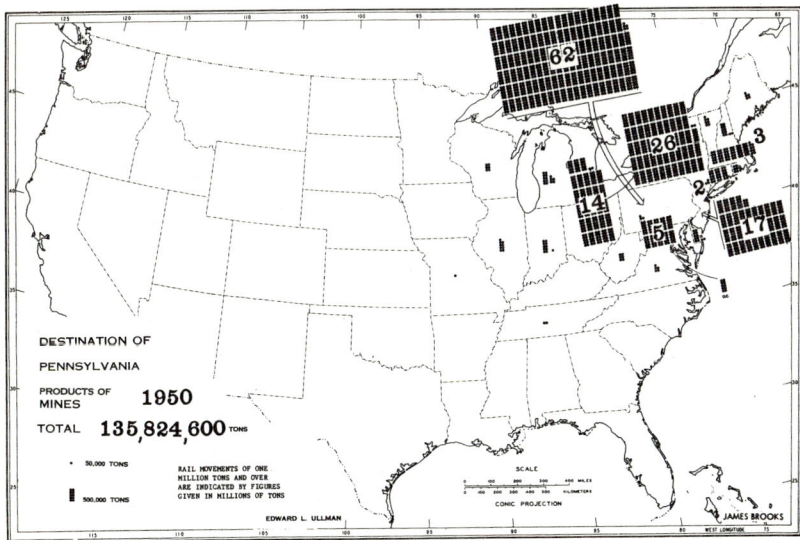

DESTINATION OF
PENNSYLVANIA
PRODUCTS OF
MINES   1950
TOTAL   135,824,600 TONS

• 50,000 TONS
▪ 500,000 TONS

RAIL MOVEMENTS OF ONE
MILLION TONS AND OVER
ARE INDICATED BY FIGURES
GIVEN IN MILLIONS OF TONS

SCALE

CONIC PROJECTION

EDWARD L. ULLMAN

JAMES BROOKS

141

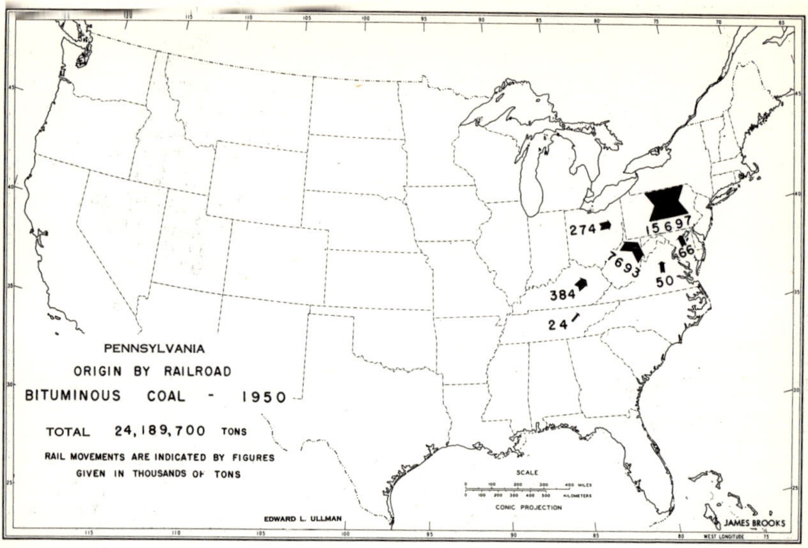

PENNSYLVANIA

ORIGIN BY RAILROAD

BITUMINOUS COAL - 1950

TOTAL 24,189,700 TONS

RAIL MOVEMENTS ARE INDICATED BY FIGURES
GIVEN IN THOUSANDS OF TONS

274 15697
1693 66
384 50
24

EDWARD L. ULLMAN   JAMES BROOKS

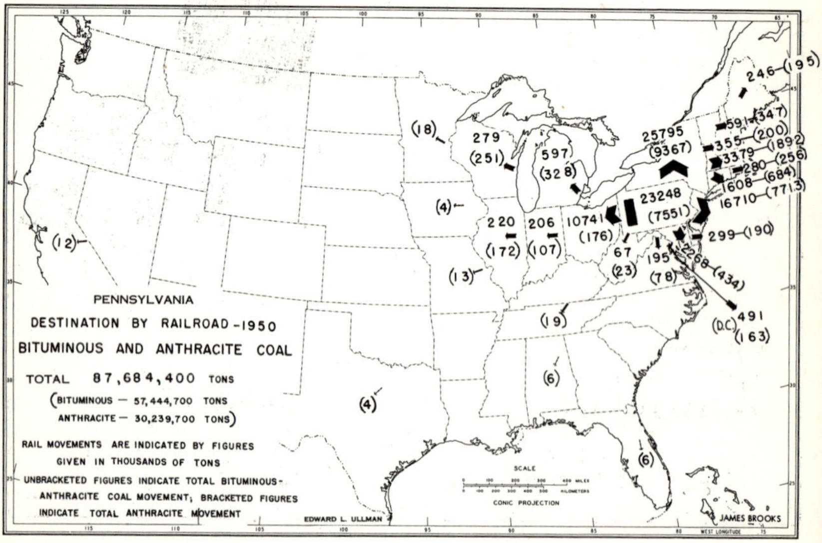

PENNSYLVANIA

DESTINATION BY RAILROAD -1950

BITUMINOUS AND ANTHRACITE COAL

TOTAL 87,684,400 TONS

(BITUMINOUS — 57,444,700 TONS
ANTHRACITE — 30,239,700 TONS)

RAIL MOVEMENTS ARE INDICATED BY FIGURES
GIVEN IN THOUSANDS OF TONS

UNBRACKETED FIGURES INDICATE TOTAL BITUMINOUS-
ANTHRACITE COAL MOVEMENT; BRACKETED FIGURES
INDICATE TOTAL ANTHRACITE MOVEMENT

246 (195)
(18) 591 (347)
279 25795 355 (200)
(251) (9367) 3379 (1892)
597 280 (256)
(328) 1608 (684)
(4) 23248 16710 (7713)
220 206 10741 (7551) 299 (190)
(172) (107) (176) 68 (434)
(12) 67 195
(23) (78)
(13) 491
(19) (DC) (163)
(4)
(6)
(6)

EDWARD L. ULLMAN   JAMES BROOKS

142

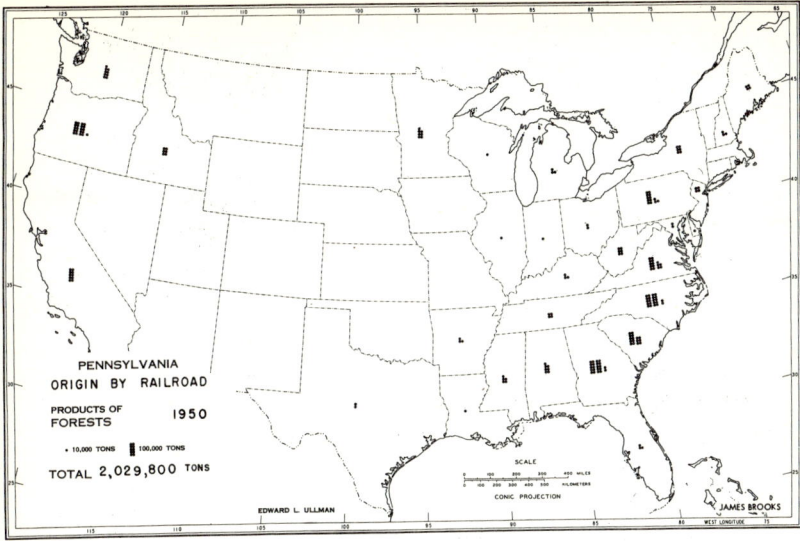

PENNSYLVANIA
ORIGIN BY RAILROAD

PRODUCTS OF
FORESTS   1950

• 10,000 TONS   ■ 100,000 TONS

TOTAL 2,029,800 TONS

SCALE

CONIC PROJECTION

EDWARD L. ULLMAN

JAMES BROOKS

WEST LONGITUDE

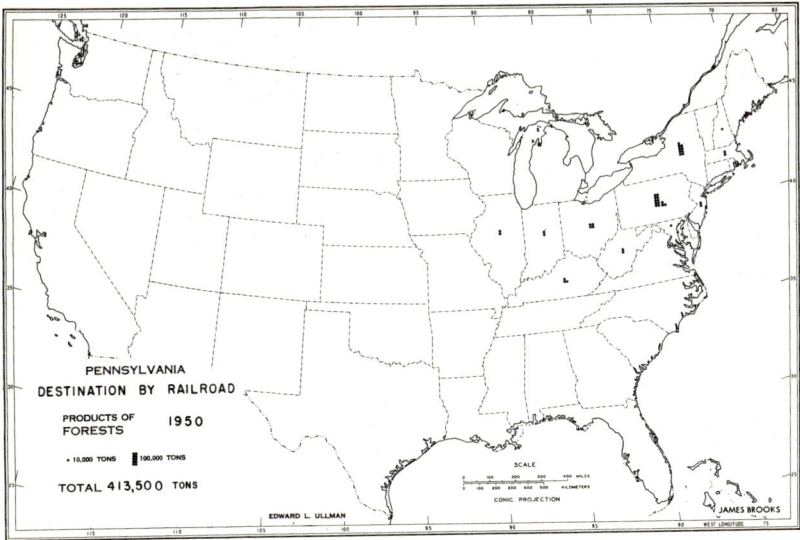

PENNSYLVANIA
DESTINATION BY RAILROAD

PRODUCTS OF
FORESTS   1950

• 10,000 TONS   ■ 100,000 TONS

TOTAL 413,500 TONS

SCALE

CONIC PROJECTION

EDWARD L. ULLMAN

JAMES BROOKS

WEST LONGITUDE

143

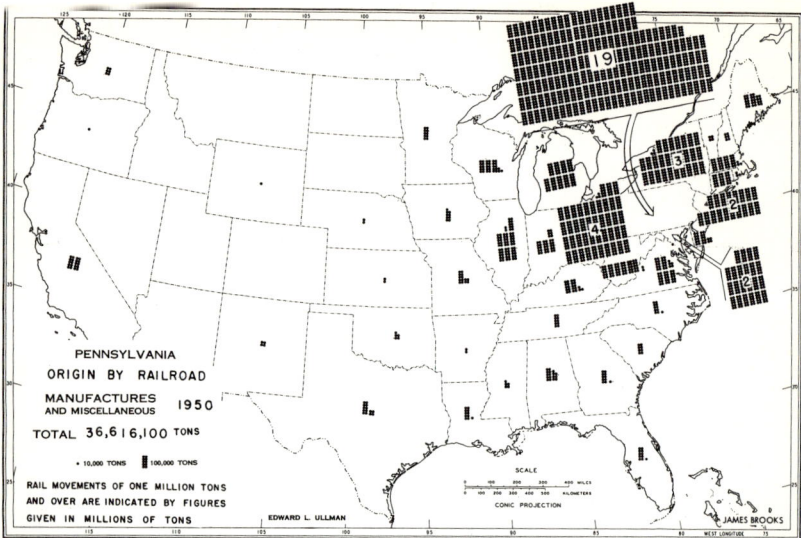

PENNSYLVANIA

ORIGIN BY RAILROAD

MANUFACTURES
AND MISCELLANEOUS 1950

TOTAL 36,616,100 TONS

• 10,000 TONS   ■ 100,000 TONS

RAIL MOVEMENTS OF ONE MILLION TONS
AND OVER ARE INDICATED BY FIGURES

GIVEN IN MILLIONS OF TONS   EDWARD L. ULLMAN

SCALE

CONIC PROJECTION

JAMES BROOKS

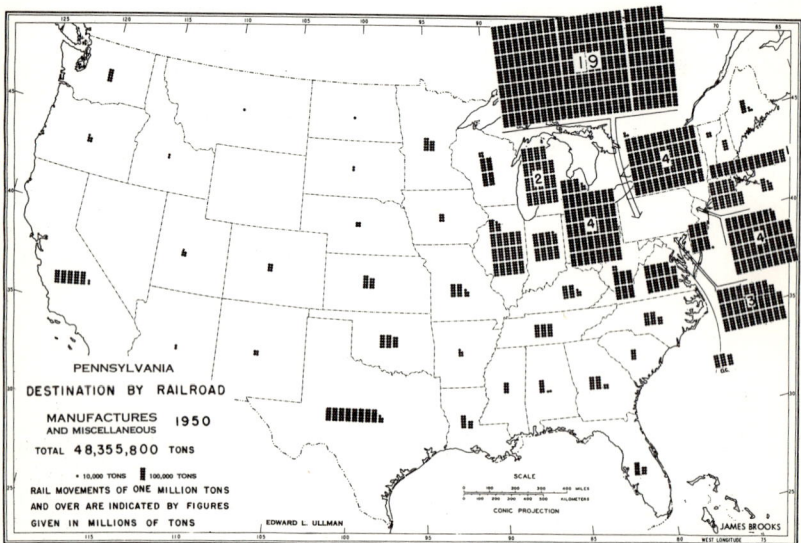

PENNSYLVANIA

DESTINATION BY RAILROAD

MANUFACTURES
AND MISCELLANEOUS 1950

TOTAL 48,355,800 TONS

• 10,000 TONS   ■ 100,000 TONS

RAIL MOVEMENTS OF ONE MILLION TONS
AND OVER ARE INDICATED BY FIGURES

GIVEN IN MILLIONS OF TONS   EDWARD L. ULLMAN

SCALE

CONIC PROJECTION

JAMES BROOKS

144

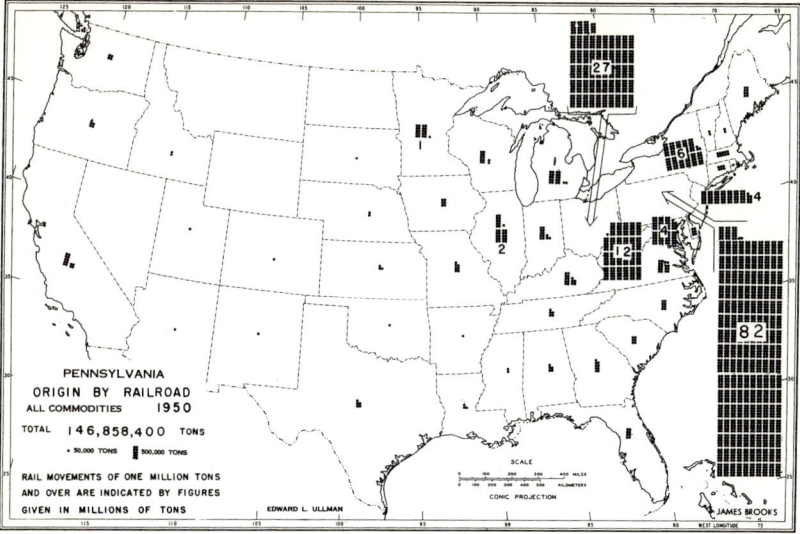

PENNSYLVANIA
ORIGIN BY RAILROAD
ALL COMMODITIES 1950
TOTAL 146,858,400 TONS
• 50,000 TONS ▌ 500,000 TONS
RAIL MOVEMENTS OF ONE MILLION TONS
AND OVER ARE INDICATED BY FIGURES
GIVEN IN MILLIONS OF TONS
EDWARD L. ULLMAN
SCALE
CONIC PROJECTION
JAMES BROOKS

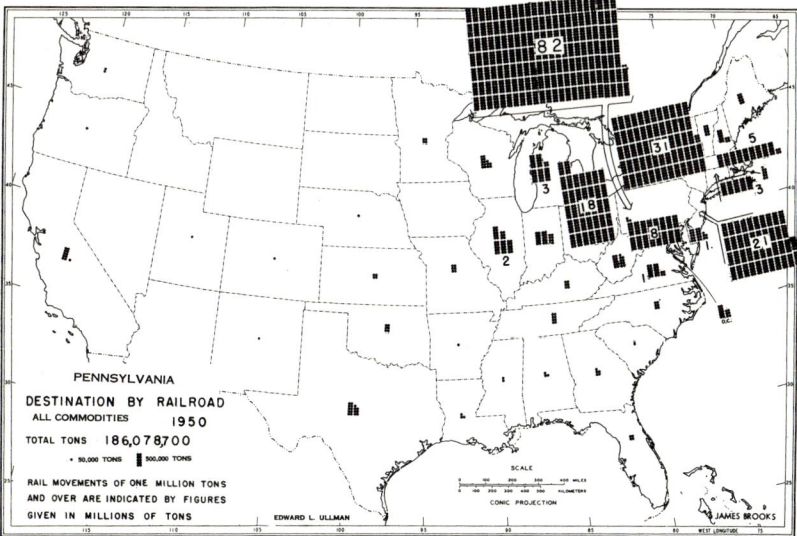

PENNSYLVANIA
DESTINATION BY RAILROAD
ALL COMMODITIES 1950
TOTAL TONS 186,078,700
• 50,000 TONS ▌ 500,000 TONS
RAIL MOVEMENTS OF ONE MILLION TONS
AND OVER ARE INDICATED BY FIGURES
GIVEN IN MILLIONS OF TONS
EDWARD L. ULLMAN
SCALE
CONIC PROJECTION
JAMES BROOKS

145

ORIGIN OF
TENNESSEE
PRODUCTS OF
AGRICULTURE
1950

EDWARD L. ULLMAN

SCALE

CONIC PROJECTION

WEST LONGITUDE

DESTINATION OF
TENNESSEE
PRODUCTS OF
AGRICULTURE
1950

EDWARD L. ULLMAN

SCALE

CONIC PROJECTION

WEST LONGITUDE

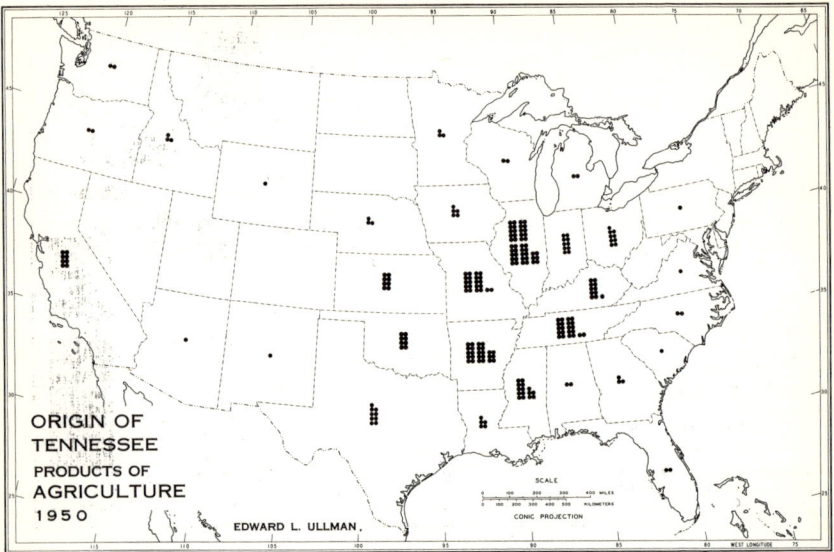

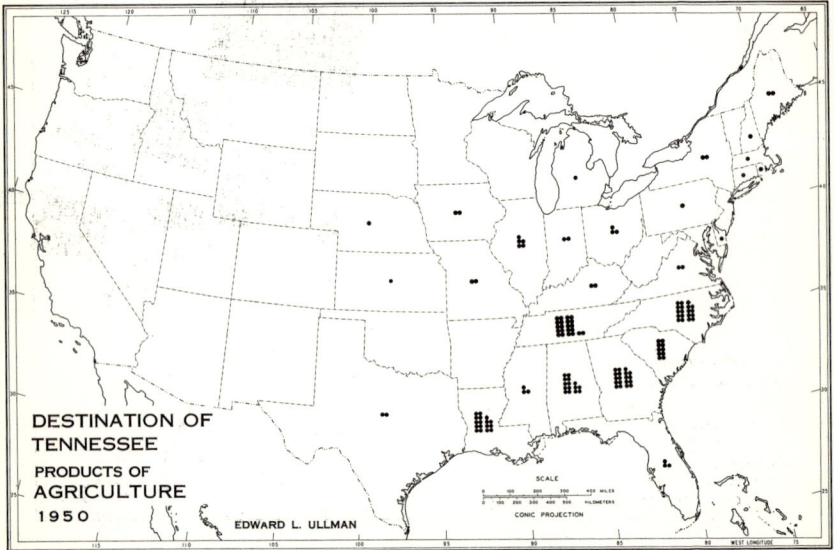

· 10,000 TONS   100,000 TONS

146

ORIGIN OF
TENNESSEE
ANIMALS
AND PRODUCTS
1950

EDWARD L. ULLMAN

SCALE
0   100   200   300   400 MILES
0   100 200 300 400 500 KILOMETERS
CONIC PROJECTION

DESTINATION OF
TENNESSEE
ANIMALS
AND PRODUCTS
1950

EDWARD L. ULLMAN

SCALE
0   100   200   300   400 MILES
0   100 200 300 400 500 KILOMETERS
CONIC PROJECTION

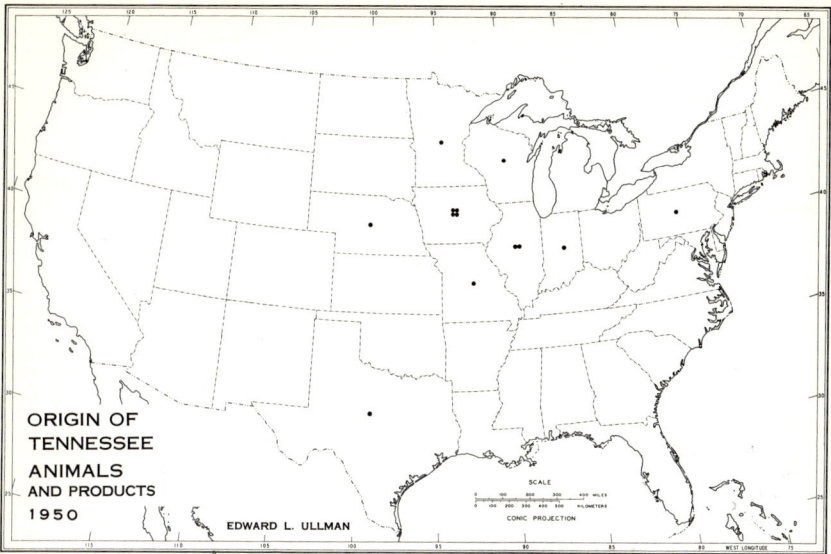

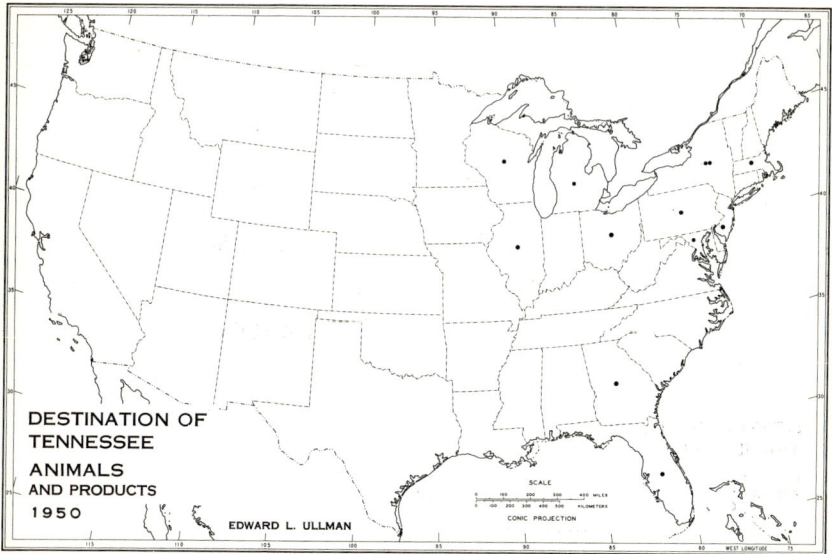

• 10,000 TONS   ▓ 100,000 TONS

147

ORIGIN OF
TENNESSEE
PRODUCTS OF
MINES
1950

EDWARD L. ULLMAN

SCALE
0   100   200   300   400 MILES
0   100 200 300 400 500
KILOMETERS
CONIC PROJECTION

WEST LONGITUDE

DESTINATION OF
TENNESSEE
PRODUCTS OF
MINES
1950

EDWARD L. ULLMAN

SCALE
0   100   200   300   400 MILES
0   100 200 300 400 500
KILOMETERS
CONIC PROJECTION

WEST LONGITUDE

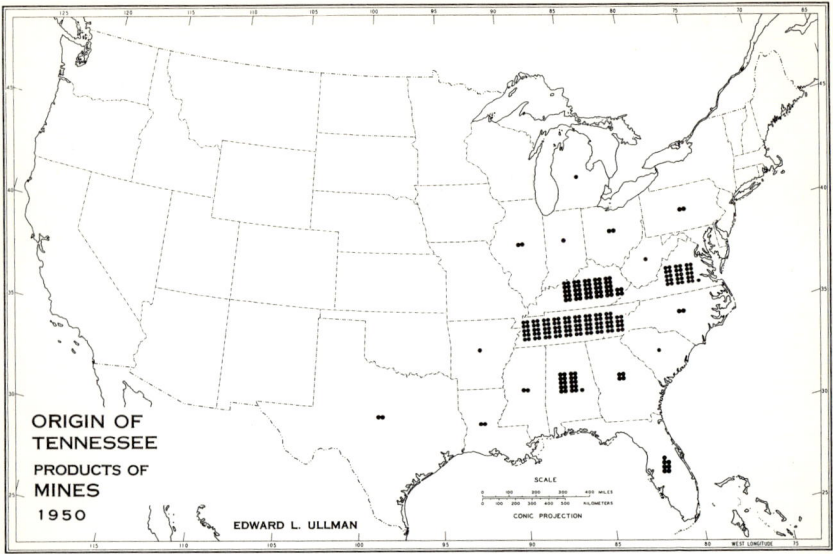

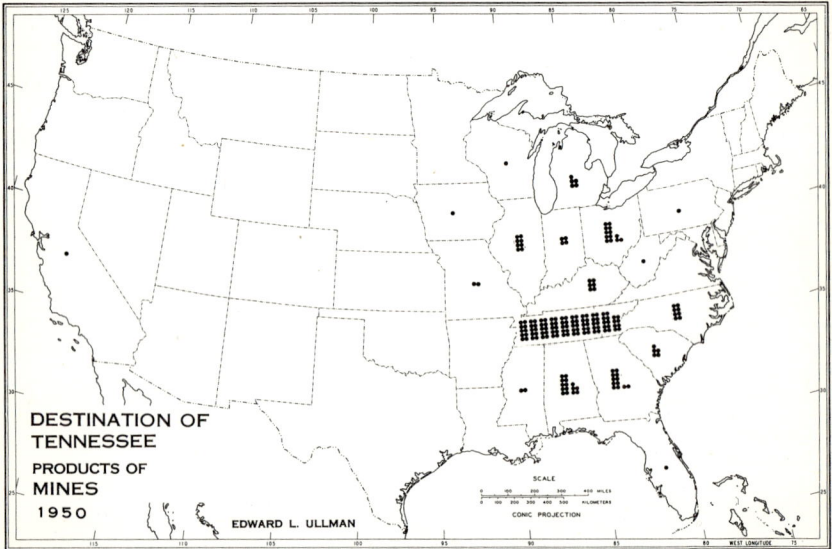

• 50,000 TONS   ▮ 500,000 TONS

148

ORIGIN OF
TENNESSEE
PRODUCTS OF
FORESTS
1950

EDWARD L. ULLMAN

SCALE

CONIC PROJECTION

DESTINATION OF
TENNESSEE
PRODUCTS OF
FORESTS
1950

EDWARD L. ULLMAN

SCALE

CONIC PROJECTION

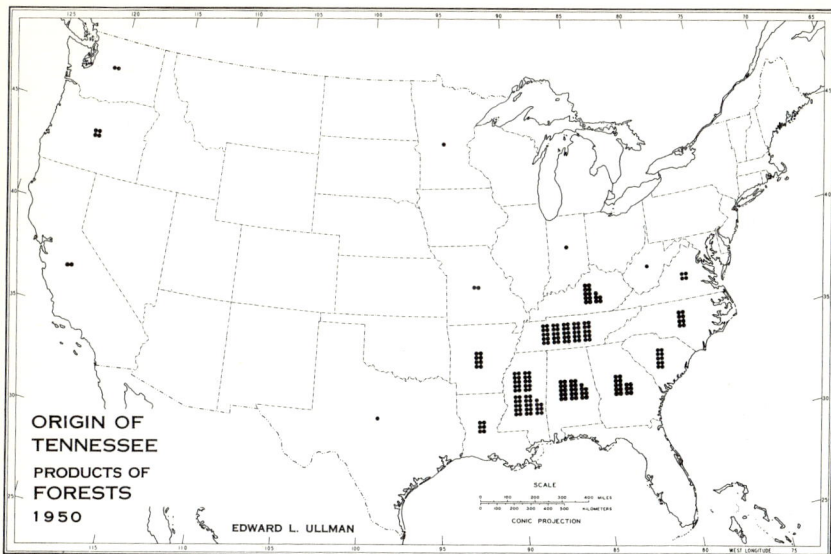

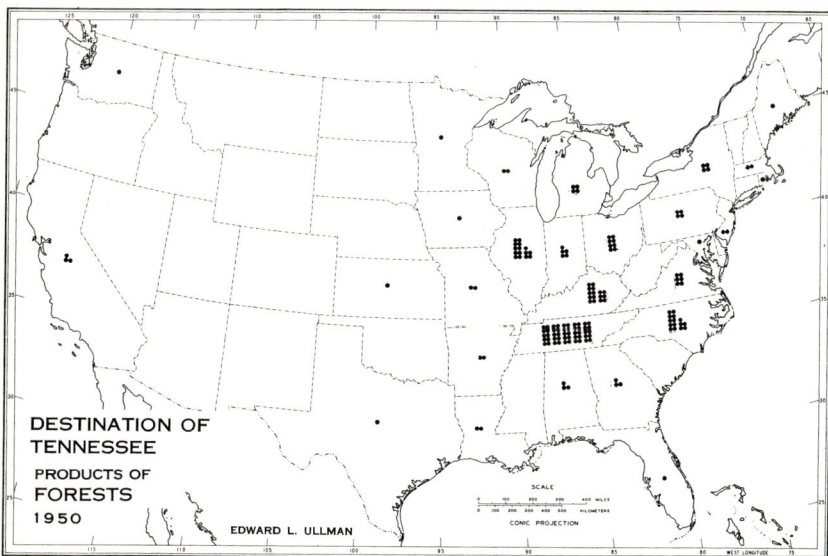

• 10,000 TONS   100,000 TONS

149

ORIGIN OF
TENNESSEE
MANUFACTURES
AND MISCELLANEOUS
1950

EDWARD L. ULLMAN

SCALE

CONIC PROJECTION

DESTINATION OF
TENNESSEE
MANUFACTURES
AND MISCELLANEOUS
1950

EDWARD L. ULLMAN

SCALE

CONIC PROJECTION

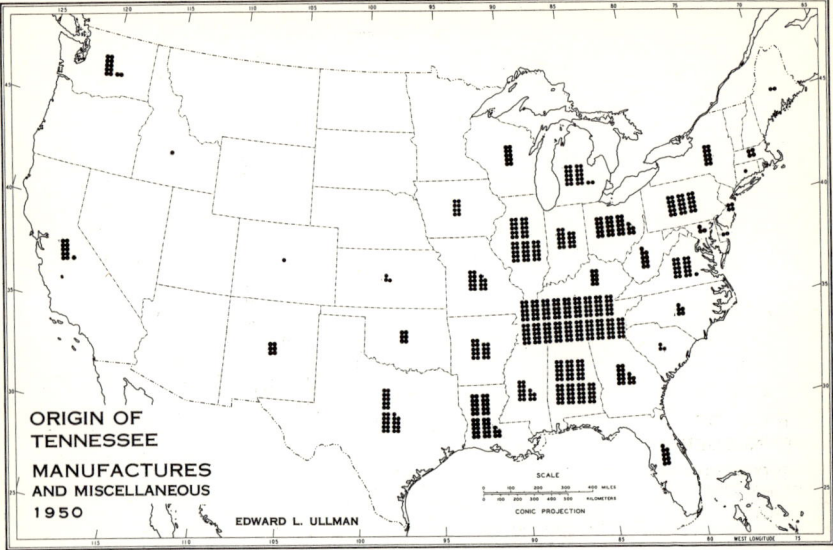

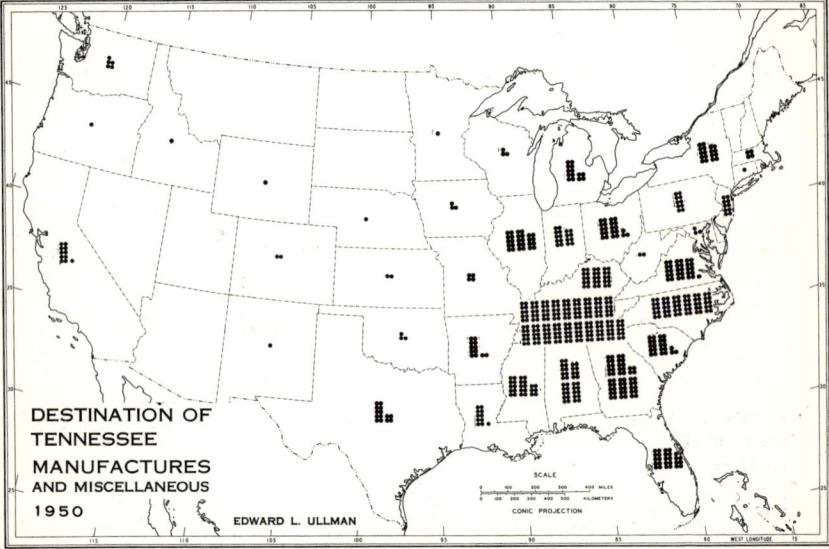

• 10,000 TONS ▊ 100,000 TONS

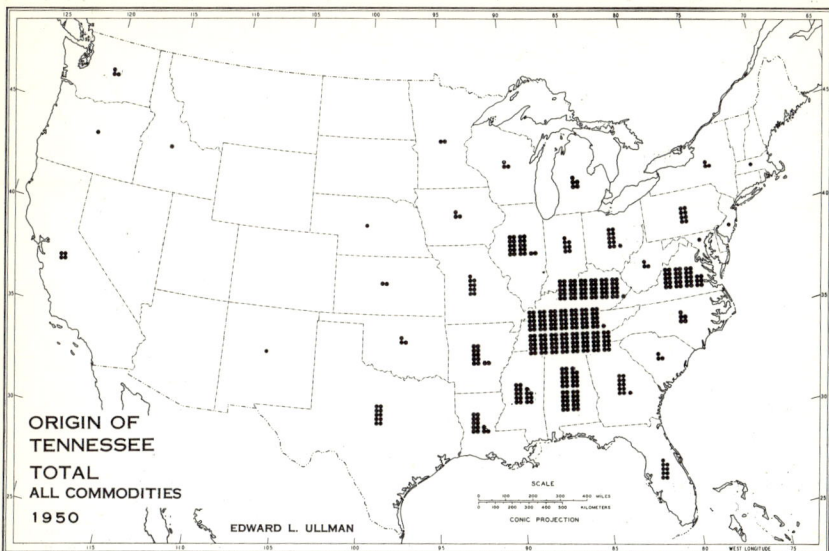

ORIGIN OF
TENNESSEE

TOTAL
ALL COMMODITIES

1950

EDWARD L. ULLMAN

SCALE

CONIC PROJECTION

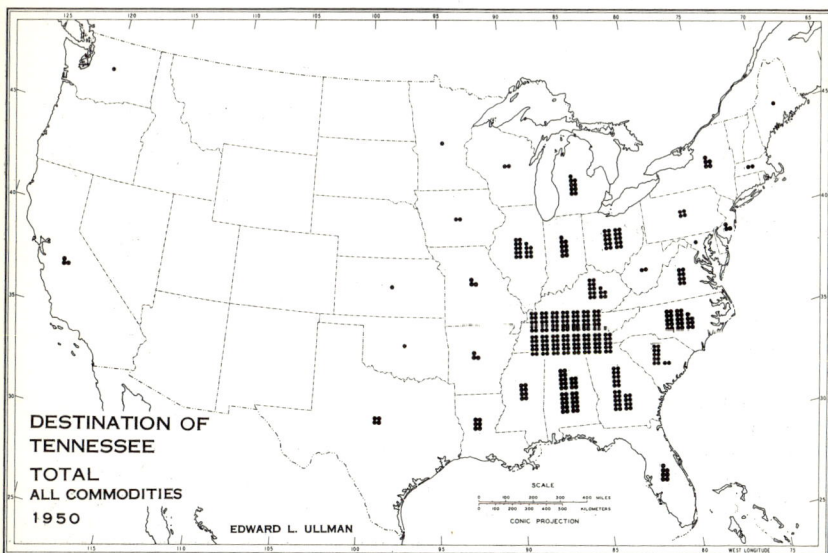

DESTINATION OF
TENNESSEE

TOTAL
ALL COMMODITIES

1950

EDWARD L. ULLMAN

SCALE

CONIC PROJECTION

• 50,000 TONS   500,000 TONS

151

ORIGIN OF
UTAH

PRODUCTS OF
AGRICULTURE
1950

EDWARD L. ULLMAN

SCALE

CONIC PROJECTION

DESTINATION OF
UTAH

PRODUCTS OF
AGRICULTURE
1950

EDWARD L. ULLMAN

SCALE

CONIC PROJECTION

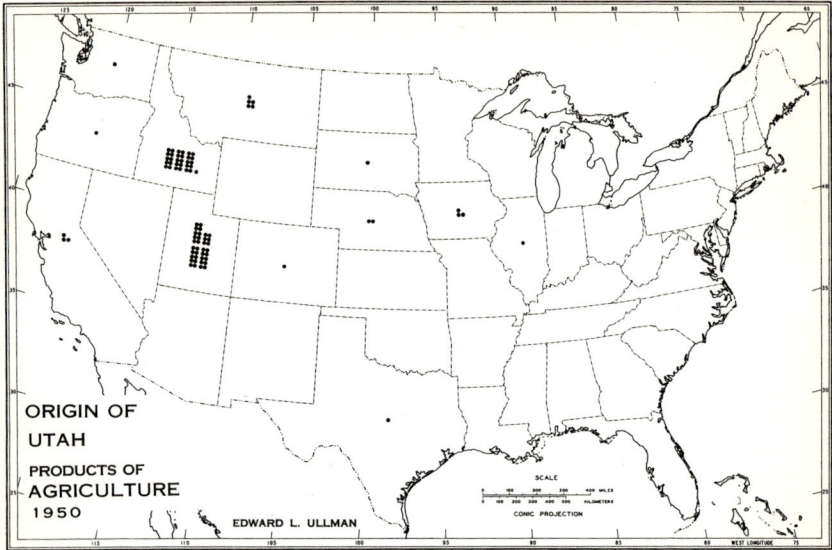

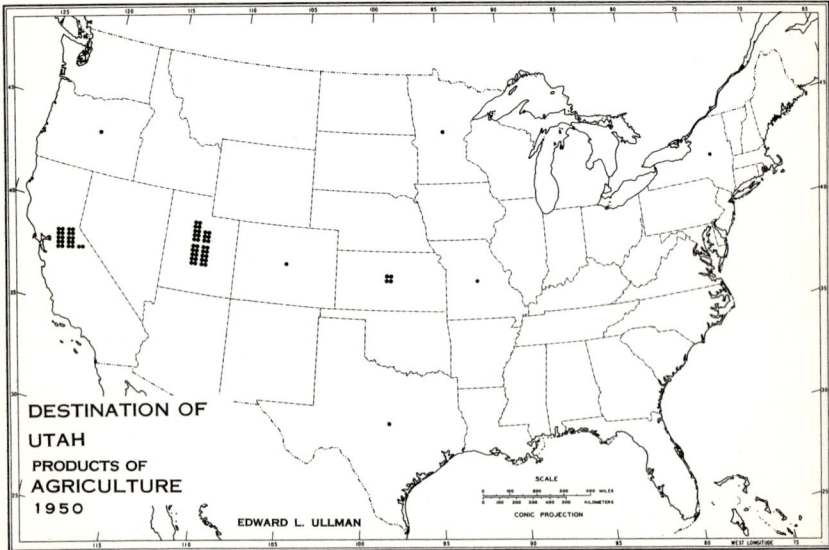

• 10,000 TONS   ▉ 100,000 TONS

ORIGIN OF
UTAH
ANIMALS
AND PRODUCTS
1950

SCALE

CONIC PROJECTION

EDWARD L. ULLMAN

DESTINATION OF
UTAH
ANIMALS
AND PRODUCTS
1950

EDWARD L. ULLMAN

SCALE

CONIC PROJECTION

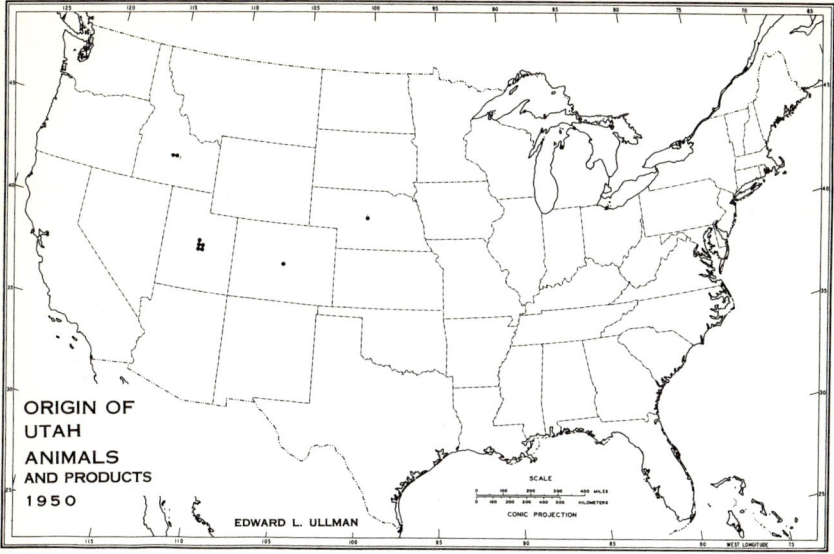

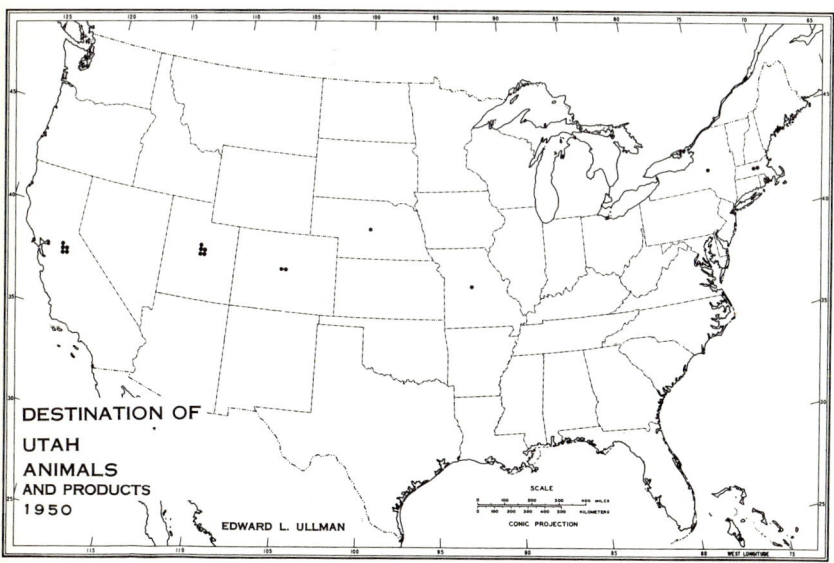

• 10,000 TONS   ▦ 100,000 TONS

153

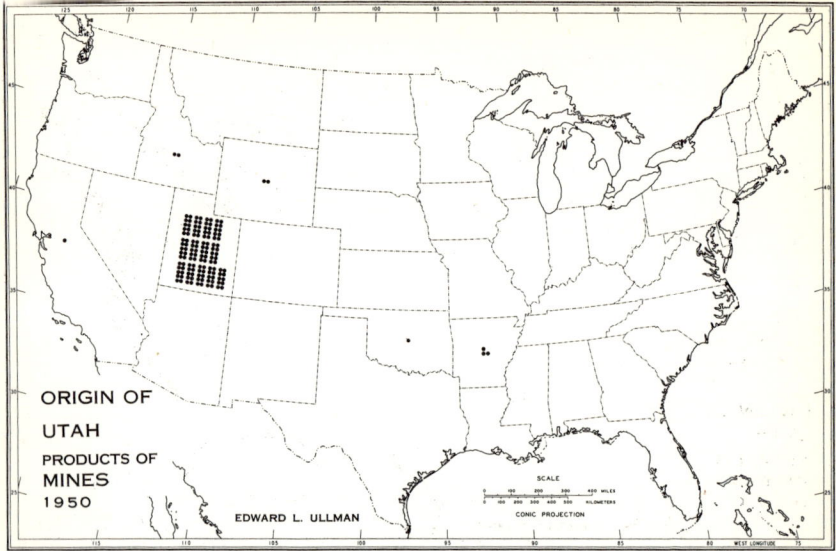

ORIGIN OF
UTAH
PRODUCTS OF
MINES
1950

EDWARD L. ULLMAN

SCALE
CONIC PROJECTION

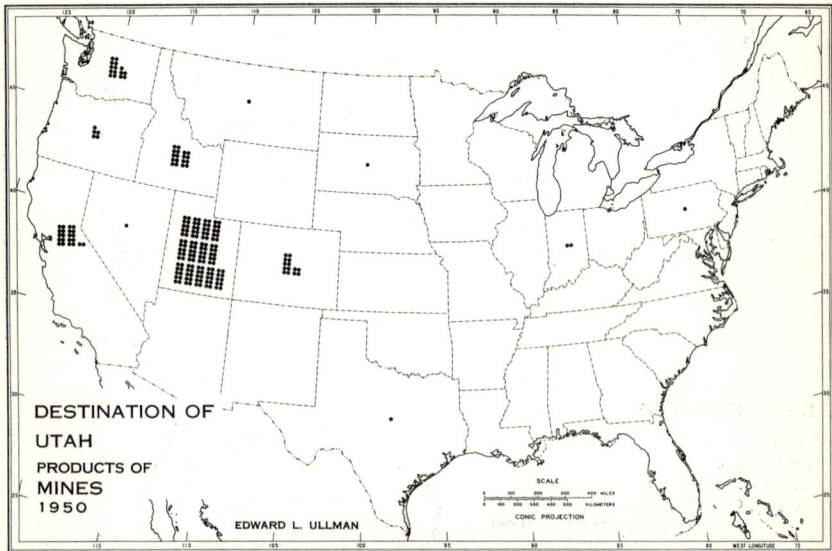

DESTINATION OF
UTAH
PRODUCTS OF
MINES
1950

EDWARD L. ULLMAN

SCALE
CONIC PROJECTION

• 50,000 TONS   500,000 TONS

154

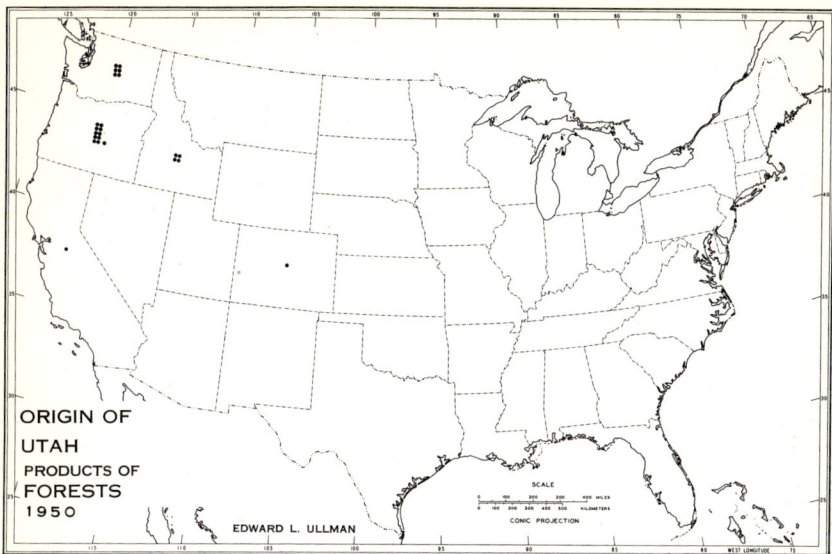

ORIGIN OF
UTAH
PRODUCTS OF
FORESTS
1950

EDWARD L. ULLMAN

SCALE

CONIC PROJECTION

• 10,000 TONS   100,000 TONS

ORIGIN OF
UTAH
MANUFACTURES
AND MISCELLANEOUS
1950

EDWARD L. ULLMAN

SCALE

CONIC PROJECTION

DESTINATION OF
UTAH
MANUFACTURES
AND MISCELLANEOUS
1950

EDWARD L. ULLMAN

SCALE

CONIC PROJECTION

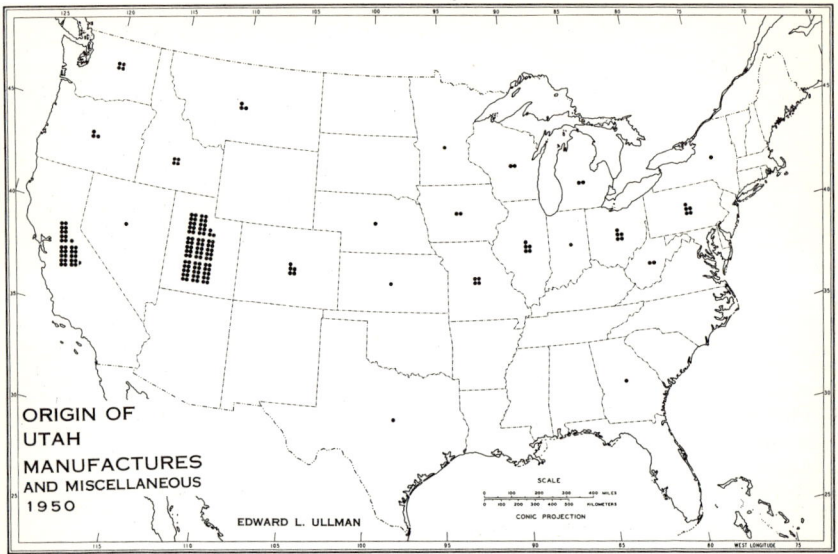

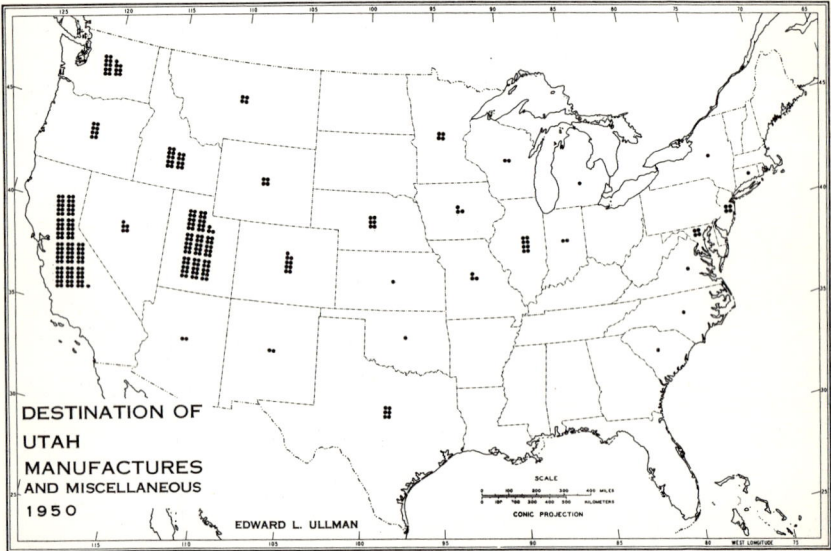

• 10,000 TONS　▓ 100,000 TONS

156

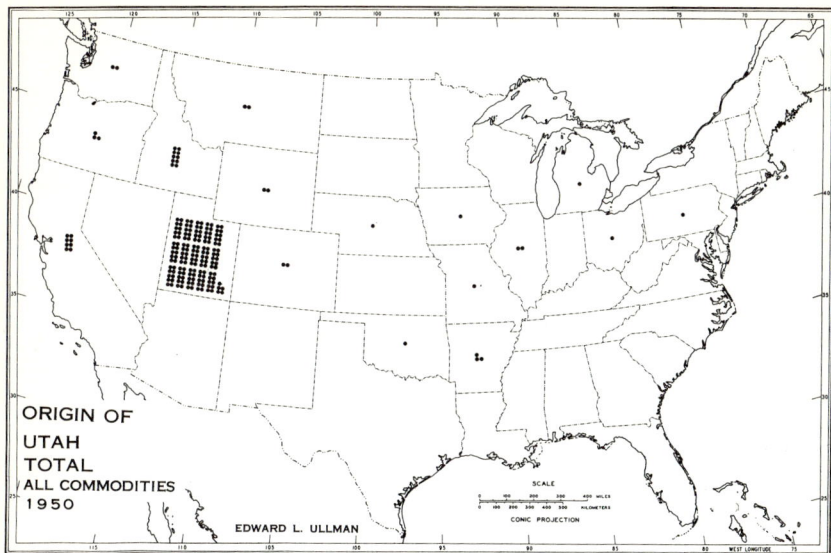

ORIGIN OF
UTAH
TOTAL
ALL COMMODITIES
1950

EDWARD L. ULLMAN

SCALE

CONIC PROJECTION

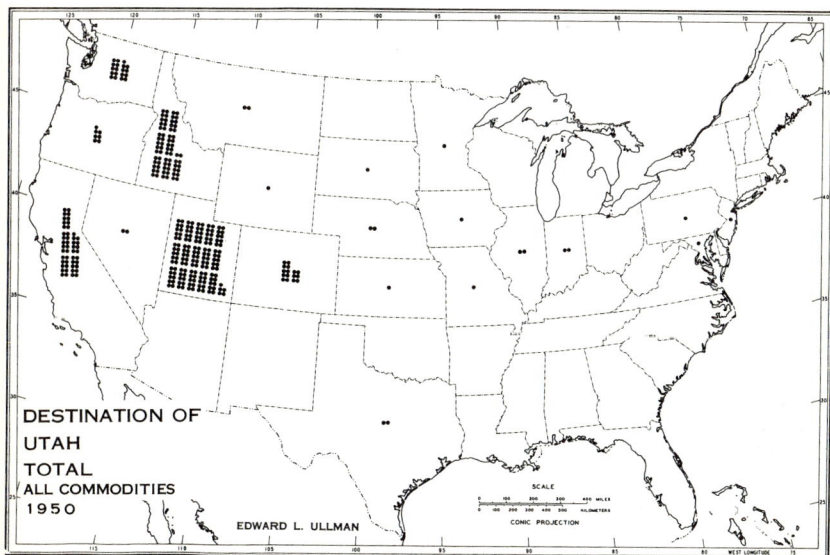

DESTINATION OF
UTAH
TOTAL
ALL COMMODITIES
1950

EDWARD L. ULLMAN

SCALE

CONIC PROJECTION

• 50,000 TONS   ▌500,000 TONS

157

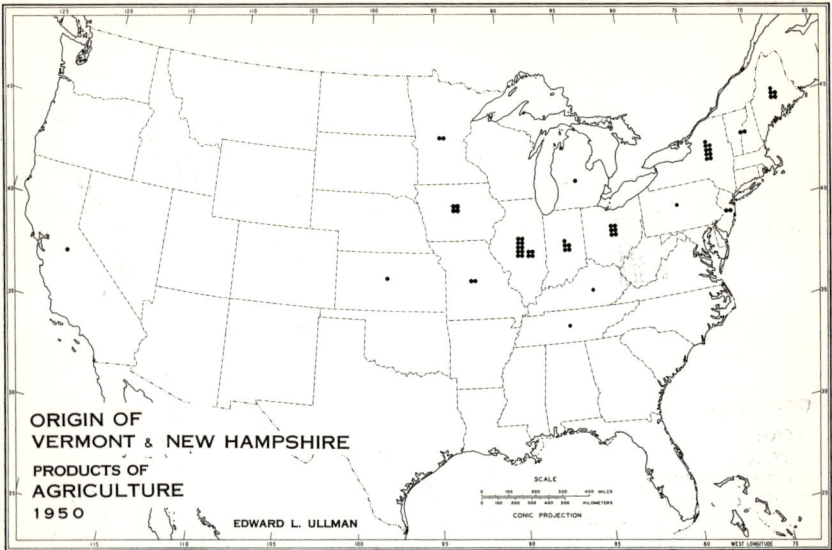

ORIGIN OF
VERMONT & NEW HAMPSHIRE

PRODUCTS OF
AGRICULTURE
1950

EDWARD L. ULLMAN

SCALE

CONIC PROJECTION

WEST LONGITUDE

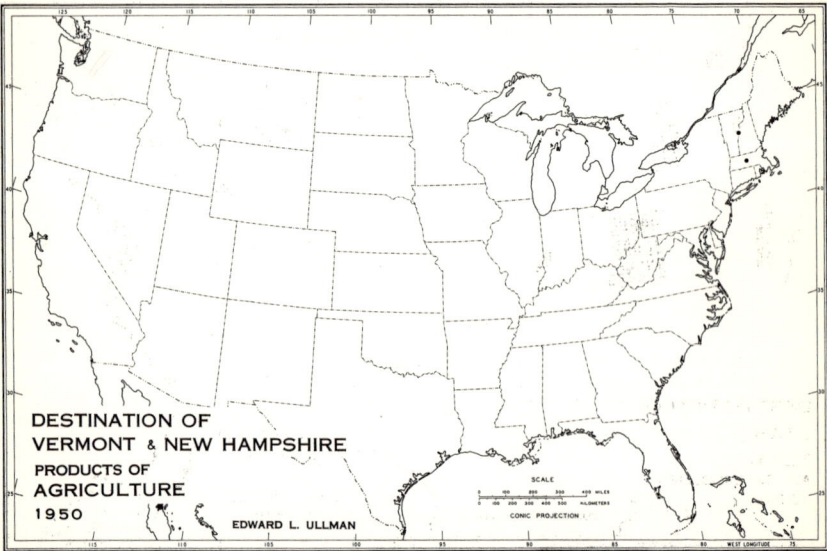

DESTINATION OF
VERMONT & NEW HAMPSHIRE

PRODUCTS OF
AGRICULTURE
1950

EDWARD L. ULLMAN

SCALE

CONIC PROJECTION

WEST LONGITUDE

• 10,000 TONS   ▌ 100,000 TONS

158

ORIGIN OF
VERMONT & NEW HAMPSHIRE
ANIMALS
AND PRODUCTS
1950

EDWARD L. ULLMAN

SCALE

CONIC PROJECTION

DESTINATION OF
VERMONT & NEW HAMPSHIRE
ANIMALS
AND PRODUCTS
1950

EDWARD L. ULLMAN

SCALE

CONIC PROJECTION

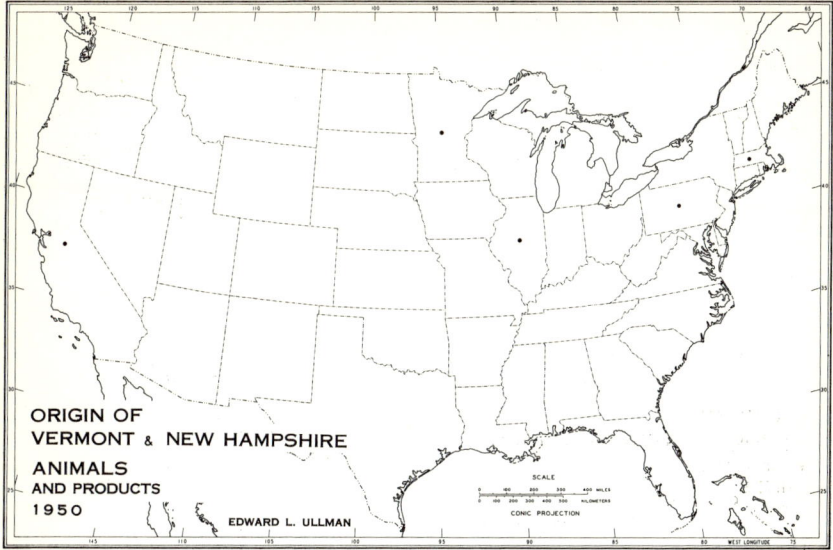

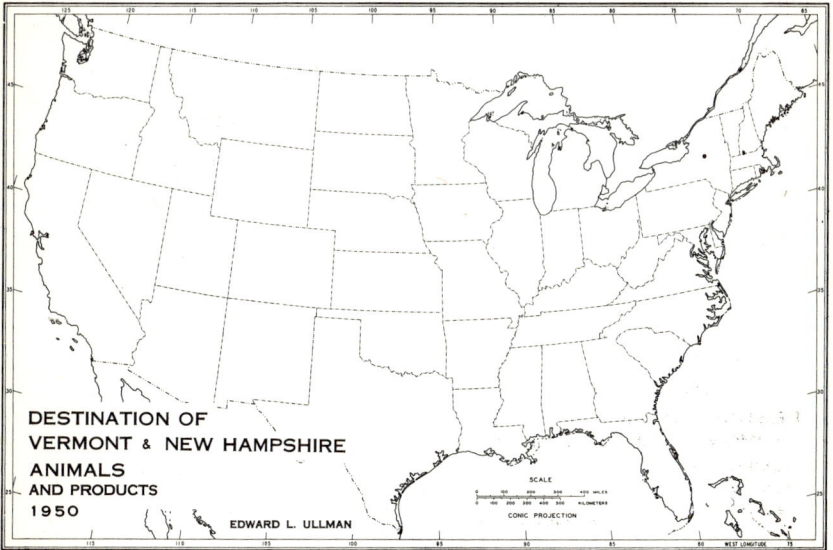

• 10,000 TONS   █ 100,000 TONS

159

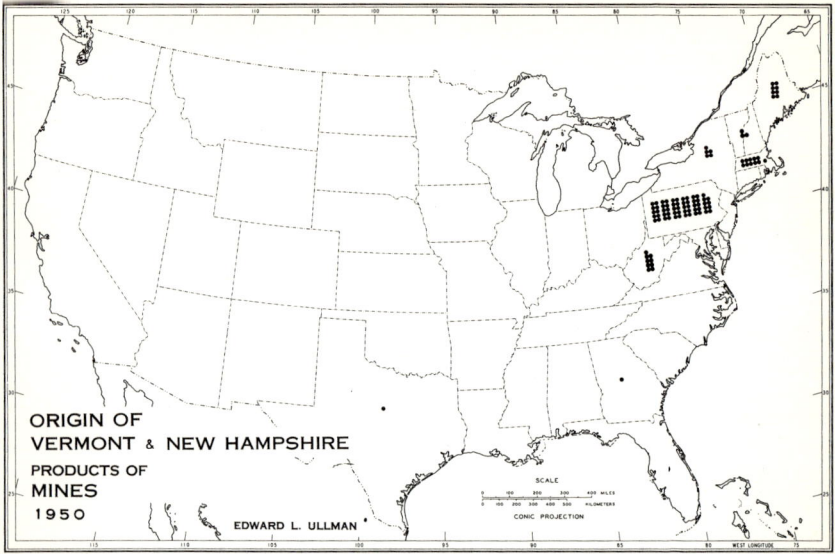

ORIGIN OF
VERMONT & NEW HAMPSHIRE
PRODUCTS OF
MINES
1950

EDWARD L. ULLMAN

SCALE

CONIC PROJECTION

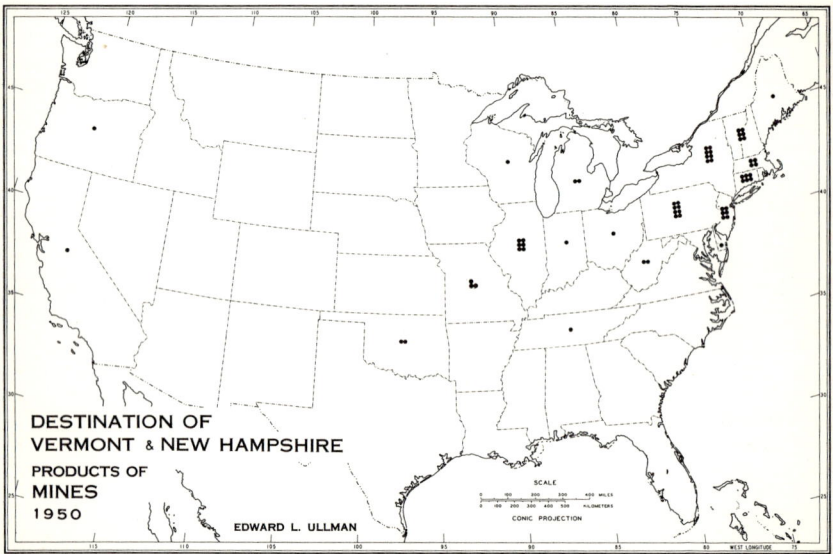

DESTINATION OF
VERMONT & NEW HAMPSHIRE
PRODUCTS OF
MINES
1950

EDWARD L. ULLMAN

SCALE

CONIC PROJECTION

• 10,000 TONS   ▮ 100,000 TONS

160

ORIGIN OF
VERMONT & NEW HAMPSHIRE
PRODUCTS OF
FORESTS
1950

EDWARD L. ULLMAN

DESTINATION OF
VERMONT & NEW HAMPSHIRE
PRODUCTS OF
FORESTS
1950

EDWARD L. ULLMAN

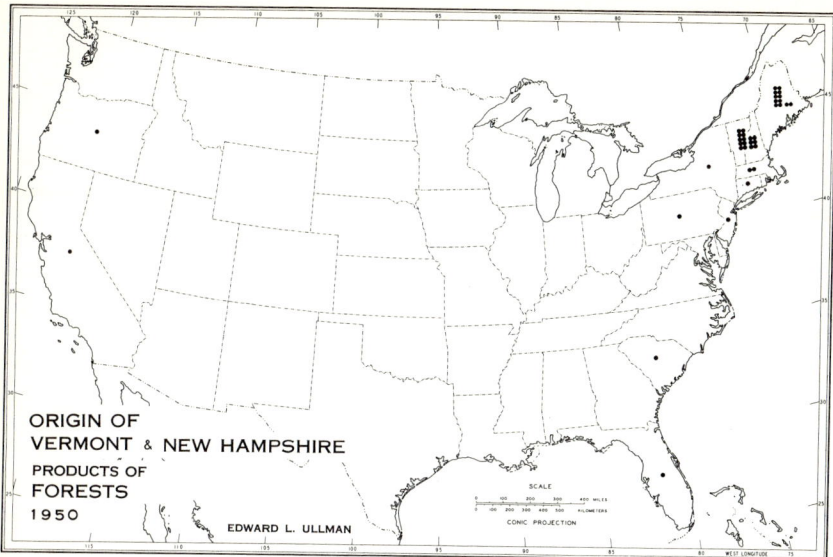

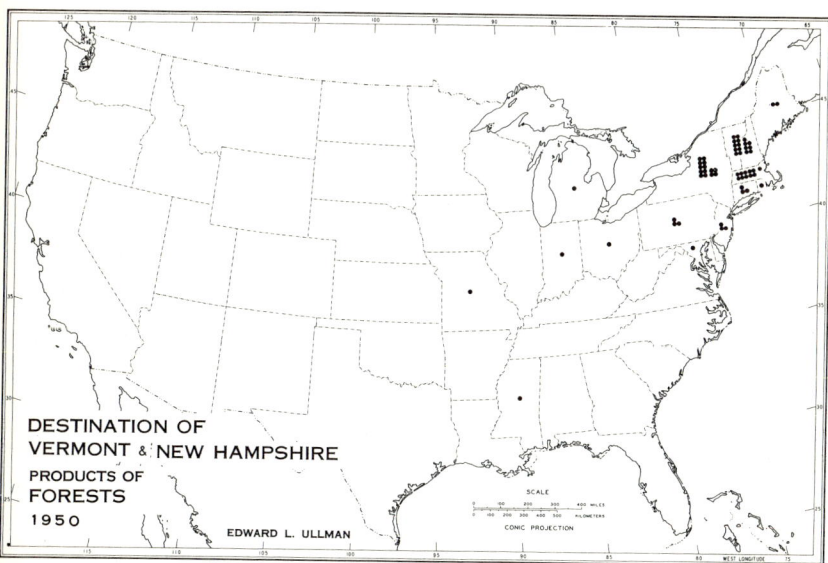

• 10,000 TONS   ▋ 100,000 TONS

161

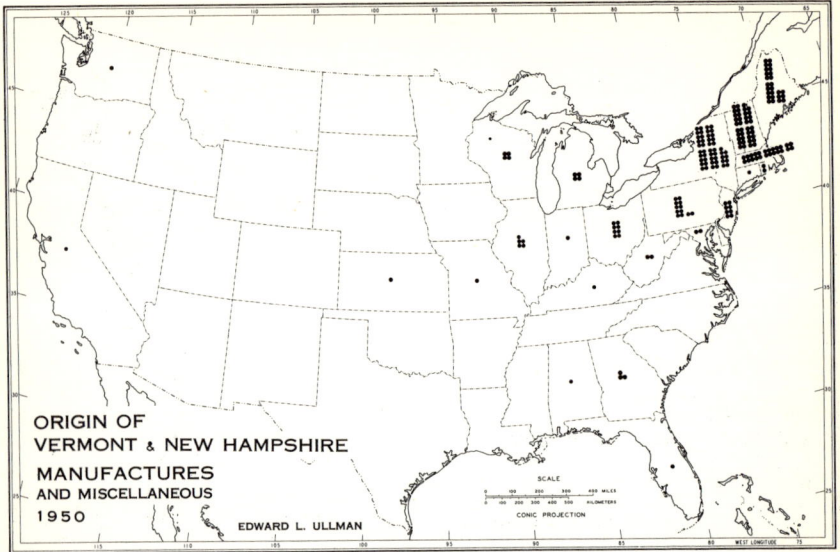

ORIGIN OF
VERMONT & NEW HAMPSHIRE
MANUFACTURES
AND MISCELLANEOUS
1950

EDWARD L. ULLMAN

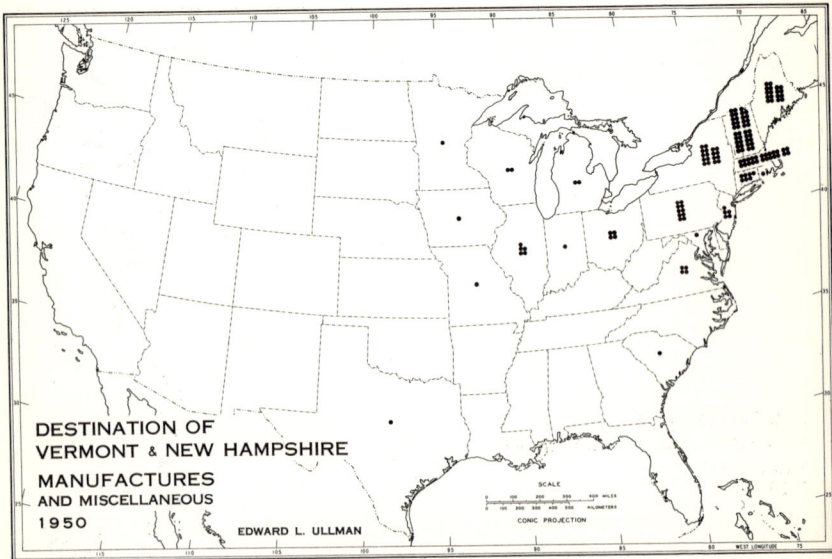

DESTINATION OF
VERMONT & NEW HAMPSHIRE
MANUFACTURES
AND MISCELLANEOUS
1950

EDWARD L. ULLMAN

• 10,000 TONS   ▮ 100,000 TONS

162

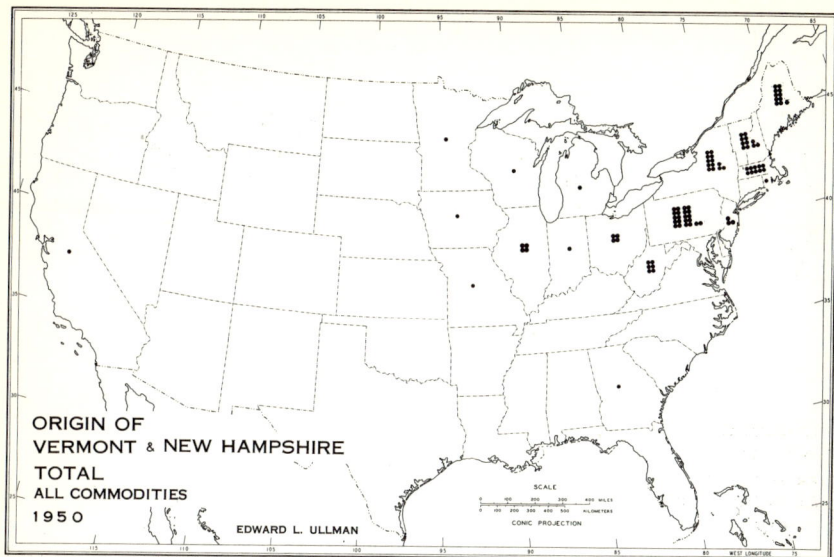

ORIGIN OF
VERMONT & NEW HAMPSHIRE
TOTAL
ALL COMMODITIES
1950

EDWARD L. ULLMAN

SCALE

CONIC PROJECTION

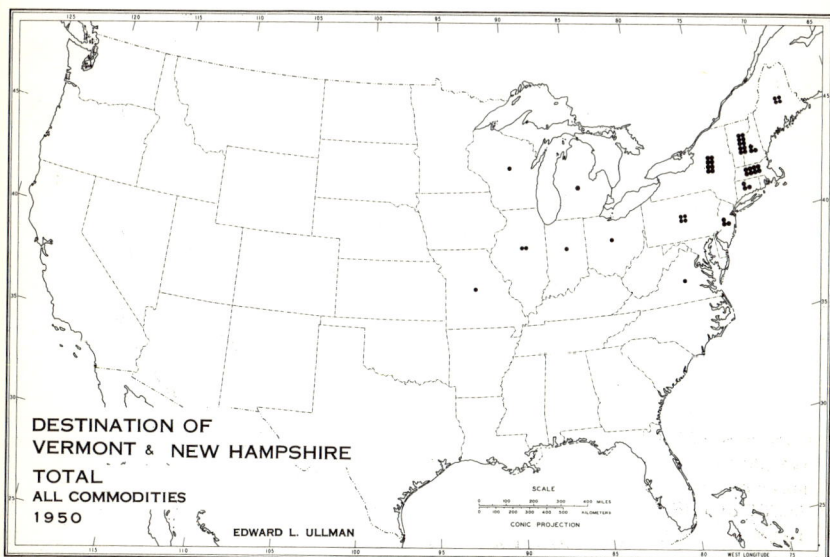

DESTINATION OF
VERMONT & NEW HAMPSHIRE
TOTAL
ALL COMMODITIES
1950

EDWARD L. ULLMAN

SCALE

CONIC PROJECTION

• 50,000 TONS   500,000 TONS

163

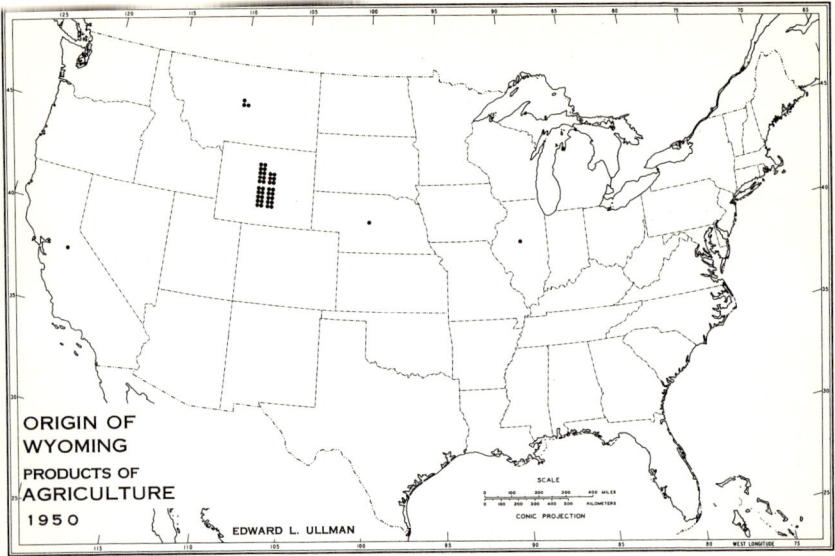

ORIGIN OF
WYOMING
PRODUCTS OF
AGRICULTURE
1950

EDWARD L. ULLMAN

SCALE
CONIC PROJECTION

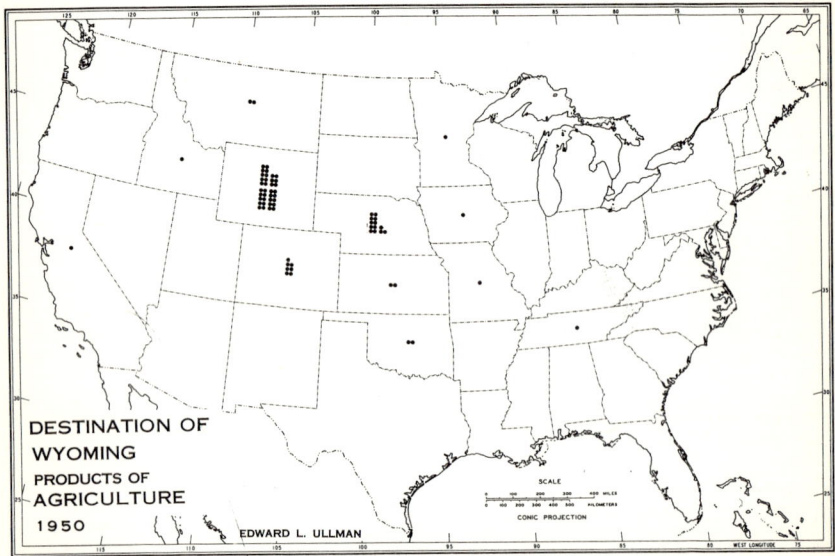

DESTINATION OF
WYOMING
PRODUCTS OF
AGRICULTURE
1950

EDWARD L. ULLMAN

SCALE
CONIC PROJECTION

• 10,000 TONS   ▮ 100,000 TONS

164

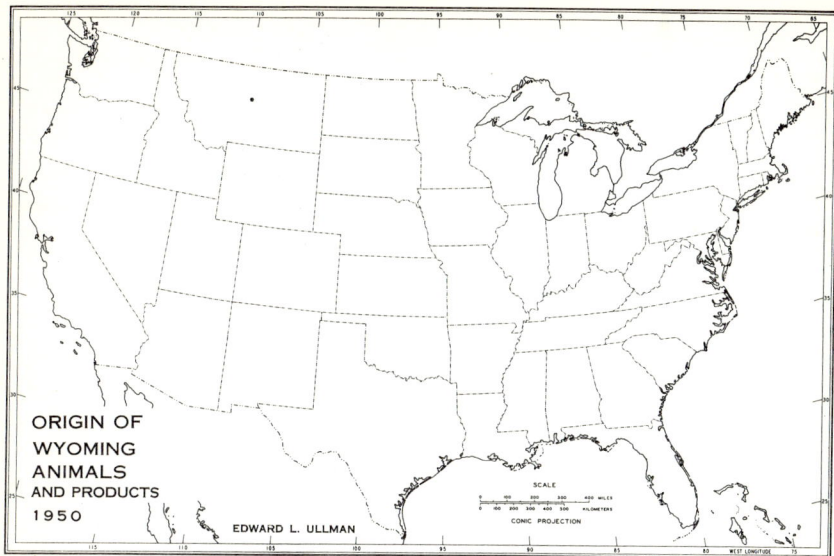

ORIGIN OF
WYOMING
ANIMALS
AND PRODUCTS
1950

EDWARD L. ULLMAN

SCALE

CONIC PROJECTION

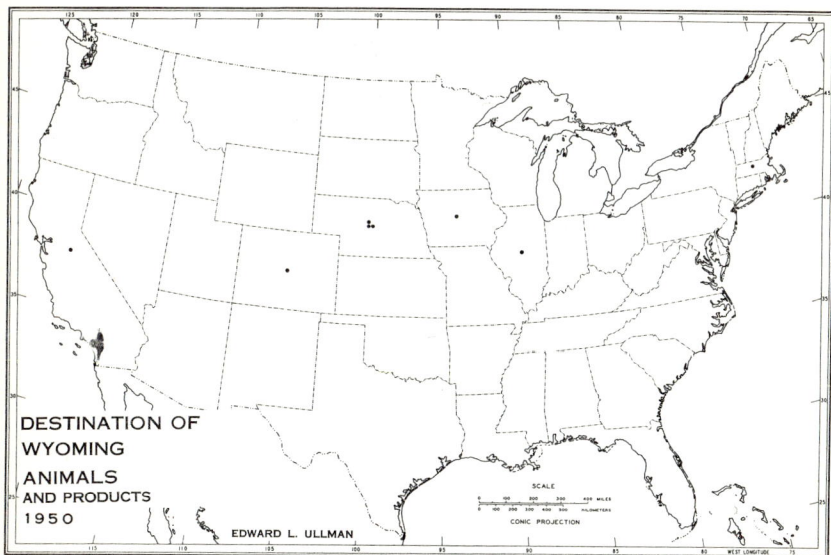

DESTINATION OF
WYOMING
ANIMALS
AND PRODUCTS
1950

EDWARD L. ULLMAN

SCALE

CONIC PROJECTION

• 10,000 TONS   ▮ 100,000 TONS

165

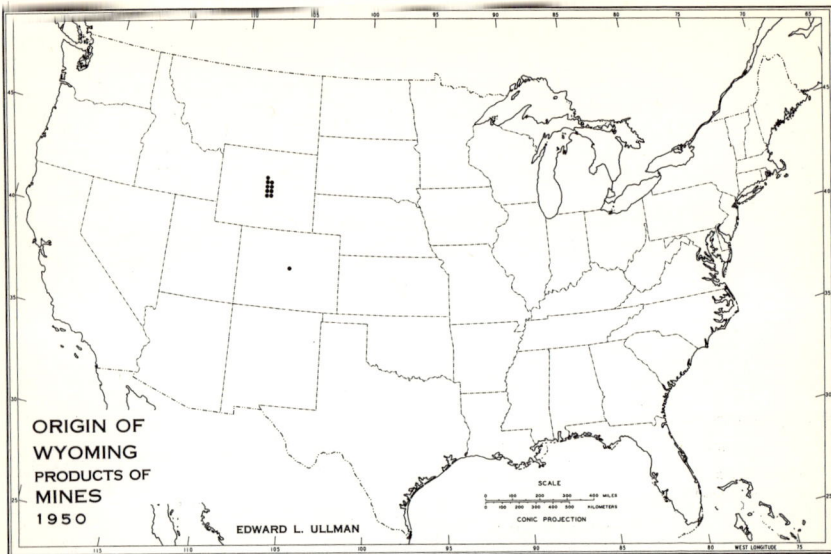

ORIGIN OF
WYOMING
PRODUCTS OF
MINES
1950

EDWARD L. ULLMAN

SCALE

CONIC PROJECTION

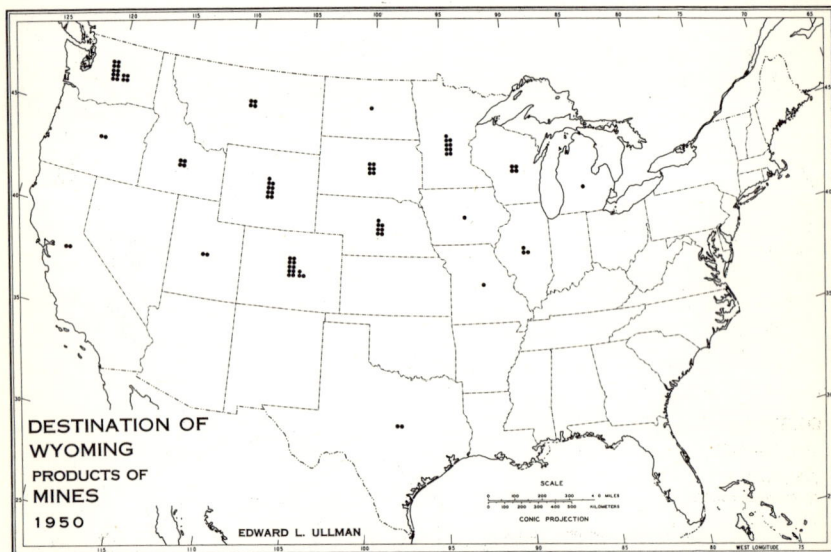

DESTINATION OF
WYOMING
PRODUCTS OF
MINES
1950

EDWARD L. ULLMAN

SCALE

CONIC PROJECTION

• 50,000 TONS   500,000 TONS

166

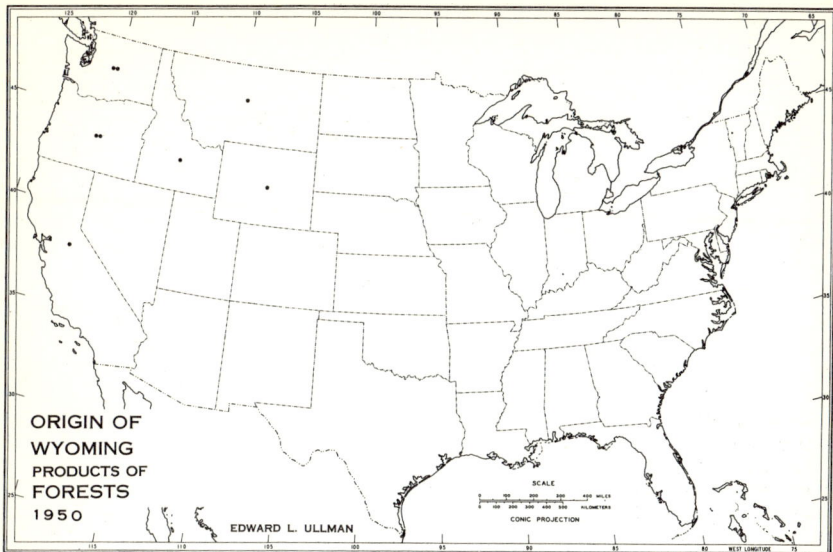

ORIGIN OF
WYOMING
PRODUCTS OF
FORESTS
1950

EDWARD L. ULLMAN

SCALE

CONIC PROJECTION

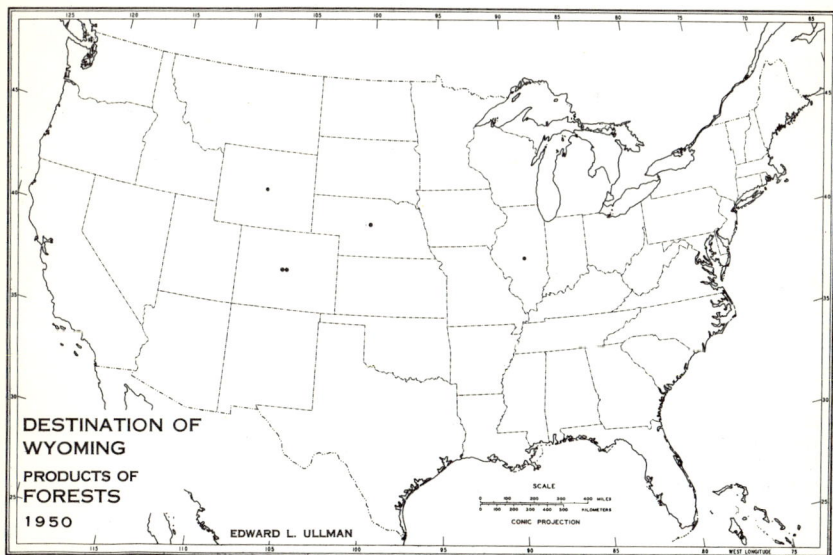

DESTINATION OF
WYOMING
PRODUCTS OF
FORESTS
1950

EDWARD L. ULLMAN

SCALE

CONIC PROJECTION

• 10,000 TONS   100,000 TONS

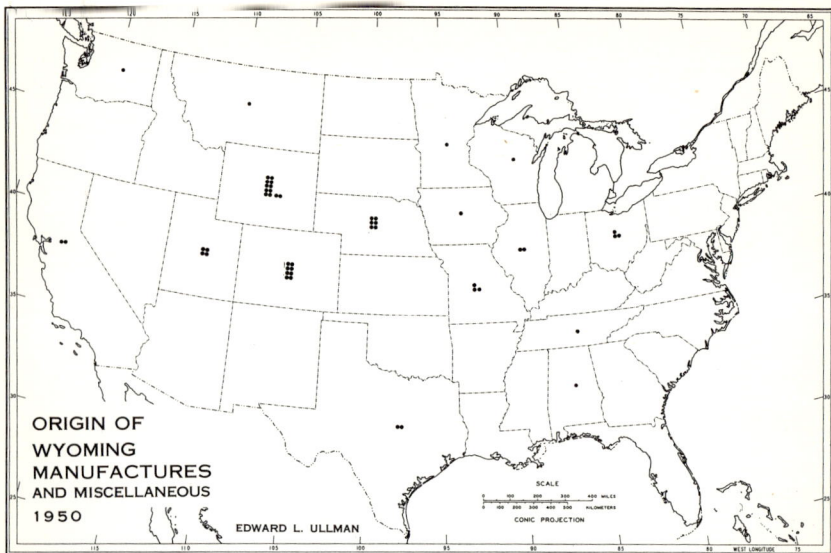

ORIGIN OF
WYOMING
MANUFACTURES
AND MISCELLANEOUS
1950

EDWARD L. ULLMAN

SCALE

CONIC PROJECTION

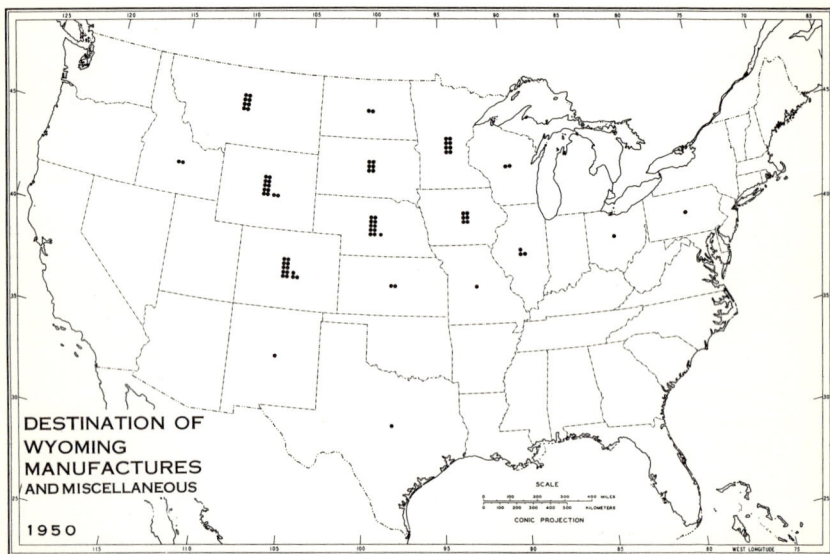

DESTINATION OF
WYOMING
MANUFACTURES
AND MISCELLANEOUS
1950

SCALE

CONIC PROJECTION

· 10,000 TONS ▮ 100,000 TONS

168

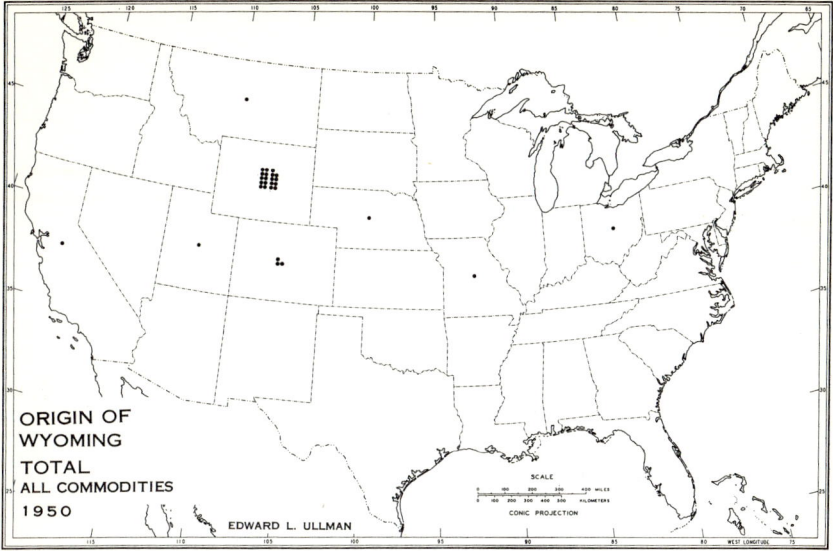

ORIGIN OF
WYOMING

TOTAL
ALL COMMODITIES
1950

EDWARD L. ULLMAN

SCALE

CONIC PROJECTION

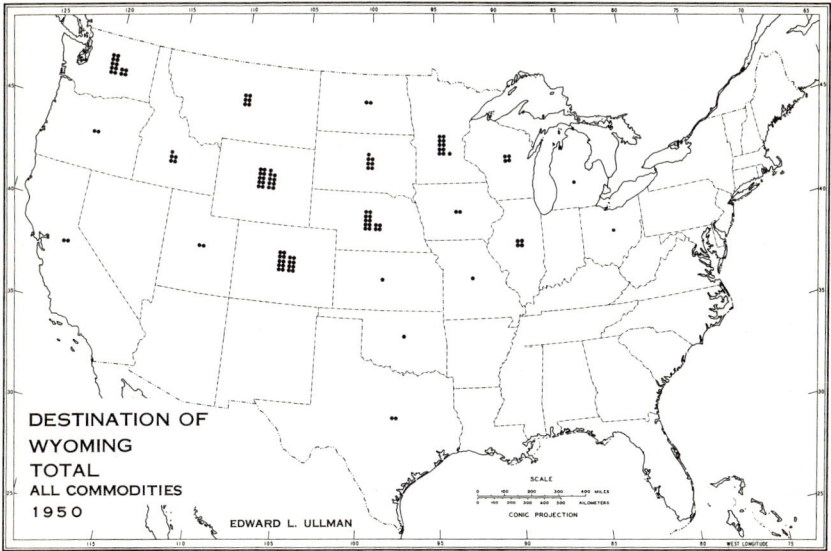

DESTINATION OF
WYOMING

TOTAL
ALL COMMODITIES
1950

EDWARD L. ULLMAN

SCALE

CONIC PROJECTION

• 50,000 TONS   ▓ 500,000 TONS

V

American Ocean Freight Traffic

THIS CHAPTER contains maps showing: (1) flow of United States foreign ocean-borne trade for dry cargo in 1948; (2) tanker traffic flow in 1947; (3) United States domestic ocean traffic flow in 1950; and (4) origin and destination by United States coastal areas for domestic ocean traffic in 1950. The years chosen are fairly representative, except for certain foreign trade routes, and were the only ones for which data were available to the author. Only a brief analysis of the flows will be given; general principles incorporating data from the maps have already been discussed in Chapter III, and mention has been made in Chapters I and IV of some specific domestic flows.

DOMESTIC TRADE

United States domestic or coastwise ocean trade between coastal ports is heavy, about the same as total foreign trade in most postwar years, even if Great Lakes and noncontiguous areas (Puerto Rico, Hawaii, Alaska) are excluded, as well as the short-haul categories of internal, intraport, and local. Bulk products, especially petroleum, are the main commodities handled, a characteristic of water traffic even more than of rail.

Of the coastal sectors the North Atlantic coastal region has the heaviest trade. It is the gateway to the industrial belt and naturally has the heaviest ocean traffic, just as it has the heaviest land traffic. It also receives more than it ships in a ratio of about 3 to 1, much the same as for rail traffic, a natural corollary when an industrial area imports raw materials. The Gulf is second, but is a heavy exporter of raw materials, principally petroleum, and its total outbound tonnage therefore exceeds its inbound almost 7 to 1.

The volume of trade for 1950 of all the coastal regions is shown in Table 4. (Great Lakes and noncontiguous traffic are also shown for comparative purposes but are not mapped, except for Alaska.)

TABLE 4
DOMESTIC DEEP-SEA AND LAKEWISE TRAFFIC, 1950*
(1, 000's of short tons of 2, 000 lbs.)

Coastal Region	Shipments	Receipts
North Atlantic	40, 815	119, 041
South Atlantic	622	10, 539
Gulf	97, 938	14, 860
South Pacific	35, 573	20, 997
North Pacific	4, 182	11, 873
Total Coastal Regions	179, 130	177, 310
Alaska	200	1, 210
Puerto Rico & Virgin Is.	1, 287	1, 630
Hawaii & other Pacific Is.	1, 895	2, 320
Total Noncontiguous	3, 382	5, 160
Great Lakes†	169, 909	169, 950

*Data for this table and the ensuing discussion from Water-Borne Commerce of the United States, Domestic, Deep-Sea and Lakewise Traffic, Calendar Year 1950, Board of Engineers for Rivers and Harbors, Corps of Engineers, Department of the Army (Washington, D. C., June, 1952). Data include intraregional traffic as well as interregional; Great Lakes therefore has virtually identical shipments and receipts. This is also virtually true for the total for all coastal regions, the approximately 1, 820, 000 tons greater shipments representing essentially greater receipts by the noncontiguous regions.
†Domestic only; excludes about 25, 000, 000 tons to Canada and 4, 000, 000 from Canada.

Domestic trade for 1950, in short tons of 2, 000 pounds, is shown on flow maps with both directions combined and on origin and destination dot maps, which can be used to indicate direction of flow and also to show the volume of intraregional trade. (For example, the heavy coal movement from Hampton Roads, Virginia, up the Atlantic Coast, as shown on the map in Chapter I, does not show on the flow maps which indicate interregional trade only, and Hampton Roads is within the North Atlantic region; its volume, however, is included

171

(in the origin and destination dot map for the North Atlantic region, in the category of tonnage shipped with the region.)[1]

Data are reported for coastal areas: North Atlantic (from the Canadian border to the North Carolina border); South Atlantic (to Key West, Florida); Gulf; South Pacific (California); and North Pacific (Washington, Oregon), with trade to Alaska also shown. (Puerto Rico and Hawaii are also listed in the source data but are not mapped.) The extent of the individual coastal sectors is shown on the various origin and destination maps.

North Atlantic

The greatest volume of dry cargo traffic handled in the North Atlantic region is intraregional. Of this almost one-half (approximately 12, 000, 000 tons) is coal, principally from Hampton Roads, received by rail from the Pocahontas coal fields and shipped up the coast to Middle Atlantic and New England ports (see heavy flows on the railway traffic map, frontispiece, and the discussion in Chapter I). Sand, gravel, and rock (approximately 8, 000, 000 tons)--ubiquitous, volume, short-haul commodities--account for about one-third, with the remaining one-sixth of dry cargo divided up among lesser commodities.

The biggest traffic of all is in petroleum, both crude and refined (approximately 70, 000, 000 tons), from the Gulf and some (approximately 4, 000, 000 tons) in 1948 from California. Even intraregionally in the North Atlantic, more than 14, 000, 000 tons are handled, almost all refined products, presumably from local refineries, a testimonial to the importance of the commodity.

A variety of other items is received from the whole country, as will be noted subsequently.

---

1. Source of data for domestic traffic is U.S. Department of the Army, Corps of Engineers, Water-Borne Commerce of the United States, Domestic Deep-Sea and Lakewise Traffic, Calendar Year 1950 (Washington, D.C., June, 1952). This report also lists shipments by individual commodities. Tanker traffic was obtained by adding together the various liquid petroleum products, as reported in Group 5. The remainder of total traffic is classified as dry cargo, although a tiny fraction of this may be liquid.

South Atlantic

South Atlantic trade is the smallest of all coastal regions. No single commodity exceeds 30,000 tons to or from the North Atlantic except gasoline (320,000 tons) and coal tar products (74,000 tons), both from the North Atlantic. By far the largest receipts are petroleum and products from the Gulf, almost entirely refined (approximately 38,000,000 tons) in contrast to the crude receipts of the North Atlantic, which has refineries. Other items from the Gulf are sulfur (approximately 155,000 tons) from Texas or Louisiana and phosphate (approximately 66,000 tons) from Tampa, which together account for about three-fourths of the dry cargo trade. Trade with the Pacific is negligible and from the North Pacific almost nonexistent, since the latter is primarily a forest products shipper and the South has its own forests. Complementarity does not exist, just as was the case for rail shipments.

Gulf

The principal commodity shipped from the Gulf is petroleum and products to the North Atlantic and secondarily to the South Atlantic, as already noted, with heavy intraregional movements also. Petroleum, because it is so easily loaded or unloaded (pumped), and because it moves in such enormous volume, moves short distances by water, as well as long, in contrast to most other commodities.

In dry cargo, intraregional Gulf trade, phosphate (428,000 tons) and sulfur (186,000 tons) account for more than three-fourths of the flow, almost as large a proportion as to the South Atlantic. To the North Pacific sulfur also predominates (144,000 tons), accounting for more than three-fourths of the total volume, presumably being used in the paper industry of that area. Iron and steel products account for almost all of the remainder to the North Pacific and represent most of the volume (73,000 tons) to the South Pacific. This is primarily Birmingham iron and steel, shipped through Mobile. [2]

2. For details of this trade, which was larger before the war, before the Pacific Coast built its own blast furnaces, see Edward L. Ullman, Mobile--Industrial Seaport and Trade Center (1943; privately printed).

By far the leading commodity handled in the South Pacific (California) region is petroleum and products, shipped intra-regionally (mostly in crude form) and to the Pacific Northwest (mostly in refined form), with a small amount (mostly refined, but mainly fuel oils) to the North Atlantic. This latter flow was important before the war but has been declining and is probably even less today (although no data are available), as California uses its own for its growing population. The same is true, or will be shortly, of the flow to the Pacific Northwest, where Alberta oil is now coming in via pipeline (see Chapter IV, discussion of Washington).

In the United States ocean petroleum flow pattern as a whole, the Gulf essentially supplies the East Coast, along with imports from Venezuela, and California the West Coast, with some exports to the Pacific.

Other leading shipments from the South Pacific are canned fruits and vegetables (600,000 tons) to the North Atlantic and canned fruits (50,000 tons) to the Gulf, practically the entire water export of California to these two regions, and a natural product of produce-specializing California. Fresh produce, as has been noted, goes by rail. To the North Pacific the two most important shipments, accounting for two-thirds of the volume, are cement (231,000 tons) and salt (190,000 tons), both from San Francisco Bay. The cement goes largely to Puget Sound to supplement inadequate local supplies, and the salt is part of the movement which reflects San Francisco Bay as the salt supplier for the Pacific Coast, just as Great Salt Lake is for the intermountain area. The salt is virtually the only sea salt produced by natural evaporation in the United States. Other items to the North Pacific include automobiles (68,000 tons) from California's branch plants and lumber (29,000 tons), presumably redwood, which is not grown in the North Pacific and is renowned for its keeping and other qualities.

North Pacific and Alaska

The North Pacific outbound trade is dominated by lumber, just as is its rail trade, although the inbound volume of petroleum (almost all refined--see the discussions under South Pacific and in Chapter IV) is far greater than all other trade, as is the case with all coastal shipping in the United States. For dry cargo, however, the North Pacific is overwhelmingly

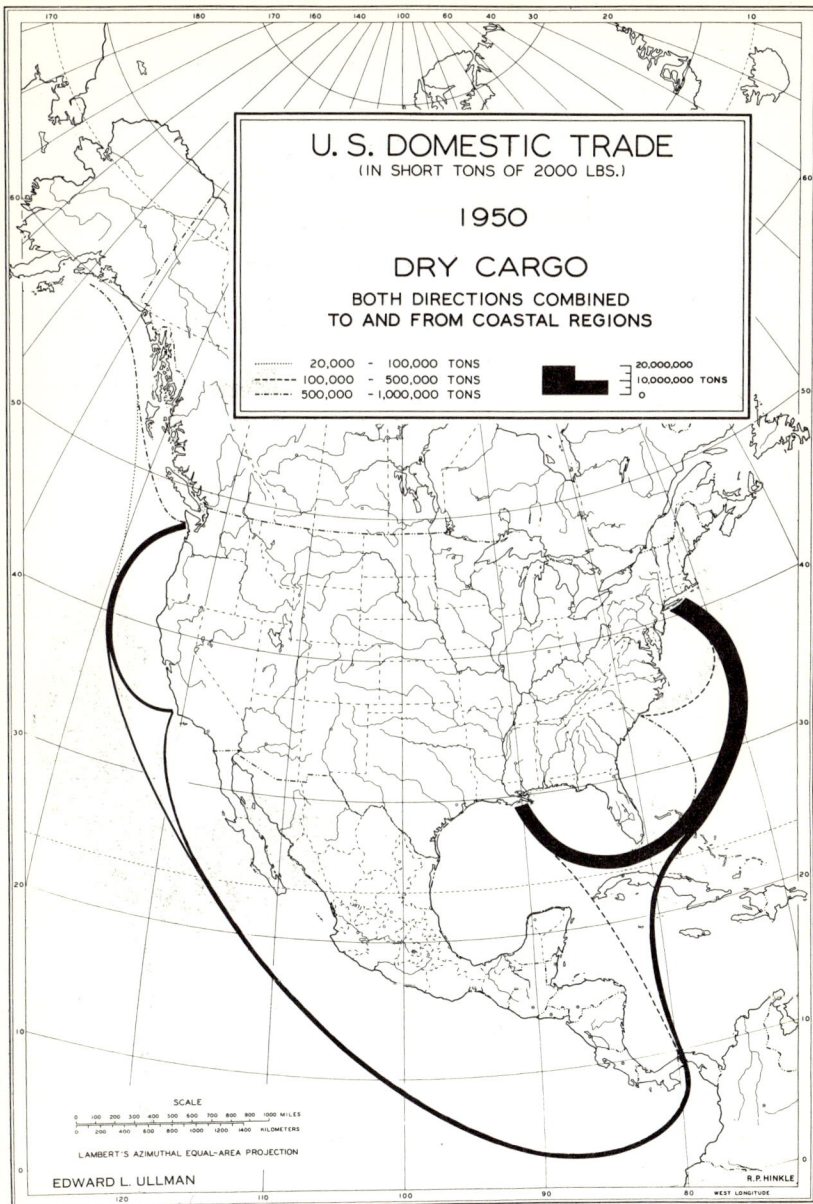

U. S. DOMESTIC TRADE
(IN SHORT TONS OF 2000 LBS.)

1950

DRY CARGO

BOTH DIRECTIONS COMBINED
TO AND FROM COASTAL REGIONS

20,000 - 100,000 TONS
100,000 - 500,000 TONS
500,000 - 1,000,000 TONS

20,000,000
10,000,000 TONS
0

SCALE

0 100 200 300 400 500 600 700 800 1000 MILES
0   200   400   600   800   1000 1200 1400 KILOMETERS

LAMBERT'S AZIMUTHAL EQUAL-AREA PROJECTION

EDWARD L. ULLMAN

R.P. HINKLE

WEST LONGITUDE

175

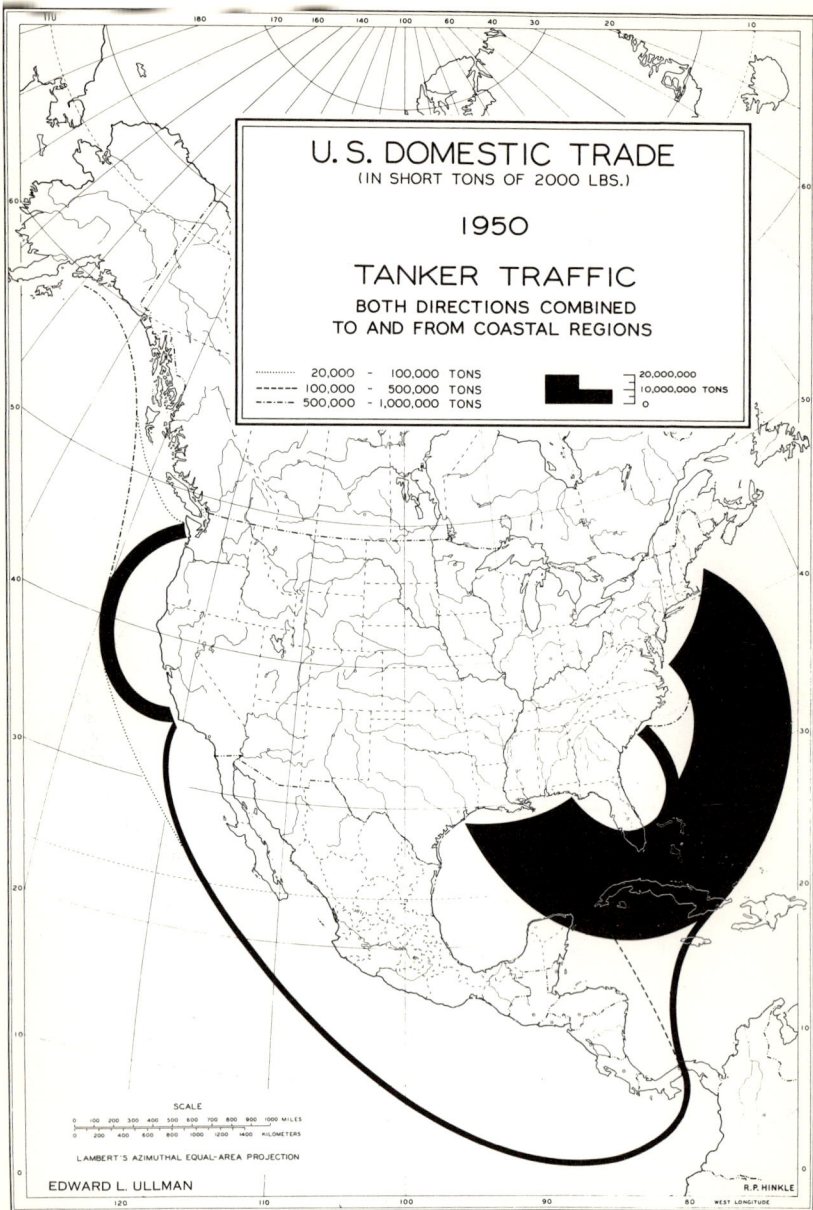

U. S. DOMESTIC TRADE
(IN SHORT TONS OF 2000 LBS.)

1950

TANKER TRAFFIC
BOTH DIRECTIONS COMBINED
TO AND FROM COASTAL REGIONS

.... 20,000 - 100,000 TONS
- - - - - - 100,000 - 500,000 TONS
-·-·-·- 500,000 - 1,000,000 TONS

20,000,000
10,000,000 TONS
0

SCALE

LAMBERT'S AZIMUTHAL EQUAL-AREA PROJECTION

EDWARD L. ULLMAN

R.P. HINKLE

WEST LONGITUDE

176

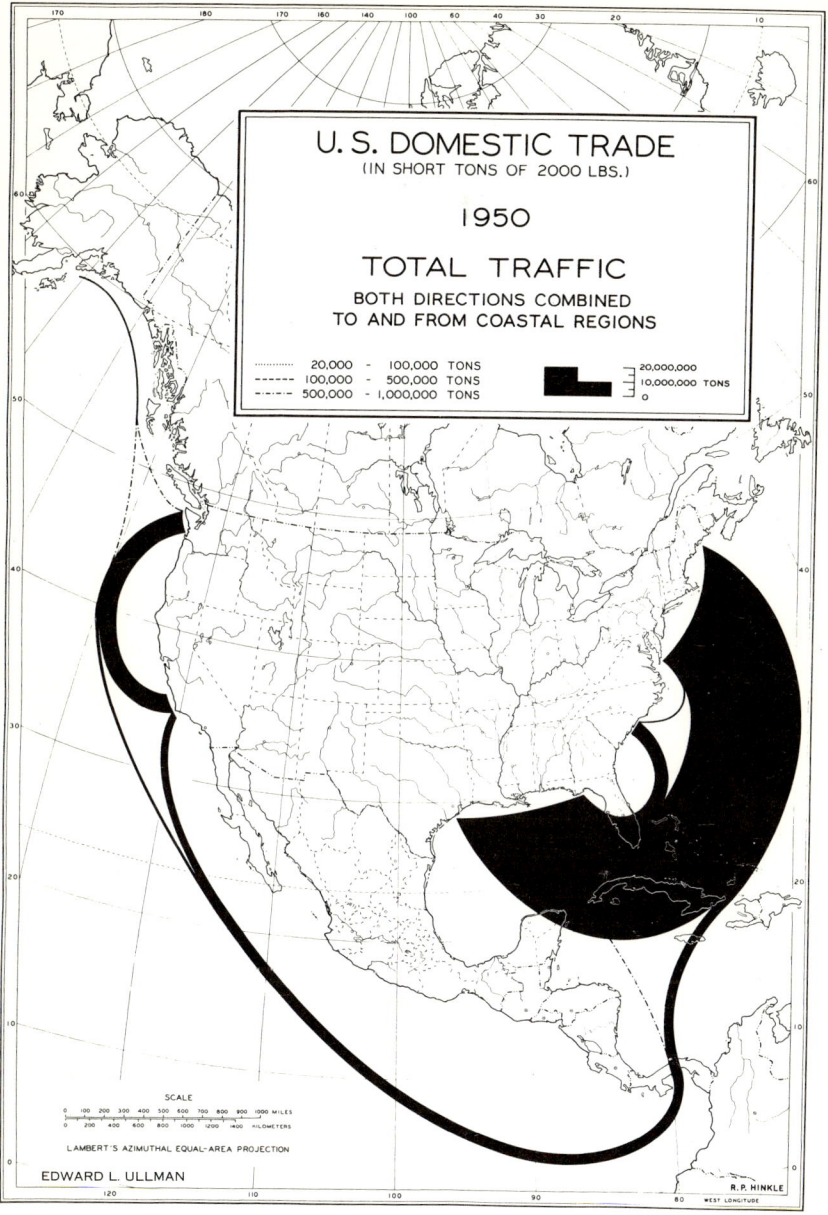

U. S. DOMESTIC TRADE
(IN SHORT TONS OF 2000 LBS.)

1950

TOTAL TRAFFIC
BOTH DIRECTIONS COMBINED
TO AND FROM COASTAL REGIONS

.... 20,000 - 100,000 TONS
- - - - - - 100,000 - 500,000 TONS
-·-·-·- 500,000 - 1,000,000 TONS

20,000,000
10,000,000 TONS
0

SCALE

0 100 200 300 400 500 600 700 800 900 1000 MILES
0 200 400 600 800 1000 1200 1400 KILOMETERS

LAMBERT'S AZIMUTHAL EQUAL-AREA PROJECTION

EDWARD L. ULLMAN

R. P. HINKLE

WEST LONGITUDE

177

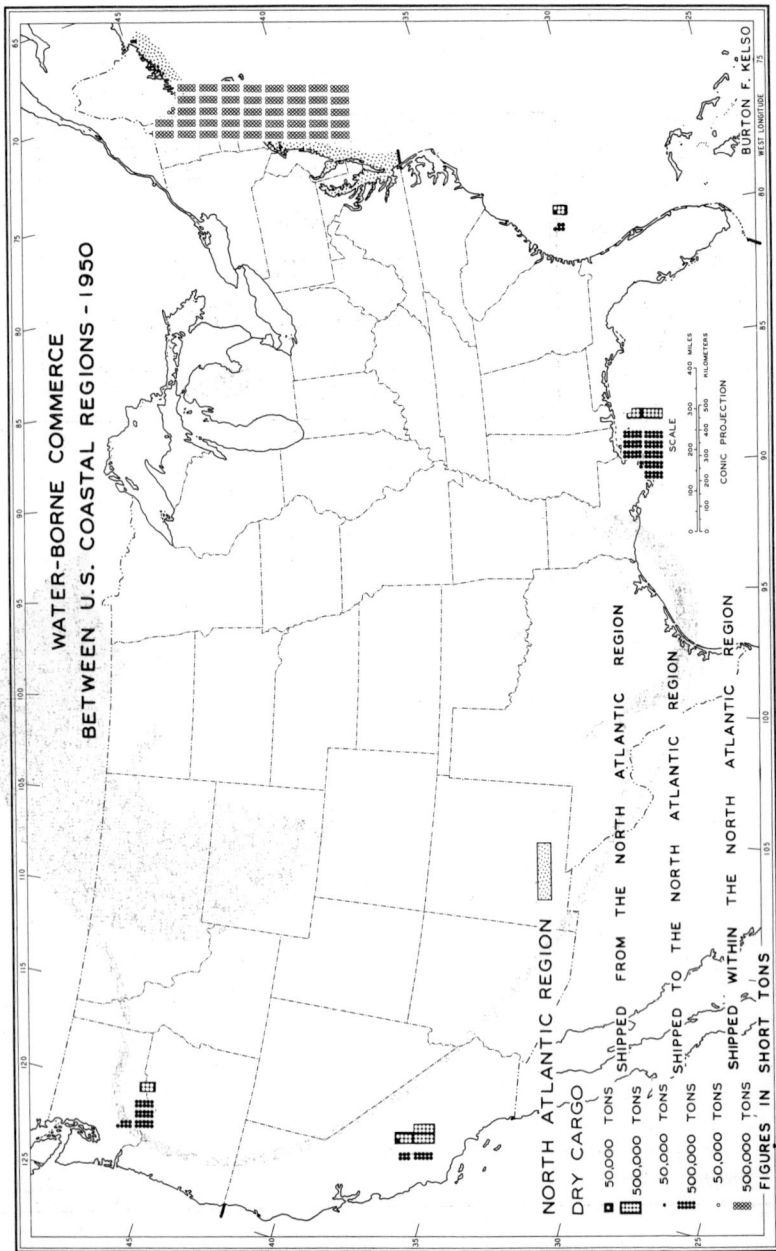

WATER-BORNE COMMERCE
BETWEEN U.S. COASTAL REGIONS - 1950

NORTH ATLANTIC REGION
DRY CARGO

50,000 TONS
500,000 TONS SHIPPED FROM THE NORTH ATLANTIC REGION
50,000 TONS
500,000 TONS SHIPPED TO THE NORTH ATLANTIC REGION
50,000 TONS
500,000 TONS SHIPPED WITHIN THE NORTH ATLANTIC REGION

FIGURES IN SHORT TONS

SCALE
CONIC PROJECTION

BURTON F. KELSO

WEST LONGITUDE

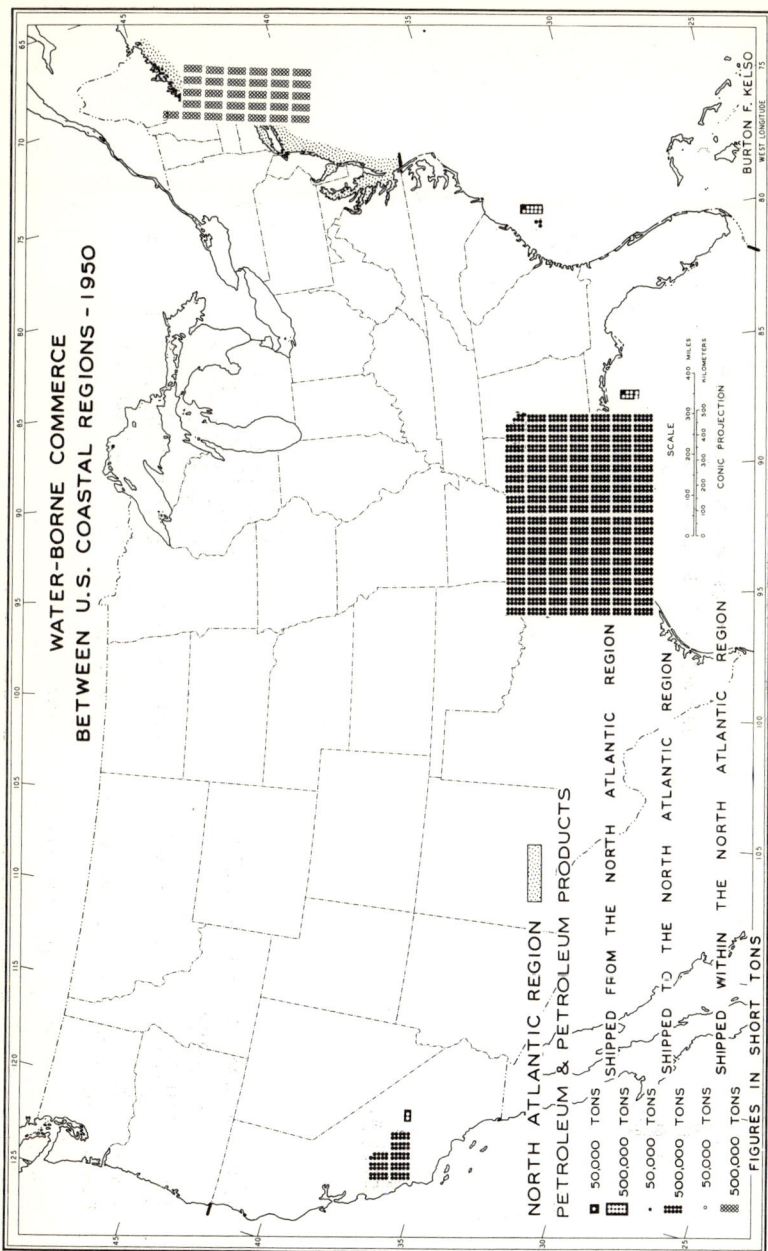

WATER-BORNE COMMERCE
BETWEEN U.S. COASTAL REGIONS - 1950

BURTON F. KELSO

NORTH ATLANTIC REGION

PETROLEUM & PETROLEUM PRODUCTS

NORTH ATLANTIC REGION

50,000 TONS SHIPPED FROM THE NORTH ATLANTIC REGION

500,000 TONS SHIPPED TO THE NORTH ATLANTIC REGION

50,000 TONS SHIPPED WITHIN THE NORTH ATLANTIC REGION

500,000 TONS

FIGURES IN SHORT TONS

SCALE

CONIC PROJECTION

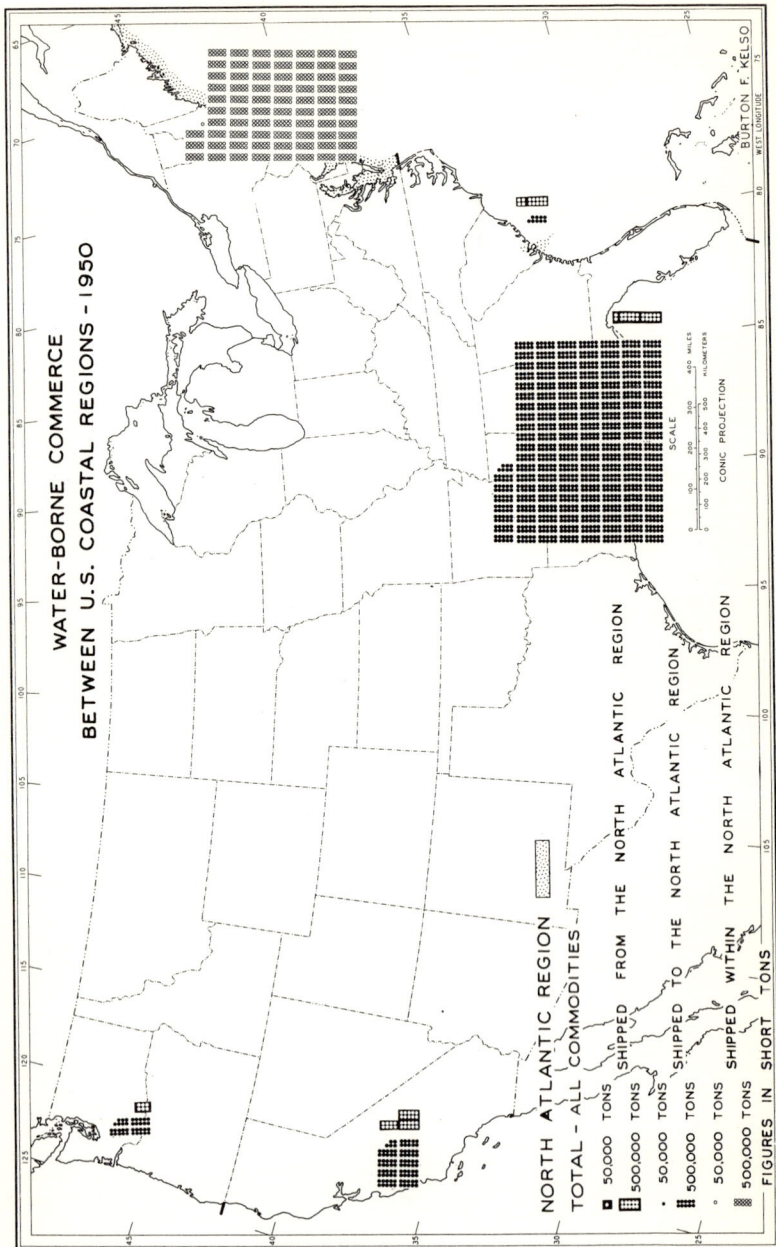

WATER-BORNE COMMERCE
BETWEEN U.S. COASTAL REGIONS - 1950

NORTH ATLANTIC REGION
TOTAL - ALL COMMODITIES

50,000 TONS
500,000 TONS } SHIPPED FROM THE NORTH ATLANTIC REGION

50,000 TONS
500,000 TONS } SHIPPED TO THE NORTH ATLANTIC REGION

50,000 TONS
500,000 TONS } SHIPPED WITHIN THE NORTH ATLANTIC REGION

FIGURES IN SHORT TONS

BURTON F. KELSO

SCALE
CONIC PROJECTION

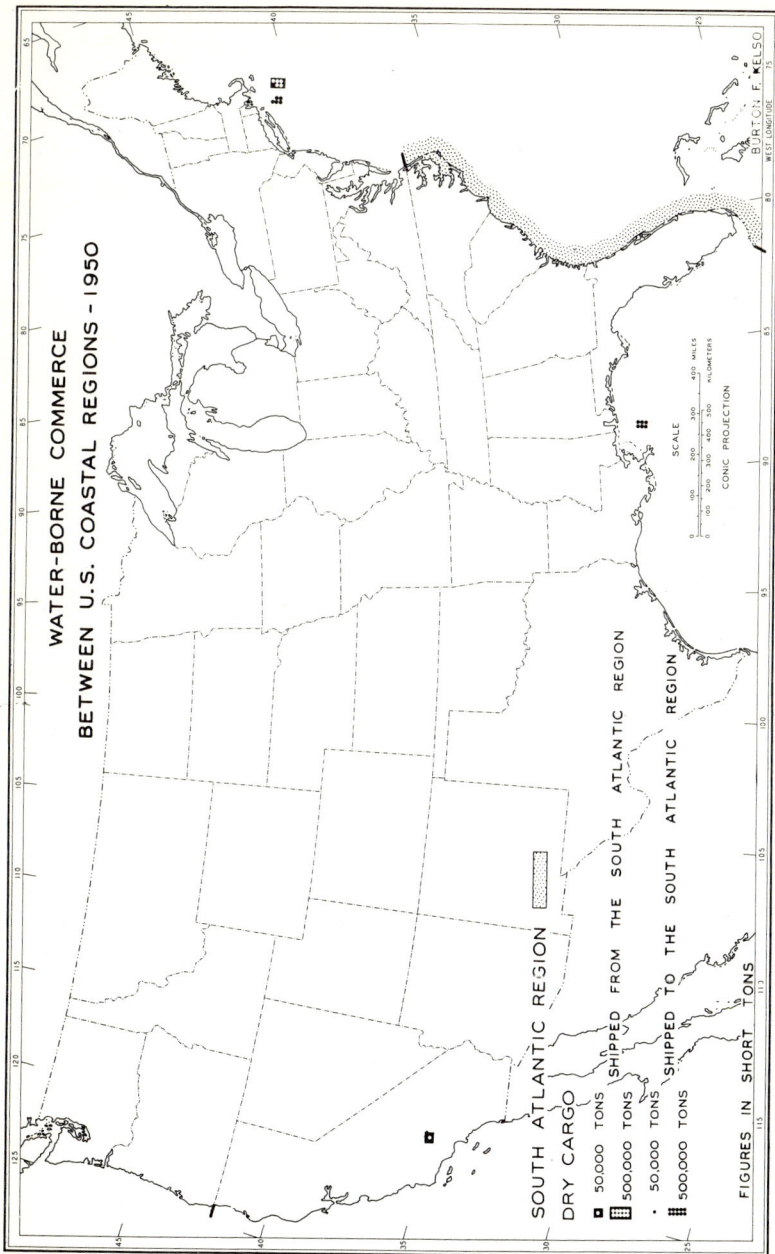

WATER-BORNE COMMERCE
BETWEEN U.S. COASTAL REGIONS - 1950

SOUTH ATLANTIC REGION

DRY CARGO

SHIPPED FROM THE SOUTH ATLANTIC REGION
□ 50,000 TONS
▦ 500,000 TONS

SHIPPED TO THE SOUTH ATLANTIC REGION
· 50,000 TONS
▦ 500,000 TONS

FIGURES IN SHORT TONS

SCALE

CONIC PROJECTION

BURTON F. KELSO

WEST LONGITUDE

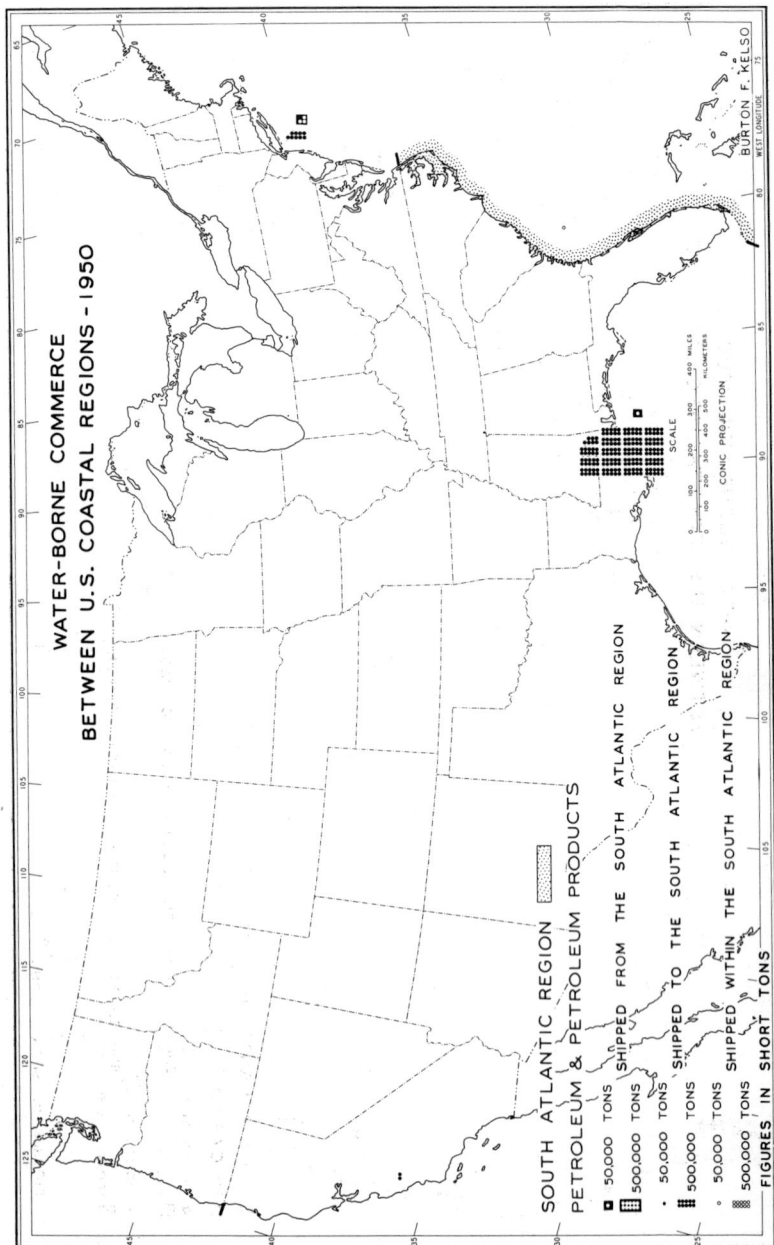

WATER-BORNE COMMERCE
BETWEEN U.S. COASTAL REGIONS - 1950

SOUTH ATLANTIC REGION
PETROLEUM & PETROLEUM PRODUCTS

■ 50,000 TONS
▦ 500,000 TONS   } SHIPPED FROM THE SOUTH ATLANTIC REGION

· 50,000 TONS
▦ 500,000 TONS   } SHIPPED TO THE SOUTH ATLANTIC REGION

○ 50,000 TONS
▨ 500,000 TONS   } SHIPPED WITHIN THE SOUTH ATLANTIC REGION

FIGURES IN SHORT TONS

BURTON F. KELSO

SCALE
CONIC PROJECTION

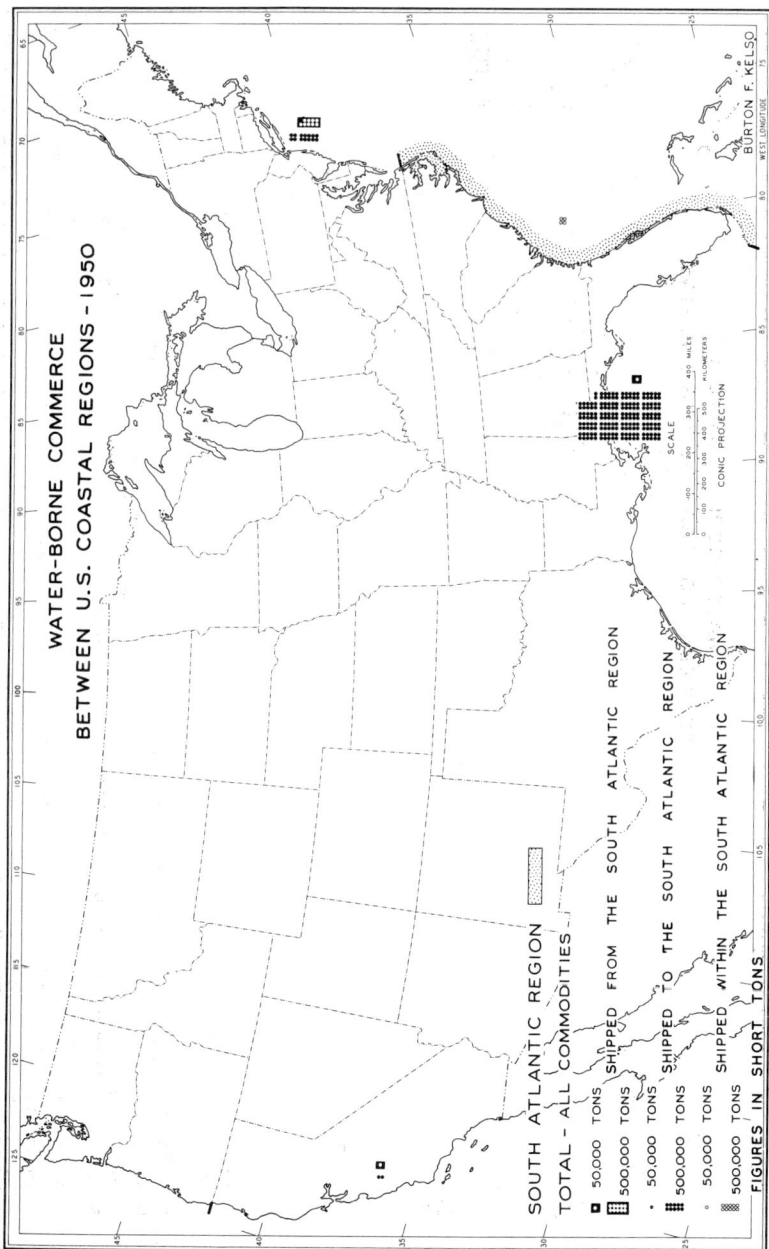

WATER-BORNE COMMERCE
BETWEEN U.S. COASTAL REGIONS - 1950

BURTON F. KELSO

SOUTH ATLANTIC REGION

TOTAL - ALL COMMODITIES

■	50,000 TONS
▦	500,000 TONS
·	50,000 TONS
▦	500,000 TONS
○	50,000 TONS
▨	500,000 TONS

SHIPPED FROM THE SOUTH ATLANTIC REGION

SHIPPED TO THE SOUTH ATLANTIC REGION

SHIPPED WITHIN THE SOUTH ATLANTIC REGION

FIGURES IN SHORT TONS

SCALE

CONIC PROJECTION

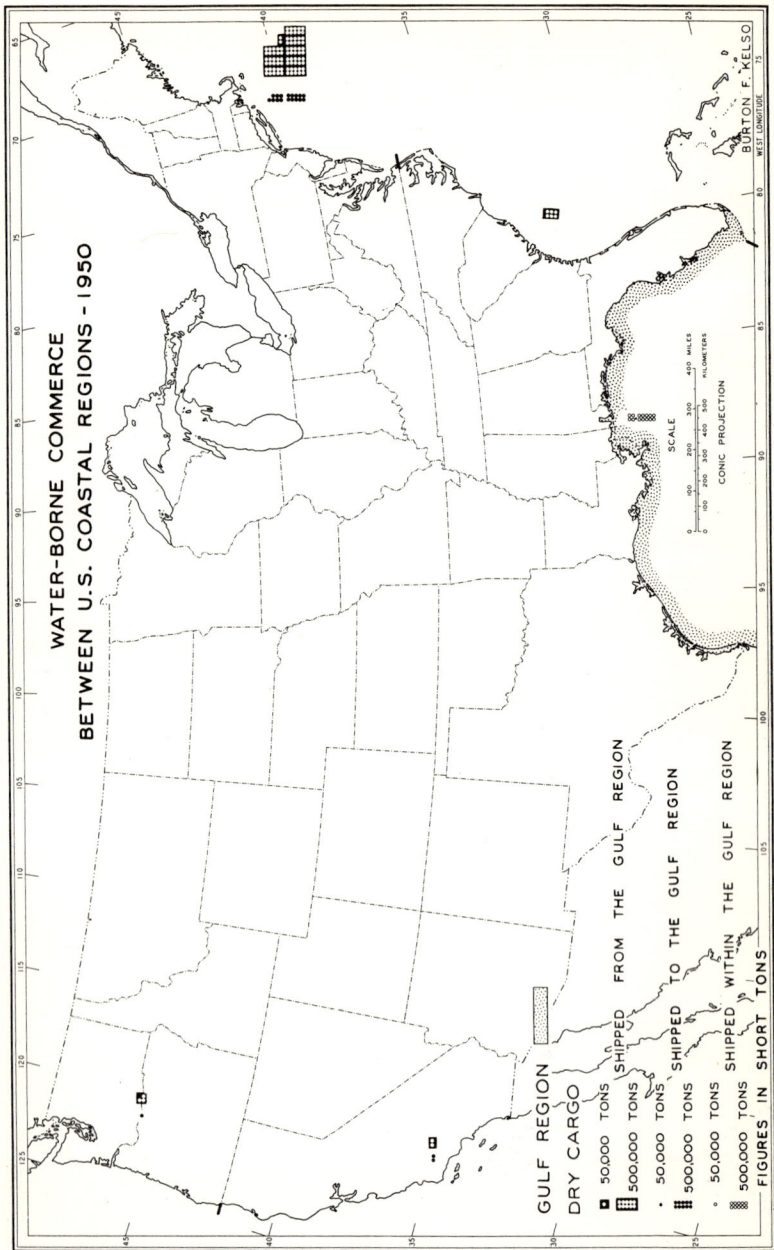

WATER-BORNE COMMERCE
BETWEEN U.S. COASTAL REGIONS - 1950

BURTON F. KELSO

SCALE
CONIC PROJECTION

GULF REGION
DRY CARGO

50,000 TONS   SHIPPED FROM THE GULF REGION
500,000 TONS

50,000 TONS   SHIPPED TO THE GULF REGION
500,000 TONS

50,000 TONS   SHIPPED WITHIN THE GULF REGION
500,000 TONS

FIGURES IN SHORT TONS

184

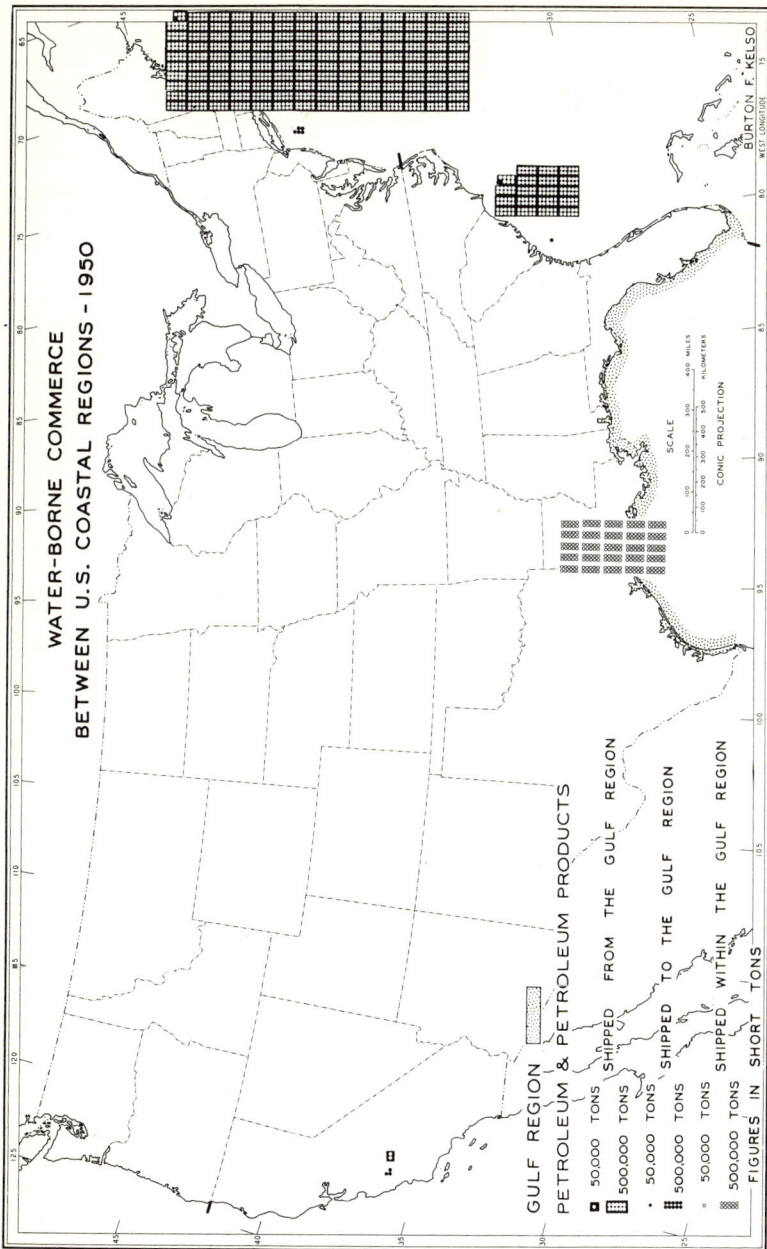

WATER-BORNE COMMERCE
BETWEEN U.S. COASTAL REGIONS - 1950

GULF REGION

PETROLEUM & PETROLEUM PRODUCTS

50,000 TONS
500,000 TONS SHIPPED FROM THE GULF REGION
50,000 TONS
500,000 TONS SHIPPED TO THE GULF REGION
50,000 TONS
500,000 TONS SHIPPED WITHIN THE GULF REGION

FIGURES IN SHORT TONS

SCALE

CONIC PROJECTION

BURTON F. KELSO

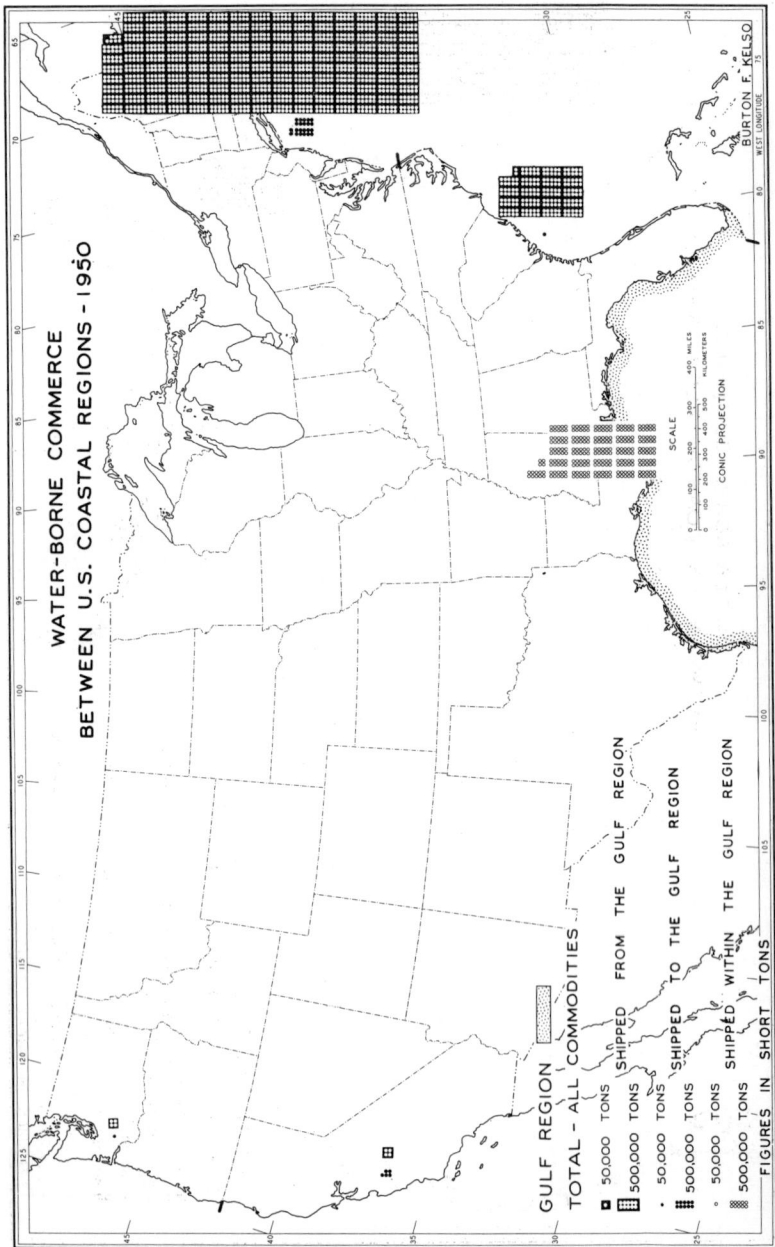

WATER-BORNE COMMERCE
BETWEEN U.S. COASTAL REGIONS - 1950

BURTON F. KELSO

WEST LONGITUDE

SCALE

MILES
0   100   200   300   400   500
KILOMETERS
CONIC PROJECTION

GULF REGION
TOTAL - ALL COMMODITIES

☐ 50,000 TONS
▦ 500,000 TONS   SHIPPED FROM THE GULF REGION

· 50,000 TONS
▦ 500,000 TONS   SHIPPED TO THE GULF REGION

○ 50,000 TONS
▩ 500,000 TONS   SHIPPED WITHIN THE GULF REGION

FIGURES IN SHORT TONS

186

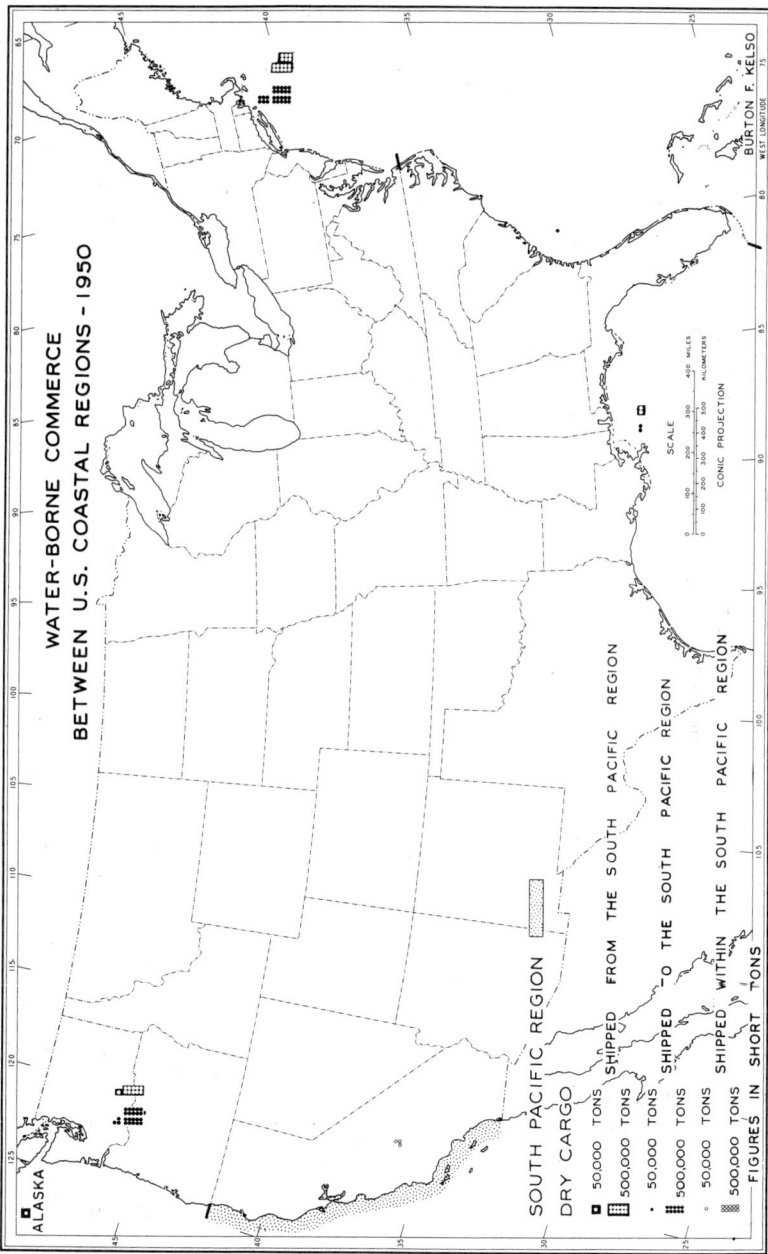

WATER-BORNE COMMERCE
BETWEEN U.S. COASTAL REGIONS - 1950

ALASKA

SOUTH PACIFIC REGION

DRY CARGO

50,000 TONS   SHIPPED FROM THE SOUTH PACIFIC REGION

500,000 TONS

50,000 TONS   SHIPPED TO THE SOUTH PACIFIC REGION

500,000 TONS

50,000 TONS   SHIPPED WITHIN THE SOUTH PACIFIC REGION

500,000 TONS

FIGURES IN SHORT TONS

SCALE

CONIC PROJECTION

BURTON F. KELSO

WEST LONGITUDE

187

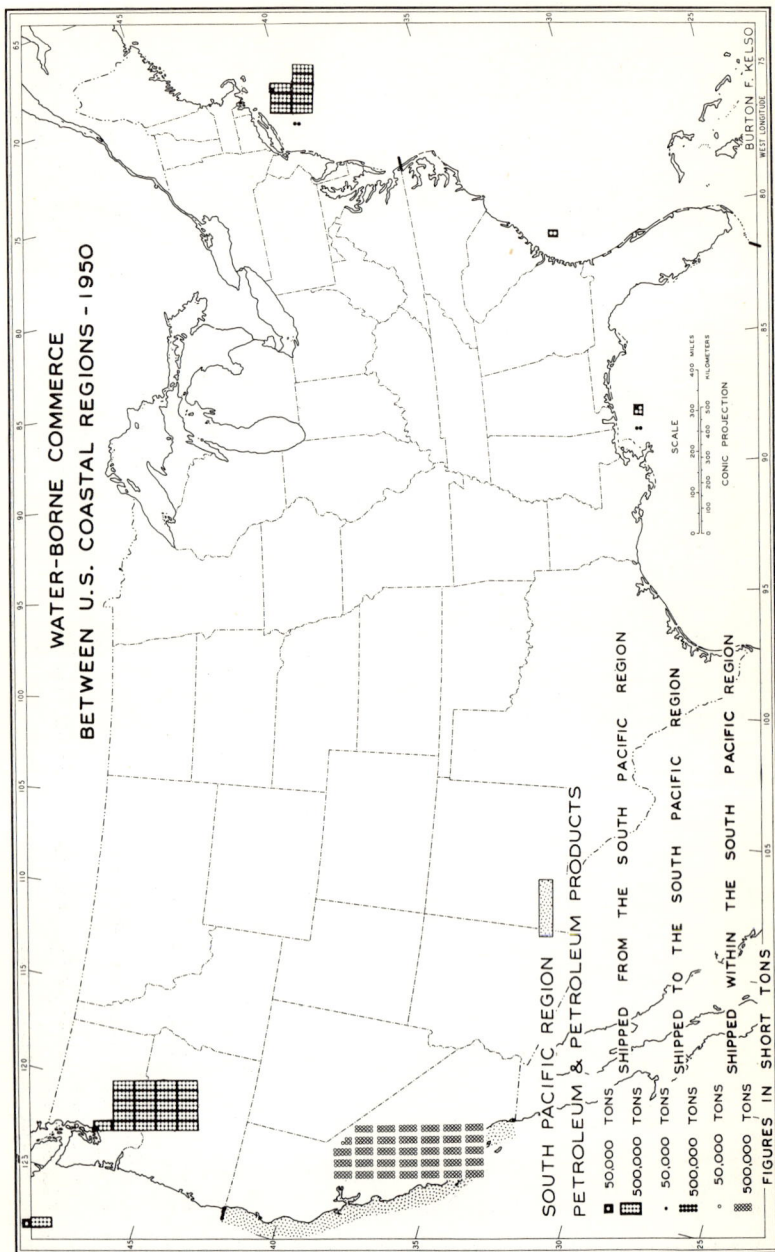

WATER-BORNE COMMERCE
BETWEEN U.S. COASTAL REGIONS - 1950

SOUTH PACIFIC REGION
PETROLEUM & PETROLEUM PRODUCTS

☐ 50,000 TONS SHIPPED FROM THE SOUTH PACIFIC REGION

▦ 500,000 TONS SHIPPED FROM THE SOUTH PACIFIC REGION

· 50,000 TONS SHIPPED TO THE SOUTH PACIFIC REGION

▩ 500,000 TONS SHIPPED TO THE SOUTH PACIFIC REGION

○ 50,000 TONS SHIPPED WITHIN THE SOUTH PACIFIC REGION

▦ 500,000 TONS SHIPPED WITHIN THE SOUTH PACIFIC REGION

FIGURES IN SHORT TONS

SCALE

BURTON F. KELSO

CONIC PROJECTION

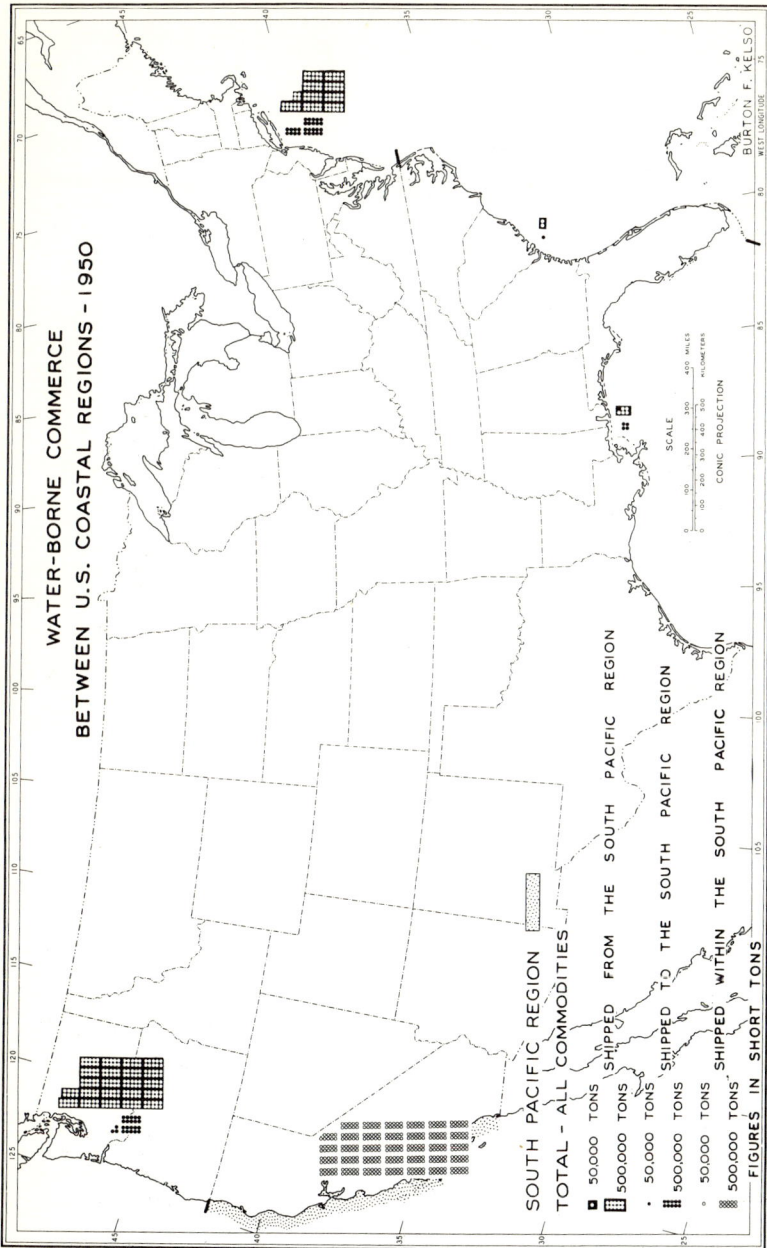

WATER-BORNE COMMERCE
BETWEEN U.S. COASTAL REGIONS - 1950

SOUTH PACIFIC REGION
TOTAL - ALL COMMODITIES

■ 50,000 TONS ┐
▦ 500,000 TONS ┘ SHIPPED FROM THE SOUTH PACIFIC REGION

· 50,000 TONS ┐
▦ 500,000 TONS ┘ SHIPPED TO THE SOUTH PACIFIC REGION

□ 50,000 TONS ┐
▨ 500,000 TONS ┘ SHIPPED WITHIN THE SOUTH PACIFIC REGION

FIGURES IN SHORT TONS

SCALE
MILES
KILOMETERS
CONIC PROJECTION

BURTON F. KELSO
WEST LONGITUDE

189

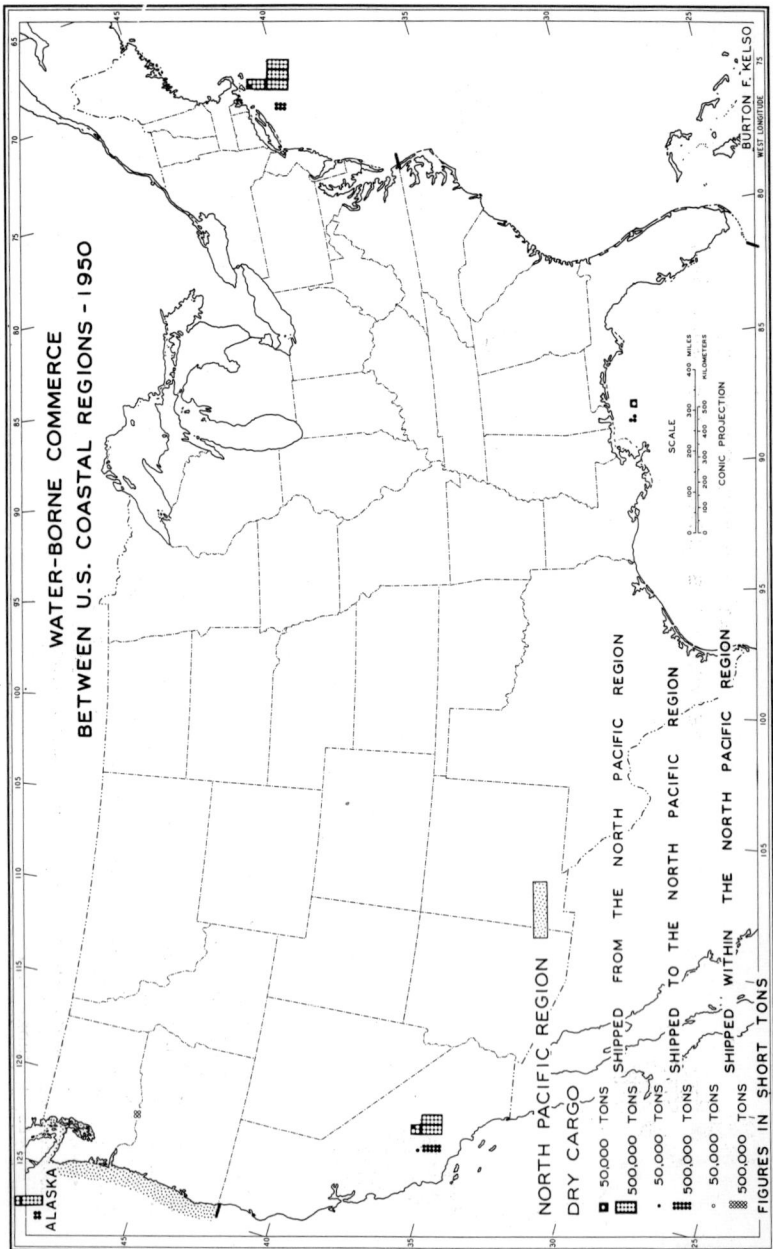

WATER-BORNE COMMERCE
BETWEEN U.S. COASTAL REGIONS - 1950

BURTON F. KELSO

ALASKA

NORTH PACIFIC REGION

DRY CARGO

□ 50,000 TONS   SHIPPED FROM THE NORTH PACIFIC REGION
⊞ 500,000 TONS

· 50,000 TONS   SHIPPED TO THE NORTH PACIFIC REGION
⊞ 500,000 TONS

∘ 50,000 TONS   SHIPPED WITHIN THE NORTH PACIFIC REGION
▨ 500,000 TONS

FIGURES IN SHORT TONS

SCALE

0   100   200   300   400   MILES
0 100 200 300 400 500 600 KILOMETERS

CONIC PROJECTION

WEST LONGITUDE

190

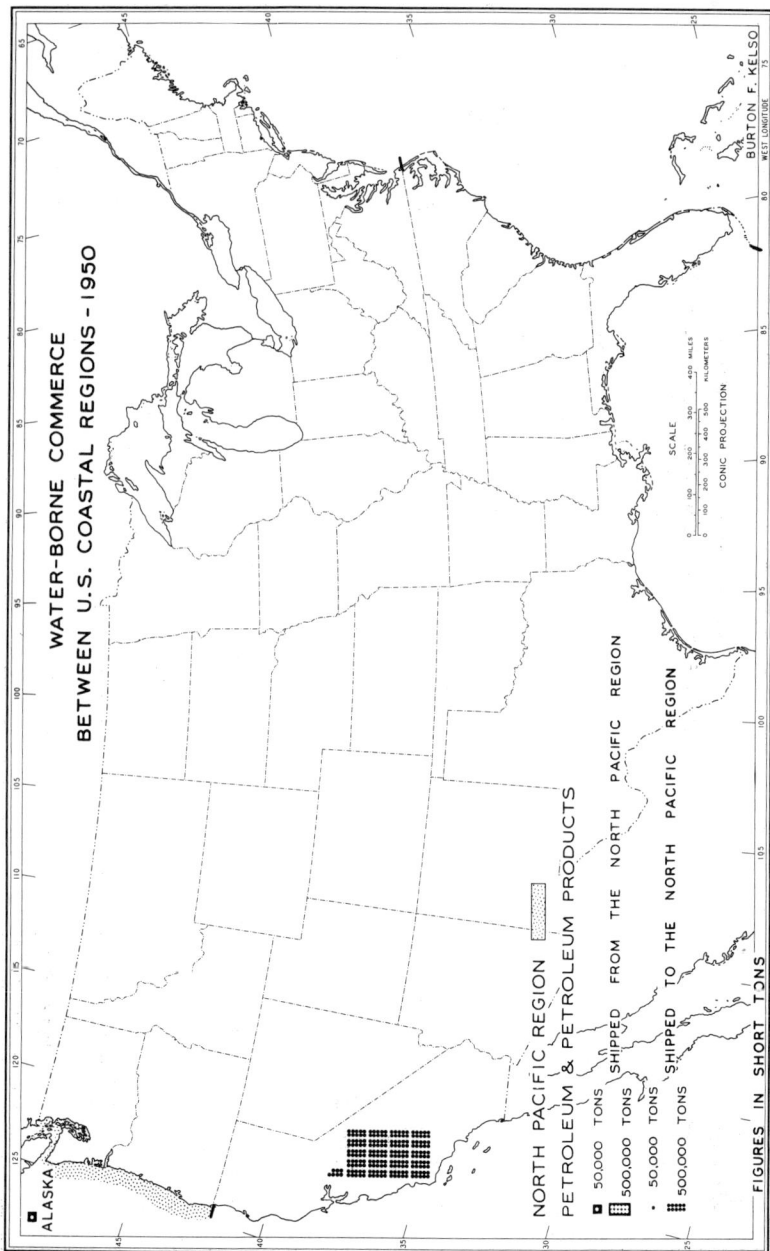

WATER-BORNE COMMERCE
BETWEEN U.S. COASTAL REGIONS - 1950

NORTH PACIFIC REGION
PETROLEUM & PETROLEUM PRODUCTS

□ 50,000 TONS
▦ 500,000 TONS   SHIPPED FROM THE NORTH PACIFIC REGION
· 50,000 TONS
▥ 500,000 TONS   SHIPPED TO THE NORTH PACIFIC REGION

FIGURES IN SHORT TONS

ALASKA

SCALE
0 100 200 300 400 MILES
0 100 200 300 400 500 KILOMETERS
CONIC PROJECTION

BURTON F. KELSO
WEST LONGITUDE

191

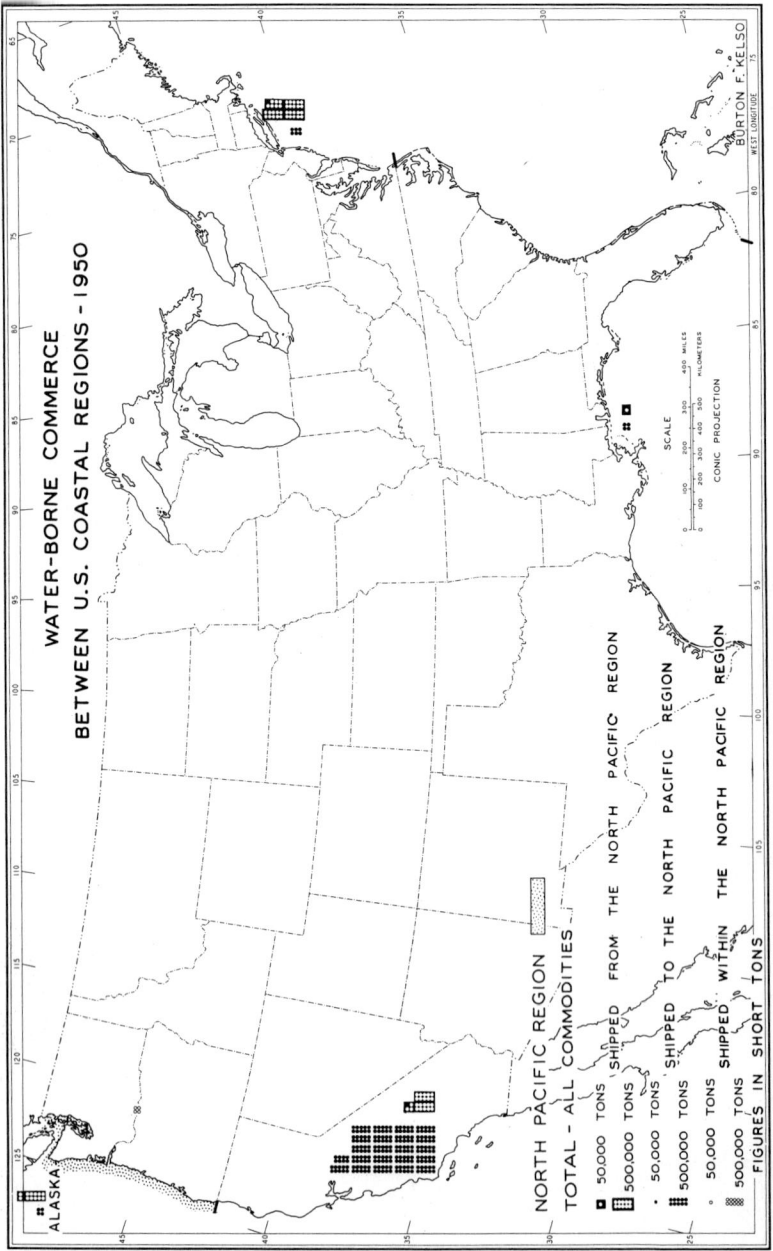

WATER-BORNE COMMERCE
BETWEEN U.S. COASTAL REGIONS - 1950

NORTH PACIFIC REGION
TOTAL - ALL COMMODITIES

50,000 TONS SHIPPED FROM THE NORTH PACIFIC REGION
500,000 TONS

50,000 TONS SHIPPED TO THE NORTH PACIFIC REGION
500,000 TONS

50,000 TONS SHIPPED WITHIN THE NORTH PACIFIC REGION
500,000 TONS

FIGURES IN SHORT TONS

ALASKA

BURTON F. KELSO

SCALE

CONIC PROJECTION

192

an area of shipping, even more than of rail traffic (noted in Chapter IV).

Almost all the exports to California are forest products of one sort or another (resembling the rail trade): lumber (917,000 tons), newsprint (142,000 tons), and other paper (approximately 40,000 tons). The biggest flow is to the North Atlantic, with forest products accounting for more than two-thirds, consisting of lumber (1,600,000 tons), wood pulp (55,000 tons), and paper (47,000 tons), with canned fruits and vegetables accounting for 71,000 tons.

Practically all of Alaska's trade, except for heavy movements of refined petroleum out of California, is with the North Pacific, principally Seattle, the traditional gateway to Alaska. Traffic is overwhelmingly outbound to Alaska rather than inbound (a ratio of 3 to 1), a circumstance somewhat surprising for such a virgin territory, but reflecting the essentially consuming, military, undeveloped character of the economy. Half the inbound commodities are canned fish (salmon), 98,000 tons, with lumber, including rafted logs, accounting for another one-fourth. Principal items shipped to Alaska are iron and steel products (125,000 tons), lumber (65,000 tons), and cement (61,000 tons), which together make up about 40 per cent of the shipments by weight. The remainder, consisting of a large variety of items from food to machinery, mirrors the fact that Seattle serves essentially as the metropolis and wholesale center of Alaska, even though it is a thousand or more miles away.

FOREIGN TRADE

Dry cargo data

The dry cargo flow map (p. 204) shows ocean traffic carried by vessels of all nationalities on essential United States trade routes as defined by the United States Maritime Administration. [3] The great bulk of American foreign trade is indicated

---

3. Figures are reported for the thirty-one essential trade routes, totaling 72,414,000 cargo tons (of 2,240 pounds each). Other trade routes not specifically delineated account for 4,623,000 cargo tons, or about 6 per cent of the volume of the thirty-one essential routes. (Total foreign trade is 77,037,000 cargo tons, including the nonessential trade routes.) Thus

reasonably well. The major exception is the abnormally large
flow of coal to Europe and the Mediterranean, normally very
slight, but exceptionally heavy in most of the postwar years,
including 1948. Data on the map are plotted by generalized
coastal areas. The character of the data prevents a more precise allocation. Thus, all of Atlantic Europe from Spain to the

the map represents the majority of the flows, although one
might wonder whether the 6 per cent in other trade routes
accounts for all the contract, private, tramp, and nearby
ocean traffic. (Note the absence of flows to and from Canada
on the dry cargo map, for example, a fairly heavy movement
on both coasts.) The Corps of Engineers reports for 1948
about 89,000,000 short tons of 2,000 pounds each; converting
this to cargo tons of 2,240 pounds each gives about 79,000,000,
only about 2,000,000 tons more than the Maritime Commission
figures, so that the remainder is negligible, although there
may be minor differences in reporting. In either case the
Great Lakes-Canada trade is excluded (about 25,000,000 short
tons of exports, of which coal is more than 20,000,000 and
iron ore more than 3,000,000 tons, and about 4,000,000 tons
of imports, with pulp wood and iron ore making up more than
half). Also, none of the figures in this report includes cargo
handled by military freighters. For maps and descriptions of
routes see U.S. Maritime Commission, Essential Foreign
Trade Routes of the American Merchant Marine (Washington,
D.C., 1949). Source of data for foreign dry cargo maps in
this report is U.S. Maritime Commission, United States and
Foreign Flag Vessels Participation in Commercial Dry Cargo
Freight Traffic on Essential U.S. Foreign Trade Routes, July
1947 to December 1948 (Washington, D.C., n.d.). Figures
for the two half years of 1948 were combined to get figures for
calendar year 1948. For maps on a slightly different basis
see Edward L. Ullman et al., "Flow Maps of the United States
Ocean-Borne Foreign Trade 1938," Report No. 4, ONR Transportation Geography Project (1951; privately distributed).
Three of these maps, showing total United States foreign trade,
dry bulk and liquid bulk commodities, have been published
in American Geography: Inventory and Prospect, P. E. James
and C. F. Jones, eds. (Syracuse, N.Y.: Association of American Geographers and Syracuse University Press, 1954), chap.
xiii, pp. 310-32.

Baltic and Scandinavia is lumped into one region, as are various other areas such as the Mediterranean, parts of the Caribbean, East Coast of South America, West Coast of South America, Far East, etc. The same applies to the United States, where the finest possible breakdown is: North Atlantic (from Canada to Hampton Roads), South Atlantic (to Key West), Gulf, and Pacific Coast. This is the same breakdown as for domestic trade, except that South and North Pacific are combined into one coastal region. On the Atlantic Coast for some trade routes even this fine a breakdown is impossible, since some individual trade routes originate and terminate in several coastal regions. Where Atlantic Coast in general is specified, the routes have been terminated in the North Atlantic sector, the overwhelming contributor of traffic. Where Atlantic-Gulf or South Atlantic-Gulf is specified, the routes are arbitrarily terminated in the South Atlantic sector, as explained on the map for specific trade routes. Likewise, precise routes of flow cannot be shown. Thus it is possible to give only a generalized picture, but one in greater geographical detail than has been hitherto available, since at least Atlantic and Pacific coasts are separated.

For volume of trade from all United States coastal ports combined, to the individual foreign coastal regions, see Table 5. This table should be referred to in the brief discussion that follows and in studying the map of dry cargo foreign trade. Table 5 will be found particularly useful to indicate direction, since it shows both exports and imports, which the map does not, and to indicate recent change because it gives data for 1953 as well as for 1948.

Dry cargo routes

A detailed analysis of dry cargo foreign trade will not be attempted, since the main purpose of this study is to describe American internal commodity flow, a neglected and more important movement; foreign trade, at least for other countries and the world, has been much more intensively analyzed by others.[4] Moreover, suitable data were not available to the

4. For world patterns see Tore Ouren and Axel Sømme, Trends in Interwar Trade and Shipping (Bergen: J. W. Eides Forlag, 1949); Johannes Humlum, Kultur Geografisk Atlas (4th ed.; 2 vols.; Copenhagen: Gyldendalske Boghandel Nordisk

TABLE 5
DRY CARGO FOREIGN TRADE OF THE UNITED STATES
BY FOREIGN COASTAL REGIONS*
(In 1,000's of short tons of 2,000 lbs.)

Coastal Region	1948		1953	
	Imports	Exports	Imports	Exports
Caribbean	7,830	4,535	12,889	3,807
East Coast South America	2,262	4,158	2,041	2,515
West Coast South America	4,802	905	5,948	1,154
West Coast Central America and Mexico	708	138	1,060	210
Gulf Coast Mexico	280	310	331	521
United Kingdom and Eire	518	2,051	872	2,804
Baltic, Scandinavia, Iceland, and Greenland	2,663	1,829	3,598	1,285
Bayonne-Hamburg Range	960	17,685	3,823	10,871
Portugal and Spanish Atlantic	262	720	262	329
Azores, Mediterranean, and Black Sea	2,196	10,895	1,811	6,897
West Coast Africa	522	638	2,346	397
South and East Africa	860	1,366	1,640	943
Australasia	323	657	640	610
India, Persian Gulf, and Red Sea	1,139	2,237	2,428	2,167
Straits Settlements and Netherlands East Indies	1,011	464	752	321
South China, Formosa, and Philippines	1,433	1,451	2,541	1,437
North China including Shanghai and Japan	222	1,375	540	8,646
Pacific Canada	1,246	182	2,269	290
Atlantic Canada and Newfoundland	3,964	1,604	4,811	1,098
TOTAL	32,751	53,204	50,604	46,307

*U.S. Water-Borne Trade by Trade Area, Current Summary Reports, FT. 973 (for 1948); FT. 985 (for 1953), Bureau of the Census, Department of Commerce, Washington, D.C. (as reported in Statistical Abstract, Bureau of Census, Tables 650-51, 1952; Tables 722-23, 1955. The calculations in this table were made from the latter source.).

writer for detailed mapping of foreign trade, either in terms of commodity distribution by suitable coastal regions or for a more representative recent year. Foreign trade fluctuates

Forlag, 1955); the map section has appeared in an English edition with the title Atlas of Economic Geography (London: Meiklejohn & Son, Ltd., 1955). The older classic is A. J. Sargent, Seaways of the Empire (2nd ed.; London: A. C. Black, Ltd., 1930), for British shipping.

196

more violently from year to year, decade to decade, or war to war, than does American domestic trade. These fluctuations are often reflections of wars and international political changes. Another probable factor is the relative ease with which vessels can be shifted from route to route, in comparison with the more fixed paths of land trade, although even in ocean trade the regularly scheduled liner predominates.

In 1948 United States exports of dry cargo exceeded imports; about 53,000,000 short tons of exports were shipped, compared to 32,000,000 tons of imports; however, if the approximately 21,000,000 tons of coal export, most of which was abnormal, are discounted, imports equal exports. By 1953 coal had indeed declined to 14,000,000 short tons and imports had risen, so that total imports were 50,000,000 short tons and exports only 46,000,000. In any case, the United States is exporter and importer of both raw materials and finished products, although raw or semiraw materials dominate our imports more, a fact which indicates the change in our economy since the nineteenth century.

The East Coast of the United States, including the Gulf, dominates United States foreign trade, as can be seen from the map, just as it does domestic water and land trade. This is not surprising, since there are about 140,000,000 persons in the eastern half of the country, compared to only about 20,000,000 in the western half, with probably about the same differential in resources and an even greater concentration of industry. Likewise, the Atlantic Ocean, particularly the North Atlantic and its offshoots, has far greater traffic than the Pacific, reflecting particularly the much greater development around the margins of the Atlantic. Distances are also shorter than across the Pacific, but in ocean trade this greater ease of transferability is not nearly as important as in land trade.

The two main regions of all American ocean dry cargo foreign trade are, therefore: (1) the North Atlantic, with about 37,000,000 short tons of total trade in 1948 and about 31,000,000 in 1953; and (2) Latin America (especially the Caribbean), with 27,000,000 in 1948 and 30,000,000 in 1953 (Table 5). In direction of trade, however, the two regions contrast sharply; imports from Latin America (especially the Caribbean) were almost twice the exports in 1948, and almost three times in 1953, reflecting heavy importation of raw and semiraw materials, while exports to Europe were more than five times the imports in 1948 and more than twice in 1953, reflecting the manufacturing character of Europe.

The North Atlantic trade route, connecting the two industrial hearts of the world, is the greatest route not only of American commerce but also traditionally of world commerce. Exports to Europe include coal, wheat, iron and steel products, machinery, and other items; imports are made up of a variety of commodities in lesser volume. However, the 21,000,000 short tons (approximately 18,000,000 cargo tons) of coal exported from the United States in 1948, already alluded to, are predominantly on the North Atlantic and Mediterranean runs; their removal would cut sharply into this route. The great volume of this flow in 1948 and in other postwar years mirrored the distressed condition of Europe after the war as well as American volume mining methods on thick seams, and the use of superior energy sources, petroleum and natural gas, to meet America's increased requirements--a source which Europe could not tap as readily to meet its increased needs. As Europe recovered, coal production there increased. Exports of coal from the United States declined by more than one-third, but other trade picked up, so that the North Atlantic is still the premier route in weight volume (Table 5) and even more so in value, the conventional measure.

The heavy trade between the United States and Europe may seem surprising in view of the competitive rather than complementary nature of these two leading industrial areas of the world. Transferability, it is true, is good, since there are many competing shipping services, but it is not markedly superior to that between most overseas points, and it is in many instances inferior because of the artificial trade barriers between competing economies.

Some complementarity, however, does exist. In the first place, each area has a great range of natural and cultural differences. This normally promotes trade with the nearest intervening opportunity, the local continent, stretching from Scandinavia and Canada to and beyond the margins of the Mediterranean and the Caribbean, respectively. It also results in intercontinental transfer, as of wood pulp from Sweden, watches from Switzerland, olives from Spain; or apples from Washington and cotton from southern United States. Second, the two areas, as the centers of world economic development, are the main sources of innovation, of new products. Innovation creates demands for interchange before the products can be duplicated, although trade barriers hamper these movements more seriously than they do the flow of complementary raw materials. Third, the economies of scale permitted by differential demands for some products (for example, for small automobiles and motor scooters in Europe) apparently promote some interchange since duplicate producers in the small market continent would be submarginal.

Finally, since the two areas are the largest productive centers in the world, even a small or temporary complementarity creates a large absolute potential for interchange.

A persistent feature of the trade since the war has been America's supplying of many goods as a part of Europe's recovery. European recovery has gone far and has obviated the need for many imports. However, the recovery itself results in demands for certain essential goods, as, for example, fuel. Even a 10 per cent deficit in European coal production results in an enormous demand for coal from America, so great is industrial Europe's consumption. Thus irregularities in European production, whether owing to shortage of energy, seasonal crop failures, innovations, irregular advances in standard of living, or political crises and their effects, create demands for interchange.

Perhaps one of the best ways to consider trade relations between the two hearts of the world, therefore, is to think of them as linked on a recurring, quasi-emergency or stand-by basis, with America's increasing production supplying most of the emergency needs thus far. For each area the other is the largest ready source of many industrial and other Western-style goods, whether raw, semifinished, or (particularly in the case of innovations) completed.

What the effect of the integration of Europe and the consequent scale economies would be it is difficult to predict. Europe would become more competitive and at the same time would increase its buying and selling power. The countries of Europe, comparable in general to the states of the United States, would become even greater intervening opportunities for each others' trade within a common trade barrier. Trade between the two large areas thus could not be strongly supported by long-range complementary relations, since each continent has such a diversity of complementarity within its own borders, but might rather depend, in part, on the stand-by, innovation basis discussed above, and on the policies of the partners in allowing such interchange.

In the meantime, the two competitive areas operate somewhat as parts of one world core, as represented in the political and military sphere by NATO, to give one example. Such
interchanges, although outside the scope of this analysis, undoubtedly help to create some of the environment for physical
interchange, particularly on an emergency aid basis. The most
striking physical interconnection is the flow of coal between the
two leading coal producers of the world in defiance of the classic complementary injunction against "carrying coals to New-
castle." Thus one of the fundamental natural bases of the
American industrial belt, coal, performs part of the same
function for the other great industrial area. The same high-
grade Pocahontas coal that has served such a wide area in
eastern United States, from North Dakota to Maine to Georgia,
now also reaches Europe. In view of the low value and conse-
quently relatively high transfer costs of such a commodity,
this is a surprising relationship, presumably temporary, although the flow has been proceeding irregularly in large volume for more than ten years and shows no sign of abating in
the immediate future. Large volume, excellent bulk loading
facilities, and relatively low transfer costs by water of course
facilitate the flow.

The European industrial belt is also dependent on petroleum
from outside its borders, mainly from the Middle East, which
is about the same distance away as the Southwest Gulf fields
are from the United States industrial belt. A vital difference
is that Europe's oil supplies, unlike those of the United States,
are outside its political jurisdiction. Thus interruption of supplies from the Middle East also tends to force Europe to look
to the United States, not only for petroleum but also for still
more coal to make up for some of the loss of petroleum.

The North Atlantic coastal sector of the United States, as
the gateway to the industrial belt, has the greatest share of
the traffic and the highest percentage of imports of any United
States coastal region; New York is traditionally not only America's greatest port, but particularly its greatest import port.
The Gulf, however, has a surprisingly large traffic, but one
heavily outbound to Europe; wheat and other grains, sulfur,
coal, cotton, phosphate, lumber, and other materials predominate.

The other great area for American overseas trade, the
nearby Caribbean and Latin America (Table 5), is tied to both
the North Atlantic and the Gulf coasts of the United States.

(If tanker traffic is also counted, the Caribbean becomes the leading area for United States tonnage; see Table 6.) Heavy inflows of raw materials and tropical products dominate: bauxite to the Gulf from Dutch Guiana, America's principal source; iron ore, sugar, and bananas from the Caribbean; iron ore, copper ore, and nitrate from the west coast of South America, particularly Chile; coffee, especially from Brazil; and a host of manufactured and other products including iron and steel, lumber, and coal, sent southward.

From the remotest parts of the world--Australasia, South and Central Africa, Malaya, India, Japan, and the Philippines--ores and raw materials also come; although of lesser volume than the Atlantic-Caribbean flows, many of the products are critical to our economy--manganese, chrome and other ferroalloys, and additional necessary products not produced in the United States. Many United States products are also shipped out to these remote areas, so cheap is ocean transport. Even from across the Pacific, however, the flows are heavier to and from the Atlantic Coast than the Pacific Coast.

The completion of the St. Lawrence Seaway will also bring deep sea traffic to the heart of America and, by reducing transferability costs, afford still more opportunity for export of many commodities noted above, as well as for import of critical raw and other materials and general exchange of manufactured products with the heart of America by water. [5]

Tanker traffic

Tanker traffic on the foreign map is about 97 per cent petroleum and products. The map again is by generalized coastal areas, although the data permit a somewhat more specific depiction and avoidance of the few ambiguities of the dry cargo map. Data arc not restricted to essential trade routes, as are the dry cargo figures. All commercial movements are shown; only Great Lakes and military tanker cargoes, a relatively small percentage of the total, are not represented.

Direction of flow is also shown by arrows on the map and by Table 6, showing movements for the whole country for 1948 and 1953. Comparison of total tanker movements of 1947,

---

5. See Harold M. Mayer, "Great Lakes-Overseas: An Expanding Trade Route, " Economic Geography, XXX (1954), 117-43.

1948, and 1953 with 1938 shows a reversal of the United States position, with imports now more important than exports as follows:[6]

U. S. FOREIGN TANKER TRAFFIC
(Millions of short tons of 2,000 lbs.)

	1938	1947	1948	1953
Exports	23	15	10	11
Imports	10	28	31	61

Since 1947 and 1953 other fluctuations have occurred, with movements of Middle East oil and development of Canadian supplies, including a pipeline to Vancouver and Washington which cuts down the relative contribution of California to British Columbia.

The American pattern, as shown on the maps for 1947 and in the table for 1953, is quite simple: heavy imports from Venezuela to the nearby North Atlantic, exports in much lesser volume from the Gulf to Northwest Europe, and still smaller exports from California to the Pacific area. Total flow is by far the greatest of any American foreign commodity movement and is increasing. In 1953, with some 72,000,000 tons, it was equal to three-quarters of all dry cargo trade, and in imports, the heavy direction, it was 20 per cent greater than all dry cargo imports. Indirectly this mirrors the greatly increased use in the American economy of petroleum, which has already equaled coal as a source of United States

---

6. Source of 1938 and 1947 tanker data is: U. S. Maritime Commission, Bureau of Government Aids, Division of Traffic, Tankship Traffic in United States Foreign Trade (Washington, D. C., June, 1949). Figures for 1948 are taken from U. S. Department of the Army, Corps of Engineers, Commercial Statistics, Water-Borne Commerce of the United States for the Calendar Year 1948, Part II of The Annual Report of the Chief of Engineers, 1949 (Washington, D. C., 1950); figures for 1953 are taken from U. S. Department of the Army, Corps of Engineers, Water-Borne Commerce of the United States, Calendar Year 1953 (Washington, D. C., n. d.). Canadian Great Lakes and military traffic are excluded. Maritime Commission figures are converted to short tons.

energy. Domestic petroleum supplies continue to be the main source, but so great is the demand and so cheap are the transfer costs that nearby foreign areas (Venezuela) are also heavily drawn upon by American companies.

TABLE 6
TANKER FOREIGN TRADE OF THE UNITED STATES
BY FOREIGN COASTAL REGIONS*
(In 1,000's of short tons of 2,000 lbs.)

Coastal Region	1948 Imports	1948 Exports	1953 Imports	1953 Exports
Caribbean	26,015	1,310	39,990	1,559
East Coast South America	......	415	1	242
West Coast South America	12	59	20	361
West Coast Central America and Mexico	8	466	21	860
Gulf Coast Mexico	1,076	3	3,066	21
United Kingdom and Eire	153	2,284	281	1,519
Baltic, Scandinavia, Iceland, and Greenland	14	702	57	216
Bayonne-Hamburg Range	43	1,121	608	728
Portugal and Spanish Atlantic	......	78	1	30
Azores, Mediterranean, and Black Sea	89	242	2,360	295
West Coast Africa	......	107	......	116
South and East Africa	......	......	......	116
Australasia	2	243	......	277
India, Persian Gulf, and Red Sea	3,300	......	3,543	802
Straits Settlements and Netherlands East Indies	......	......	523	......
South China, Formosa, and Philippines	......	198	61	36
North China including Shanghai and Japan	......	195	......	1,703
Pacific Canada	......	1,940	1	2,381
Atlantic Canada and Newfoundland	3	508	5	682
TOTAL	30,719	9,872	61,647	11,023

*U.S. Water-Borne Trade by Trade Area, Current Summary Reports, FT. 973 (for 1948); FT. 985 (for 1953), Bureau of the Census, Department of Commerce, Washington, D.C. (as reported in Statistical Abstract, Bureau of Census, Tables 650-51, 1952; Tables 722-23, 1955. The calculations in this table were made from the latter source.).

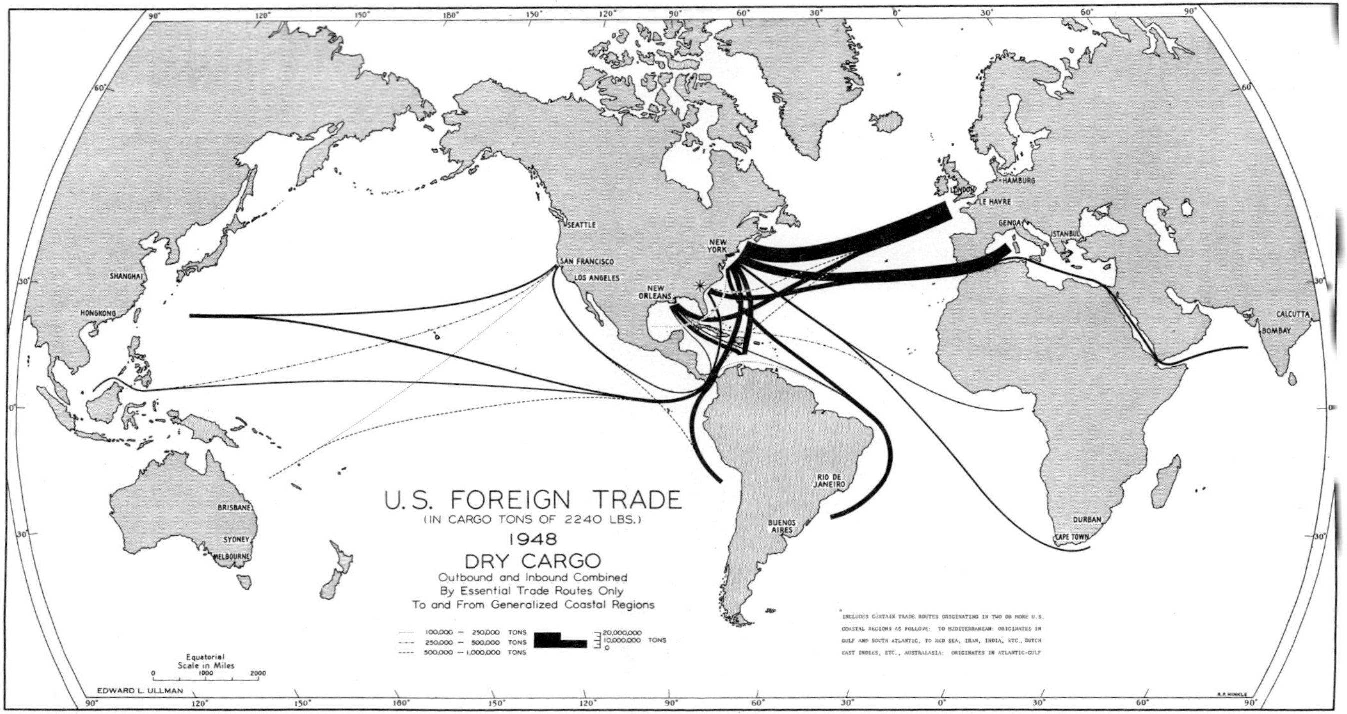
U.S. FOREIGN TRADE
(IN CARGO TONS OF 2240 LBS.)
1948
DRY CARGO
Outbound and Inbound Combined
By Essential Trade Routes Only
To and From Generalized Coastal Regions
100,000 – 250,000 TONS
250,000 – 500,000 TONS
500,000 – 1,000,000 TONS
20,000,000
10,000,000 TONS
0
*INCLUDES CERTAIN TRADE ROUTES ORIGINATING IN TWO OR MORE U.S. COASTAL REGIONS AS FOLLOWS: TO MEDITERRANEAN: ORIGINATES IN GULF AND SOUTH ATLANTIC; TO RED SEA, IRAN, INDIA, ETC., DUTCH EAST INDIES, ETC., AUSTRALASIA: ORIGINATES IN ATLANTIC-GULF
Equatorial Scale in Miles
0 1000 2000
EDWARD L. ULLMAN
SEATTLE
SAN FRANCISCO
LOS ANGELES
NEW YORK
NEW ORLEANS
LONDON
LE HAVRE
HAMBURG
GENOA
ISTANBUL
CALCUTTA
BOMBAY
DURBAN
CAPE TOWN
RIO DE JANEIRO
BUENOS AIRES
SHANGHAI
HONGKONG
BRISBANE
SYDNEY
MELBOURNE

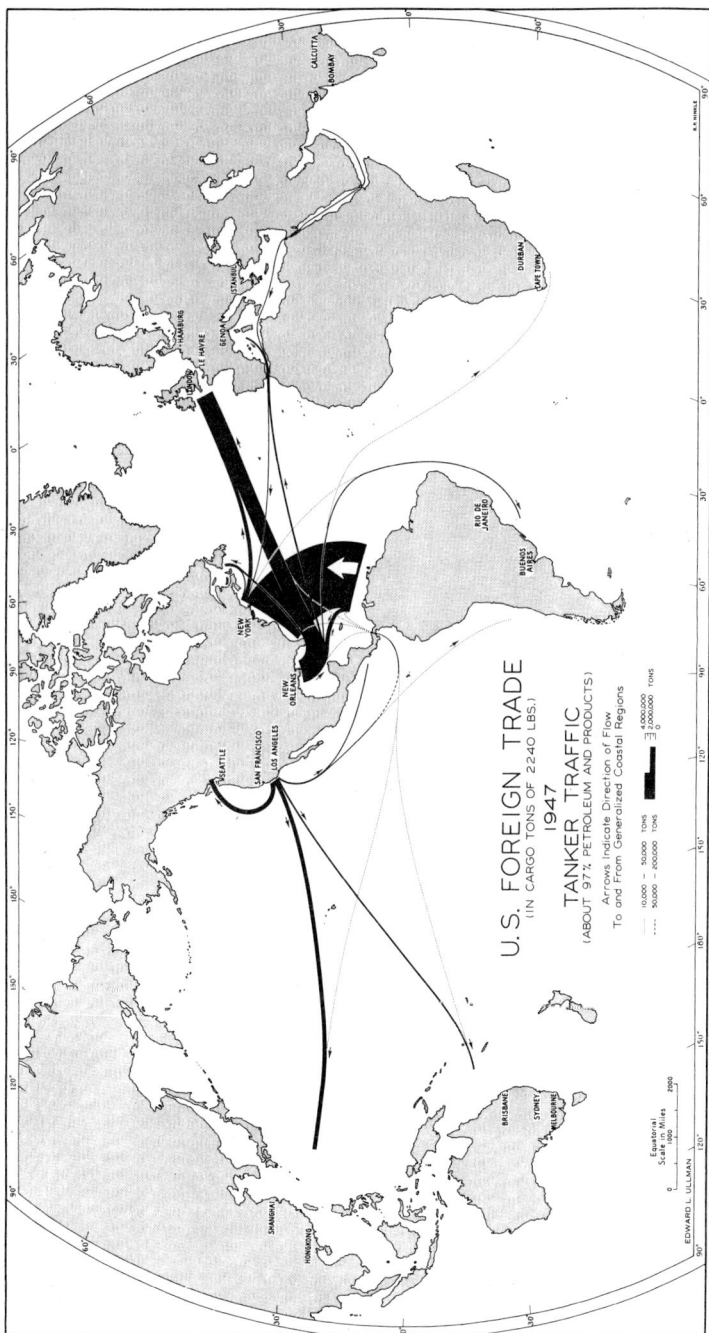

U.S. FOREIGN TRADE
(IN CARGO TONS OF 2240 LBS.)
1947

TANKER TRAFFIC
(ABOUT 97% PETROLEUM AND PRODUCTS)

Arrows Indicate Direction of Flow
To and From Generalized Coastal Regions

10,000 — 50,000 TONS
50,000 — 200,000 TONS

2,000,000 TONS
4,000,000 TONS
0

Equatorial
Scale in Miles
1000   2000

EDWARD L. ULLMAN

Bibliography

Aagesen, Aage. Geografiske Studier over Jernbanere i Danmark. (Det Kongelige Danske Geografiske Selskab, Kulturgeografiske Skrifter, Vol. V.) Copenhagen: H. Hagerups Boghandel, 1949.

Association of American Railroads. Transportation in America. Washington, D.C., 1947. Chap. viii, pp. 103-207, "Freight Traffic."

Ballert, Albert G. "The Soo and the Suez," Science, CXXII (October 28, 1955), 822-23.

Becht, J. E. Commodity Origins, Traffic, and Markets Accessible to Chicago Via the Illinois Waterway. Urbana, Ill.: University of Illinois Press, 1952.

Beckerman, W. "Distance and the Pattern of Intra-European Trade," Review of Economics and Statistics, XXXVIII (February, 1956), 31-40.

Bright, Arthur, Jr., and George Ellis, eds. See National Planning Association.

Capot-Rey, R. Géographie de la circulation sur les continents. Paris: Gallimard, 1946.

Carlson, Knute E. Interregional and Intraregional Traffic of the Mountain-Pacific Area in 1939. Research directed by James C. Nelson and Paul M. Zeis, under U.S. Department of Commerce, Transportation Division. Pullman, Wash.: State College of Washington.

Castiglioni, Bruno. La Rete ferroviaria italiana e il movimento dei viaggiatori. Padua: R. Zannoni, Editore, 1936.

Cavanaugh, Joseph A. "Formulation, Analysis and Testing of the Interactance Hypothesis," American Sociological Review, XV (1950), 763-66.

Cooley, C. H. The Theory of Transportation. (Publications of the American Economic Association, Vol. IX.) Baltimore, Md., 1894.

Daggett, Stuart. Principles of Inland Transportation. 4th ed. New York: Harper & Bros., 1955.

--------, and John P. Carter. The Structure of Transcontinental Railroad Rates. Berkeley, Calif.: University of California Press, 1947.

Dodd, Stuart C. "The Interactance Hypothesis: A Gravity Model Fitting Physical Masses and Human Groups," American Sociological Review, XV (1950), 245-56.

Ellsworth, P. T. "The Structure of American Trade: A New View Re-examined," Review of Economics and Statistics, XXXVI (August, 1954), 279-85.

Harris, Chauncy D. "The Market as a Factor in the Localization of Industry in the United States," Annals of the Association of American Geographers, XLIV (1954), 315-48.

--------. Salt Lake City: A Regional Capital. Published Ph. D. dissertation, Department of Geography, University of Chicago, 1940. (Privately printed.)

Hartshorne, Richard. "The Significance of Lake Transportation to the Grain Trade of Chicago," Economic Geography, II (1926), 274-91.

Humlum, Johannes. Kultur Geografisk Atlas. 4th ed. 2 vols. Copenhagen: Gyldendalske Boghandel Nordisk Forlag, 1955; the map section has appeared in an English edition with the title Atlas of Economic Geography. London: Meiklejohn & Son, Ltd., 1955.

James, Preston E., and Clarence F. Jones, eds. American Geography: Inventory and Prospect. Syracuse, N. Y.: Association of American Geographers and Syracuse University Press, 1954. Chap. xiii, pp. 310-32, "Transportation Geography," by Edward L. Ullman.

Jones, Clarence F. "The Grain Trade of Montreal." Economic Geography, I (1925), 53-72.

Kelley, Ray S., Jr. Origins and Destinations of New England's Rail Traffic. (National Planning Association, Committee of New England, Staff Memorandum No. 1.) Boston, 1952.

Lambie, Joseph T. From Mine to Market: A History of Coal Transportation on the Norfolk and Western Railway. New York: New York University Press, 1954.

Leontieff, Wassily W. "Domestic Production and Foreign Trade," Proceedings of the American Philosophical Society, XCVII (1953), 332-49; reprinted in Economia Internazionale, VII (February, 1954), 9-45.

Lewis, Edwin H. Minnesota's Interstate Trade. (University

of Minnesota Studies in Economics and Business, No. 16.)
Minneapolis: University of Minnesota Press, March, 1953.

Mayer, Harold M. "Great Lakes-Overseas: An Expanding
Trade Route," Economic Geography, XXX (1954), 117-43.

McFall, R. J. See U. S. Bureau of Foreign and Domestic
Commerce.

National Planning Association, Committee of New England.
The Economic State of New England, ed. Arthur Bright,
Jr., and George Ellis. New Haven: Yale University Press,
1954.

-------. Origins and Destinations of New England's Rail Traffic. See Kelley, Ray S., Jr.

Official Guide of the Railways and Steam Navigation Lines of
the United States, The. New York: National Railway Publication Co., 1950- . (Published monthly.)

Ohlin, Bertil. Interregional and International Trade. (Harvard Economic Studies, Vol. XXXIX.) Cambridge, Mass.:
Harvard University Press, 1933 (reprinted 1955).

Ouren, Tore, and Axel Sømme. Trends in Inter-war Trade
and Shipping. (Norwegian University School of Business,
Geographical Series, Publication No. 5.) Bergen: J. W.
Eides Forlag, 1949.

Patton, Donald J. "The Traffic Pattern on American Inland
Waterways," Economic Geography, XXXII (1956), 29-37.

Sampson, Roy J. "Expanding Domestic Markets for Northwestern Lumber," Pacific Northwest Business, XV (January, 1956), 3-8.

Sargent, A. J. Seaways of the Empire. 2nd ed. London: A. C.
Black, Ltd., 1930.

Scheu, Erwin. Deutschlands wirtschaftsgeographische Harmonie. Breslau: F. Hirt, 1924.

Simpson, Paul B. Regional Aspects of Business Cycles and
Special Studies of the Pacific Northwest. A study prepared
for the Bonneville Administration and supported by the University of Oregon and the Social Science Research Council,
1953. (Mimeographed.)

Social Science Research Council. Interregional Linkages:
Proceedings of the Western Committee on Regional Economic Analysis. Berkeley, Calif., 1954. (Mimeographed.)

Stanton, William L. "The Purpose and Source of Seasonal
Migration to Alaska," Economic Geography, XXXI (1955),
138-48.

Stevens, W. H. S. "Commodity Flow Analysis," in Changing

Perspectives in Marketing, ed. Hugh Wales. Urbana, Ill.: University of Illinois Press, 1951. Pp. 139-57.

Stewart, John Q. "Empirical Mathematical Rules concerning the Distribution and Equilibrium of Population," Geographical Review, XXXVII (1947), 461-85.

Stouffer, Samuel A. "Intervening Opportunities: A Theory Relating Mobility to Distances," American Sociological Review, V (1940), 845-67.

Sweeney, Leo W. "The Iowa Economy as Portrayed by Rail Freight Traffic Movement," Iowa Business Digest (Bureau of Business and Economic Research, University of Iowa), XXII, No. 12 (December, 1951), 1-8.

Swerling, Boris C. "Capital Shortage and Labor Surplus in the United States," Review of Economics and Statistics, XXXVI (August, 1954), 286-89.

Taylor, George R. The Transportation Revolution, 1815-1860. Vol. IV of The Economic History of the United States. New York: Rinehart & Co., 1951.

Thomas, William L., Jr., ed. Man's Role in Changing the Face of the Earth. Chicago: University of Chicago Press, 1956. Pp. 862-80.

Ullman, Edward L. "American Commodity Flow: The Cases of Connecticut, Iowa and Washington." (ONR Transportation Geography Project, Contract No. Nonr-477[03], Report No. 12.) Seattle: University of Washington, May, 1955. (Mimeographed; privately distributed.) Also published in German in Die Erde, No. 2, (1955), pp. 129-64.

-------. "Geography as Spatial Interaction," Annals of the Association of American Geographers, XLIV (1954), 283-84.

-------. "Maps of State-to-State Rail Freight Movement for 13 States of the United States in 1948." (ONR Contract No. N5 ORl-07633, Report No. 3.) Cambridge, Mass.: Harvard University, June, 1951. (Mimeographed; privately distributed.)

-------. Mobile: Industrial Seaport and Trade Center. Published Ph. D. dissertation, Department of Geography, University of Chicago, 1943. (Privately printed.)

-------. "The Railroad Pattern of the United States," Geographical Review, XXXIX (1949), 242-56.

-------. "Rivers as Regional Bonds: The Columbia-Snake Example," Geographical Review, XLI (1951), 210-25.

-------. "The Role of Transportation and the Bases for Interaction," in Man's Role in Changing the Face of the Earth, ed. William L. Thomas, Jr. Chicago: University of Chicago Press, 1956. Pp. 862-80.

-------. "Transportation Geography." See James, Preston E., and Clarence F. Jones.

-------. U. S. Railroads Classified according to Capacity and Relative Importance. (Map.) New York: Simmons-Boardman Publishing Corp., 1950.

-------, et al. "Flow Maps of United States Ocean-borne Foreign Trade, 1938." (ONR Transportation Geography Project, Contract No. Nonr-477[03], Report No. 4.) Cambridge, Mass.: Harvard University, June, 1951. (Mimeographed; privately distributed.) Three of these maps have been published in American Geography: Inventory and Prospect, ed. Preston E. James and Clarence F. Jones (q.v.).

U. S. Board of Investigation and Research. The Economics of Coal Traffic Flow. 79th Cong., 1st sess., Senate Doc. 82. Washington, D. C.: Government Printing Office, 1945.

-------. The National Traffic Pattern. 79th Cong., 1st sess., Senate Doc. 83. Washington, D. C.: Government Printing Office, 1945.

U. S. Bureau of the Census. Statistical Abstract of the United States. Washington, D. C.: Government Printing Office. (Published annually.)

-------. Foreign Trade Division. U. S. Foreign Trade: Waterborne Trade by Trade Area, 1948. (Summary Report FT. 973.) Washington, D. C.: Bureau of the Census, n. d. (Mimeographed.)

-------. U. S. Foreign Trade: Water-borne Foreign Trade Statistics, 1953. (Summary Report FT. 985.) Washington, D. C.: Bureau of the Census, n. d. (Mimeographed.)

U. S. Bureau of Foreign and Domestic Commerce. The External Trade of New England, by R. J. McFall. (U. S. Department of Commerce, Domestic Commerce Series, No. 22.) Washington, D. C.: Government Printing Office, 1928.

-------. Transportation Factors in the Marketing of Newsprint. (Transportation Series, No. 2.) Washington, D. C.: Government Printing Office, 1952.

U. S. Department of the Army, Corps of Engineers. Commercial Statistics, Water-borne Commerce of the United States for the Calendar Year 1948, Part II of The Annual Report of the Chief of Engineers, 1949. Washington, D. C.: Government Printing Office, 1950.

211

--------. Transportation on the Great Lakes. (Transportation Series, No. 1, prepared by the Board of Engineers for Rivers and Harbors.) Washington, D. C.: Government Printing Office, 1932 (revised 1937).

--------. Water-borne Commerce of the United States, Calendar Year 1953. Washington, D. C.: Corps of Engineers, n. d.

--------. Water-borne Commerce of the United States, Domestic Deep-Sea and Lakewise Traffic, Calendar Year 1950. Prepared by the Board of Engineers for River and Harbors. Washington, D. C.: Corps of Engineers, June, 1952.

U. S. Federal Reserve Bank of San Francisco. "Twelfth District Interregional Trade, 1950," Monthly Review, September, 1952, pp. 79-81.

U. S. Interstate Commerce Commission, Bureau of Transport Economics and Statistics. Carload Waybill Statistics, One Per Cent Sample of Terminations. Various sections published separately with subtitles. Washington, D. C.: ICC. (Published annually.)

--------. Sixty-third Annual Report of the Statistics of Railways in the United States for the Year Ended December 31, 1949. Washington, D. C.: Government Printing Office, 1951.

--------. The Transportation of Fresh Apples. (Statement No. 468, File No. 40-C-2.) Washington, D. C.: ICC, March, 1946.

--------. Volume of Intercity Freight Traffic, Public and Private, by Kinds of Transportation, 1939-49. (Statement No. 5046, File No. 10-D-7.) Washington, D. C.: ICC, September, 1950. (Mimeographed.)

--------. Waybill Statistics, Their History and Uses. (Statement No. 543, File No. 40-A-3.) Washington, D. C.: ICC, February, 1954.

U. S. Maritime Administration. Review of Essential United States Foreign Trade Routes. Washington, D. C.: Government Printing Office, May, 1953.

U. S. Maritime Commission. Essential Foreign Trade Routes of the American Merchant Marine. Washington, D. C.: Maritime Commission, 1949.

--------. United States and Foreign Flag Vessels Participation in Commercial Dry Cargo Freight Traffic on Essential U. S. Foreign Trade Routes, July 1947 to December 1948. Washington, D. C.: Maritime Commission, n. d. (Mimeographed.)

--------, Bureau of Government Aids, Division of Traffic. Tankship Traffic in United States Foreign Trade. Washing-

ton, D. C.: Maritime Commission, June, 1949. (Mimeographed.)

Zipf, George K. Human Behavior and the Principle of Least
Effort. Cambridge, Mass.: Addison-Wesley Press, Inc.,
1949.

Index

61

Date Due
